Understanding and responding to drug use: the role of qualitative research

PLANNING GROUP

Jane Fountain
Richard Hartnoll
Deborah Olszewski
Julian Vicente

SCIENTIFIC EDITOR

Jane Fountain

EDITORS

Gloria Greenwood
Kathy Robertson

E.M.C.D.D.A.
European Monitoring Centre
for Drugs and Drug Addiction

Information on the EMCDDA can be found on its website (**http://www.emcdda.org**).

A great deal of additional information on the European Union is available on the Internet.
It can be accessed through the Europa server (http://europa.eu.int).

Cataloguing data can be found at the end of this publication.

Luxembourg: Office for Official Publications of the European Communities, 2000

ISBN 92-9168-088-5

Printed in Belgium

PRINTED ON WHITE CHLORINE-FREE PAPER

CONTENTS

Part VIII: Methodological issues

Part IX:
Qualitative research within a global research agenda

FOREWORD

I t is with great pleasure that I present this scientific monograph, which reflects the breadth and variety of qualitative research on drug use patterns and responses currently under way in the European Union. The monograph reveals that the qualitative approach is increasingly recognised in many EU countries as a useful tool for understanding the drug phenomenon. Its very publication also illustrates a general commitment to qualitative research and a desire to provide a more profound knowledge base across Europe on which to promote rational and effective interventions.

These pages would not have been possible without the thorough and dedicated work of Jane Fountain, who brought together and edited the contributions into a coherent manuscript. Thanks are also due to the individual contributors for their time and effort, as well as to the participants in the scientific seminars which provided the stimulating context around which many of these contributions were produced. Last but not least, I would like to thank the staff of the European Monitoring Centre for Drugs and Drug Addiction (EMCDDA) who initiated and followed through the projects which resulted in this comprehensive and insightful compilation.

Georges Estievenart
Director
EMCDDA

GENERAL INTRODUCTION

GENERAL INTRODUCTION

Richard Hartnoll

One of the major objectives of the EMCDDA is to promote useful knowledge for developing rational policies and effective interventions in response to drug use and drug problems in Europe. Qualitative research focuses on the meanings, perceptions, processes and contexts of the 'world of drugs' and offers ways of understanding drug use patterns and related responses. It can be an effective first step towards generating hypotheses or identifying issues that require more extensive and systematic data collection. However, its main value is to complement quantitative data and statistical analyses by helping to reveal and interpret developments behind the statistics.

These factors lay behind a decision taken by the EMCDDA in 1996 to include qualitative research in its epidemiology work programme and to embark on a project to obtain a comprehensive overview of qualitative research on drugs in Europe. Between 1996 and 1999, the Centre's work on this topic developed and expanded through several phases and projects, all of which were key to developing an EU-wide network of qualitative researchers. The projects helped the Centre and its partners draw together the rather scattered initiatives that have been, or are being, undertaken by researchers across Europe today and start raising the profile of qualitative research as a valuable and necessary complement to quantitative epidemiology and evaluation. This monograph is a key product of these activities.

The projects involved compiling or organising:

- inventories of recent or current research projects and researchers in Europe;
- an annotated bibliography of published and 'grey' literature;
- reviews of qualitative research on drugs in each EU Member State;
- three substantial scientific seminars (Bologna, July 1997; Lisbon, October 1998; Lisbon, October 1999);
- three thematic reviews of qualitative research undertaken by three working groups on new drug trends, drugs and crime, and risk behaviours and health; and
- a qualitative research project on drug demand-reduction interventions.

Information on these initiatives can now be found on an EMCDDA website especially designed to disseminate their results (http://www.qed.org.uk).

Structure of the monograph

The monograph opens by highlighting in Part I the multiple roles of qualitative research, presenting it as a prerequisite for understanding and responding to drug use.

In Part II, which addresses the impact of qualitative research on policy-making, the nature of the relationship between research and policy is examined using the discipline of history. The development of qualitative research is also described via practical examples of its impact on policy.

Part III, on new drug trends, reflects the growing concern regarding the timeliness of information in this area. It summarises the work of the EMCDDA's workgroup on new drug trends set up in 1997 to explore the role of qualitative research in the identification and tracking of new trends in drug consumption in the EU. This section provides examples of research conducted in different cities and Member States that has been specifically designed to identify and verify new trends. It also includes a description of an endeavour to construct a theory that will explain these trends and offer useful knowledge to those responsible for responding to them.

Part IV, on risk behaviour, demonstrates how qualitative research methods, and observation techniques in particular, have made a considerable contribution to the knowledge and understanding of health risks associated with drug injecting. However, it reveals that the use of qualitative methods varies widely between EU countries and that major gaps exist, particularly with regard to overdoses, hepatitis C, HIV, gender differences and user perspectives on treatment and harm-reduction services. Various aspects of risk behaviour are addressed in other sections of this monograph. This section of the book contains relatively few papers, due to the fact that the EMCDDA is planning a separate publication exclusively on this theme.

Part V is dedicated to the theme of social exclusion and incorporates a wide range of issues. These include: an examination of theoretical concepts associated with social exclusion; qualitative action research projects among ethnic minority communities; ethnographic research located in a specific geographical context; and a multiple data-source method to explore the relationship between heroin use and social exclusion. An evaluation of a day programme aimed at reintegrating long-term problem drug users into the wider community is also presented in this section.

Part VI, focusing on drug markets, highlights the dearth of studies on the drugs–crime relationship. It addresses the problems of collecting such data and identifies the methods, themes and contributions already apparent in various EU countries. The data presented here demonstrate how different types of qualitative research can contribute to understanding the development of the supply side of the illegal drug market and the people involved. The results, which contrast with official theories and dogmas, provide the means for rational responses to illegal drug markets. EU collaborative studies are now being funded to explore the real differences in the way in which the drug problem is defined and tackled, both between and within Member States.

Drug services evaluation is the theme of Part VII, which contains contributions from researchers who have evaluated a range of services targeted at a variety of problem drug users. These chapters show how qualitative evaluation leads to a deep understanding of drug users, which, in turn, enables service planners to provide efficiently for apparently contradictory needs. Such understanding has been shown to lead to more successful results than the adoption of restricted outcome measures which may jeopardise a client's chance of success and consequently lead to relapse.

Qualitative techniques and methods are the focus of Part VIII. This section addresses specific methods that may be adopted in the course of qualitative research. Caution is given about applying the 'medical paradigm' to service evaluations and using computer programs for qualitative data analysis. Problems and new developments in sampling techniques and employing drug users as fieldworkers are also described and ethical dilemmas discussed.

The final section of the monograph, Part IX, is devoted to qualitative research on drug use within a global research agenda. It reveals that the scale of qualitative drug research varies greatly between countries, that little is published in the drug-specific scientific journals and that high-quality work often appears to fail to influence policy. The debate between those wishing to make the qualitative approach more scientific and those wishing to preserve the 'purity' of the ethnographic approach is addressed. It concludes that a comprehensive approach should include the training of individual experts and research teams and exchanges of experience between researchers across and beyond Europe.

I hope that this monograph enhances understanding of drug use and the problems and responses to it, and encourages a wider appreciation of the contribution that qualitative research can make.

THE ROLE OF QUALITATIVE RESEARCH

PART I

INTRODUCTION

*I*n Chapter 1, Tim Rhodes describes the development of qualitative research and the multiple roles it plays in understanding and responding to illicit drug use.

These roles include:

- *reaching and researching hidden populations;*
- *understanding the experience and meaning of drug use;*
- *understanding the social context of drug use;*
- *informing the design of quantitative research;*
- *complementing and questioning the results of quantitative research; and*
- *developing effective interventions and policy responses.*

In short, qualitative research is seen as a prerequisite for understanding and responding to drug use.

THE MULTIPLE ROLES OF QUALITATIVE RESEARCH IN UNDERSTANDING AND RESPONDING TO ILLICIT DRUG USE

Tim Rhodes

It is said that the beginnings of modern qualitative research on drug use can be traced to De Quincey's *Confessions of an English Opium Eater* (1822), where the method employed was akin to participant observation (Feldman and Aldrich, 1990). As applied research, the methodological origins of qualitative research may be traced to social interactionism in sociology, which emerged in the 1920s and 1930s, led by the Chicago school (Znaniecki, 1934; Carey, 1975). These developments emphasised the socially situated nature of individual action, and demonstrated the value of integrating multiple qualitative methods to understand the subjective meanings and social contexts of behaviour, giving rise to a number of ethnographies in criminality and deviance (Anderson, 1923; Shaw, 1930; Whyte, 1955). The experience of addiction and dependency itself, for example, was found to have a social, rather than merely physiological, basis in socially situated understandings of what constituted withdrawal (Lindesmith, 1947). This was the genesis of qualitative research as a means of understanding drug use and its interpretation as socially constructed, and of encouraging intervention developments coherent with local practices in different cultural settings.

Building on the principles of social and symbolic interactionism, qualitative studies in the field of illicit drug use have been of note, not only for the social explanations of drug use and addiction they provided, but also for their insights into applied qualitative methodology and theorising on deviance (Becker, 1953; 1963; Agar, 1973; 1980; Weppner, 1977).

The clandestine nature of many drug use behaviours and subcultures has provided ideal terrain for the development of what are now considered classic ethnographies of drug use, deviance and normality (Becker, 1953; Sutter, 1966; Preble and Casey, 1969; Agar, 1973; Jackson, 1978). In the tradition of ethnography, the focus of such research was to 'make sense' of the social world of drug use from the perspectives of drug users. Drawing on a variety of techniques, including direct observations and face-to-face interviews, these studies sought to describe the everyday context of behaviours and lifestyles otherwise misunderstood or hidden from view.

Popular perceptions of drug users as passive or deviant were countered by drug ethnographies of the 1960s and 1970s which discovered purposeful and active meanings in drug use in the context of the drug user's lifestyle (Hughes, 1961; Becker, 1963; Preble and Casey, 1969; Feldman et al., 1979). As demonstrated by ethnographies of the use of LSD (Becker, 1970), PCP (phencyclidine) (Feldman et al., 1979), heroin in urban areas (Hughes, 1961; Preble and Casey, 1969; Agar, 1973), methadone (Preble and Miller, 1977) and alcohol (Spradley, 1970), popularly mis-understood behaviours were found to be rational and normal when understood from the perspectives of drug users, and when 'situated' within the social contexts in which they occurred.

While the dominant methodological approach in contemporary drugs research remains quantitative, there has been increasing receptivity to the use of qualitative methods as a means of understanding and responding to drug use (Agar, 1980; 1995; Rosenbaum, 1981; Adler, 1985; Pearson, 1987; Power, 1989; Moore, 1993; Ratner, 1993; Taylor, 1993; Gamella, 1994; 1997; Kaplan and Verbraek, 1999; Rhodes, 1999; Roldan and Gamella, 1999). This is particularly the case with regard to informing the development of policy and community interventions (Hughes, 1977; Atkins and Beschner, 1980; Feldman and Aldrich, 1990; Brooks, 1994; Agar, 1999).

The public health urgency surrounding HIV transmission associated with drug use provides a key example. Here, qualitative research has been demonstrated to be ideally suited to conducting studies among hidden populations 'at risk', as well as a means of identifying and interpreting 'risk behaviours' associated with drug use, and of developing social interventions in response (Murphy, 1987; Ouellet et al., 1991; McKeganey and Barnard, 1992; Sterk, 1993; Rhodes, 1995; 1997; Grund et al., 1996; Koester, 1996; Power et al., 1996; Wiebel, 1996; Bourgois, 1997). Research into AIDS has highlighted the role of qualitative research in both understanding the social context of drug use and risk behaviours, as well as in responding with prag-matic recommendations for intervention and policy developments.

At its most fundamental, the role of qualitative research into illicit drug use can therefore be envisaged as a means of understanding the lived experiences and meanings of drug use from the perspectives of drug users themselves. Additionally, as a means of understanding action as socially organised, qualitative research aims to understand how the lived experiences and meanings associated with drug use are influenced by different social, cultural and economic contexts. At the outset, quali-tative research aims to describe the context-based nature of drug use and the social meanings that such behaviours are perceived to have. Qualitative research thus pro-ceeds on the assumption that it is possible to gain insight into the factors producing social behaviour primarily through engaging with the lives of participants them-selves. The role of ethnography, for example, has been described as an attempt to 'record how individuals perceive, construct, and interact within their social and economic environment' (James, 1977, p. 180).

While ethnography may have a higher status in the field of addictions than else-where, there still very much remains a 'divide' between quantitative and qualitative approaches to drugs research (Heath, 1995; McKeganey, 1995; Pearson, 1995). This is neither helpful nor appropriate in developing understanding of the interplay of individual, social and contextual factors influencing drug use (Agar, 1995). All methods are tools, and each necessarily reveals and conceals different aspects of the phenomena under study (Denzin, 1970). The challenge for future drugs research is to recognise the pragmatic utility and methodological desirability of using multiple methods, in order to encourage research which understands the epidemiology and the social context of drug use. With this in mind, the multiple roles of qualitative research in understanding and responding to drug use are summarised below.

The multiple roles of qualitative drugs research

Reaching and researching hidden populations

The first consideration is both methodological and practical. Illicit drug use is a hidden activity and, in most countries, the majority of drug users remain hidden from treatment and agency-based services. Those in contact with services are often unrepresentative of the broader population of drug users, and this may be the case with regard to patterns of drug use, risk behaviour and health status. This has led researchers to consider sampling designs capable of reaching hidden populations, whose 'membership is not readily distinguished or enumerated based on existing knowledge and/or sampling capabilities' (Wiebel, 1990, p. 6). Overcoming such sampling problems, including those of access, bias and trust, has encouraged considerable methodological innovation in sampling design (Lambert, 1990; Carlson et al., 1994; Council of Europe, 1997; Sifaneck and Neaigus, 1999). A key characteristic of such innovation is the use of ethnographic theoretical sampling techniques, emphasising inductive approaches to targeted social networks and snowball, purposive and quota sampling (Biernacki and Waldorf, 1981; Carlson et al., 1999).

In the absence of pre-existing or representative sampling frames, sampling methods in surveys of drug use largely utilise data from multiple sources, in order to target theoretically driven quotas of drug users and/or social networks using a variety of chain-referral techniques (Biernacki and Waldorf, 1981; Cohen, 1989; Diaz et al., 1992; Hendriks et al., 1992). Emphasising theoretical and methodological realism over scientific idealism, such approaches commonly use ethnography to inform the development of numeric sampling quotas — in particular geographical or social environments — as well as in participant recruitment and follow-up (Carlson et al., 1999).

The use of ethnographic fieldworkers and key informants, including those with indigenous or privileged access, has become a common feature of such designs, aiming to maximise access and rapport as well as ethnographic descriptions of networks and settings (Hughes, 1977; Hendriks et al., 1992; Griffiths et al., 1993; Power, 1995; see also Chapter 36 in this monograph). While the use of snowball sampling methods borrows from ethnographic methodology, particularly as far as gaining access, rapport and informing sampling design are concerned, such studies need not be 'ethnographic' in the data they collect, nor in the analyses they undertake. However, qualitative sampling methods have become key features of quantitative studies of drug use (Biernacki and Waldorf, 1981; Carlson et al., 1994; 1999).

Understanding the experience and meaning of drug use

Behaviours communicate social meanings. Both the nature of knowledge itself and the process by which it is acquired shape the lived experience and perceived meanings of drug use. Two key tenets of qualitative research are to describe the social meanings participants attach to drug use experiences and the social processes by which such meanings are created, reinforced and reproduced (Moore, 1993; Rhodes, 1995; Agar, 1997). Illicit drug use is a social activity and the process of drug taking derives symbolic importance, and has social meaning, depending on the contexts of use (Becker, 1953; Grund, 1993). Qualitative research is therefore concerned with descriptions of how drug use is 'lived' and interpreted through social interactions. Whereas epidemiological research concentrates on delineating the distribution of patterns of drug use and its consequences, qualitative research aims to appreciate why such behaviours occur and how they are understood in different contexts among different social groups (Rhodes, 1995).

Because of their inductive and iterative approach to data collection and hypothesis generation, qualitative methods are ideally suited to identifying and describing the lived experience of drug use from participant perspectives. Whereas deductive designs, as well as most quantitative research, tend to be construct-driven — defining categories or variables of interest a priori on the basis of pre-existing hypotheses and theoretical frameworks — inductive designs aim to construct interpretations on the basis of data as they emerge from participant descriptions and observations (Agar, 1980; Layder, 1993). To oversimplify, the ethnography of drug use is data-driven, and thus hypothesis-generating, and leads to the discovery of subjective meaning, whereas the epidemiology of drug use is construct-driven, and thus hypothesis-testing, and leads to the charting of (presumed-to-be) objective measures of drug use.

Examples abound of the contribution of qualitative research to discovering how the meanings of drug use are socially organised. The ethnographies conducted by Howard Becker on marijuana and LSD use, for example, describe how drug use behaviours are a function of the social meanings they are perceived to communicate to participants (Becker, 1953; 1963; 1970). As his studies illustrate, the lived experience of the effects of drugs only comes to have meaning in the context of individuals' expectations of drug effects, which are themselves a function of the social organisation of knowledge in particular social networks or settings (Becker, 1953; 1970). The subjective meanings participants attach to their drug use, as with any behaviour, 'arise in the course of social interaction which itself is situated within wider cultures — "or subcultures" — of meaning and understanding' (Becker, 1970, p. 311). Qualitative research is therefore necessary if researchers and interventionists are to grasp how drug use experiences are differently interpreted by social groups in different settings.

A more recent example concerns ethnographic descriptions of HIV-related risk behaviour associated with injecting drug use. These studies have shown that needle and syringe sharing is not simply the product of risk perception or risk calculus, but that such practices also depend on the symbolic meanings they are perceived to have among participants (Murphy, 1987; Zule, 1992; Barnard, 1993; Grund, 1993). While commonly categorised a priori as 'risk behaviour' by construct-driven research paradigms, syringe sharing may alternatively be interpreted by participants as a symbol of trust and reciprocity, particularly within close friendships and sexual relationships (Zule, 1992; Grund, 1993). Qualitative understandings of the social meanings of epidemiologically defined risk behaviours help provide an appreciation of why such practices occur in certain situations or contexts, even given individuals' knowledge of the health risks involved (Rhodes, 1997).

Understanding the social contexts of drug use

The social meanings of behaviours are context-dependent. As noted, qualitative research aims to understand the nexus of meaning and context (Agar, 1995; 1997). Here, the role of qualitative research is to distinguish how drug use patterns, and their meaning and interpretation, differ by social, cultural and economic context. The social context of drug use is made up of an interplay of factors, including individual and group subjective interpretations of drug use, the physical, interpersonal and social settings in which drug use occurs, and wider structural and environmental factors. Building on notions of symbolic interactionism — the study of how the social meanings of behaviour are created and reinforced through social interaction itself (Denzin, 1970) — social context is viewed as a key process, influencing how the meanings and practices of drug use are socially organised (Becker, 1963; 1970).

A variety of studies have illustrated how individuals' beliefs and interactions associated with drug use are influenced by context. Following the example above, the meanings and practices of needle and syringe sharing have been found to depend on the influence of perceived social or network norms and expectations (Barnard, 1993; Wiebel, 1996; Rhodes and Quirk, 1996; Power et al., 1996); particular interpersonal and social relationships (Zule, 1992; Barnard, 1993; Rhodes and Quirk, 1998); the physical and social settings in which drug use occurs (Ouellet et al., 1991; Ruggiero, 1993; Turnbull et al., 1996; Wiebel, 1996); and wider structural, economic and policy factors (Pearson, 1987; Fraser and George, 1988; Grund et al., 1992; Gamella, 1994; Bourgois, 1997). The ethnographic work of Ouellet et al. (1991) and Wiebel (1996), for example, shows how different Chicago 'shooting galleries' have different rules for the sale or rent of injecting equipment, which, in turn, sustain different social norms influencing individuals' drug use and HIV risk behaviour. Here, the 'micro-setting' is envisaged as a key contextual factor influencing proximity to risk and opportunities for risk reduction. In contrast, studies by Grund et al. (1992) and Watters (1996) illustrate how the 'macro-setting' — in this case, the policy and economic context — influences the formation of drug users' social and support networks, which, in turn, impact on individual and group opportunities for risk reduction.

Other examples concern the contribution of qualitative findings to understanding the influence of social context on drug trends. Studies by Pearson (1987), Fraser and George (1988) and Gamella (1994), for example, show how exogenous factors — such as policing, housing and heroin availability — influence the social relationships maintained or lost within particular geographical or social networks, which, in turn, influence patterns of purchasing and dealing, and the diffusion of new drug trends. Of key interest here is the dual importance of social relationships in mediating initiation and use, and the influence of macro contextual factors in creating or sustaining social relationships conducive to drug use (Pearson, 1987; Gamella, 1994). In a quite different study, Henderson (1996) describes how patterns of ecstasy use are, to a large extent, socially organised within the social mores of rave and dance club cultures. Like Becker's work on LSD and marijuana (Becker, 1953; 1970), she finds the behavioural manifestations of the effects of ecstasy are contained within this particular context. The social contexts of drug use environments mediate the social meanings and practices of drug use, and qualitative research has a pragmatic contribution to make to the development of interventions and policies that are coherent with ideas of social and environmental change.

Informing quantitative research

A well-established role of qualitative research is to inform the design of quantitative measures of drug use. Here, qualitative research aims to inform the construction of meaningful constructs or measures in quantitative studies, as well as to shape appropriate analyses and their interpretation (Wiebel, 1990; 1996). A key example in HIV prevention research concerns the identification and interpretation of risk behaviours associated with drug use. The practices of 'front-loading' and 'back-loading', for example, were identified on the basis of direct observations of drug injecting in Rotterdam (Grund et al., 1991). Similarly, ethnographic observations in Denver and El Paso identified a variety of other 'indirect' sharing practices, at the time previously unexplored (Koester et al., 1990; Koester, 1996; Wiebel, 1996). These included the shared use of 'cookers', 'cottons' and rinse water among participants, even after they had made attempts to reduce HIV transmission risks by flushing out their syringes with bleach. In each case, drug injectors were found to be unwittingly engaging in risk behaviour (Wiebel, 1996). These practices have since entered the battery of epidemiological measures designed to assess the prevalence and distribution of risk associated with equipment sharing (Jose et al., 1993; Hunter et al., 1995; Ingold and Toussirt, 1997).

In addition to identifying drug use behaviours or theoretical constructs for subsequent epidemiological measurement, qualitative data play a key role in interpreting the findings generated from quantitative research. It has been demonstrated, for example, that data from qualitative interviews may be used to help interpret and substantiate the findings of quantitative surveys and statistical models (Barnard and

Frischer, 1995). While statistical modelling may identify correlational relationships between variables, it does not adequately assess why or how these relationships exist, nor explain what these associations mean. The triangulation of multiple methods and data sources, and the combined use of quantitative and qualitative methods in particular, enables the researcher to cross-check findings in order to increase the validity of the interpretations made (Denzin, 1970).

Complementing and questioning quantitative research

As a complement to epidemiological research, which traditionally centres on the interplay between 'agent', 'host' and 'environment', the role of qualitative research has been described as an attempt to provide closer understandings of how 'host' interacts with 'environment' (Agar, 1997). As noted above, qualitative understandings of the meaning and context of drug use are crucial for informing epidemiological studies. This has led towards the development of 'ethno-epidemiologies' of drug use (Agar, 1995; 1997). These involve attempts to better situate epidemiological measures and analyses within participant, rather than outsider, frameworks of interpretation, as well as attempts to encourage paradigm shifts in contemporary epidemiology from an overemphasis on risk factor approaches towards emphasising the social–environmental determinants of drug use (Agar, 1995; Pearce, 1996; Susser and Susser, 1996). As Michael Agar indicates, 'ethnography isn't just a methodological add-on; it is a conceptual and theoretical means to a necessary epidemiological end' (Agar, 1997, p. 1166). In this respect, ethnography and epidemiology converge, where the 'failures' of modern risk factor epidemiology (Susser and Susser, 1996) encourage a realisation of the need for epidemiological constructs to be ethnographically explored, as well as for ethnography to inform the development of epidemiological measures.

> *The first need is to restore 'host' and 'environment' to central importance in epidemiological analysis, to defocus on 'agent' and celebrate the two other corners of the epidemiological triad. From 'host' it isn't difficult to derive a focus on 'meaning', for it is a truism that human hosts live in a symbolic and material world. And it isn't difficult to arrive at 'context' from 'environment', since a concern with context reveals the layers of circumstance, ranging from immediate situation to political economy, in which the 'hosts' shape their lives. The need to restore the importance of host and environment, then, requires the study of meaning and context. And the investigation of meaning and context is exactly the research task that ethnography is designed to accomplish.* (Agar, 1997, p. 1166)

There is general consensus that quantitative methods can learn from qualitative methods, as well as vice versa, and that methods provide a set of complementary tools to investigation, rather than necessarily indicating a particular logic of inquiry or explanation (Hartnoll, 1995). There is agreement that 'methodological identity' should not be preserved at 'the cost of greater understanding' (McKeganey, 1995). However, the long-standing divide between 'qualitative-inductive' and 'quantitative-deductive' approaches exists for a reason. Every method, to some extent, shapes the findings it produces, yet qualitative methods are better suited to questioning deductive modes of explanation than the other way round (Pearson, 1995; Rhodes, 1995). Quantitative–qualitative differences are helpful if all methods are appropriately applied to the research question in hand and if both can be scientifically critical of the other (Hartnoll, 1995; Pearson, 1995).

An ethnographically informed epidemiology of drug use is a challenge which continues to escape most drugs research, and few contemporary epidemiological studies of drug use either attempt or adequately achieve an understanding of drug use in its environment (ACMD, 1998). An additional role played by qualitative research, therefore, is that it has the potential to question the application and interpretation of a priori epidemiological constructs, as well as the logic of deductive research (Moore, 1993; Rhodes, 1995; 1997; Bloor, 1997; Romaní, 1997). This is particularly important given the considerable resistance to paradigm shifts within epidemiology, and the paradigm predominance of positivism more generally (Susser and Susser, 1996).

The tenets of induction and hypothesis generation encourage analyses grounded in the perspectives of participants, of which the researcher is one, and thus aim to make visible the subjective and inter-subjective meanings of action (Agar, 1997). Qualitative drugs research is both iterative and reflexive (Moore, 1993). In adopting a different epistemological logic in the formation of interpretation and judgment from deductive approaches, it both complements and challenges the assumed objectivity of common-sense understandings of drug use. Induction enables the discovery of plural — and competing — interpretations of drug use and addiction which often fall outside the interpretative frameworks championed by positivist and conventional epidemiological research. As David Moore has noted of his ethnography of recreational drug use, whereas dominant research and policy discourses talk of 'drug-related "problems" and "harm" and how to reduce their incidence', participants were found to emphasise the benefits of drug use in their 'talk of "big nights" and "speeding"' (Moore, 1993, p. 17). Studies oriented to explorations in ethno-epidemiology have illustrated how 'drug use', 'addiction' and 'problems' associated with drug use are, in part, socially constructed by the paradigms, methods and findings of research (Bloor, 1997). Qualitative methods are, of course, not immune to this process (since all acts of research are forms of interaction and interpretation), but they aim to be reflexive about the process of interpretation, and do not blindly purport to capture objectivity.

It is important to reiterate that drug users are the experts on their lived experiences of drug use. No research method or design has the capacity to capture objective empirical 'facts', and it is pretence or rhetoric which says otherwise (Moore, 1993). This is obviously of concern when particular methods or forms of research purport to capture objectivity by virtue of their own claims, institutional self-legitimation, and symbolic or scientific capital. There remains very much a divide in paradigms of inductive and deductive science, as well as in applied qualitative and quantitative methods (McKeganey, 1995; Heath, 1995; Pearson, 1995). The role of qualitative methods is undervalued, and they rarely reach their potential, because they are commonly envisaged as a mere complement or supplement to positivist research (viewed as producing hard or objective facts and as 'real science'). The challenge for the future clearly involves the use of multiple methods in drugs research and this also requires recognition of the paradigmatic differences under-pinning induction and deduction. Not only is there a need to ground epidemiology within participant interpretative frameworks of what is meaningful, but there is an equal need to realise the contribution of qualitative research in questioning 'expert' understandings, the discourses of drug use within which they operate, and their per-petuation by an over-reliance on positivist paradigms.

Developing effective intervention and policy responses

The pivotal role of qualitative research in informing the design of drug interventions and policies is twofold. Firstly, it is important to target interventions in accord with local drug use norms and practices. This also demands an appreciation of how dif-ferent social and economic contexts influence drug use, as well as drug users' capacity for initiating and sustaining behaviour change. Secondly, an understanding of the social processes shaping everyday drug use is a necessary prerequisite for developing interventions which are meaningful and useful to drug users themselves. A wealth of research highlights the pragmatic contribution of qualitative research to intervention and policy development, particularly with regard to the design and evaluation of community-based initiatives (Hughes, 1977; Feldman and Aldrich, 1990; Brooks, 1994; Larson, 1999).

In keeping with the multiple roles of qualitative research summarised above, ethno-graphic contributions to drug intervention developments — including policy — have emphasised the importance of:

- understanding drug users' perceived needs for, and experiences of, interven-tions;
- understanding service providers' perceptions of service need, organisation and effectiveness; and
- exploring the social and contextual processes influencing the effectiveness of intervention delivery and impact (as with qualitative process evaluation).

Examples have included: treatment ethnographies exploring drug users' experiences of methadone and other forms of drug treatment (Preble and Miller, 1977; Korf and Hoogenhout, 1990; Keene and Raynor, 1993; Schroers, 1995); help-seeking and service utilisation (Hartnoll and Power, 1989); general practice (McKeganey, 1988); health promotion and community interventions (Jamieson et al., 1984; Brooks, 1994; Blanken and Tenholter, 1995; De Ruyver et al., 1995; Sheridan and Barber, 1996; Shiner and Newburn, 1996); responses to policy (Grund et al., 1992; Bieleman et al., 1993); developing links between ethnography and community out-reach (Hughes, 1977; Sterk, 1993; Wiebel, 1996); and understanding the impact of prison settings on drug use (Turnbull et al., 1996).

Here, qualitative research is viewed not as a means of knowledge generation for its own ends but as a means of 'action-oriented' research and intervention development (Power, 1995; Rhodes et al., 1999). The increasing receptivity to the use of qualitative methods is less indicative of wider paradigm shifts in method than it is an outcome of the realisation that qualitative methods in particular have immense practical utility for developing local responses to drug use (Feldman and Aldrich, 1990; Wiebel, 1996). This has led to the development of models of qualitative action research (Power, 1995) and of rapid assessment and response using multiple qualitative methods (Rhodes et al., 1999). The development and evaluation of effective responses require an understanding of the interplay between the meanings and contexts of drug use, as well as of intervention need, feasibility and appropriateness. Qualitative research is ideally positioned to provide the data necessary for evidence-based practice.

Conclusions

In conclusion, I envisage multiple roles for qualitative research in understanding and responding to drug use. Qualitative methods are viewed as a complement to quantitative methods, and it should be emphasised that all methods are tools for capturing different aspects of drug use and its consequences. The challenge for future drugs research is to enlist qualitative methods as fundamental components of multi-method studies of drug use. Qualitative methods and, more generally, inductive designs, complement their quantitative and deductive counterparts in capturing the interplay between the meanings and contexts of drug use.

If one challenge for future drugs research is to realise the opportunities afforded by multiple methods, a second challenge is to recognise the importance of developing ethno-methodological studies of drug use. To deny the differences between inductive and deductive designs, as well as their respective links with qualitative and quantitative methods in contemporary drugs research, is also to underplay the additional role of qualitative research in challenging common-sense interpretations of drug use, often unwittingly reinforced and reproduced by positivist paradigms. In the absence of qualitative research, there is a danger of perpetuating understandings of drug use which are devoid of relevance or meaning for participants. This, in turn, can encourage the formation of policy or the development of interventions which are inappropriate or ineffective, and, at worst, counterproductive. Qualitative research is a prerequisite for understanding and responding to drug use.

The author is Senior Research Fellow at the Centre for Research on Drugs and Health Behaviour, Department of Social Science and Medicine, Imperial College School of Medicine, University of London, UK.

Acknowledgements

Sections of this introduction draw on Rhodes, T. and Moore, D. (1999, forthcoming) 'On the qualitative in drugs research', *Addiction Research*, special issue on qualitative research in the addictions.

References

Adler, P. (1985) *Wheeling and Dealing: an Ethnography of an Upper-Level Drug Dealing and Smuggling Community*, New York: Columbia University Press.

Advisory Council on the Misuse of Drugs (ACMD) (1998) *Drug Use and the Environment*, London: Home Office.

Agar, M. (1973) *Ripping and Running: a Formal Ethnography of Urban Heroin Users*, New York: Academic Press.

Agar, M. (1980) *The Professional Stranger: an Informal Introduction to Ethnography*, New York: Academic Press.

Agar, M. (1995) 'Recasting the "ethno" in "epidemiology"', *Medical Anthropology*, 16, 1–13.

Agar, M. (1997) 'Ethnography: an overview', *Substance Use and Misuse*, 32, 1155–1173.

Agar, M. (1999, forthcoming) 'Qualitative research and public policy', in T. Rhodes (Ed.) *Qualitative Methods in Drugs Research,* London: Sage.

Anderson, N. (1923) *The Hob*, Chicago: University of Chicago Press.

Atkins, C. and Beschner, G. (Eds.) (1980) *Ethnography: a Research Tool for Policy-Makers in the Drug and Alcohol Fields*, US Department of Health and Human Services (Publication No ADM 80–946).

Barnard, M. A. (1993) 'Needle sharing in context', *Addiction*, 88, 805–812.

Barnard, M. and Frischer, M. (1995) 'Combining quantitative and qualitative: researching HIV-related risk behaviours among drug injectors', *Addiction Research*, 2, 351–362.

Becker, H. (1953) 'Becoming a marijuana user', *American Journal of Sociology*, 59, 235–242.

Becker, H. (1963) *Outsiders: Studies in the Sociology of Deviance*, London: Free Press.

Becker, H. (1970) 'History, culture and subjective experience: an exploration of the social bases of drug-induced experiences', in H. Becker (Ed.) *Sociological Work,* Chicago: Aldine.

Bieleman, B., ten Den, C. and Kroes, L. (1993) 'De wijze waarop heroïnegebruikers reageren op drugsmaatregelen (The way in which heroin users react to drug policy measures)', *Tijdschrift voor Alcohol, Drugs en andere Psychotrope Stoffen*, 19(2), 107–115.

Biernacki, P. and Waldorf, D. (1981) 'Snowball sampling: problems and techniques of chain referral sampling', *Sociological Methods and Research*, 10, 141–163.

Blanken, P. and Tenholter, J. (1995) 'Convenience advertising als medium voor AIDS-preventie onder risico jongeren (Convenience advertising as a medium for AIDS prevention among youth at risk)', Rotterdam: Addiction Research Institute (IVO)/Erasmus University.

Bloor, M. (1997) 'Addressing social problems through qualitative research', in D. Silverman (Ed.) *Qualitative Research: Theory, Method and Practice,* London: Sage.

Bourgois, P. (1997) 'Social misery and the sanctions of substance abuse: confronting HIV risk among homeless heroin addicts in San Francisco', *Social Problems,* 44, 155–173.

Brooks, C. (1994) 'Using ethnography in the evaluation of drug prevention and intervention programs', *International Journal of the Addictions,* 29, 791–801.

Carey, J. (1975) *Sociology and Public Affairs: the Chicago School,* London: Sage.

Carlson, R., Wang, J., Siegal, H., Flack, R. and Guo, J. (1994) 'An ethnographic approach to targeted sampling: problems and solutions in AIDS prevention research among injection drug and crack-cocaine users', *Human Organisation,* 53, 279–286.

Carlson, R., Wang, J., Siegal, H., et al. (1999, forthcoming) 'Ethnography and targeted sampling', in T. Rhodes (Ed.) *Qualitative Methods in Drugs Research,* London: Sage.

Cohen, P. (1989) *Cocaine Use in Amsterdam in Non-Deviant Subcultures,* Amsterdam: Instituut voor Sociale Geografie, Universiteit van Amsterdam.

Council of Europe, Pompidou Group (1997) *The Handbook on Snowball Sampling,* Strasbourg: Council of Europe.

De Ruyver, B., Soenens, A., Van Daele, L. and Vanderbeken, T. (1995) *Straathoek werk in Vlaanderen: Opstellen van een theoretische concept voor straathoek werk. Inhoudelijke en methodische ondersteuning van de veldwerkers en hun coodinatoren (Outreach projects in Flanders: Formulating a theoretical concept of outreach work in view of intrinsic and methodological support to workers and their employers),* King Baudouin Foundation, Research Group Drug Policies.

Denzin, N. (1970) *The Research Act,* Chicago: Aldine.

Diaz, A., Barruti, M. and Doncel, C. (1992) *The Lines of Success? A Study on the Nature and Extent of Cocaine Use in Barcelona,* Barcelona: Laboratori de Sociologia.

Feldman, H. W., Agar, M. and Beschner, G. M. (Eds.) (1979) *Angel Dust: an Ethnographic Study of PCP Users,* Lexington, MA: Heath/Lexington Books.

Feldman, H. and Aldrich, M. (1990) 'The role of ethnography in substance abuse research and public policy', in E. Lambert (Ed.) *The Collection and Interpretation of Data from Hidden Populations,* Rockville: National Institute on Drug Abuse (Monograph 98).

Fraser, A. and George, M. (1988) 'Changing trends in drug use: an initial follow-up of a local heroin community', *British Journal of Addiction,* 83, 655–663.

Gamella, J. (1994) 'The spread of intravenous drug use and AIDS in a neighbourhood in Spain', *Medical Anthropology Quarterly,* 8, 131–160.

Gamella, J. (1997) *Las rutinas del yonqui activo: un modelo cognitivo, Jornadas sobre Programas de Intercambio de Jeringuillas,* Ministerio de Sanidad y Consumo.

Griffiths, P., Gossop, M., Powis, B. and Strang, J. (1993) 'Reaching hidden populations of drug users by privileged access interviewers', *Addiction,* 88, 1617–1626.

Grund, J.-P. C. (1993) *Drug Use as a Social Ritual: Functionality, Symbolism and Determinants of Self-Regulation,* Rotterdam: Instituut voor Verslavingsonderzoek.

Grund, J.-P. C., Friedman, S. R., Stern, L. S., Jose, B., Neaigus, A., et al. (1996) 'Syringe-mediated drug sharing among injecting drug users: patterns, social context and implications for transmission of blood-borne pathogens', *Social Science and Medicine*, 42, 691–703.

Grund, J.-P. C., Kaplan, C., Adriaans, N. F. P. and Blanken, P. (1991) 'Drug sharing and HIV transmission risks: the practice of "frontloading" in the Dutch injecting drug user population', *Journal of Psychoactive Drugs*, 23, 1–10.

Grund, J.-P. C., Stern, L. S., Kaplan, C. D., Adriaans, N. F. P. and Drucker, E. (1992) 'Drug use contexts and HIV-consequences: the effect of drug policy on patterns of everyday drug use in Rotterdam and the Bronx', *British Journal of Addiction*, 87, 381–392.

Hartnoll, R. (1995) 'A difficult business', *Addiction*, 90, 762–763.

Hartnoll, R. and Power, R. (1989) *A Study of Help-Seeking and Service Utilisation*, London: Institute for the Study of Drug Dependence.

Heath, D. (1995) 'Quantitative and qualitative research on alcohol and drugs: a helpful reminder', *Addiction*, 90, 753–755.

Henderson, S. (1996) '"E types and dance divas": gender research and community prevention', in T. Rhodes and R. Hartnoll (Eds.) *AIDS, Drugs and Prevention: Perspectives on Individual and Community Action*, London: Routledge.

Hendriks, V. M., Blanken, P. and Adriaans, N. F. P. (1992) *Snowball Sampling: a Pilot Study on Cocaine Use*, Rotterdam: Addiction Research Institute, Erasmus University.

Hughes, H. (1961) *The Fantastic Lodge: the Autobiography of a Drug Addict*, New York: Fawcett World Library.

Hughes, P. (1977) *Behind the Wall of Respect: Community Experiments in Heroin Addiction Control*, Chicago: University of Chicago Press.

Hunter, G. M., Donoghoe, M. C. and Stimson, G. V., et al. (1995) 'Changes in the injecting risk behaviour of injecting drug users in London, 1990–1993', *AIDS*, 9, 493–501.

Ingold, F. R. and Toussirt, M. (1997) *Étude Multi-Centrique sur les Attitudes et les Comportements des Toxicomanes Face au Risque de Contamination par la VIH et les Virus d'Hépatites*, Paris: IREP.

Jackson, B. (1978) 'Deviance as success: the double inversion of stigmatised roles', in B. A. Babcock (Ed.) *The Reversible World*, Ithaca: Cornell University Press.

James, J. (1977) 'Ethnography and social problems', in R. Weppner (Ed.) *Street Ethnography*, Beverly Hills, CA: Sage.

Jamieson, A., Glanz, A. and MacGregor, S. (1984) *Dealing with Drug Misuse: Crisis Intervention in the City*, London: Tavistock.

Jose, B., Friedman, S. R. and Neaigus, A., et al. (1993) 'Syringe-mediated drug-sharing (backloading): a new risk factor for HIV among injecting drug users', *AIDS*, 7, 1653–1660.

Kaplan, C. and Verbraek, H. (1999) 'The changing nature of Dutch drugs ethnography', *Addiction Research* (submitted).

Keene, J. and Raynor, P. (1993) 'Addiction as a "soul sickness": the influence of client and therapist beliefs', *Addiction Research*, 1, 77–87.

Knipe, E. (1995) *Culture, Society and Drugs: the Social Science Approach to Drug Use*, Prospect Heights, IL: Waveland Press.

Koester, S. (1996) 'The process of drug injection: applying ethnography to the study of HIV risk among IDUs', in T. Rhodes and R. Hartnoll (Eds.) *AIDS, Drugs and Prevention: Perspectives on Individual and Community Action*, London: Routledge.

Koester, S., Booth, R. and Wiebel, W. (1990) 'The risk of HIV transmission from sharing water, drug mixing containers and cotton filters among intravenous drug users', *International Journal on Drug Policy*, 1, 28–30.

Korf, D. J. and Hoogenhout, H. P. H. (1990) *Zoden aan de dijk: Heroïnegebruikers en hun ervaringen met en waardering van de Amsterdamse drughulpverlening (What good is that? Heroin users and their experiences with and appraisal of the drug treatment services in Amsterdam)*, Amsterdam: Instituut voor Sociale Geografie, Universiteit van Amsterdam.

Lambert, E. (Ed.) (1990) *The Collection and Interpretation of Data from Hidden Populations*, Washington, DC: National Institute on Drug Abuse.

Larson, A. (1999, forthcoming) 'Fostering ownership of illicit drug research by marginalised communities', in T. Rhodes (Ed.) *Qualitative Methods in Drugs Research,* London: Sage.

Layder, D. (1993) *New Strategies in Social Research*, Cambridge: Polity Press.

Lindesmith, A. (1947) *Opiate Addiction*, Bloomington, IN: Principia Press.

McKeganey, N. (1988) 'Drug abuse in the community', in S. J. Cunningham-Burley and N. McKeganey (Eds.) *Readings in Medical Sociology*, London: Routledge.

McKeganey, N. (1995) 'Quantitative and qualitative research in the addictions: an unhelpful divide', *Addiction*, 90, 749–751.

McKeganey, N. and Barnard, M. (1992) AIDS, *Drugs and Sexual Risk: Lives in the Balance*, Milton Keynes: Open University Press.

Moore, D. (1993) 'Ethnography and illicit drug use: dispatches from an anthropologist in the field', *Addiction Research*, 1, 11–15.

Murphy, S. (1987) 'Intravenous drug use and AIDS: notes on the social economy of needle sharing', *Contemporary Drug Problems*, 14, 373–395.

Ouellet, L., Jimenez, A., Wendell, J. and Wiebel, W. (1991) 'Shooting galleries and HIV disease: variations in places for injecting illicit drugs', *Crime and Delinquency*, 37, 64–85.

Pearce, N. (1996) 'Traditional epidemiology, modern epidemiology and public health', *American Journal of Public Health*, 86, 678–683.

Pearson, G. (1987) *The New Heroin Users*, London: Blackwell.

Pearson, G. (1995) 'The quantitative–qualitative dispute: an unhelpful divide, but one to be lived with', *Addiction*, 90, 759–761.

Plant, M. (1975) *Drug Takers in an English Town*, London: Tavistock.

Power, R. (1989) 'Participant observation and its place in the study of illicit drug use', *British Journal of Addiction*, 84, 43–52.

Power, R. (1995) 'A model of qualitative action research amongst illicit drug users', *Addiction Research*, 3, 165–181.

Power, R., Jones, S., Kearns, G. and Ward, J. (1996) 'An ethnography of risk management amongst illicit drug injectors and its implications for the development of community-based interventions', *Sociology of Health and Illness*, 18, 86–106.

Preble, E. and Casey, J. (1969) 'Taking care of business: the heroin user's life on the street', *International Journal of the Addictions*, 4, 1–24.

Preble, E. and Miller, T. (1977) 'Methadone, wine and welfare', in R. Weppner (Ed.) *Street Ethnography*, Beverly Hills: Sage.

Quirk, A., Holland, J. and Hartnoll, R. (1991) *Hard to Reach or Out of Reach?* London: Tufnell Press.

Quirk, A., Lily, R., Rhodes, T. and Stimson, G. V. (1998) *Opening the Black Box: a Qualitative Study of Methadone Treatment Process*, London: Centre for Research on Drugs and Health Behaviour.

Ratner, M. (1993) *Crack Pipe as Pimp*, New York: Lexington.

Rhodes, T. (1995) 'Researching and theorising "risk": notes on the social relations of risk in heroin users' lifestyles', in P. Aggleton, G. Hart and P. Davies (Eds.) *AIDS: Sexuality, Safety and Risk*, London: Taylor and Francis.

Rhodes, T. (1997) 'Risk theory in epidemic times: sex, drugs and the social organisation of risk behaviour', *Sociology of Health and Illness*, 19, 208–227.

Rhodes, T. (Ed.) (1999, forthcoming) *Qualitative Methods in Drugs Research,* London: Sage.

Rhodes, T., Hartnoll, R. and Holland, J. (1991) *Hard to Reach or Out of Reach? An Evaluation of an Innovative Model of Outreach Health Education*, London: Tufnell Press.

Rhodes, T. and Moore, D. (1999) 'On the qualitative in drugs research', *Addiction Research* (submitted).

Rhodes, T. and Quirk, A. (1996) 'Heroin, risk and sexual safety: some problems for interventions encouraging community change', in T. Rhodes and R. Hartnoll (Eds.) *AIDS, Drugs and Prevention*, London: Routledge.

Rhodes, T. and Quirk, A. (1998) 'Drug users' sexual relationships and the social organisation of risk', *Social Science and Medicine*, 46, 161–183.

Rhodes, T., Stimson, G. V., Fitch, C., et al. (1999) 'Rapid assessment, injecting drug use and public health', *The Lancet.*

Roldan, A. A. and Gamella, J. (1999) 'The limits and scope of ethnography', *Addiction Research* (unpublished paper).

Romaní, O. (1997) 'Etnografía y drogas: discursos y prácticas', *Nueva Antropología*, 16(52), 39–66.

Rosenbaum, M. (1981) *Women on Heroin*, Brunswick, NJ: Rutgers University Press.

Ruggiero, V. (1993) 'Brixton, London: a drug culture without a drug economy', *The International Journal of Drug Policy*, 4, 83–90.

Schroers, A. (1995) *Szenealltag im Kontaktcafe (Everyday life of the scene in a street corner agency)*, Berlin: Verlag für Wissenschaft und Bildung.

Shaw, C. (1930) *The Jack-Roller*, Chicago: University of Chicago Press.

Sheridan, J. and Barber, N. (1996) 'Drug misusers' experiences and opinions of community pharmacists and community pharmacy services', *The Pharmaceutical Journal*, 2370, 325–327.

Shiner, M. and Newburn, T. (1996) *Young People, Drugs and Peer Education: an Evaluation of the Youth Awareness Programme*, London: Home Office.

Sifaneck, S. J. and Neaigus, A. (1999) 'Assessing, sampling and screening hidden populations: heroin sniffers in New York City', *Addiction Research* (submitted).

Silverman, D. (1985) *Qualitative Methodology and Sociology*, Aldershot: Gower.

Spradley, J. P. (1970) *You Owe Yourself a Drunk: an Ethnography of Urban Nomads*, Boston: Little Brown.

Sterk, C. (1993) 'Outreach among drug users: combining the role of ethnographic field assistant and health educator', *Human Organisation*, 52, 162–168.

Susser, M. and Susser, E. (1996) 'Choosing a future for epidemiology: from Black Box to Chinese Boxes to Eco Epidemiology', *American Journal of Public Health*, 86, 674–677.

Sutter, A. (1966) 'The world of the righteous dope fiend', *Issues in Criminology*, 2, 177–222.

Taylor, A. (1993) *Women Drug Users: an Ethnography of Female Injecting*, Oxford: Clarendon.

Thrasher, F. (1927) *The Gang*, Chicago: University of Chicago Press.

Turnbull, P., Dolan, K. A. and Stimson, G. V. (1991) *Prisons, HIV and AIDS: Risks and Experiences in Custodial Care*, Horsham: AVERT.

Turnbull, P., Power, R. and Stimson, G. V. (1996) '"Just using old works": injecting risk behaviour in prison', *Drug and Alcohol Review*, 15, 251–260.

Watters, J. (1996) 'Americans and syringe exchange: roots of resistance', in T. Rhodes and R. Hartnoll (Eds.) *AIDS, Drugs and Prevention: Perspectives on Individual and Community Action*, London: Routledge.

Weppner, R. S. (Ed.) (1977) *Street Ethnography*, Beverly Hills, CA: Sage.

Whyte, W. F. (1955) *Street Corner Society*, Chicago: University of Chicago Press.

Wiebel, W. (1990) 'Identifying and gaining access to hidden populations', in E. Lambert (Ed.) *The Collection and Interpretation of Data from Hidden Populations*, Washington, DC: National Institute on Drug Abuse.

Wiebel, W. (1996) 'Ethnographic contributions to AIDS intervention strategies', in T. Rhodes and R. Hartnoll (Eds.) *AIDS, Drugs and Prevention: Perspectives on Individual and Community Action*, London: Routledge.

Znaniecki, F. (1934) *The Method of Sociology*, New York: Farrer and Rhinehart.

Zule, W. A. (1992) 'Risk and reciprocity: HIV and the injection drug user', *Journal of Psychoactive Drugs*, 24, 243–249.

THE IMPACT OF QUALITATIVE RESEARCH ON POLICY-MAKING

PART II

I n Chapter 2, the first in this section, Virginia Berridge uses the discipline of history to examine the nature of the relationship between research and policy and what this means for the impact of qualitative research. She surveys some theories on the relationship between research and health policy and looks at four case studies from the post-war period which suggest that research made its mark during that period.

However, the track record of qualitative research in relation to policy is uncertain. Berridge highlights the fact that policy interests may package a 'message' from qualitative research but that qualitative research, by its very nature, is rarely so specific about guiding policy. Moreover, qualitative research can be ignored in one decade and be centre stage in the next. She concludes that policy-makers and interest groups who have a key influence on the definition of acceptable science and its policy applications should become the subjects of study alongside drug users.

Chapter 3, by Ton Cramer, himself a policy adviser to the Dutch Ministry of Health, describes the development of qualitative research since the 1970s and offers practical examples of its impact on policy in the Netherlands. He stresses the importance of developing a strategy involving high-level research expertise to ensure that the findings of narrowly focused qualitative research studies do not give rise to spurious alarms about widespread drug use.

THE IMPACT OF QUALITATIVE RESEARCH ON POLICY-MAKING: SETTING THE SCENE

Virginia Berridge

Discussion on the relationship between science and policy is currently much in vogue in some western countries, most noticeably in Britain and North America. Qualitative research forms some part of those discussions. This chapter will use one 'innovative qualitative methodology' — that of history — to examine the nature of the relationship between research and policy and what this means for the impact of qualitative research. First of all, it will briefly survey some theories of the relationship between research and policy, then it will look at four case studies from the post-war period, where research does indeed seem to have made its mark, and, finally, it will suggest what this might mean for qualitative research in this type of relationship.

Theories of the research/policy relationship

Interest in the research/policy relationship has come from a number of different directions (Berridge and Stanton, 1999). These can be segmented in a number of different ways, but here four models are surveyed. These are:

- the 'evidence-based medicine'/health policy model;
- the 'journalist' school;
- the sociology of scientific knowledge (SSK); and
- policy–science/science–policy approaches.

There are areas of overlap between all of these approaches.

The evidence-based medicine model is much concerned with the concept of clinical effectiveness and is increasingly allied with the particular methodology of the randomised controlled trial. Underlying these moves are positivist models of science and rational models of policy-making. Research, if properly funded and correctly positioned, can, and should, have an influence on policy — either directly or in some more diffuse way; the problem is simply to secure a working relationship between the two.

The 'journalist' school also sees the relationship as desirable, but in a more partisan way. When a hiatus appears, conspiracy theories abound. There is talk of 'delay', and blame is attached to key participants for failure to act. This is a common approach, not only in journalistic accounts but also in academic analyses. AIDS and BSE provide recent examples.

The third model, that of the sociology of scientific knowledge, does not presuppose this rationality. Latour's *Science in Action,* for example, provides a model of the 'actor networks' which sustain the research process (Latour, 1987). The strength of any scientific claim is based on the resources — whether people, organisations, other disciplines or objects — from which its proponents are able to derive support. Much of this work is concerned with themes of emergence and resistance in science: an inward-looking perspective that does not take account of policy development.

This has been a concern of the policy–science/science–policy literature. Here, the policy dimension of the production of knowledge and its validation has been more central. Jasanoff (1990), for example, has drawn attention to the differential impact of the 'same science' in different national and policy contexts. There is the 'co-production' of knowledge where government agencies also negotiate the meaning and the boundaries of science. The concept of the 'policy community', linking scientific communities and government in various forms, is of importance here (Jordan and Richardson, 1987).

Four examples of the research/policy relationship

What are the key paradigmatic pieces of research that we will consider in this the-oretical context (Berridge and Thom, 1996)? Firstly, there is the research by Doll and Hill, published in 1950: a case control and subsequently a prospective epidemi-ological study that demonstrated the connection between the rise in lung cancer and the habit of smoking. This led ultimately to a new policy agenda for smoking, and for public health more generally, stressing price mechanisms, advertising controls, the role of the mass media and of health education. Through a focus on epidemi-ological modes of proof and on public health epidemiology, rather than the genetic and hereditarian modes of biostatistics, it marked a decisive paradigm shift both for science and for policy.

Secondly, there is the Ledermann hypothesis, which had little influence when first advanced in the 1950s but which came to prominence in the 1970s. In the 1950s, the disease view of alcoholism was dominant, while population approaches such as those which Ledermann proposed had connotations of temperance, of morality rather than of science. Only in the 1970s did the policy agenda change. Limitation of availability and harm, via the Ledermann hypothesis, became the rallying point for a coalition of alcohol doctors, civil servants, the alcohol voluntary sector, the police and the law.

Thirdly, the controlled trial by Hartnoll and Mitcheson of heroin versus methadone prescribing, carried out in the 1970s in a drug dependence unit in London, ran-domly allocated addicts to injectable heroin or oral methadone. This research was widely credited with changing prescribing policy in the drug dependence units from heroin to oral methadone, towards what was seen as a more 'confrontational' treatment response. This was, however, not the intention of the researchers themselves. The study coincided with the introduction of oral methadone and there is some evidence that this change in policy began before the research was complete and the results disseminated. Here was research support for a change that was already under way.

Finally, from more recent times, there was a needle-exchange evaluation, hastily funded by the UK Department of Health in 1987, to gauge whether such harm-reduction approaches would be an appropriate means of dealing with the threat of the spread of HIV into the general population via drug users. The research appeared to prove that syringe exchange 'worked' and was a significant factor in unlocking government support for harm reduction and for increased funding for services. Here, apparently, was a classic example of the influence of research on policy (Berridge, 1996).

Why did the research have an impact?

Let us look now to see if we can deconstruct these historical episodes. Are there any common variables which can be drawn out, or any specific factors which appear to have influenced particular situations? It should be noted that we are talking about different forms of 'research impact'. Some, like the research on needle exchange, had a very direct impact. Others, like the smoking and alcohol examples, changed the climate of opinion in which policy was formed, rather than directly affecting policy.

Given this difference, we can identify some common variables and also some issues specific to particular cases. In all our case studies, the primary methodology has been quantitative rather than qualitative, and this reflects the dominant statistical/epidemiological paradigm of post-World War II research, a paradigm for which the Doll and Hill research was significant.

But methodology alone is far from the full explanation. The case studies demonstrate the importance of the policy alliances supporting science within government — and also of the ways in which science/research has, in turn, provided coherence for policy communities.

Within that relationship, the perspective of change over time is important. Science, which had little impact in the 1950s, developed the status of orthodoxy by the 1970s, when the policy situation itself had altered. The smoking and alcohol case studies provide examples of this process. By the 1970s, the smoking research was emblematic of a 'new public health' constituency in the UK, which strongly advanced the policy case. Likewise, Ledermann, who was ignored in the 1950s, was the watchword of the new alcohol lobby by the 1970s. Our other case studies also illustrate these processes at work. Hartnoll and Mitcheson's research suited the aims of a clinic-worker constituency in alliance with psychiatrists, all of whom agreed on the need for new 'active treatment' policies. For AIDS, harm reduction had been the unspoken objective for some time of a new and broader health 'policy community' around drugs. The crisis of AIDS and the funding and results of research, which were carefully managed, enabled deeply held political objections to be overcome.

Here we have a symbiotic process where the validation of science is not just an internal matter (as in Latour's model) but, rather, a process of mutual accommodation with alliances and interests in policy. Let us look at how this process operates in a little more detail.

In Britain, the role of civil servants and of expert committees has been important. In the case of smoking, the role of the Chief Medical Officer, Sir George Godber, was of central importance to the new public health agenda. Later, in the AIDS/drugs era, the medical civil servant responsible for drug policy, Dr Dorothy Black, was important in ensuring that research results were presented in ways and situations acceptable to politicians.

Committees have been important too. Reports by the Royal College of Physicians on smoking (particularly those published in 1962 and 1971, which had considerable impact) gave independent authority to 'scientific facts' and made them widely available through the media. For Hartnoll and Mitcheson, the committee of London drug psychiatrists, which met at the Department of Health in the 1980s, was important in determining prescribing policy. Likewise, reports by the Advisory Council on the Misuse of Drugs on AIDS and drug misuse (particularly Part I of the 1998 report) provided important legitimacy for the research results and the concept of harm reduction.

These gatekeeping institutions or individuals have been important in the research/policy process. In the post-war period, the media was an important mediator between research and policy, for instance when the scientific 'facts' were put into the public and policy domain (Berridge, 1998) concerning the early Royal College of Physicians' reports on smoking.

Some areas of policy have their own particular traditions. British health policy has been characterised by its tension between central management and local self-determination. The drugs field shows this clearly, with policy initiatives often emerging initially at the local level — as with the Hartnoll and Mitcheson research and its support by a local London-based committee. Needle exchange also began as a local initiative.

Crisis, too, is an important variable, and is well known to historians who have analysed and debated its impact in, for example, wartime situations. The crisis of war has often led to more radical change in policy than would otherwise have been tolerated. The AIDS and harm-reduction situation shows the effect of a crisis clearly: it enabled what was essentially a political change to be masked as a technical issue, as a matter of research results, made essential by the crisis of the day.

Clearly, the operative factors in different policy arenas may well be different. These case studies show that the arenas of alcohol and smoking have been historically more diffuse than that of drugs, with a greater variety of interests involved, not least the industrial and legitimate economic interests within government. The absence of these for drugs has given it a smaller and potentially more cohesive 'policy community' where the research/policy relationship has been perhaps easier to establish.

But this is to write from the British perspective. The nature of the structures and the interrelationships with government will obviously be different in different national cultures. In some European countries, the Netherlands for example, the recent relationship between researchers and policy-making civil servants has been close. In others, it has not been possible for research to form part of these processes. In the United States, although there were moves in New York to establish needle exchange as a 'controlled trial' — i.e. as a scientific procedure — these foundered on the opposition of local political interests, most notably black politicians, who condemned harm reduction as potential genocide for their constituency. The different institutions and structures and the different national and local or federal political cultures have also to be taken into account.

What has been the role of researchers in these processes? Here again there has been change over time. The role of the researcher as an 'activist' in the policy process developed in the post-war period. Sir Austin Bradford Hill, in the 1950s, was firmly of the opinion that his role was to conduct scientific research: it was the role of the Chief Medical Officer and other policy interests to promote the policy options. Too great a closeness to policy would undermine the independence and unbiased nature of science. Researchers such as Mitcheson took the view that their results were 'hijacked' by policy interests to draw conclusions which they had not intended. Changes in research policy since the 1970s have drawn researchers more closely into the policy process than was the case when the first smoking results were published in the 1950s, but they appear rarely to have been in control of the use to which their results have been put.

It is clear from this discussion that the type of 'rational' relationship between research and policy, presupposed by the evidence-based medicine and policy model, is hardly the case. Policy alliances, both around science and in relation to policy, are variable, and the contexts of time, culture and country have to be considered.

What role for qualitative research?

The examples cited here appear to show little of a role for qualitative research per se, although it should be noted that quantitative questionnaire-based studies are usually founded on initial qualitative pilot studies. In the field of history, the track record of qualitative research in relation to policy is uncertain. At one level, history could be seen as having had quite an impact. The history of British drug policy, and in particular the 1926 'Rolleston Report', was used in US drug policy in the 1970s to argue that a more liberal, medicalised approach 'worked'. The history of US Prohibition has also been used to argue that systems of control based on prohibition of substances 'don't work'. Do historians sit back and preen because historical examples have had this impact? No, they do not. In both instances, historical 'events' have been used for policy purposes in a way that is not in accord with the conclusions of historical research. There are some good arguments that Prohibition did operate quite well for a time, and that Rolleston was not, in the opinion of some historians, solely responsible for a liberal system which worked. Here, policy interests have packaged a 'message' or a 'lesson of history'. Qualitative research, by its very nature, is rarely so specific.

My last example, one from the smoking area, illustrates some of the complexities around the issue of the impact of such research. Hilary Graham's work on smoking and lone mothers, where she used interviews to show the importance that smoking had in these women's lives, was published in the 1980s in its fullest version (Graham, 1987). It was unpopular with the public health lobby because it challenged the dominant abstentionist ethos and drew attention to issues of poverty and low income, which were not on the political agenda at the time. In the late 1990s, inequalities were back on the agenda and public health smoking interests moved towards a harm-reduction stance. The time-specific context, the change in policy alliances, has given the qualitative research of the 1980s greater policy influence. Ironically, though, the issue is now seen in policy terms in a medicalised way and nicotine replacement therapy will be offered free to poor people. The justification for such policy moves now is through the scientific construct of dependence and through the use of survey data, rather than the initial qualitative interview material which revealed the culture of working-class lives.

Conclusions

So what conclusions can we draw? Clearly, the rational model of any form of research, qualitative or quantitative, feeding neatly into policy will not do. In that process of scientific legitimation, the alliances within science are important — in the Latourian model — but, in terms of policy, the relationships within policy communities and with gatekeepers within government are crucial. The role of particular science/policy 'product champions' has been central. All of this underlines the essentially symbiotic relationship between policy alliances and the prominence of particular variants of science.

The time-specific context is also important. Research can be ignored in one decade and centre stage in the next. There seem to be periods in recent history when qualitative research of all types has had a greater legitimacy with policy-makers. The 1970s was certainly a productive time for this style of working and we may be due for a revival, even though biomedical and genetic influences are also strong. Qualitative research seems to be synonymous in the drugs area with means of studying 'hidden populations' of users. As this introductory chapter indicates, the real 'hidden populations' are the policy-makers, the civil servants, and the members of organisations and interest groups who have a key influence on the definition of acceptable science and its policy application. They, too, should be under the qualitative microscope.

The author is Professor of History at the London School of Hygiene and Tropical Medicine, University of London, UK.

References

Berridge, V. (1996) *AIDS in the UK: the Making of Policy 1981–1994*, Oxford: Oxford University Press.

Berridge, V. (1998) 'Science and policy: the case of post war smoking policy', in S. Lock, L. Reynolds and E. M. Tansey (Eds.) *Ashes to Ashes: the History of Smoking and Health*, Amsterdam: Rodopi.

Berridge, V. and Stanton, J. (1999) 'Science and policy: historical insights', *Social Science and Medicine*, 49, 1133–1138.

Berridge, V. and Thom, B. (1996) 'Research and policy: what determines the relationship?', *Policy Studies*, 17(1), 23–34.

Graham, H. (1987) 'Women's smoking and family health', *Social Science and Medicine* 25(1), 47–56.

Jasanoff, S. (1990) 'American exceptionalism and the political acknowledgement of risk', Daedalus, autumn, 61–81.

Jordan, A. G. and Richardson, J. J. (1987) *British Politics and the Policy Process*, London: Allen and Unwin.

Latour, B. (1987) *Science in Action: How to Follow Scientists and Engineers through Society*, Milton Keynes: Open University Press.

How qualitative research has influenced Dutch drug policy

Ton Cramer

In the 1960s and early 1970s, Dutch drug policy was largely based on theoretical concepts. Since 1972, research, often of a qualitative nature, has played an increasingly important role in the process of formulating Dutch drug policy at national level. The 1972 report of the Baan Committee, which laid the foundation of Dutch drug policy, was mainly based on social scientific research and theories. In the 1985 policy paper 'Drug policy in motion', guiding concepts were formulated for the period 1985–95. This paper was based on a qualitative typology developed by the criminologists Janssen and Swierstra (1982).

The study of the lifestyle and economic behaviour of opiate addicts in Amsterdam by Grapendaal et al. (1991), combining quantitative and qualitative methods, played a significant role in shaping the targeted approach to drug-related public nuisance, formulated in a 1993 policy memorandum. Qualitative research also figures prominently in the list of studies referred to in the 1995 Green Paper 'Dutch drug policy: continuity and change'. As a last example, small-scale qualitative studies, as well as impressionistic reports, have played a part in the formulation of the 1998 policy paper on so-called ecological or 'smart' drugs.

Thus, since the early 1970s, Dutch drug policy has been increasingly developed on the basis of scientific research, often of a primarily qualitative nature. It has become the rule to start with the question 'what do we know?'. As the central goal of our policy is the reduction of risks related to drug use, a risk analysis almost always forms the basis of policy decisions. The risk analysis now being formalised, in the process of developing the national assessment function for synthetic drugs, is based on both quantitative and qualitative criteria.

Quantitative versus qualitative research

From a policy perspective, qualitative research and quantitative research are complementary. Obviously, statistics are not sufficient for an in-depth view of drug problems. On the basis of ethnographic studies, however, it is complicated to make generalisations or draw conclusions about the size of any problem. Fortunately, social scientific drug research in the Netherlands has a long tradition of combining qualitative and quantitative methodologies.

The remainder of this chapter will discuss two topics:

- the influence of qualitative research on drug policy; and
- its role in monitoring and prevention efforts.

The influence of qualitative research on drug policy

A direct relationship between research and policy measures occurs only in exceptional cases. Such a case will be illustrated by reviewing in more detail the role of the study of Janssen and Swierstra (1982). In 1985, the Dutch Government published a policy paper, 'Drug policy in motion: towards a normalisation of drug problems'. The paper discussed the results and policy recommendations of a criminological study commissioned by the government and undertaken by Janssen and Swierstra in 1982.

In this qualitative study, based on in-depth interviews with heroin users, Janssen and Swierstra treated heroin use as a form of behaviour that is rational and meaningful from the viewpoint of the users. Secondly, they studied factors contributing to the spread of heroin use, notably the importance of subcultures for young people. Thirdly, they examined the development of the so-called heroin structure, the network of groups that have some kind of stake in the perpetuation of the heroin problem.

On the basis of this analysis, they developed a cultural typology of the lifestyles of heroin users. The researchers concluded that the existing policy measures for reducing supply and demand were rather unsuccessful in terms of dealing adequately with mechanisms at the three levels. They therefore discussed alternative policy options, ranging from legalisation of drugs to compulsory treatment. They proposed the 'cultural integration of heroin use' as the most promising, as well as the most politically feasible, option. Janssen and Swierstra, judging that heroin use had entrenched itself permanently in Dutch society, reasoned that attempts at the complete elimination of heroin use would be futile. 'Cultural integration' would be a pragmatic way of managing the risks of drug use in society.

The government accepted this recommendation, although it chose to speak of the 'cultural integration of heroin problems' to avoid the impression that it was calling for legalisation. This cultural integration, or normalisation as it was also called, has led to the policy intention of treating heroin problems as 'normal' social problems, calling for a businesslike, pragmatic approach. Important aspects were the intentions to try to de-mythologise drug problems, reduce the harmfulness of illegal drugs and restrict the development of specific policy measures aimed exclusively at drug addicts.

Although the government did not accept all the recommendations made by Janssen and Swierstra, their study has significantly influenced Dutch drug policy, at least at the national level. In addition to the adoption of the normalisation approach, the study also led to the official recognition that drug policy always entails the balancing of conflicting interests, and that it is important to minimise the negative side-effects that drug policy inevitably produces. This has reinforced the importance of risk-reduction initiatives. For instance, the development of needle-exchange systems and other forms of HIV prevention for drug addicts has been amply funded by the government.

The Janssen and Swierstra experience represents a rather exceptional case in which a qualitative study has had a strong and direct effect on the formulation of drug policy at national level. This study had been specifically commissioned by the government to be used for an evaluation of drug policy, in a period, moreover, in which drug policy was not a political rallying theme. Normally, the influence of qualitative research, indeed of research in general, on policy at national level is of a more indirect nature. The situation at local level will probably be comparable to the situation at national level, although it is possible that the influence of research in formulating local policy is more subject to political constraints.

The role of qualitative research in monitoring and prevention

For monitoring and prevention purposes, it is important to obtain information about the types of drugs that are available, their health and social risks, and trends or patterns in their use. Prevalence studies, if repeated over time, can show trends in the use of 'old' drugs and can provide the policy-maker with hard data on the size of the phenomenon, its geographical spread, etc. On the other hand, qualitative studies appear more appropriate for identifying the use of 'new' drugs at an early stage, and providing insight into the set and setting of use. Thus, qualitative research can provide key data for risk analysis, the first phase of developing policy. Moreover, specific risk factors, as well as protective factors, can be identified, enabling the development of targeted early intervention efforts.

Currently, several qualitative methods are used in the Netherlands. Two projects will be discussed here: the DIMS project and the panel studies of the Amsterdam Antenna project, both of which are important instruments for early intervention and prevention.

The DIMS project

The Drugs Information Monitoring System (DIMS) has two objectives: to monitor which drugs are in circulation (with special emphasis on synthetic drugs) and to prevent health damage owing to their use. DIMS is coordinated at national level by the Netherlands Institute of Mental Health and Addiction and comprises 21 test services throughout the country.

One of the participant organisations is the Amsterdam Drug Advice Bureau, which combines chemical analysis of drug samples at the office with testing 'on the spot' at large-scale dance events. The test service is part of the Safe House Campaign, which entails an array of preventive efforts. When potentially harmful developments in drug-using behaviour are detected, so-called red-alert campaigns can be undertaken, with publicity varying from low to high key. For instance, in the autumn of 1997, pills containing caffeine caused very odd effects. The staff of the Safe House Campaign reported that these effects could not be explained by the presence of caffeine and proposed a laboratory search for other substances. Upon receipt of this additional information, the laboratory was able to demonstrate the presence of atropine in these pills. On the basis of this, a red-alert campaign was started.

The DIMS project not only provides insight into the supply side of the synthetic drug market, but direct contact between the testers and the users, especially 'on the spot', also provides a lot of valuable information on trends and patterns within the dance culture. These qualitative data are used in targeting preventive measures, as in the example of the caffeine pills cited above.

In the near future, the Ministry of Health, Welfare and Sport intends to discuss the possibility of gathering and interpreting these data in a more scientific format. Of course, test results are important, but adding a more elaborate qualitative component to the DIMS project may serve to contextualise the quantitative data and achieve cross-fertilisation.

The Amsterdam Antenna project

The reports of the Antenna project of the Amsterdam Jellinek Centre are based on four kinds of data:

- a school survey;
- a survey among customers of cannabis coffee shops or another specific sub-population;
- a panel study; and
- data from the care and prevention sector of the Jellinek Centre, including results from chemical analyses of illegal drugs.

A special committee analyses the data and formulates policy recommendations for preventive interventions and local drug policy. The recommendations are presented to representatives of the city council of Amsterdam and to other interested parties. In this way, Antenna serves as an instrument to monitor trends in the use of alcohol, drugs and excessive gambling behaviour in Amsterdam (see Chapter 6 in this monograph).

Drawing on my experience as a policy adviser, I can say that local panel studies provide useful information to enable the relevant organisations to be prepared in case a disturbing new drug trend should indeed become popular. On the other hand, it seems that panel studies alone do not provide a basis for policy conclusions. Even in conjunction with the quantitative data of the Antenna studies, it is difficult to interpret the results. It is like receiving some pieces of a jigsaw puzzle without knowing what the total picture is. As certain media and other parties have been eager to draw far-reaching conclusions on the basis of such studies, it seems to be essential to work out a reporting procedure, as foolproof as possible, to reduce the chance of unwarranted conclusions influencing public opinion. Obviously, this applies to all qualitative methods that are used for monitoring.

Of course, the abuse of data in this complicated field of 'new trends' cannot be totally prevented. However, researchers should take a critical look at the way they state the limitations of their results and should also educate policy-makers and their other 'customers' on this issue. This education should be a two-way process, as researchers would also benefit from learning more about the situation of policy-makers and advisers.

Conclusions

The formulation of policy is often a very hasty process. In such cases, policy advisers have to work with data that have been gathered in a very short time, often at the expense of scientific quality. Advisers may find it difficult to determine the boundaries between data from monitoring systems, scientific ethnographic studies, impressionistic field data and journalistic reports. This situation needs a strategy for improvement. The importance of a high level of expertise for researchers in this field should be emphasised here. One of the risks at present would be that small-scale 'research and consultancy' bureaus without significant expertise could take over the market for rapid research.

When we speak of a trend in drug use that necessitates a public health (or other) intervention, we encounter the issue of myth or fact. The popular media regularly purport to identify new drug trends, often on the basis of isolated incidents or rumours. For instance, the Dutch media have portrayed the use of substances such as khat and nitrous oxide, as well as the licking of toads, as having reached epidemic proportions among young people over a short period of time and as presenting unacceptable risks. Qualitative research can do much to reduce such reports to realistic proportions. Of course, quantitative studies, especially in the form of 'quick scans', may also be very useful in this regard.

On the other hand, small-scale trends that need careful monitoring to prevent the situation from worsening can be put on the policy agenda by qualitative research. Of course, qualitative research, if not carefully stating its limitations, may itself provoke unwarranted conclusions on new drug trends. For instance, reports on drug trends in exclusive, trendsetting urban circles, viewed under a microscope so to speak, may, if not presented properly, give rise to false alarms about a 'drug crisis' in public opinion and among politicians.

The author is a drug policy adviser in the Dutch Ministry of Public Health, Welfare and Sport.

Acknowledgements

In preparing this chapter, I have benefited from the support and critical comments of my colleague (and former drug researcher) Marcel de Kort.

References

Grapendaal, M. E., Leuw, E. and Nelen, H. (1991) *De economie van het drugsbestaan: criminaliteit als expressie van levensstijl en loopbaan,* WODC-reeks, 115, Arnhem: Gouda Quint.

Janssen, O. J. A. and Swierstra, K. (1982) *Heroïnegebruikers in Nederland: een typologie van levensstijlen,* Rijks Universiteit Groningen (National University Groningen).

Further reading

Het Nederlandse drugbeleid. Continuïteit en verandering (1995), The Hague: SDU.

Interdepartementale Stuurgroep Alcohol en Drugbeleid (1985) *Drugbeleid in beweging: naar een normalisering van de drugproblematiek* (copies of this policy paper can be obtained at cost price from the library of the Dutch Ministry of Public Health, Welfare and Sport. Tel. (31-70) 340 79 11).

Korf, D. J., Nabben, T. and Berdowski, Z. (1997) *Antenne 1996: Trends in alcohol, tabak, drugs en gokken bij jonge Amsterdammers,* Amsterdam: Jellinek Reeks, No 6.

Nota inzake het beleid gericht op het verminderen van door verslaafden veroorzaakte overlast (1993), Handelingen Tweede Kamer 1993–94 (Proceedings of the House of Representatives) 22 684, No 12, 31597F, The Hague: SDU (ISSN 0921-7371).

Werkgroep Smart Shops (1998) *Smart shops en nieuwe trends in het gebruik van psychoactieve stoffen,* Rijswijk: Ministerie van Volksgezondheid, Welzijn en Sport (copies of this policy paper can be obtained at cost price from the library of the Dutch Ministry of Public Health, Welfare and Sport. Tel. (31-70) 340 79 11).

Werkgroep Verdovende Middelen (1972) *Achtergronden en risico's van druggebruik,* The Hague: SDU.

NEW DRUG TRENDS

PART III

INTRODUCTION

*T*his section includes six chapters on new drug trends. Chapter 4 is a summary of the work of an EMCDDA workgroup on this topic, which was set up to explore the role of qualitative research in the identification and tracking of new trends in drug consumption in the EU. This paper concludes with a call for more attention to be paid to developing theoretical models to guide the collection and analysis of information on new drug trends.

Michael Agar describes, in Chapter 5, his endeavours to construct a trend theory built upon a range of information including: information about the subjective effects of the chemical; the world of drug use; the social position of high-risk groups; global and local distribution networks; and policy. His paper suggests that a theory based on complexity will explain trends and advance useful knowledge for those charged with responding to them. Qualitative research plays an essential part in understanding trends.

In Chapter 6, Dirk Korf and Ton Nabben provide examples of research designed to identify new trends. New trends in drug use are likely to evolve among specific groups that are scarcely represented, if at all, in samples drawn from general populations (e.g. school and household surveys). Nor can broad surveys include specific questions on new drugs (or ways of taking them) until more information is available. This chapter describes the panel study methodology implemented in Amsterdam to gather information continually from a number of different sources.

In Chapter 7, Reiner Domes and Ludwig Kraus describe the implementation and testing of a proposed approach to setting up a national early recognition system in Berlin. This was undertaken in the context of the work of the EMCDDA. The approach integrates qualitative and quantitative research approaches where hypotheses about trends have to be verified by an independent database, such as surveys of schoolchildren or drug users and a study of groups at risk. It represents an attempt to produce data to harmonise with other existing early monitoring systems in Germany and Europe.

Howard Parker documents, in Chapter 8, the British response to 'rumours' of new heroin outbreaks in three small cities and uptake among very young new users in numerous small towns with no heroin history. In the absence of any formalised early warning system in the UK, a rapid audit was conducted. The audit methods are described and the audit's success is attributed to: its flexible design; strong support for the audit from the police and government; and the timelines of the research.

In the last chapter in this section, Chapter 9, Amador Calafat and Paolo Stocco describe ongoing work funded by the European Commission which looks at drugs taken in recreational environments. The work represents a thematic and conceptual broadening towards more sociological and anthropological spheres. The authors describe their methods and present findings collected from over 1 500 respondents about the characteristics and social representations of ecstasy use in five European cities (Coimbra, Modena, Nice, Palma de Mallorca and Utrecht).

CHAPTER 4

NEW DRUG TRENDS
AND QUALITATIVE RESEARCH

EMCDDA workgroup on new drug trends, edited by Louise Vingoe

This chapter summarises the discussions of an EMCDDA workgroup on new drug trends set up in 1996. The workgroup was charged with exploring the role of qualitative research in the identification and tracking of new trends in drug consumption.

The timely identification of new trends in drug consumption may allow a more rapid response to the potential health and social problems that can accompany such changes. It has been suggested that qualitative methods may be particularly appropriate for this task. Here, we outline some of the issues raised over a series of meetings exploring this topic.

In some countries, qualitative inquiry is poorly developed or lacks credibility. As such, it may be difficult to conduct qualitative studies of new patterns of drug use, or data from such work may fail to influence responses.

A significant problem faced by those seeking to develop the use of qualitative research to identify new trends in drug use across the EU is that the development and credibility of this form of inquiry vary greatly between countries. Whilst, in some countries, there is a tradition of conducting qualitative studies on drug use, in others, such activity is uncommon and it may be difficult to obtain support for such work.

Obviously, this problem is common to qualitative research on drug use per se and not just to studies of new trends, but it may be that the nature of research into new trends exacerbates it. For example, exploring HIV risk behaviour among chronic drug injectors may be seen as a more legitimate task than studying drug use among young people attending dance events. Even in those countries where qualitative research is relatively well-established, the legitimacy and importance of studies outside chronic drug-using populations may be explicitly or implicitly called into question.

The absence of a qualitative drugs research tradition was identified in a number of countries contributing to the workgroup's review. In Italy, for example, the lack of training in this area and a lack of faith in the reliability of qualitative research results are reflected in the absence of a significant qualitative research programme. Similarly, in Germany, the reputation of qualitative research results is poor and the impact of qualitative data on policy decisions is minimal. There are few recent social research studies on new drug trends in the country, but considerable quantitative research activity: reports about new drugs are mainly derived from epidemiological prevalence studies or police data (Rabes, 1995).

This suggests that, if qualitative techniques are to become more developed for identifying and understanding new drug trends, the challenge is not restricted to the development of appropriate methodological techniques. If research is to be funded and the results utilised, then policy-makers and those commissioning research activity have to be convinced of its value. It may well be that the growing acceptance of the need to improve the monitoring of important changes in drug consumption, together with the demonstrable utility of qualitative approaches in this area, will prove useful in promoting qualitative inquiry among those who currently remain unconvinced of its value.

Qualitative research offers unique insights into the emergence of new trends

One of the strengths of qualitative research, in terms of its ability to identify new trends, is the proximity of the researchers to the study population. Qualitative researchers often work in the field directly with drug users, who tend to be aware of and discuss new products and innovations, even if they are not using them themselves.

Qualitative research studies locate information on drug use within the broader contexts of subcultural sets of rules, meanings and affiliations. For example, the potential spread of ecstasy use, at least in the early years of the availability of the drug, must be understood in relation to its role in the new 'dance culture' that was developing at the same time. Recognising how the drug was understood by young people and the contexts in which it was used are important considerations when assessing the potential for the trend to develop. Qualitative research is unique in this respect and can provide insight into new drug consumption patterns that is not available from other techniques more concerned with prevalence or incidence estimation. Simply observing that a new substance or consumption pattern exists is not helpful in evaluating its potential to spread and cause problems.

The contention that qualitative studies do have the potential to identify emerging patterns of drug use has been demonstrated in a number of countries. For example, qualitative studies in the Netherlands have often proved to be the first to pinpoint new drugs and new patterns of use. In some respects, this can be seen as stemming from the more flexible nature of qualitative inquiry, which allows the research gaze to be responsive to new developments.

Quantitative studies, such as general population surveys, often require considerable preparation time and the instruments used are rarely flexible. Good methodological and practical arguments exist for not changing existing questionnaire formats, as this allows comparable data to be generated over time. This does mean, however, that the introduction of new questions about trends into surveys is often a time-consuming process. In addition, there may be a tendency for the populations in which new trends originate to be overlooked by quantitative studies, either because of sampling strategies or because the behaviour is occurring at low frequency.

In Spain, since 1987, the most important contribution to quantitative research has been in the form of studies conducted by the *Plan Nacional sobre Drogas (PNSD)* (National Plan on Drugs). This includes regular survey work on the drug use of young people, school populations and the general population. Pallarés and Romaní (1998) argue that, despite the establishment of the PNSD, qualitative research has continued to provide equally valuable results for far lower resource investment. In particular, qualitative studies have been more sensitive to the emergence of new trends and have offered analysis of the potential treatment needs associated with new patterns of use. This research has been influential with respect to changes made in Spanish treatment and harm-reduction policies during the 1990s.

Similarly, in Finland, qualitative research has contributed to knowledge about drug trends at street level, the lifestyles of users, patterns of drug use and the characteristics of drug cultures. Interviews, memoirs and newspaper articles have supplied more precise information on the emergence of new drug trends, drug scenes and changes in patterns of use, and, in this way, have helped in recording their historical development. Qualitative research has thus emphasised that drug use is a heterogeneous phenomenon, including different groups of users and patterns of use.

Increases in consumption of synthetic drugs in Germany in the early to mid-1990s encouraged qualitative research. Epidemiological prevalence studies could show the quantitative status of the problem, but politicians, scientists and experts lacked an understanding of the new drug 'wave'. Qualitative studies in 1993–94 described the population, including motives, settings, psycho-pharmacological short- and long-term effects, subcultural ideologies, etc. This kind of understanding was important in formulating policy responses to this 'new' population of drug consumers.

Determining the appropriate areas for observing innovation

Whilst qualitative researchers are generally regarded as having good access to drug-using populations, this does not necessarily imply that research will be conducted with the groups in which new drug patterns emerge. Research activity is directed towards those areas seen as most important. Often this will be the chronic use of drugs by marginalised populations, accompanied by high levels of health and other social problems. This has, historically, been the case in the UK, for example, although this is now changing to some extent, and a number of qualitative studies are focused on drug consumption patterns among young people.

When innovation occurs in populations or contexts that have previously not been associated with drug use, it may not be visible to existing researchers, regardless of their methodological perspective. For example, cocaine use among city business-men or drug use in gymnasia may be unobserved by qualitative researchers more accustomed to working with street heroin users. Access problems still exist for qual-itative researchers, even if, traditionally, they have developed considerable expert-ise in this area. The assumption that detailed knowledge about one particular pop-ulation of drug users necessarily implies knowledge about patterns of use elsewhere is as likely to lead to error as to insight.

Analysing new drug trends within a broader context of social inquiry

Whilst qualitative research can provide useful insight into new drug trends, clearly there are difficulties in drawing firm conclusions from any one methodological tech-nique. It appears likely that qualitative research techniques will prove most useful in exploring and identifying new drug consumption patterns when juxtaposed against information from other sources. The credible identification of new trends may be best achieved by triangulating data from qualitative and quantitative stud-ies and ongoing monitoring activity.

This approach is not new and has been influential in other areas of social inquiry. Rapid assessment methods (RAMs) have been developed to utilise diverse data sources and produce quick, practically oriented assessments in areas where epi-demiological systems are poor. The World Heath Organisation has been developing resources that facilitate assessments in relation to drugs and health risk behaviours, such as HIV infection among drug injectors. Others have adopted a similar approach in relation to new drug trends. For example, considerable concern is cur-rently being expressed about the possibility that the UK is experiencing a new her-oin epidemic, although no systematic evidence exists to support this contention. A recent study conducted by Howard Parker and his colleagues represents an inter-esting example of how qualitative techniques can be combined with other method-ologies to audit quickly what information exists to support the suggestion that a new trend is occurring (see Chapter 8). This research has proved influential in informing the current debate in the UK on new patterns of heroin use and demonstrates the strengths of qualitative methods combined with other techniques in allowing a rapid exploration of potential new trends in drug consumption.

Models incorporating both qualitative and quantitative data sources can place new patterns of drug use within a dynamic understanding of changing patterns of youth culture and associated lifestyle information. Such a perspective may enhance our ability to predict the potential for further diffusion of the behaviour. Indeed, in prac-tice, the rigid theoretical divide between the two approaches may be somewhat artificial. Many qualitative studies often include quantitative elements and, increas-ingly, quantitative studies may include some qualitative procedures.

The problem of reporting

Often, considerable time periods elapse before studies are disseminated, regardless of the methodological approach adopted. For example, in Ireland, the most systematic data available on illicit drug use are the annual reports from the National Drug Treatment Reporting System, but the time lag between a new trend and/or a new drug appearing on the street and its appearance in treatment centres can be extensive. This could be a particular problem for qualitative studies, as considerable time may be spent in observing and gaining access to the field. Most researchers aim to publish their work in scientific journals and the time taken to prepare, submit and publish research articles is often lengthy.

Such problems are shared by both qualitative and quantitative researchers, who may become aware of new trends not directly relevant to the concerns of their current investigations and which, therefore, often go unreported.

Cultural monitoring

Qualitative research studies of drug users have tended to focus on observation or interview techniques. A rich body of literature on other qualitative research techniques explores how the cultural and symbolic meanings of social behaviour can be understood. Drug use, for example, is generally located within specific subcultural groups whose members may share affiliations to particular styles of fashion, music and language. Evidence of new drug trends may be found, and the trends themselves better understood, by monitoring such cultural areas. An example of this can be found in *Characteristics and Social Representation of Ecstasy in Europe* (Calafat et al., 1998; see also Chapter 9 in this monograph), which explores cultural and social phenomena associated with new synthetic drugs in five European countries.

Panels of drug users

One area of monitoring new drug trends that has proved successful in some countries, but has not been systematically developed elsewhere, is the utilisation of drug users themselves to report on new patterns of drug consumption. Two techniques have been used in this area: the use of drug users themselves as peer researchers who collect structured or semi-structured information from their contacts; and the recruitment of panels of drug users who regularly report on new trends and developments.

The Rotterdam Drug Monitoring System (DMS) continually collects information on drugs, drug consumption patterns and drug-using populations (predominantly daily opiate users) in their 'natural environment'. The system employs various research methods using networks of key contact persons (drug users, dealers, treatment workers, police), community fieldwork (see Chapter 19) and small sample surveys. Similarly, the Antenna drugs and gambling project is a monitoring system for tracking and understanding new trends and developments in consumption of alcohol, tobacco, illicit drugs and gambling among youngsters aged 25 or under in Amsterdam. This system also uses a range of qualitative and quantitative research (see Chapter 6).

New drug trends in the European Union: the importance of migrants, tourists and refugees

The potential for innovations in drug consumption to be diffused by the mixing of different population groups is well known. In Europe, all areas of life have been influenced by changes in the demographics of communities. Some of these population changes result from long-term migration, others from relatively recent developments in the tourist industry. For example, holiday resorts popular with young people may allow different nationalities to become aware of drug consumption patterns common elsewhere. Similarly, social and political changes occurring outside the EU have resulted in refugee status being granted to groups who may bring with them their own drug consumption patterns. For example, Somalian refugees in London have maintained their traditional khat (qat) chewing habits (Griffiths, 1998).

It is likely that studying the drug use of migrants, tourists and refugees will be a fruitful area for identifying potential new trends in terms of the influence of the host community on newly arrived or visiting individuals and vice versa. Methodological difficulties may exist in accessing such populations, but this is an area in which qualitative research techniques are likely to be particularly appropriate.

Internet and research discourses

One new development that may be useful to those seeking to identify and understand new drug consumption patterns is the development of the Internet, or world wide web. The Internet may prove useful in two ways:

- as a tool for facilitating networking activities between groups of researchers;
- as a means of allowing researchers to engage in dialogue with drug consumers that may help detect or confirm the existence of a new consumption pattern.

This area of work has not, to date, been systematically developed and the potential of the Internet as a research tool remains largely speculative. However, this appears to be an area in which developments are likely and in which resource investment is merited.

Gilman (1998) has been using the Internet to examine a key research question that relates to trends in new heroin addiction — in other words 'new' trends with an 'old' drug. He has been exploring the role of youth culture and fashion in influencing drug choices and examining the possible policy implications. He suggests that, once a product becomes available (e.g. cheap, high-quality, smokable brown heroin), culture and fashion will play a critical role within the diffusion of the product and the patterns of its use. Methodologically, he has relied heavily on the usenet news groups on the Internet to gather information and reaction to hypotheses in relation to routes into heroin addiction. Gilman states that, 'if youth culture and fashion significantly influence drug choices, then there is clear potential for imaginative use of advertising in drugs education'. However, if most heroin addicts come to heroin not from broader 'macro' drug cultures (e.g. the dance culture and synthetic drugs) but from the 'micro' worlds of socially excluded communities and 'high-risk' families, then one must question how useful a significant investment in drugs education would be.

Theory development and modelling

Perhaps one of the areas most in need of attention in terms of our ability to detect, monitor and understand new drug trends is our ability to place such developments in a theoretical context. Whilst some theoretical models exist in this area — such as diffusion theory — in general, it is fair to say that theoretical developments are poor and their predictive value negligible.

There is a need to better develop theory in this area and to examine how existing theoretical understanding can be better translated into practice. For example, diffusion theory suggests that certain groups of individuals may be important for the adoption and future spreading of innovations, and certain conditions are more likely to lead to diffusion than others. These models could direct research attention to particular study areas and assist in the 'risk analysis' of whether new consumption patterns are likely to spread.

Conclusions

Considerable attention has been given recently to new theoretical developments spreading from the information technology field and the study of complex structures. It is to be hoped that this work could marry qualitative methodology with complex computer models and that this could lead to a better understanding of how new drug trends may spread and develop.

Acknowledgements

Acknowledgements go to the other members of the workgroup on new drug trends: Jane Fountain, Mark Gilman, Paul Griffiths, Pekka Hakkarainen, Hans-Volker Happel, Dirk Korf, Aileen O'Gorman, Joan Pallarés Gómez, Oriol Romaní Alfonso, Paolo Stocco and Colin Taylor. The full version of the workgroup's review, which includes profiles for each participating country (Germany, Spain, Ireland, Italy, the Netherlands, Finland and the UK), can be found on the web (http://www.qed.org.uk).

References

Calafat, A., Stocco, P., Mendes, F., Simon, J., van de Wijngaart, G., Sureda, P., Palmer, A., Maalste, N. and Zavatti, P. (1998) *Characteristics and Social Representation of Ecstasy in Europe,* Irefrea and the European Commission.

Gilman, M. (1998) EMCDDA workgroup review, in J. Fountain and P. Griffiths (Eds.) *Coordination of Working Groups of Qualitative Researchers to Analyse Different Drug Use Patterns and the Implication for Public Health Strategies and Prevention,* Lisbon/London: EMCDDA/NAC (also available on http://www.qed.org.uk).

Griffiths, P. (1998) *Qat Use in London: a Study of Qat Use among a Sample of Somalis Living in London,* Drugs prevention initiative paper 26, London: Central Drugs Prevention Unit, Home Office.

Pallarés, J. and Romaní, O. (1998) EMCDDA workgroup review, in J. Fountain and P. Griffiths (Eds.) *Coordination of Working Groups of Qualitative Researchers to Analyse Different Drug Use Patterns and the Implication for Public Health Strategies and Prevention,* Lisbon/London: EMCDDA/NAC (also available on http://www.qed.org.uk).

Rabes, M. (1995) 'Ecstasy und Partydrogen', in *Jahrbuch der Suchtgefahren,* Geesthacht: Deutsche Hauptstelle gegen die Suchtgefahren.

CHAPTER 5

TOWARDS A TREND THEORY

Michael Agar

Drug trends are the engines that drive planning, intervention and evaluation in the drug field, whether one thinks of prevention, treatment or law enforcement. We typically monitor trends with a 'number trail' from the institutions that deal with drug users. Useful as such data may be, well-known problems exist in reading trends from the quantitative record. These relate to the fact that:

- indicators are typically lagging rather than leading;
- institutions that maintain records usually over-represent long-term users from impoverished groups;
- institutional processes may change the numbers (e.g. arrest statistics fluctuate with policy and shifting police priorities); and
- the numbers do not reveal the changing worlds of use that are needed to interpret them.

In short, the normal epidemiological surveillance systems are deficient for several reasons, given the needs of action-oriented policy. Firstly, they will not pick up new trends, yet new trends clearly matter for planning purposes. Secondly, most indicators tap into the world of illicit drug use among the urban poor, yet we know that problematic licit and illicit drug and alcohol use are distributed throughout society. Thirdly, when numbers do change, it is not clear if they change because something in the world is different or because something in the reporting institutions is different. Finally — and most important for intervention and evaluation — indicators usually focus on a single drug. Who is using what drugs, in what ways, in what circumstances — the world of use — plays no role in the indicator data.

Programme design and evaluation involve intercultural communication: translating between public health models and local realities. Indicators do not tell us how to make contact, communicate sensibly and interpret appropriately in the context of those realities. Suppose we jump up a level, from chemical to user. Suppose we investigate who the users are, their world, their styles of communication and the role drugs play. Now we know something about whether use of a particular drug will increase or decrease, we know how to target prevention efforts, and we have learned something about what kinds of intervention might be locally appropriate.

The investigation of actual worlds of use calls into play a style of research called by a variety of terms, including ethnography, grounded theory, phenomenology, and qualitative research. Such work has been, and can be, done well, as a scan of the

European Monitoring Centre for Drugs and Drug Addiction (EMCDDA) compendium of qualitative work in the European Union shows (Fountain and Griffiths, 1999). With support and focus, this style of research can comprehensively and continually answer questions that link drug/alcohol use, specific local communities and planning, intervention and evaluation needs. This is all well and good. Indeed, the EMCDDA is now designing a system to link indicators and qualitative investigations of drug use, based on models already tested by members of their network of qualitative researchers, and similar efforts — multi-site studies in US cities that coordinated with epidemiological and planning issues — have already been completed (Feldman et al., 1979; Ratner, 1993; Agar et al., 1998; Agar and Kozel, 1999). I should emphasise that the reason these multi-site studies were successful was that experienced ethnographers were recruited who knew their cities well. Without their prior experience and community contacts, the short-term studies would not have been possible. A more elaborate description of the strengths and weaknesses of the US multi-site studies unfortunately goes beyond the limits of this chapter.

A 'trend' signals a shift in the use of a drug. But why does the shift occur? Why are the worlds of use there at all? We need still more levels in the theory — which will be referred to here as a 'trend theory'. The first level involves the chemicals (including their neuro-physiological and psycho-pharmacological basis, which is not addressed here). The next level is the lived world of user and use — a level which is handled well by qualitative research.

Historical conditions that produce risk groups

What is next? This is an epidemiological question with a political, economic and historical answer. Use of a particular drug is never randomly distributed throughout a population. To some extent, use occurs in clusters, and more in some groups than in others. Why is this? Let us consider the history of opiate use in the United States, something that has inspired a number of recent books to add to Musto's classic work (1987). Indeed, it is almost as if the United States only recently discovered that it has a drug history. Several groups stood out with comparatively higher proportions of opiate addicts. Around the turn of the century, middle-class housewives showed the highest rate of opiate addiction in US history, for the most part due to widely available patent medicines. In the 1920s, young, white working-class men in the cities used the newly available heroin, and, immediately after World War II, heroin use took off in African-American communities in the cities.

There are other examples — both in the United States and in other countries, at other times — but these three cases illustrate the point. Note how different they are, in gender, in class, in race. Nothing inherent in the chemical itself explains the variation. Hence something else must, and to articulate this 'something else' we turn to the historical context of the three groups.

Each of these groups, in their historical context, shared a particular social position. Let us refer to it here as 'open marginality', for reasons that will be explained below.

As far as women were concerned, in their traditional housewife/homemaker roles, it was the time of the suffragette movement, with such items of popular culture in the air as Ibsen's *The Doll's House.* For the working-class men, most of them immigrants or their descendants, it was the time of the anti-immigrant reaction, new restrictive laws, accusations of Bolshevik sentiments behind the growing labour union movement, and so on. For the African-Americans, mostly recent arrivals from the South or their descendants, they had just returned from a role as liberators of Europe to racism at home.

All three groups were 'marginal' in the sense that their members were not visible at the centres of government, corporate or academic power. However, all three groups, in their respective times, lived when alternatives were also visible and possible, when their own communities and the national discourse contained messages that marginality need not be, or should not be, accepted. Their marginality was a public issue. Some 'tokens' existed: a few members appeared at the centres of power, living proof of a possible future that was all too rare. However, these possibilities were limited at a time when opiate trends increased. For most members of these groups, the possibilities were not, in fact, probabilities. Hence the term 'open marginality'. It is clear to members that there is a door in the marginality, a way out and up. It is also clear that the opening is not very wide and that not many have moved through it. There is an awareness of the negative aspects of marginality, of the possibility that things could be different, but also of the probability that they will not be, for that person in his or her lifetime.

This preliminary hypothesis needs to be qualified and expanded in many ways. However, at least for these three groups in the history of US opiate addiction, the hypothesis is a plausible one. Risk groups for opiate addiction change over time. Yet the historical conditions of each group may well form a pattern, in this case of a social position of open marginality. The hypothesis, then, is that members of such groups would find, in the effects of opiates, some relief from the existential contradiction of open marginality, and that, therefore, a higher proportion of group members would continue use to the point of physical dependence. In short, changing historical situations also explain why trends shift.

Now we have three levels of trend theory: the chemicals; the world of use; and the historical conditions that produce risk groups within which those worlds of use take their shape (neuro-physiological, ethnographic and historical research). What else is needed? We need to know where the chemicals came from, which is the traditional domain of the 'supply-side' intelligence analysts.

Shifts in supply

Again, the stories are legion and space is too limited in this chapter for anything more than an example or two. Let us consider the immigrant men, or their descendants, who used heroin in the 1920s. According to one history (Jonnes, 1996), once heroin became illegal in the United States, an entrepreneurial gangster in New York organised the first international narcotics distribution system with purchases of the drug in Europe, where it was still legally manufactured.

Let us also consider the African-Americans. Immediately after the war, as another history shows (McCoy, 1991), the Central Intelligence Agency (CIA) helped the Corsicans take power in Marseilles to combat communism. With alliances to the Mafia, reinstated in the south of Italy to aid the US invasion and support the occupation, the 'French Connection' trail to New York was established, something that would serve American heroin markets for the next two decades. Shifts in supply, from global to local, are additional candidates to explain why trends shift.

Drug policy

Drug policy may also make a difference. In a re-evaluation of the Nixon era, some now argue that it represented one of the saner moments in US drug policy (Massing, 1998). Nixon acted internationally to shut down the French Connection and, at the same time, supported treatment, especially the new use of methadone for maintenance, rather than withdrawal. I stepped into this changing situation when I began ethnographic work in New York City in 1973 (Agar, 1977). Heroin use declined as a result of these policies, though methadone programme enrolments mushroomed. To some extent, methadone replaced the market niche vacated by the dwindling supply of heroin. Clearly, drug policy can change trends as well.

The chemical, the world of use, the social position of a high-risk group, global/local distribution networks and policy: probably not a complete list, but certainly one whose components may play a role in the rise or fall of a drug trend. A trend theory — that is, a theory that explains trends in a way that is useful for planning, prevention and intervention — must take at least these mechanisms into account. In fact, it is plausible that social position, distribution and policy may well explain more of the variance represented by a particular trend than either chemical or user.

The usual quantitative indicators are the tip of an unknown trend iceberg. If we want to understand trends — or anticipate them, even — in useful ways, we need a trend theory at least as complicated as that I have outlined, and what I have outlined has been preliminary. Further, we are not dealing with a linear causal model, where the sum of the factors gives us a value for the trend. Instead, we are dealing with a model that specifies interactions among factors, iteratively over time, where feedback processes routinely occur, and where emergent properties of the interactions surprise us with the unexpected. We are, in short, in the realm of non-linear dynamic systems made up of purposeful learning agents: the realm of complexity theory (Waldrop, 1992).

Complexity is a topic that cannot be fully developed here; however, two points will be covered. Firstly, forecasting a drug trend is seen in a new light. Like weather and the economy, complex systems can be forecast within a limited time range, after which the system veers off into the unexpected. The time range varies with the phenomenon. To forecast drug trends, we will need to establish a time range and develop monitoring systems that tap into the various factors outlined in trend theory — chemical, world of use, social position, distribution and policy. Only this strategy will yield forecasts with a known range of accuracy.

Secondly, complex systems have leverage points: areas where a small input has large effects on the system's trajectory. Without a solid trend theory, we do not know where those points are. We do know that, in the United States at any rate, recent attempts to leverage drug trends have not been effective. At least with opiates, which are truly dangerous drugs because of physical dependence and its consequences, an understanding of effective leverage points would be worth its weight in gold. As one tentative example, I have occasionally worked as a 'drug educator', offering heroin lectures to the substance abuse curriculum required of Baltimore County youth arrested for a drug or alcohol offence. I have learned that the 'leverage point' of crossing over into physical dependence is a powerful tool, one reflected in music and film and observed by the young people in the class among their peers. This leverage point in an addict's biography also serves as a leverage point in drug education.

At the moment, my associate, Heather Schacht Reisinger, and I are trying to develop a trend theory for heroin epidemics in the Baltimore region. We have learned that all the factors discussed in this paper need to be included in the theory, and, the more we learn, the more we believe that complexity theory is the only formal model that stands a chance of representing the processes that underlie those trends. We are looking at the newest heroin trend among white youth resident in the suburbs, and we would like to hazard a forecast. There is clearly an epidemic of experimentation, in the sense of a rapid increase in those who have 'ever used' heroin. However, we think that physical dependence will increase to the frequently mentioned level of around 10 % among youth in the eastern part of the metropolitan area, the area where working-class populations have been marginalised by the decline in the manufacturing industry over the last 20 years. Physical dependence will seldom occur, or will occur and be 'cured', in the suburban areas to the north, the areas that represent a suburban boom development as middle- and upper-middle-class families have left the urban area. The youth in the east are more marginal, as that term was defined earlier.

Conclusions

This brief summary sketches a large amount of material in a limited space, and it does so based on an ongoing study. Preliminary though it might be, this chapter does suggest that a trend theory, based on complexity, will explain trends and add useful knowledge for those charged with responding to them.

On the issue of qualitative research, I hope that this chapter demonstrates two points. Firstly, 'qualitative' knowledge is an essential part of trend theory. The subjective effects of the chemical, the nature of the world of use, the knowledge required to understand high-risk groups, the nature of distribution systems and drug policies — these are patterns made of propositions, not variables converted to a numerical representation. Secondly, quantitative data are clearly a relevant and important part of the picture as well, including the traditional indicators. They have been neglected here because of the general goal of foregrounding how qualitative data fit into the picture. At any rate, I would rather not discuss when and how 'qualitative' and 'quantitative' data are the right way to go. I would rather discuss the importance of developing a trend theory, for both researchers and practitioners, and then gather and use whatever data are necessary to get the job done.

The author is Professor Emeritus at the University of Maryland and a consultant with Ethknoworks in Takoma Park, Maryland, USA.

Acknowledgements

The support of grant 1 RO1 DA10736 from the National Institute on Drug Abuse (NIDA), National Institute of Health, is gratefully acknowledged.

References

Agar, M. H. (1977) 'Going through the changes: methadone in New York', *Human Organisation,* 36, 291–295 (with commentary by R. Basham and reply).

Agar, M. H., Bourgois, P., French, J. and Murdoch, O. (1998) 'Heroin addict habit size in three cities: context and variation', *Journal of Drug Issues,* 28, 921–940.

Agar, M. H. and Kozel, N. (Eds.) (1999) 'Ethnography and substance use: talking numbers', *Substance Use and Misuse,* 34, 1935–1949.

Feldman, H., Agar, M. H. and Beschner, G. (Eds.) (1979) *Angel Dust,* Lexington, MA: Lexington Press.

Fountain, J. and Griffiths, P. (Eds.) (1999) 'Synthesis of qualitative research on drug use in the European Union: report on an EMCDDA project', *European Addiction Research,* 5(4), 4–10.

Ibsen, H. J. (1996 edition) *The Doll's House,* London: Faber.

Jonnes, J. (1996) *Hep-Cats, Narcs, and Pipe Dreams: a History of America's Romance with Illegal Drugs,* New York: Scribner.

McCoy, A. W. (1991) *The Politics of Heroin: CIA Complicity in the Global Drug Trade,* Chicago: Lawrence Hill Books.

Massing, M. (1998) *The Fix,* New York: Simon and Schuster.

Musto, D. F. (1987) *The American Disease: Origins of Narcotic Control* (expanded edition), New York: Oxford University Press.

Ratner, M. S. (1993) *Crack Pipe as Pimp: an Ethnographic Investigation of Sex-for-Crack Exchanges,* New York: Maxwell Macmilian International.

Waldrop, M. M. (1992) *Complexity,* New York: Viking.

CHAPTER 6

ANTENNA: A MULTI-METHOD APPROACH
TO ASSESSING NEW DRUG TRENDS

Dirk Korf and Ton Nabben

New trends in drug use are likely to evolve among specific groups that are scarcely represented, if at all, in samples drawn from general populations, such as school and household surveys. Commonly, the small numbers of drug users in general surveys make it difficult to reach an understanding of their backgrounds, lifestyles and the social contexts in which they consume their drugs. Furthermore, the questionnaires used for such broad surveys cannot include specific questions on new drugs (or new ways of taking drugs) until more detailed information about them is available.

The rapid rise in the use of ecstasy and various other synthetic drugs in the 1980s, and of 'ecodrugs' (euphoric, libido-enhancing and hallucinogenic vegetable-based substances) in the late 1990s, made drug consumption increasingly complex (Parker et al., 1998). Within a short time, new youth subcultures sprang up. 'House music' (also called 'acid', 'techno' or 'rave' music) caused a revolution in the music business. The existing drug care, drug prevention and drug education agencies in the Netherlands, as in many other countries, were virtually unable to keep track of the new drug trends that were simultaneously emerging. As emphasis in the 1980s was focusing more and more on caring for a group of ageing drug addicts, outreach among younger users was often neglected, as were investigations into new youth trends and the drug use that accompanied them. When the new youth subcultures proved to be more than a short-lived phase, and ecstasy rapidly became the most popular illicit drug in entertainment circles after cannabis, drug workers began deliberating on how to respond more quickly and adequately.

A critical stocktaking within various drug care institutions in the Netherlands in the early 1990s revealed a number of shortcomings in the existing approaches to data collection and in the availability and utility of information. In short, drug prevention and education agencies were virtually out of touch with the environments where drug trends were evolving, and most data (e.g. law enforcement, treatment, surveys) were inadequate and/or became available too late for an effective response.

A multi-method approach

To be able to respond quickly to current developments in illicit drug use in Amsterdam, in collaboration with the Prevention Department of the Jellinek Centre, we developed and implemented a methodology which enabled us to gather information continuously from a number of different sources.

The cornerstone of this approach is the qualitative component: a panel study among lay and professional experts who are well-informed about drug use among some specific group of drug users or in specific settings. The first goal of the panel study is the early detection and contextual understanding of new drug trends. Qualitative findings from the panel study are validated and further explored by quantitative methods. Every two years, a survey is conducted in secondary schools, deliberately targeting older pupils (average age 17 years), since, in the Netherlands, illicit drugs are rarely used by young adolescents. Every year, a survey of one selected 'high-risk population' is carried out (e.g. clients in youth assistance centres, visitors to trendy dance clubs and raves). This quantitative picture is supplemented by statistical data drawn from questions asked by users and their families or friends when they telephone Jellinek Prevention's helpline, and by data on the quality of ecstasy pills.

The panel study: objectives and methodology

In a panel study, 'a sample of respondents is selected and interviewed, then re-interviewed and studied at later times' (Kerlinger, 1972). Our panel study has three main objectives.

- *Early identification:* monitoring current developments in the interests of policy, prevention and care. The panel method enables us to collect data on new trends in drug use quickly and flexibly.

- *Orientation to context and practice:* mapping out trends to improve drug prevention and education among young people. The panel method is well-suited to acquiring in-depth information on the nature of both current and new drug use, and on the contexts in which they take place.

- *Prompt updating of survey questionnaires:* making it possible for our surveys to respond promptly and adequately to new developments. When the panel study reveals that the use of a new drug is spreading rapidly among trend-setters, then questions about this drug can be added to the school survey at very short notice, allowing us to obtain a quantitative picture of its more general prevalence.

Panel studies are used in diverse areas of research, and they may be quantitative or qualitative in nature (Diekmann, 1997). In our case, the study is mainly a qualitative one, although quantitative data are also collected. The panel study serves as an information system by which data are constantly being gathered on drugs, drug use and networks of users, covering a specific geographical area (in our case, Amsterdam) and a specific time period (in our case, twice a year since 1993). In contrast to most panel studies, our respondents are interviewed not so much about themselves as about the settings they frequent and the networks to which they belong. This demands certain qualities of the panel members, including:

- insider insight on new drugs, an overall view, and reflective faculties;
- special and up-to-date knowledge pertaining to certain aspects of drug use and its evolution within specific networks of users or in settings where users congregate; and
- good observation qualities (e.g. a well-informed panel member can determine whether a dance club is trendy or mainstream, whether it attracts a predominately gay or straight crowd, and which of the visitors are interested in, or experiment with, drugs).

In addition, in order to obtain valid data from independent sources, panel members should not know one another, nor should they be getting information from the same circuits and locations.

The research process of the panel study is divided into the following four successive stages.

Formulating and operationalising research questions and target populations

The more specific the research questions and the target populations are, the more rigorously one can search for suitable scenes and panel members. Key questions are: What do we need to know more about (e.g. the use of new drugs, new consumption techniques, problems and risks, polydrug use)? Which are the target populations (e.g. school drop-outs, homeless youth, ethnic minority youth, avant-garde youth, mainstream youth)?

Preparing the panel

The panel members are the mainstays of the panel study. They can be recruited from diverse sources: networks of drug-using groups; persons in touch with certain groups of users (e.g. dealers); dance club, discotheque and rave staff; outreach workers, neighbourhood and youth workers; the police; or those working in the fashion industry (hairdressers, etc.). It is important for the panel to have a well-balanced composition. The following steps should be taken to achieve this:

- compilation of an inventory of potential networks and settings;
- selection of networks and settings (trendy, mainstream, alternative, etc.);
- guarantee of sufficient diversity and geographical dispersion (different subcultures, ethnicities, ages, genders, sexual orientations);
- identification of potential panel members and verification of the quality of their information; and
- formation of a well-balanced panel, where members are informed about the purpose and operation of the study, and whose commitment is ensured.

Data collection, analysis and quick reporting

A team of researchers and prevention workers critically discuss data on a regular basis. This serves two purposes: not only do the prevention workers get information about new developments in time to orientate their approach to them, but also researchers can adapt their data-collection activities to accommodate these developments. The results are published once a year (Korf and van der Steenhoven, 1994; Korf et al., 1995; 1996; 1997; 1998).

Continuation of the study, revision of research questions if needed, panel maintenance and expansion, and member replacement

In the meetings of prevention workers and researchers, the objectives and methods of the prevention work of the previous year are evaluated and, if necessary, new goals and prevention strategies are articulated. The panel method is an instrument for longitudinal research. One of the key problems is panel attrition (also called panel mortality): the loss of study participants through non-response to subsequent measurements (Freedman et al., 1980; Call et al., 1982; Thornton et al., 1982; Morgan and Duncan, 1983). We try to minimise attrition by giving specific consideration to the continuity of panel members' participation at the time they are selected. In addition, the research team has regular, informal contacts with the panel members to maximise their involvement in the study. Important, too, is continuity in the research team itself. For example, a suggestion to enlist students to interview the panel was rejected, since they would probably only be involved in the research for a relatively brief period.

Panel attrition cannot always be avoided. Our panel study is not concerned with the behaviour of the panel members themselves, but with the situations they encounter and developments within their environment. If a panel member withdraws from the group or setting about which he/she is being interviewed, this person is replaced by someone from the same group or setting (among users, 'scene' is the more common word). Despite this individual attrition, the replacement provides for continuity in the information. Sometimes panel attrition is desirable. Since new trends often arise in new scenes, constant alertness as well as the ability to make ethnographic observations are demanded. On the basis of these observations and other information, we expand the panel with new members from new scenes. On the other hand, new trends may become mainstream, or they may lose popularity and disappear. In such cases, the further participation of a panel member may no longer be worthwhile.

The Amsterdam panel: avant-garde and marginalised youth

Each round of panel interviews are held with 25 to 30 key informants. The panel members can be classified into four clusters: party-goers and ravers, trendy club- and disco-goers, neighbourhood youth and problem youth (although in practice these clusters are not entirely separate). The clusters vary with regard to the number of users they cover, their age, gender and ethnicity. Panel members also differ in respect of their backgrounds (see Figure 1). Through the panel, we have access to a sustained, high-quality stream of information about drug trends as they are currently evolving from the insider's perspective. Within this body of information, we differentiate between *rumour* (hearsay, stories of a general nature not verified by the respondent), *signals* (verifiable, episodic information and individual observations of respondents), and concrete, verifiable, more systematic *observations*.

Figure 1: Four clusters in the Amsterdam panel (the situation in autumn 1998)

Cluster	N	Average age	Females (%)	Ethnic background	Panel members
Trendy club- and disco-goers (9 'scenes')	850	26	40	70 % white; also Surinamese, Moroccan	Bar staff, active visitors, DJs, VJs, fashion industry employees, drug dealers, doorkeepers
Party-goers and ravers (11 'scenes')	675	22	40	Mainly ethnic Dutch and other whites (mostly British)	Active ravers, DJs, drug dealers, party staff, 'eco-shop' staff
Neighbourhood youth (7 'scenes')	750	20	25	Mainly segregated groups of ethnic Dutch, Surinamese or Moroccan	Youth workers, people living or working in the neighbourhood, coffee shop staff
Problem youth (4 'scenes')	400	20	10	Mostly ethnic minorities or white foreigners (Germans, East Europeans)	Outreach workers

If all the rumours about 'new drugs' in the mass and underground media, or which panel members hear about, were true, then Amsterdam would by now have been overrun by all kinds of designer drugs such as cyber, flea, B-sting, chrystel, nexus and dolce vita. However, the popularity of many drugs can prove to be short-lived, or often the drugs are in extremely short supply. Not infrequently, many people have heard of a drug but have never seen it, let alone used it.

Sometimes data seem to signal a possible new trend, for example a drug may become known in a short time, but it may then disappear from the market just as rapidly. This occurred with GHB (gamma-hydroxybutyric acid) in 1996. In the spring, a large number of panel members had heard of GHB, or 'liquid ecstasy', but it was observed in only a few networks. By autumn, GHB was scarcely available. Normally, we only speak of a 'trend' if several panel members independently and persistently cite the same phenomenon, at around the same time, in different settings.

In recent years, there have also been observations of drugs that were gradually gaining in popularity.

- In 1994 a renewed interest in magic mushrooms was observed. Since then, the trend has intensified, as is evident in our surveys (Figure 2).

- The availability of laughing gas (N_2O) on the nightlife circuit initially became known in the spring of 1995, although today a more strict distribution policy by its producers has led to a decrease in its use.

- In 1995–96 cocaine was once again a focus of attention. Nearly half of our panel members signalled an increasing use of the drug, both in networks of disco-goers and ravers, and among neighbourhood and problem youth. More recently, panel members observed that more cocaine is being consumed in many different networks — and this is verified by surveys (Figure 2). Cocaine is now 'cool' and 'in'.

- Although, according to some panel members, the popularity of ecstasy is starting to wane, it is still the most popular illicit drug after cannabis (Figure 2).

- In addition to being sniffed, cocaine has increasingly been reported being smoked in the form of a cigarette. In networks of marginalised youth, there is a growing interest in freebase cocaine (also known as crack). As yet, however, these are only small cliques.

- Among the hallucinogenic drugs, magic mushrooms are the most frequently used. The use of LSD remains marginal. Mushrooms are preferred because their effects can be controlled better than those of LSD.

- There is increasing interest in other 'ecodrugs'. More and more varieties of 'energy drinks' and all kinds of herbal variants of ecstasy (such as X4, X7 and Cloud 9) are appearing on the market.

- A more general trend observed by panel members, primarily in discotheque and party circles, is the increasing use of several drugs simultaneously, in particular stimulants and alcohol. Ecstasy is used more and more as a basis drug, or 'starter': the desired feeling can then be extended and strengthened with hallucinogens or stimulants.

Figure 2:
Prevalence of some drugs, according to Antenna surveys in Amsterdam 1995–98

		Older pupils		Clubbers and ravers	
Year		1995	1997	1995	1998
N		586	862	462	456
Age in years (median)		17	17	23	25
Ecstasy	Ever	7 %	10 %	50 %	66 %
	Last year	6 %	7 %	41 %	55 %
	Last month	3 %	3 %	33 %	41 %
Magic mushrooms	Ever	5 %	11 %	29 %	45 %
	Last year	4 %	9 %	19 %	28 %
	Last month	1 %	3 %	6 %	8 %
Laughing gas	Ever	n.a.	10 %	n.a.	45 %
	Last year	n.a.	6 %	n.a.	31 %
	Last month	n.a.	2 %	n.a.	8 %
Cocaine	Ever	5 %	6 %	33 %	48 %
	Last year	3 %	4 %	25 %	37 %
	Last month	1 %	2 %	14 %	24 %
LSD	Ever	5 %	3 %	23 %	21 %
	Last year	2 %	2 %	9 %	3 %
	Last month	<.5 %	<.5 %	2 %	1 %

NB: n.a. = not applicable.

Conclusions

In the Amsterdam panel study, four clusters of 'scenes' were defined. At a more the-oretical level, they can be reduced to two main groups: avant-garde and margin-alised youth. Avant-garde youth appear to be predominantly of white origin, where-as immigrants and ethnic minorities are strongly represented among marginalised youth. As yet, few Moroccan, Surinamese and Antillean young people — who, together with Turks, are the largest ethnic minorities in Amsterdam (Holt and Scholten, 1996; O+S, 1996) — attend raves, which might explain why few use ecstasy.

From the experience in Amsterdam, a general model for diffusion of 'new' drugs (and revival of 'old' drugs) can be deduced (Figure 3). Most commonly, new drugs are introduced among avant-garde trendsetters; they are then taken over by middle-class trend followers and further diffused among the lower classes. This diffusion brings about decreasing popularity among the original trendsetters, who then search for new drugs. However, not all new drugs end their career among the lower classes, and some start their career there. In particular, drugs that are predominantly defined as a social problem, such as heroin and crack, are introduced among marginalised groups and often remain restricted to them. Consequently, new 'avant-garde drugs' often make a downwards career movement, whereas new 'problem drugs' rarely fol-low an upwards career pattern.

Figure 3: General model for diffusion of new drugs

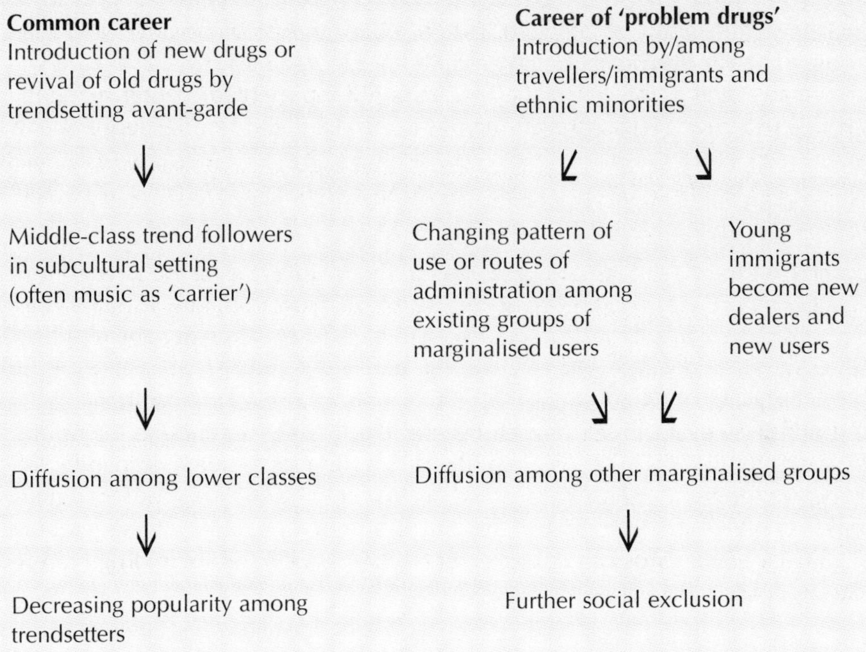

Common career
Introduction of new drugs or
revival of old drugs by
trendsetting avant-garde

↓

Middle-class trend followers
in subcultural setting
(often music as 'carrier')

↓

Diffusion among lower classes

↓

Decreasing popularity among
trendsetters

Career of 'problem drugs'
Introduction by/among
travellers/immigrants and
ethnic minorities

↙   ↘

Changing pattern of   Young
use or routes of   immigrants
administration among   become new
existing groups of   dealers and
marginalised users   new users

↘   ↙

Diffusion among other marginalised groups

↓

Further social exclusion

Dirk Korf is Associate Professor at the University of Amsterdam, Bonger Institute of Criminology, the Netherlands. At the time of writing, Ton Nabben was a researcher at the Amsterdam Bureau of Social Research and Statistics (O+S), the Netherlands.

References

Call, V. R. A., Otto, L. B. and Spenner, K. I. (1982) *Tracking Respondents: a Multi-Method Approach,* Lexington, MA: Lexington Books.

Diekmann, A. (1997) *Empirische Sozialforschung,* Reinbek: Rowohlt.

Freedman, D. S., Thornton, A. and Camburn, D. (1980) 'Maintaining response rates in longitudinal studies', *Sociological Methods and Research,* 9, 87–98.

Holt, J. and Scholten, D. (Eds.) (1996) *Etnische Groepen in Amsterdam,* Amsterdam: Bureau voor Strategisch Minderhedenbeleid.

Kerlinger, F. N. (1972) *Foundations of Behavioural Research,* London: Holt, Rinehart & Winston.

Korf, D. J. and van der Steenhoven, P. (1994) *Antenne 1993: Trends in alcohol, tabak, drugs en gokken bij jonge Amsterdammers,* Amsterdam: Jellinek Reeks, No 2.

Korf, D. J., Nabben, T. and Schreuders, M. (1995) *Antenne 1994: Trends in alcohol, tabak, drugs en gokken bij jonge Amsterdammers,* Amsterdam: Jellinek Reeks, No 3.

Korf, D. J., Nabben, T. and Schreuders, M. (1996) *Antenne 1995: Trends in alcohol, tabak, drugs en gokken bij jonge Amsterdammers,* Amsterdam: Jellinek Reeks, No 5.

Korf, D. J., Nabben, T. and Berdowski, Z. (1997) *Antenne 1996: Trends in alcohol, tabak, drugs en gokken bij jonge Amsterdammers,* Amsterdam: Jellinek Reeks, No 6.

Korf, D. J., Nabben, T., Lettink, D. and Bouma, H. (1998) *Antenne 1997: Trends in alcohol, tabak, drugs en gokken bij jonge Amsterdammers,* Amsterdam: Jellinek Reeks, No 7.

Morgan, J. N. and Duncan, G. J. (1983) *User Guide for the Panel Study of Income Dynamics,* Michigan: Survey Research Centre, University of Michigan.

O+S (1996) *De Amsterdammers in acht etnische groepen,* 1 January 1996, Amsterdam: The Amsterdam Bureau of Social Research and Statistics.

Parker, H., Aldridge, J. and Measham, F. (1998) *Illegal Leisure: the Normalization of Adolescent Recreational Drug Use,* New York: Routledge.

Thornton, A., Freedman, D. S. and Camburn, D. (1982) 'Obtaining respondent cooperation in family panel studies', *Sociological Methods and Research,* 11, 33–51.

AN EARLY RECOGNITION SYSTEM FOR DRUG TRENDS IN BERLIN

Reiner Domes and Ludwig Kraus

The drug market, like other markets, is subject to periodic fluctuations and trends. Both 'old' and 'new' substances (such as designer drugs) become popular at irregular intervals. For example, the amount of the hallucinogen LSD confiscated by the police in Germany has risen sharply in recent years. At the same time, as certain drug combinations, habits and methods of use appear, they are accompanied by new risks, such as the danger of HIV or hepatitis infection through intravenous use. Some trends do not remain restricted to a limited social milieu, but instead spread among new and previously less visible drug-using groups. Changing drug-using behaviour has the potential to burden the lives of new groups of users with new or different psychological and social risks than they previously experienced. The risk of coming into contact with drugs and later developing problematic forms of use depends upon a number of factors (e.g. unemployment, homelessness, gender, migration). Recognising these factors allows the identification of groups at risk of developing patterns of problem drug use.

Timely recognition of new developments in drug use is imperative for planning and implementing substance abuse prevention measures. The emergence of new synthetic drugs in the early 1990s, in particular, demonstrated the need for sensitive and reliable instruments for recognising such new trends (Drogen- und Suchtbericht des Landes Berlin, 1997). As a rule, statistics on trends from the police and documentation from out-patient and in-patient drug treatment units are available only after a delay. In addition, they supply only limited information on the social context in which such changes are taking place. The historic changes of 1989 exposed drug-using habits in West Berlin to a previously highly protected generation from the eastern part of the formerly divided city. This situation seemed likely to lead to changes in drug-using patterns in the restored capital. The implementation and testing of the proposed approach is a first step in the process to set up a national early recognition system in the context of the work of the EMCDDA in this area (EMCDDA/NAC, 1998).

Background and objectives

Due to the illegality of drug use, access to drug-using groups is methodologically demanding. For this reason, one can expect denials when questioning previously inconspicuous drug users, who first have to be identified and then agree to be questioned. In addition, one must take into account that revelations of new trends and the related criminal prosecution are not in the direct interest of the drug users and can lead to distortions in response behaviour. It can thus be assumed that representative surveys underestimate the true number of drug users. A frequent and extensive survey of all potential and manifest drug-using groups would be necessary to discover new trends that first appear in very small groups but could spread relatively quickly. Yet, as a rule, the financial cost of research does not allow for such an approach.

In Berlin, a wide range of facilities have daily contact with groups of potential or manifest drug users. These services include drug prevention initiatives, health services and outreach programmes in schools and community settings, but their knowledge concerning drug users' realities is seldom communicated to colleagues from other facilities in order to broaden their perspectives. At the same time, existing statistical data from the police and drug outreach programmes could be included in the overall picture of drug use, and media reports and personal observations could also be considered and analysed. Predictions from an early recognition system could be checked retrospectively using these data.

Access

There is the potential for new scenes to develop around new drugs, drug combinations and methods of preparation and use. These subcultures can be formed by groups that are not particularly visible, making access accordingly difficult. Drug-using groups in which few serious physical, psychological or social crises occur are identified very late or not at all. Still, to a certain extent, problems are visible in other areas of life (school, family, leisure activities), which is why we are aiming at a wide range of approaches for the early recognition system in Berlin. Potential contributors (interview partners) could include not only doctors and medical personnel, street outreach workers, drug counsellors and therapists, but also employees from youth outreach and other counselling centres, the police and other individuals who have insight as empirical social researchers into specific youth scenes. All interview partners deal with potential or manifest drug users in their careers and their multiplicity makes it possible to access a very broad range. In addition, case studies can be considered in a larger context and filtered through specific criteria.

Model

Little is known about the factors leading to the spread of new trends into larger groups of users. In the face of the low number of relevant individual observations, a growth rate or a threshold value of observed cases is a priori indefinable. An observation will be judged relevant when several interview partners can credibly confirm that they made the corresponding observations during the same time period. If this is the case, potential trends can then be more closely examined. Not until a trend hypothesis has proven significant in a further study can a trend be confirmed.

Focus

The existing survey instruments that gather data on known dimensions are considered relevant for patterns of use (amount of use, frequency of use, combinations used simultaneously or 'on the side', etc.). Yet, new trends can possibly be better described with the addition of new dimensions. In the qualitative part of the study, the definitions of problems given by the interview partners will be considered. In doing so, new aspects and descriptive patterns can be developed.

Establishing a network

Trends in drug use that first appear in smaller groups do not always assert themselves in larger segments of the population in the same manner. Reports on new trends can stimulate interest and encourage their spread. Little is known about the conditions under which a limited trend develops into an epidemiologically significant phenomenon. In order to reach an acceptable level of prediction accuracy, an important element of the early recognition system is the creation of a network between the institutions and facilities involved. The observations reported to the institutions and facilities can subsequently be used to sensitise staff in their work.

Scope

The system is structured as broadly as possible in order to be able to spot possible new drug-using groups — a compelling priority for the situation in Berlin. The early recognition system identifies potential trends in all areas of illicit drugs.

Efficiency and cost-effectiveness

Given the circumstance of limited financial resources, a maximally cost-efficient procedure has been chosen. In addition, existing structures will be used to the greatest possible extent.

Avoiding false alarms

The system should be as resistant as possible to interference and aim at a balance between sensitivity and overreaction. In order to achieve this, it is necessary to have reliable information from a variety of sources.

Concordance with existing data collection

Existing information systems will be used and supported. Investigations can be coordinated for the benefit of other studies — for example, the modification of surveys — where applicable.

A dynamic process of data collection, analysis and exchange

The early recognition system explores drug use in very different groups of people and would hardly be possible as a result of standardised data collection from the same populations. Rather, it is conceived of as a dynamic process in which data collection, the generating of hypotheses, and networking continually supplement one another (Griffiths and Vingoe, 1997).

Design

The early recognition system does not define a trend in the sense of a statistical threshold value for describing long-term changes in measurable data, but instead in the broader sociological sense of changing currents in society and in subcultures. Against a backdrop of changing material and immaterial values, these changes lead to a new self-concept and thus to related changes of behaviour in the affected group of people. For this reason, an ethnographically oriented research design was chosen to describe the context of life in which such radical changes occur. In the exploration and networking of the observations made by the members of various organisations connected with drug use, and in the hypotheses directing our actions, an overall view can be developed of the drug-using groups, substances, patterns of use, and social and geographical surroundings, as well as individual and common sub-cultural motivations for use.

In contrast to research questionnaires for broad population surveys, the focus of the early recognition system is on the potential and manifest drug users themselves: new developments in groups of drug users *(who?)*; the substances and combinations being used *(what?)*; patterns of use *(how?)*; the social and geographical environment *(where?)*; and the motivating factors for use *(why?)* (Korf et al., 1998).

Data collection

Quantitative approach

Data obtained from the various services working with drug users on a daily basis can be analysed within the framework of the early recognition system. Along with publications of the Criminal Police Office (LKA) on confiscated quantities, data from treatment centres' documentation (Destas, EBIS, SEDOS) will also be considered during the course of the study.

Qualitative approach

A total of 20 to 25 interview partners, from facilities as diverse as possible, will be questioned. The criteria for the selection of the institutions include their early contact with potential and manifest drug users, their distribution across the neighbourhoods of Berlin, their emphasis on working with certain scenes or users of specific substances and their particular access to certain risk groups. In order to avoid unnecessary overlap of information, some facilities that are important for Berlin's drug awareness and treatment system are not included in the pool of interview partners. The selection in no way reflects any judgment on the quality of work of these facilities.

Research questionnaires

Interview partners will be asked to describe the type of contact they have with the affected groups of persons and to provide information about typical subgroups or scenes. In the last section of the research questionnaire, there will be questions on new drugs and atypical forms of use and procedures. To broaden the scope, the research questionnaire will be discussed within the selected facilities, if possible. The questionnaire's main objective is to prepare for the interview (see below) and to focus on the aspects of their work most relevant to the early recognition system.

Interview

The interview will explore the interview partner's subjective categories of description. The scenes and subgroups will be described in terms of their realities and habits of use, their value systems, and in regard to the corresponding risks and problems. Here, the focus is on more recent developments and corresponding changes in each field of work.

Methods of analysis

All data will be analysed together. Descriptions will be analysed qualitatively on content, examined for common factors in the facilities' observations, and condensed into a report. The resulting overview of any changes in drug use will be reported back to the facilities involved in an anonymous form and could have a sensitising function for their work. This yields a dynamic process of data collection, analysis and exchange. The observations of change that are described in the report can then be examined in other studies for their general application and relevance. The data collection is conceptualised as a repeated survey and should be carried out at regular intervals.

Conclusions

The early recognition system for drug trends in Berlin integrates qualitative and quantitative research approaches: hypotheses about trends in Berlin have to be verified by an independent database, such as surveys of schoolchildren or drug users and a study of groups at risk. This design will yield data on the range of potential new drug trends and will be cost-effective. It also represents an attempt to produce data to harmonise with other existing early monitoring systems in Germany and Europe.

The authors are members of the Department of Social Epidemiology, Institute for Therapy Research, Munich, Germany.

References

Drogen- und Suchtbericht des Landes Berlin (1997) Drucksache 13/1606 des Abgeord-netenhauses von Berlin.

EMCDDA/NAC (National Addiction Centre) (1998) 'Feasibility study on detecting, tracking and understanding emerging trends in drug use', report prepared for the EMCDDA.

Griffiths, P. and Vingoe, L. (1997) 'Developing a rapid reporting methodology to respond to new patterns of drug use, new substances of use and changes in routes of drug administration', paper presented at the EMCDDA seminar 'Qualitative research: methodology, practice and policy', Bologna.

Korf, D. J., Kemmesies, U. E. and Nabben, T. (1998) 'Trendstudie Drogen', *Sucht,* 44, 280–284.

CHAPTER 8

INCORPORATING QUALITATIVE METHODS INTO A RAPID AUDIT OF NEW HEROIN OUTBREAKS AMONGST BRITISH YOUTH

Howard Parker

During the 1980s, several urban regions based around large cities in the UK hosted extensive heroin outbreaks that primarily involved socially excluded young adults (17–25 years) becoming heroin users. These heroin outbreaks, in sum, represented the UK's first heroin epidemic, which impacted right across the 1980s.

The social impact of around 150 000 heroin users in Britain was considerable. Users funded their drug habits by supplementing State benefits with significant rates of acquisitive crime and drug dealing. Some female users became involved in the sex industry, particularly in London and the Scottish cities. Demand for treatment services grew, further fuelled by a gradual switch from smoking to injecting heroin that coincided with the HIV/AIDS epidemic near the end of the 1980s. Eventually, these heroin outbreaks settled, with incidence falling away, but they left an endemic heroin-using population in the affected areas. This population has since been reasonably and successfully 'managed' with extensive methadone prescribing (Parker et al., 1988).

Over the first half of the 1990s, the UK experienced a 'quiet' (endemic) period vis-à-vis heroin and most young Britons largely eschewed the drug and all injecting, being well aware of heroin's addictiveness and the health dangers of injecting. Aside from the 'old' heroin sites, the rest of the UK saw little heroin use. This period was dominated by extensive 'recreational' drug use, namely of cannabis, amphetamines and ecstasy, although crack cocaine joined the repertoires of many city-based 'problem' drug users.

However, from around 1995–96, 'rumours' of new heroin uptake began to circulate amongst drugs professionals and the police. At least three small cities (with a heroin 'footprint' from the 1980s by way of availability through a handful of dealers) experienced full-scale local outbreaks and numerous small towns with no heroin history saw very young new users emerge. As these rumours grew, and in the absence of any formalised early warning system, the UK Government commissioned a rapid audit of the situation in England and Wales (Parker et al., 1998).

Mixing methods

There are dangers in the quantitative–qualitative bifurcation found in so many discussions on research methods, in that many of the most effective investigations into drug misuse utilise a range of techniques and often combine quantification with softer, qualitative techniques. So whilst, clearly, we have the classic stand-alone ethnographies, on the one hand, and the standardised survey with its totally descriptive statistics, on the other, the reality in much drugs research is a blend of approaches. To this we must add that the experienced career drugs researcher often brings with her or him accumulated knowledge and experience which allows an additional intuitive or creative dimension to play a role. In this case, having researched the UK heroin outbreaks of the 1980s and drugs in youth culture during the 1990s, the author was able to design the research instruments and techniques and interpret the findings with, hopefully, a sociological imagination. This again is borne of embracing both the quantitative and qualitative traditions, and locating and interpreting statistics in an understanding of human behaviour vis-à-vis drug initiation, drugs careers and heroin epidemiology (e.g. Hunt and Chambers, 1976).

The audit focused on those aged under 19, and involved a national postal survey of all police forces and drugs action teams (DATs, statutory local inter-professional drugs response networks) in England and Wales. The questionnaire was designed to elicit both hard data (e.g. arrests, seizures, local research and monitoring information) and perceptions and informed opinion. It also provided open questions and 'open space' to allow elaboration, which was well-used by many respondents, who offered cameos of their local heroin situation. This postal survey was followed up with telephone calls, both to increase the response rate (e.g. by completing the questionnaire over the phone) and elaborate on returns. Moreover, numerous telephone interviews were conducted as a consequence of survey returns identifying key local informants (e.g. a detached worker or a drugs agency manager).

As the national picture was pieced together from the survey — based on an eventual 80 % return rate from the police and 73 % from the DATs — and regional mapping was begun, fieldwork visits were undertaken to identifiable heroin 'hotspots'. Thus, three small cities with full-scale outbreaks, involving adolescent and young adult heroin users counted in thousands, were visited, as were minor towns with only very small, but currently rising, numbers. Numerous key professionals were interviewed and a small number of interviews with young heroin users/dealers were undertaken in each area. Thus, the survey, although concerned with some quantification, was 'open' enough to produce more complex assessments of how heroin use might be spreading in particular areas, the social profiles of new users, the way heroin is being distributed and marketed, its price and purity, etc. In short, because these new heroin outbreaks are often only just unfolding and few new users have been 'captured' in crime and treatment profiling, the qualitative element in the survey and fieldwork encouraged perceptions and impressions held by key local actors to be disclosed.

Had this mixed-methods approach and the reliance on local actors' perceptions and descriptions produced a jumble of unrelated idiosyncratic data, the analysis and conclusions would have been highly problematic. In fact, there was a remarkable uniformity in the findings, and clear patterns and profiles emerged which fitted well with the previous epidemiological knowledge about heroin outbreaks and the knowledge base about young Britons' drug wisdom and drug use during the 1990s.

Findings

Some 80 % of the DAT networks and 81 % of police forces making returns reported new or recent clusters of heroin users in their jurisdictions. The 200 plus returns, despite the non-return rate, covered almost every area of England and Wales. The geographical mapping which flowed from the data analysis showed that the old heroin sites from the 1980s were least likely, along with isolated rural areas, to report new outbreaks. Conversely, those regions hardly affected during the first epidemic — large to small towns in north-east England, Yorkshire, west Midlands, Avon and south-west England — repeatedly reported new heroin uptake.

During the 1980s epidemic, the social profile of the young heroin users had matched what is now termed 'social exclusion'. Most users were undereducated, unemployed, living in poor neighbourhoods and many had delinquent antecedents even prior to heroin use. However, this time, whilst such a profile was clearly apparent, many non-city reports were describing heroin trying and use amongst relatively conformist 'bonded' young people from, if not affluent, then certainly not poor neighbourhoods/backgrounds. It was also widely reported that the age of onset was routinely including young people of 15 to 17, far younger than previously identified in the UK. This was borne out during fieldwork visits, whereby social histories with young users often identified first experimentation with heroin prior to 16 years of age.

Most of the young users in these outbreak areas are currently smoking (or 'tooting') heroin but with injecting becoming more likely through time and experience. Heroin careers appear to be taking some time to develop, with many young people initially using only occasionally and then, even with regular usage, being able to function on one bag (GBP 10 EUR 16, containing 0.1 gram of 30–40 % pure heroin) a day. As in the 1980s, more young men than young women are being identified as users, but this time around there is an involvement amongst Asian youth where there are significant Asian communities in the affected towns and cities (see Chapter 13).

Conclusions

In the absence of a systematic 'early warning' system of new drug trends or problems for the UK, this rapid audit approach becomes a feasible, and certainly a cost-effective, device. Clearly, however, a stimulus is required before government — local or national — will commission such a review. In this case, with heroin seizures and new treatment presentations rising and, most of all, drugs professionals' stories generating rumours, the catalysts were present.

The audit purposefully utilised a mixed-methods approach because it was recognised that, with no sustained research and few effective monitoring systems functioning on the ground, 'hard' data would be scarce. The high return rate and unusual willingness of local informants to provide additional 'soft' anecdotal and impressionistic information was probably the result of the flexible instrument design, the strong support for the audit from the police and government, but, most of all, the timelines of the research. The right questions were asked at the right time and so potential returnees were motivated to express their concerns and share their intelligence in both senses of the word.

This report has refocused UK Government strategy towards acknowledging a second heroin epidemic which may be beginning to unfold in the UK. It has also alerted those working in the drugs field to be watchful for heroin uptake in local youth populations. It can do no more than this, because, at the early stages of heroin outbreaks, usage remains hidden and secretive, with new users being some time away from presenting for treatment or being willing to disclose their drugs status to 'officials' of any sort. Quantification of the scale and size of these outbreaks is unlikely to take place in the near future because of the major cost of what would be qualitative research in numerous areas of the country. Ironically, it will only be when full-scale outbreaks have unfolded in a particular city or town that the far more accurate capture–recapture or multi-agency enumeration (supported by qualitative 'snowballing' interviewing) will become feasible. Then, with users being identified in the criminal justice system, at treatment agencies, needle exchanges, etc., counting heads will become feasible (Parker et al., 1988). In the meantime, strategic response possibilities include public health messages to give heroin a bad name and explain its dependency potential to a young audience, most of whom know little about 'brown' (heroin), and, most importantly, developing young people's drug services in those areas already experiencing outbreaks.

The author is Research Professor and Director of the Social Policy Applied Research Centre (SPARC) in the Department of Social Policy and Social Work at Manchester University, UK.

References

Hunt, S. and Chambers, C. (1976) *The Heroin Epidemics: a Study of Heroin Use in the United States*, New York: Spectrum.

Parker, H., Bakx, K. and Newcombe, R. (1988) *Living with Heroin: the Impact of a Drugs Epidemic on an English Community*, Milton Keynes: Open University Press.

Parker, H., Bury, C. and Egginton, R. (1998) *New Heroin Outbreaks amongst Young People in England and Wales*, London: Police Research Group, Home Office.

RECREATIONAL LIFE AND ECSTASY USE

Amador Calafat and Paolo Stocco

Whilst traditional patterns of drug use associated with heroin are far from disappearing, new forms of use associated with recreational activities have appeared and are increasingly associated with young people who use not only ecstasy but also alcohol, cannabis, cocaine and LSD. Recreational activities occupy an important place in the lives of young people. During the week, they study or work within an order imposed by society, but the weekends are their own, where they can create their own experiences, their own identity and give their lives significance. For many of them, legal or illegal drugs are an element of group cohesion and facilitate their recreational desires.

Research

A European network of professionals interested in research and prevention has been carrying out surveys on ecstasy use, funded by the European Commission, since 1997. The first survey focused on ecstasy, described the characteristics of users, and studied the social representations which users and non-users had of this drug. The 1998 study, 'Sonar Project 98', was not exclusively concerned with ecstasy, but looked at all drugs taken in recreational environments since the first survey showed that ecstasy users use other drugs too. These surveys are continuing, and qualitative methodology plays an important part in them.

Researching the use of drugs in recreational environments immediately forces us to explore the culture of users and forms of use, which are both in constant evolution. The extent of, and cultural backing for, ecstasy use specifically has progressed surprisingly quickly. Sampling, at a national level, of both students and the population in general is clearly insufficient to understand the full complexity of ecstasy use and the cultural framework which supports it. For this reason, qualitative elements were added to the research design. Our aim is to develop an open structure, sensitive to the context and the continuous changes: defining problems as well as acquiring knowledge are perceived as processual activities.

Having created a 'minimal quantitative framework', we found that the qualitative research approach was the most fruitful method with which to examine the complex dynamic interactions between the cultural, social, economic and other aspects of ecstasy use. The result of this pluralistic point of view is the construction of a 'common knowledge' of the phenomenon, rather than a limited technical knowledge. This knowledge is socially constructed. The first consequence of this is that both technical and interactive knowledge are useful in reforming complex problems, like those of ecstasy, and in defining strategic frameworks. The second consequence is that we realised that a plurality of subjects take part in reframing problems, and that the researcher is not the only one who has knowledge of the question.

Characteristics and social representation of ecstasy in Europe

This section describes the methodology used and presents some findings from our first research project on the characteristics and social representation of ecstasy in five European cities (Coimbra, Modena, Nice, Palma de Mallorca and Utrecht).

Social representation theory and methodology were used for the study. This theory is based on the idea that there is no break between the object and the subject: an objective reality does not exist. The aim was to gather 'common knowledge' via an analysis of the literature on the topic and by in-depth interviews with ecstasy users. The information was fed into a social representation questionnaire and analysed using a method developed by a group of researchers at the University of Aix-en-Provence, directed by Professor Flament, which allows the study of the structure of the relationships between representations.

We concluded that the characteristics of ecstasy use have not been sufficiently studied from an epidemiological point of view, so we devised a questionnaire on lifestyles and patterns of ecstasy use. The size of the sample (a total of 1 627 individuals distributed among the five cities) and the methodology used to recruit them enabled the creation of a minimal quantitative framework that permitted us to locate the qualitative analysis.

Finally, two scales which allowed quantitative analysis were included in the study: Zuckerman's Sensations Seeker Scale Version V, and the Social Deviation Scale used by the Centre on Drug and Alcohol Research at the University of Kentucky. These scales were introduced to provide a more detailed characterisation of ecstasy users.

The data from this quantitative part of the study offered us descriptive information about the characteristics of use, in different European cities, of a substance still insufficiently studied. It also served to analyse the social representation of ecstasy users and non-ecstasy users, and it established differences between ecstasy users and non-users. The data revealed that ecstasy users are more likely to be polydrug users than other young people and that they are greater abusers of other drugs (they get drunk and use other drugs with greater frequency). They are not individuals who could be considered marginal, but they present significant differences in important parameters (e.g. they are greater seekers of sensation, according to the Zuckerman scale, and score more on the Social Deviation Scale). They are less worried by the dangers associated with drug use and they are not worried about avoiding them. They are also more interested in 'house' culture.

As for social representation, the distribution of items in two blocks or chains of representations was repeated by both the ecstasy consumers' and the non-consumers' control group. This leads us to suggest that we are seeing two powerful stereotypes, with important repercussions on the behaviour of individuals, and which must be taken into account in designing prevention campaigns.

It is important to understand that, although the ecstasy consumers' and non-consumers' positions are opposed in each of the chains of representation, the structure is always respected. One of the chains of representation shows the position of respondents on the effects attributed to ecstasy. The second block shows another chain, where the central theme relates to respondents' positions on the dangers of consumption. Here, we find an association of components, such as ecstasy leads to death, or addiction, or has a long-term depressive effect. These components may also be considered 'effects' of ecstasy to a certain extent, but we believe that what leads them to be associated is the focus on the dangers — in other words, aspects which would imply that ecstasy was a supposedly dangerous drug for those who use it. The individuals in our survey think about, understand or interact with ecstasy on the basis of two chains of association or social representations — the implied 'effects' and the implied 'dangers' — to position themselves for or against using it. Ecstasy users believe that the effects of the substance are positive ones and do not evaluate the dangers associated with its use, whereas non-users believe the opposite.

Preventive implications

These data have preventive implications. One of the most important discoveries of this study, as described above, is that there is no similarity between the social representation of ecstasy users and non-users. We believe that there should be a strategy aimed at not weakening the caution of non-consumers. Further research must be undertaken to achieve a better understanding of the nature and function of social representation. Our hypothesis is that the messages transmitted by preventive campaigns will only be effective if they connect with the social representation schema of young people.

The ideal situation is to integrate ecstasy prevention strategies into a wider and comprehensive drug preventive strategy. Ways of using ecstasy, the amounts used, its simultaneous use with other drugs and its place in youth culture can change over time. Some data from our investigations concur with other epidemiological studies, indicating that ecstasy is forming part of polydrug-using repertoires. This negates the widely held stereotype in which ecstasy consumers are different from those who use other drugs (i.e. that they are using ecstasy exclusively and are capable of exercising control over the substance, and that the only dangers of this pattern of use come from adulteration of the product and ignorance of harm-minimisation procedures, such as drinking water and resting to avoid heatstroke when dancing).

Present survey

The complex relationship between synthetic drugs, house music and recreational life has contributed new dimensions to our research. Firstly, there is the importance of the recreational context in understanding the patterns of current use. There is a strong association between ecstasy (and other designer drugs), dancing, music, a youthful lifestyle and even a world concept. Not all musical styles are associated with a specific drug, but in the case of 'house' music, synthetic drugs appear to be an indispensable companion. Secondly, our study challenges the stereotype of ecstasy users, and, thirdly, it has shown the central importance of alcohol consumption within recreational polydrug-using repertoires.

Our studies show the need to continue research into the recreational lives of young people and the association with drug use. Recreational life, represented above all in the entertainment activities of weekends, is in constant expansion and has established itself as an expression of young people's needs. Thus, it is essential to have a description of this recreational world throughout Europe. This is one of the priorities of the present survey, in which we are devoting an important part to providing a description of the nightlife in those cities which are taking part (Athens, Berlin, Coimbra, Manchester, Modena, Nice, Palma de Mallorca, Utrecht and Vienna). Through these descriptions, it will be possible to see similarities and differences in forms of entertainment and enjoyment, and to identify aspects which are relevant to drug use. We can define 'recreational togetherness' as a 'community of practices', characterised by the continuous activity of sense-making shared activities, as we have seen above in users' evaluations of ecstasy's effects.

We consider that the description of the nightlife in each city should identify the different groups of young people who participate in it, ascertain the most popular places and describe participants' habits and cultures relating to entertainment and, most particularly, to legal and illegal drug use. It is also our intention to get to know the nightlife from the point of view of the population professionally involved in it, such as waiters, disc-jockeys, police officers, and club and disco owners.

Conclusions

The survey is centred on polydrug use in recreational environments. To have concentrated once again on ecstasy only, having established that its use forms part of polydrug-using patterns, would not give us the full picture. In the present survey, we have continued to employ a combination of exploratory methods, both quantitative (questionnaires) and qualitative (semi-structured interviews) in each of the nine cities. The quantitative part (300 young people sampled in each city) provides abundant direct information by those who are actually participating in the nightlife scene. The qualitative part (more than 90 interviews with key informants on the nightlife in each city) enables such information to be put into context. The present survey also represents a thematic and conceptual broadening towards more sociological and anthropological spheres, and this has contributed a more global view of trends, movements, influences and networks.

Amador Calafat is a psychiatrist and President of the European Institute for the Investigation of Risk Factors for Children and Adolescents (Irefrea) Spain. Paolo Stocco is a psychologist and President of Irefrea, Italy.

Further reading

Beck, J. (1993) *Ecstasy and the Rave Scene: Historical and Cross-Cultural Perspectives,* Proceedings, Vol. 2, Comm. Epidemiol. Work Group, San Francisco, California, 16 and 17 December 1993, pp. 421–431.

Beck, J. and Watson, L. (1991) 'New age seekers: MDMA use as an adjunct to spiritual pursuit', *Journal of Psychoactive Drugs,* 23, 261–270.

Calafat, A. (1997) 'La representación social de las drogas de diseño en Europa', *Jornadas Nacionales Socidrogalcohol,* 24, 39–61.

Calafat, A., Amengual, M., Palmer, A. and Saliba, C. (1997) 'Drug use and its relationship to other behaviour disorders and maladjustment signs among adolescents', *Substance Use and Misuse,* 32, 1–24.

Calafat, A., Stocco, P. et al. (1998) *Characteristics and Social Representation of Ecstasy in Europe,* Palma de Mallorca: Irefrea.

Calafat, A., Stocco, P., et al. (1999) *Night Life in Europe and Recreative Poly Drug Use,* Palma de Mallorca: Irefrea.

Goldstein, J. W. and Sappington, J. T. (1997) 'Personality characteristics of students who become heavy drug users: an MMPI study of avant-garde', *American Journal of Drug and Alcohol Abuse,* 4, 401–412.

Griffiths, P. and Vingoe, L. (1997) 'Amphetamines, ecstasy and LSD: strange bedfellows?', in P. Griffiths and L. Vingoe (Eds.) *The Use of Amphetamines, Ecstasy and LSD in the European Community: a Review of Data on Consumption Patterns and Current Epidemiological Literature* (UK National Addiction Centre, unpublished).

Griffiths, P. and Vingoe, L. (1997) *The Use of Amphetamines, Ecstasy and LSD in the European Community: a Data Synthesis* (UK National Addiction Centre, unpublished).

Henderson, S. (1993) 'Fun, fashion and frisson', *International Journal of Drug Policy,* 4, 122–129.

McDermott, P. and Matthews, A. (1997) 'Ecstasy in the UK: recreational drug use and cultural change' (available on http://hyperreal.com/drugs/mdma/ecstasy.uk).

McKeganey, N., Health, D. B., Ogborne, A., Stimson, G., Araya, R., Pearson, G., Darke, S. and Hartnoll, R. (1995) 'Qualitative methods in drug abuse and HIV research', *Addiction,* 90, 749–766.

Melero, J. C. and Flores, R. (1996) *Extasis y otras Drogas de Sintesis,* Bilbao: Edex Kolectiboa.

Miller, P. and Plant, M. (1996) 'Drinking, smoking and illicit drug use among 15 and 16 year-olds in the United Kingdom', *British Medical Journal*, 313, 394–397.

Moscovici, S. (1969) 'Preface', in C. Herzlich, *Santé et Maladie: Analyse d'une Représentation sociale*, Paris: Mouton.

Roig Traver, A. (1994) 'Sobre el uso recreativo de la metilendioximetanfetamina: aspectos historicos y efectos adversos', *Adicciones*, 6, 437–452.

Saunders, N. (1993) *E is for Ecstasy* (first edition), London: Nicholas Saunders.

Sherlock, K. (1997) *Psycho-social Determinants of Ecstasy Use*, Doctoral thesis, University of Central Lancashire.

Tossman, P. (1997) 'Drug affinity among youths in the techno-party scene', paper presented at the seminar 'Ecstasy, Characteristics of Consumption and Social Representations', Venice: Irefrea (unpublished).

Zuckerman, M. (1978) 'Sensation seeking in England and America: cross-cultural, age, and sex comparisons', *Journal of Consulting Psychology*, 46.

Zuckerman, M., Bone, R., Neary, R., Mangelsdorff, D. and Brustman, B. (1972) 'What is the sensation seeker? Personality trait and experience correlates of the sensation-seeking scales', *Journal of Consulting Psychology*, 39.

RISK BEHAVIOUR

PART IV

INTRODUCTION

*T*his section of the monograph on risk behaviour contains fewer chapters than the other parts due to the fact that the EMCDDA is planning a separate publication focusing exclusively on this theme. Various aspects of risk behaviour have also been addressed in many of the other chapters of the monograph.

Both chapters here emphasise the considerable contribution qualitative research has made to our knowledge and understanding of this aspect of drug-using behaviour.

Chapter 10 opens with a summary of the key points of a review undertaken by the EMCDDA's workgroup on injecting risk behaviour. This review looks at the contribution that qualitative research can make, in particular to understanding the risks associated with drug injecting, and focuses specifically on the example of needle and syringe sharing. The use of qualitative research on health risks associated with drug injecting varies widely between EU countries and major gaps exist, particularly with regard to overdose, hepatitis C, HIV, gender differences and user perspectives of treatment and harm-reduction services.

In Chapter 11, Robert Power presents a case study demonstrating how observational techniques can identify precise aspects of behaviour that have informed community-level response to risk behaviour. The same techniques help to evaluate outcomes of community-based interventions. He also refers to the need to improve ambiguous and poorly executed sampling strategies.

QUALITATIVE RESEARCH ON THE HEALTH RISKS ASSOCIATED WITH DRUG INJECTING: NEEDLE AND SYRINGE SHARING

Nuria Romo Aviles, Marina Barnard, Tim Rhodes, Fabienne Hariga, Urban Weber, Anne Coppel and Jane Fountain

Qualitative research techniques are now a commonly used and accepted means of social inquiry, particularly in the field of health behaviour. Although survey methods remain dominant, there is a recognition that qualitative research methods have the capacity both to inform survey designs and to complement survey findings. Importantly, and in their own right, they provide a means of interpreting behaviours which might otherwise seem inexplicable. This is particularly the case among 'hidden' or 'hard-to-reach' populations — such as injecting drug users (IDUs) — where there exist practical and methodological difficulties in the use of large-scale quantitative surveys and representative sampling designs.

While there is an established tradition of using qualitative methods in drugs research in some European countries (notably France, the Netherlands and the UK), there is increasing interest in using these techniques as a means of understanding and responding to public health problems associated with drug injecting in many European countries.

Here, we aim to summarise the contribution that qualitative research can make to understanding the risks associated with drug injecting, focusing specifically on the example of needle and syringe sharing. This work was undertaken as part of a larger review conducted by an EMCDDA workgroup on injecting risk behaviour, of which the authors were members. This review is available on http://www.qed.org.uk and an expanded version can be found in Rhodes et al. (forthcoming).

Qualitative research in the time of AIDS

Prior to the advent of HIV infection and AIDS, most qualitative research on drug injecting concentrated on understanding the social meanings and contexts of drug-using lifestyles. The emergence of HIV infection and AIDS brought about considerable changes in the use of qualitative methods in research on illicit drugs, as well as changes in the specific focus of applied qualitative research on injecting drug use. This shift can be traced to the mid-1980s, with the discovery that HIV was spreading 'epidemically' among populations of IDUs through the shared use of injecting equipment and unprotected sex. In Europe, this was found to be particularly the case in (West) Germany, Spain, France, Italy and in the UK (Edinburgh). From the mid-1980s onwards, the health risks associated with drug injecting were given greater policy priority, when HIV and AIDS were found to constitute a major public health issue.

This concern prompted European research activity oriented towards mapping the extent of HIV infection and HIV-related risk behaviour among IDUs. These studies indicated varying HIV prevalence among IDUs within and across Europe over time. 'Low' (under 5 %) and 'stabilised' prevalence were reported in Belgium, the former East Germany, Greece, Scotland (Glasgow), and Sweden (Lund and Stockholm) and in the UK (London) since 1994. Fluctuations in 'low' to 'medium' prevalence over time (5–20 %) were reported in the cities of Amsterdam, Berlin, Frankfurt, Hamburg, Dublin, Paris, and London prior to 1994. 'Medium' prevalence (20–40 %) was reported in Rome and Edinburgh, and 'high' prevalence (over 40 %) in Milan, Madrid, and in Edinburgh prior to about 1991.

These epidemiological studies provided an indication of the extent and frequency of HIV risk behaviour among IDUs, particularly concerning the continued use of shared injecting equipment and relatively high levels of unprotected sex. To a large extent, they also provided the backdrop for qualitative investigations of the social meanings and context of risk behaviour. If the determinants of risk behaviour were to be understood, it became apparent that the focus of research had to embrace the variety of individual, social and environmental factors that influenced IDUs' 'risk behaviours'. This clearly required more than the mapping of viral spread among populations designated 'at risk'; it also indicated the need to know how a number of behavioural and contextual factors interacted together to determine why and how injecting drug use and risk behaviours occurred. The emergence of HIV and AIDS thus brought about an increased receptivity to the use of qualitative methods in the field of illicit drug use.

Qualitative research on health and drug injecting in the European Union

The urgency to understand HIV risk behaviour among IDUs has led to an increased receptivity in the use of qualitative methods in many countries. To some extent, a tradition of qualitative research in the field of drug use has already existed in France, the Netherlands and the UK, and the workgroup's review found evidence of published qualitative studies on HIV risk behaviour associated with drug injecting in Belgium, Denmark, Germany, Spain and Ireland. However, it is important not to overstate the extent to which qualitative methods have been applied within the drugs field. We found evidence of an established interest in qualitative research on drug injecting in France, the Netherlands and the UK, evidence of increased interest since the mid-1980s in Denmark, Germany and Spain, and evidence of emerging interest since the early 1990s in Belgium, Ireland and Italy. However, we found little evidence of funded or published qualitative research on the risks associated with drug injecting in Greece, Luxembourg, Austria, Portugal, Finland or Sweden (see Figure 1).

Figure 1: Qualitative research on health and drug injecting in the EU

Member State	Established	Emerging	Scant evidence
Belgium		▓	
Denmark		▓	
Germany		▓	
Greece			▓
Spain		▓	
France	▓		
Ireland		▓	
Italy		▓	
Luxembourg			▓
Netherlands	▓		
Austria			▓
Portugal			▓
Finland			▓
Sweden			▓
United Kingdom	▓		

Thus, the public health imperative to reduce HIV infection associated with drug use has brought about renewed interest in the use of qualitative methods in the field of illicit drug use in some countries, and a recognition of their utility for the first time in others. It was recognition of a lack of knowledge about risk behaviours associated with drug injecting which initially spurred interest in undertaking small-scale qualitative projects to look specifically at needle sharing and sexual risk behaviours. Since then, qualitative projects have been instrumental in focusing the attention of researchers and interventionists on the degree to which risk behaviour is 'socially organised'. Rather than being understood from the perspective of cognitions alone, risk behaviours have been shown to be best understood as highly sensitive to the relationships drug injectors have with each other in the context of the social circumstances and environments in which they find themselves.

Case study: The sharing of injecting equipment

While the workgroup's full review (Rhodes et al., forthcoming) focuses on a variety of health risks and risk behaviours associated with drug injecting, here we focus briefly on the example of needle and syringe sharing.

The first task facing qualitative research on needle and syringe sharing was to describe the nature of sharing practices. While it had become evident by the mid-to-late 1980s that needle and syringe sharing was one of the most important risk factors in mediating HIV transmission among IDUs, little was known about sharing practices — apart from a hitherto relatively obscure piece of research undertaken in the early 1970s on needle sharing among IDUs in San Francisco, United States (see

Rhodes et al., forthcoming). By the late 1980s, it had become the task of observational and interview studies to discover the circumstances in which sharing took place, and the variety of factors influencing whether and how sharing occurred. Below we summarise some of the key points contained in our review.

Firstly, qualitative studies have proved useful in identifying and categorising sharing practices. Observational and interview studies have highlighted how the sharing of injecting equipment may mean different things to different people in different contexts. One of the most incisive examples of how ethnographic research has informed understandings of sharing is the discovery of 'front-loading', 'back-loading' and other 'indirect sharing' practices. These risk practices were initially identified on the basis of a series of 95 observations undertaken with approximately 192 IDUs in 14 different houses or squats by Jean-Paul Grund and colleagues in Rotterdam, where it was noted that approximately 80 % of observed sharing occasions involved front-loading. A fuller description of these risk practices is given in Rhodes et al. (forthcoming).

Secondly, qualitative studies have been instrumental in establishing a much keener appreciation of the relationship between risk and social context. Risk behaviour has been understood as being located firmly within particular settings and contexts. Rather than being envisaged as simply an act of individual volition or as a socially isolated event, qualitative studies have shown risk to be contextually determined and sustained. One example includes the investigation of needle and syringe sharing within the prison context. Studies have associated the institutional prohibition of drug injecting and injecting equipment with greatly increased risks of HIV transmission within EU prisons. Qualitative studies have explored drug injectors' attempts to minimise HIV risk in the prison context, as well as their relative acceptance of risk associated with the shared use of injecting equipment in this setting. Of key importance is that many qualitative studies have emphasised that a scarcity of needles and syringes is not, in itself, a sufficient explanation for the continued sharing of injecting equipment.

Thirdly, qualitative studies have found the reasons for direct and indirect sharing to be complex. To a large extent, individuals' decisions to share used equipment with others have been shown to be influenced by the nature of the situations and relationships in which sharing occurs, and by the perceived social norms and etiquette with regard to the reciprocal rights and obligations of friendship. Needle sharing has rarely been found to be a random activity, but instead tends to follow lines of kith and kin. Most sharing takes place between IDUs who are either in a sexual relationship with each other or who are friends or family. A common finding across studies has been that female injectors are more likely than men to share needles and syringes, often habitually, with their sexual partners. Local conditions of needle availability may influence the prevalence of such risk behaviour, but do not completely eliminate sharing, since the reasons for its continuance appear to be embedded in the social meanings of IDUs' interactions and relationships with their sharing partners. These findings highlight the fact that the act of sharing a needle or syringe communicates social meaning in the context of IDUs' relationships and friendships.

Fourthly, while much qualitative research points to sharing between IDUs as a positive response to the rights and obligations of friendship or sexual relationships, we are reminded by Michael Bloor that this should not blind us to the fact that some of the social relationships which pattern needle and also drug sharing, 'embrace fear and domination rather than intimacy and trust' (quoted in Rhodes et al., forthcoming).

This has led some researchers to consider power as an additional contextual variable in the negotiation of relationships and risk encounters. Patterns of sharing may also be expressive of the distribution of power and control in relationships, often running along the lines of gender. For example, in Dundee, Scotland, one study indicated a connection between domestic violence and HIV risk behaviour. It found that challenges or questions by female IDUs to their male partners about their risk behaviour could sometimes be perceived as a threat to the status quo of the relationship which could, and often did, result in violent reprisal. The distribution of power in relationships, and thus also of risk negotiation, can therefore be 'gendered'. Future research on risk reduction should consider 'power' and 'negotiation' as key categories of investigation. In addition, the social or interpersonal relationship would appear to be a useful unit of analysis for understanding risk behaviour as an outcome of 'negotiation' and 'social interaction'.

Fifthly, taking the above points together, it is clear that the difficulties IDUs have in achieving safer injecting can no longer be merely considered an outcome of the lack of availability of sterile injecting equipment, nor a lack of knowledge of the risks involved. They may relate more fundamentally to the dynamics of drug dependency and the complex set of social ties characterising an IDU's social relationships.

Qualitative studies indicate that the 'risk culture' of IDU subcultures is made up of a combination of social and structural factors. What Jean-Paul Grund describes as the 'almost universal subcultural code of sharing' has been found to exist for economic reasons (as with the availability and affordability of clean syringes), but it is also associated with the criminal and socially stigmatised nature of drug dependency. In the face of constant adversity and external pressure, IDUs are mutually dependent upon each other, both positively and negatively, for information and help in locating, financing and managing drug use. This 'dependency' has been noted in a number of ethnographic studies. While instrumental in some respects (to stave off drug withdrawals, to share costs), such sharing and reciprocity between drug users has been found to perform a wider set of social functions. So, for example, drug sharing might be used to mediate and resolve conflicts, to make and sustain alliances, and to compensate for previous violations between IDUs. The sharing of injecting equipment may also symbolise trust and reciprocity within IDU networks. The social character of sharing among drug users and its ascribed social value within IDU subcultures greatly add to the difficulties of reducing the health risks associated with this behaviour.

Conclusions

Since HIV infection is a behavioural disease, its transmission is subject to variations in the ways humans interact. This leads us to consider risk behaviour as a product of social interaction, and not merely of individuals' risk perceptions and risk calculus.

Understanding risk behaviour as socially situated — as a product of social interactions and relationships — emphasises that a variety of social and material factors influence why and how risk behaviours occur. Qualitative research has a key role to play in understanding — as well as responding to — the public health consequences of drug injecting. It aims to understand the social context of health behaviours and risk reduction as a means of developing public health policies and interventions in accord with IDUs' lived experiences of drug use and the social contexts in which risk occurs.

We have summarised some of the key points contained in the EMCDDA's workgroup review on the health risks associated with drug injecting. While we have concentrated here on the example of needle and syringe sharing, the review notes the contributions of qualitative research to understanding and responding to health risk more generally. Key examples include studies of sexual risk behaviour associated with substance use, and intervention-based studies of risk-reduction interventions.

This chapter has noted that the use of qualitative research to study the health risks associated with drug injecting varies widely between EU countries. In some countries, we could not find any evidence of qualitative studies on drug injecting (for example, Greece, Luxembourg, Austria, Portugal, Finland and Sweden), and yet, in others (notably France, the Netherlands and the UK, but also increasingly Belgium, Germany and Spain), there is evidence of a growing series of interlinked studies on the HIV risks associated with needle and syringe sharing, and to some extent on unprotected sex. It is thus difficult to generalise as to the precise focus of future EU qualitative studies. That said, it is evident that a number of topics of obvious public health relevance remain under-investigated, particularly with regard to the influence of social and contextual factors.

The workgroup concluded that the following research topics are of priority for future EU qualitative studies on the health risks associated with drug injecting:

- factors influencing the individual risk management of overdose and overdose prevention;
- risk perception, behaviour, help-seeking and treatment experience associated with hepatitis C transmission and infection;
- risk perception, behaviour, help-seeking and HIV-related treatment experience among HIV-positive IDUs;
- the influence of gender in risk behaviour and risk reduction associated with drug injecting;
- qualitative evaluation, including the IDU's experience of service use, of syringe exchange and distribution interventions; and
- qualitative evaluation, including the IDU's experience of service use, methadone and other substitution treatment interventions.

References

Rhodes, T., Barnard, M., Aviles, N. R., Hariga, F., Fountain, J. and Weber, U. (forthcoming) *Injecting Drug Use and Risk Behaviour: the Role of Qualitative Research*, Insights series, Lisbon: EMCDDA.

CHAPTER 11

QUALITATIVE RESEARCH AND COMMUNITY-LEVEL RESPONSES TO ILLICIT DRUG USE

Robert Power

Qualitative research methods are well suited to inform community-level responses to illicit drug use, especially in identifying patterns of behaviour, profiling difficult-to-access groups and targeting populations for tailored interventions. Qualitative research can provide answers to many of the questions practitioners want answered before shaping their interventions, such as: What are the patterns and trends of drug use? Who is using which drugs and how? What social networks of drug users exist and how do they relate to each other? Where do drug users congregate? What are their experiences and impressions of current service provision? Qualitative research methods also allow for the flexibility needed during fieldwork, when unforeseen questions and issues emerge. Often, nuances of behaviour are detected that might be missed by quantitative methods.

A key strength of qualitative research is its facility to study social phenomena in non-institutional settings. This is enhanced by the inductive approach commonly adopted by the qualitative researcher and the flexible and multiple research techniques available. An historical overview of qualitative drugs research might highlight the heyday of the Chicago school, particularly from the 1950s to the mid-1970s (Park, 1952). Such a review is also likely to identify the era of AIDS as a time when qualitative research enjoyed a resurgence.

In the first instance, the Chicago school emphasised the importance of context and utilising anthropological methods (such as participant observation). The AIDS epoch has highlighted the need to access the hidden population of drug users in order to understand better the nature and shades of risk behaviour. Both trends have had a major impact on the way in which qualitative research has been used in the drugs field, particularly in responding to HIV risk amongst drug injectors not in contact with services. One negative consequence has been an overemphasis on self-reports, to the detriment of direct or participant observation, and the lack of theoretical frameworks.

This chapter will illustrate the positive contribution of observational methods in informing community responses by presenting some contemporary research. In so doing, it also points to the enduring value of direct observation in qualitative studies. The illustration is a case study which investigated the social networks and lifestyles of drug users in England.

Case study: Social networks and lifestyles of injecting drug users

This qualitative study resulted from an initiative by the Department of Health of England and Wales concerning drug users who were not using established needle- and syringe-exchange programmes. Much quantitative and qualitative data had been collected on needle- and syringe-exchange clients (Paone et al., 1998), but little was known about the risk behaviours of those in the community. The main aim of this study was to describe the risk behaviours and responses of relevant networks of drug injectors (Power et al., 1995).

The study took place at three sites in England. The first phase entailed researchers contacting networks of drug users who were not in contact with syringe-exchange schemes. In good ethnographic tradition, much of this first phase of fieldwork was taken up with researchers spending time with the drug users at their homes, clubs and bars. The purpose was to get to know members of the target group and gain their trust. Methodologically, the objective was to identify potential key informants and snowball chains for interview. All the while, the researchers (as observers) were noting behaviour patterns emanating from conversations and observations, to guide the study.

By adopting an inductive analytical approach, based on the tenets of grounded theory (Glaser and Strauss, 1967), we used a range of qualitative methods, including semi-structured interviews with 100 drug users recruited through snow-balling. In addition, we conducted focus groups and a series of 24-hour recall in-depth interviews. Importantly, the three fieldworkers continued with participant observation throughout the duration of the study, compiling extensive field notes.

In line with grounded theory, we were able to describe both individual and group behaviours and created categories and sub-categories to assist the analysis. One early observation was the extent to which 'informal coping strategies' were used by these groups of drug users. Within this category, we developed a number of related sub-categories. One good example was the sub-category of 'reciprocity'. Although mainly a function of drug consumption patterns, it was clear within the group that reciprocal arrangements existed around providing clean needles and syringes. Friendship groups, especially in the smaller towns, operated to protect against high-risk behaviour. At the level of the individual, we noted a wide range of informal coping strategies, including secreting clean syringes around the home, leaving them with non-injecting friends, buying new syringes from the pharmacy when down to the last pack, and personalising individual syringes for reuse. On this last point, it was worrying to note the number of injectors who stated that they marked a cross on the syringe barrel to denote ownership. One simple health promotion response would be a campaign encouraging the use of initials as a unique identifier. On the other hand, observations and interviews noted high-risk injecting 'hotspots', such as when withdrawing from drugs, buying drugs in unfamiliar places, in prison, when intoxicated, or when injecting with a sex partner. It is worthy of note that these sub-categories of risk behaviour had not changed since the early days of HIV/AIDS (Power, 1988).

One of the main objectives of the study was to look at ways in which we could inform community-based services for drug injectors. In this context, the value of combining an inductive grounded theory framework with direct ethnographic observation became apparent. During the ongoing analysis of fieldwork, it became clear that the category of 'sharing injecting paraphernalia' was linked to the sub-categories of 'ritual' and 'social etiquette'.

It was during participant observation at the house of a dealer that one important aspect of 'social etiquette' was noted. Amongst this network, injectors who were permitted to inject in the dealer's house paid for the hospitality by leaving the used filter ('cotton') behind. These were kept by the dealer for use at a later date, as they contained a residue of heroin. These filters would previously have been shared by a number of injectors and constituted a risk of infection (especially hepatitis C) when reused. Through participant observation of this aspect of 'indirect sharing', we were able to describe hitherto undocumented behaviour which could subsequently inform, refine and tailor health promotion interventions. In the spirit of complementing qualitative data with quantitative data, we appended a question on this aspect of 'social etiquette' to a country-wide World Health Organisation study of 500 injecting drug users. This confirmed that the activity was not an isolated temporal or spatial observation, but was part of the broader drug culture (Power et al., 1994). This small example illustrates the value of participant observation. This nuance of behaviour had not previously been captured in either quantitative or qualitative studies and was able to contribute to our deeper understanding of the nature of drug-injecting risk.

Many other researchers have shown the vital importance of actual observation of drug users' behaviour to understanding their lifestyles and risk behaviours and thereby to enhancing community-based responses (Koester et al., 1990; Grund et al., 1991; Moore, 1993). Once the behaviour has been identified and practitioners begin to tailor a community-based intervention, what role is there for qualitative research?

Qualitative research and community-level intervention

The example presented above illustrates how qualitative research can identify precise aspects of behaviour that require community-based responses. In the case in point, our work was used to develop outreach health promotion around indirect sharing and to further the development of community-based peer education. It also formed the basis of two qualitative action research projects which focused on the role of peer interventions targeting community-based populations of drug users (Ward et al., 1997) and resulted in widely circulated and adopted guidelines of good practice.

More generally, qualitative research can be usefully employed at each of the stages of formative, process and outcome evaluation. In formative evaluations, rapid assessment studies have shown the key role of mapping exercises in helping to profile target populations and in identifying key issues for intervention. For example, this author has used qualitative research to describe varying patterns of drug use and injecting behaviours amongst community samples in such diverse settings as Vietnam (Power, 1998) and the Czech Republic (Tyrlic et al., 1998). Qualitative methods, especially ethnography, provide rare data for formative evaluations to help target community-based interventions.

Once the intervention is in place, qualitative research can contribute to process evaluation. Indeed, qualitative research is most often conducted during the process evaluation phase of delivering an intervention, when recruitment, training, supervision and service delivery are monitored. This is 'safe' territory for qualitative researchers, who can use the wide range of techniques available to them, such as satisfaction questionnaires, focus groups, surveys and semi-structured interviews. Again, the importance of using direct observation of service delivery to complement other available methods should be stressed.

Most qualitative researchers in the drugs field shy away from outcome evaluation. Many see the epidemiological markers and other outcome measures as the preserve of the quantitative researcher. Yet many of these outcome measures (such as a reduction in HIV infection amongst drug users) can be usefully complemented by qualitative data. Returning to our case study, we might wish to revisit our network and interview drug-injecting members about the subjective impact of any health promotion activity upon their specific behaviour of indirect sharing. We can also conduct participant observation to verify such changes. At this stage of evaluation, confirmatory focus groups can be used to gauge the extent to which the results of an outcome evaluation concur with the experiences and lifestyles of the target group. In addition, we must begin to look at the ways in which qualitative research can inform more experimental research designs, such as community-matched trials of interventions. For too long, researchers in the drugs field have resisted such evaluations, yet, where such research has been undertaken, the results have been useful in assessing the efficacy of competing interventions. Qualitative research methods can usefully complement quantitative approaches in collecting relevant data from community-derived samples.

Our case study also highlights a number of other issues regarding the future development of qualitative research. First and foremost, we need to keep ethnography alive. As alluded to above, there has been a tendency for non-observational techniques (in-depth interviews, recall, focus groups, self-reports) to gain ascendancy in qualitative research. This has been to the detriment of ethnographic approaches such as participant observation and other anthropological techniques. This becomes especially problematic when so-called 'indigenous fieldworkers' or 'privileged access interviewers' are employed (Wiebel, 1988; Griffiths et al., 1993; Power and Harkinson, 1993; Power, 1994; see also Chapter 36 in this monograph). In these cases, over-reliance on self-reports and recall, coupled with the casually employed interviewer, means there are often three, four or five stages between the event and the final analysis and writing-up of the social phenomenon itself.

Let us take an example that is all too real in the world of social research into illicit drug use. Firstly, social action takes place (such as informal supply of clean injecting equipment in the house of a drug-using friend). Secondly, the drug user is asked to recall the event (often some time after it took place) by an indigenous fieldworker (through an interview based on self-report). Thirdly, these data are interpreted and coded (often by a research assistant). Fourthly, they are analysed by another (often more experienced) researcher. Fifthly, the research report is written (often by the research team led by the grant holder or manager). This is not to deny the place and validity of self-reports but rather to promote ethnography as an integral and complementary facet of community-level research.

In a similar vein, in the quest for greater validity, reliability and rigour in qualitative research, we must be more critical of our sampling strategies. Community-level qualitative research in the drugs field is particularly weak in this area, with a tendency to refer to ambiguous and often poorly executed strategies, such as snowball or 'convenience' sampling. As early as the 1980s, Biernacki and Waldorf (1981) and Watters and Biernacki (1989) and others pointed to the need for more rigour in snowball sampling, and Cohen (1990) showed the potential for a more structured approach through 'random nomination selection' (see also Chapter 32 in this monograph). Others, such as Spreen (1992) and Carlson et al. (1994), have addressed this issue, looking to alternative solutions to sampling dilemmas in assessing hidden populations, such as link-tracing designs. Such fine-tuning of sampling techniques will be especially important if qualitative research is to be taken seriously in outcome evaluation of community-level response to drug prevention.

Conclusions

In summary, qualitative research has much to offer, and has offered much, to community-level responses to drug use. It needs to resist a new orthodoxy (where the self-report and focus group predominate) and reinstate ethnography and participant observation as significant research tools. With a comprehensive and flexible use of all available techniques, qualitative research is well placed to contribute to all facets of social behavioural research into illicit drug use.

The author is Senior Lecturer at the Department of Sexually Transmitted Diseases, Royal Free and University College Medical School, London, UK.

References

Biernacki, P. and Waldorf, D. (1981) 'Snowball sampling: problem and techniques of chain referral sampling', *Sociological Methods and Research,* 10, 141–163.

Carlson, R., Wang, J., Siegal, H., Falk, R. and Guo, J. (1994) 'An ethnographic approach to target sampling: problems and solutions in AIDS prevention research among injection drug and crack cocaine users', *Human Organisation,* 53, 279–286.

Cohen, P. (1990) *Drugs as a Social Construct,* Amsterdam: University of Amsterdam.

Glaser, B. and Strauss, A. (1967) *The Discovery of Grounded Theory: Strategies for Qualitative Research,* Chicago: Aldine.

Griffiths, P., Gossop, M., Powis, B. and Strang, J. (1993) 'Reaching hidden populations of drug users by privileged access interviewers: methodological and practical issues', *Addiction*, 88, 1617–1626.

Grund, J-P., Kaplan, C., Adriaans, N. and Blanken, P. (1991) 'Drug sharing and HIV transmission risks: the practice of frontloading in the Dutch injection drug users population', *Journal of Psychoactive Drugs*, 23, 1–10.

Koester, S., Booth, R. and Wiebel, W. (1990) 'The risk of HIV transmission from sharing water, drug mixing containers and cotton filters among intravenous drug users', *International Journal of Drug Policy*, 1(6), 28–30.

Moore, D. (1993) 'Penetrating social worlds: conducting ethnographic research into alcohol and other drug use within Australia', *Drug and Alcohol Review*, 11, 313–323.

Paone, D., Des Jarlais, D. and Shi, Q. (1998) 'Syringe exchange and HIV risk reduction over time', *AIDS*, 12, 121–123.

Park, R. (1952) *Human Communities*, Glenco: Free Press.

Power, R. (1988) 'The influence of AIDS upon patterns of intravenous use: syringe and needle sharing among illicit drug users in Britain', in R. Battjes and R. Pickens (Eds.) *Needle Sharing Among Intravenous Drug Abusers: National and International Perspectives*, Research Monograph Series 80, Washington: National Institute on Drug Abuse, pp. 75–88.

Power, R. (1994) 'Some methodological and practical implications of employing drug users as indigenous fieldworkers', in M. Boulton (Ed.) *Challenge and Innovation: Methodological Advances in Social Research on HIV/AIDS*, London: Taylor & Francis, pp. 97–111.

Power, R. (1998) 'Rapid assessment of the drug-injecting situation at Hanoi and Ho Chi Minh City, Vietnam', *Bulletin on Narcotics*, 48, 35–53.

Power, R. and Harkinson, S. (1993) 'Accessing hidden populations: a survey of indigenous interviewers', in P. Davies, G. Hart and P. Aggleton (Eds.) *Social Aspects of AIDS*, Falmer: Falmer Press.

Power, R., Hunter, G., Jones, S. and Donoghoe, M. (1994) 'The sharing of injecting paraphernalia among illicit drug users', *AIDS*, 8, 1509–1511.

Power, R., Jones, S. and Kearns, G. (1995) 'Drug user networks, coping strategies and HIV prevention in the community', *Journal of Drug Issues*, 25, 565–583.

Spreen, M. (1992) 'Rare populations, hidden populations and link-tracing designs: what and why?', *Bulletin Methodologie Sociologique*, 36, 34–58.

Tyrlic, P., Zuda, T., Bem, P. and Power, R. (1998) 'The drug-use situation in the Czech Republic', *Bulletin on Narcotics*, 48, 89–99.

Ward, J., Hunter, G. and Power, R. (1997) 'Peer education as a means of drug prevention and education among young people: an evaluation', *Health Education Journal*, 56, 251–263.

Watters, J. and Biernacki, P. (1989) 'Targeted sampling: options for the study of hidden populations', *Social Problems 1989*, 36(4), 151–166.

Wiebel, W. (1988) 'Combining ethnographic and epidemiological methods in targeted AIDS interventions: the Chicago model', in R. Battjes and R. Pickens (Eds.) *Needle Sharing Among Intravenous Drug Abusers: National and International Perspectives*, Research Monograph Series 80, Washington: National Institute on Drug Abuse, pp. 137–151.

SOCIAL EXCLUSION

PART V

INTRODUCTION

*I*n Chapter 12, Susanne MacGregor provides an overview of social exclusion by examining its different meanings and its relationship to poverty. In particular, MacGregor examines how recent research has addressed social exclusion and underlines that the concept of 'mainstream' needs to be questioned since it underestimates the degree of differentiation in 'mainstream' society. She argues that, if the concept of social exclusion is to add anything to the concept of poverty, it has to use qualitative research in order to understand the exclusion processes.

In Chapter 13, Kamlesh Patel reports on a number of qualitative and action research projects which contradict drug prevalence studies by clearly indicating the existence and increasing level of drug use among ethnic minority communities. He attributes the success of action research in this area to investment in time, adoption of a clear strategic focus and staff support and commitment.

Aileen O'Gorman describes, in Chapter 14, a study using multiple data sources to explore the relationship between heroin use and social exclusion in Dublin. This study focused on the dynamic of social process and structural forces and attempted to locate the perspectives and experiences of the heroin users within the context of the social and economic structures in which they live and operate. The findings have policy implications in that they add empirical support to existing calls for drug policy to be more cognisant of the environmental context of drug misuse.

In Chapter 15, Luís Fernandes describes how the findings of ethnographic drug research in an urban-industrial Portuguese context 'forced' an analysis of the relationship between drugs and social exclusion. He describes the methods and findings of his personal fieldwork in zones often represented by their own inhabitants as territories 'under siege'. Fernandes' fieldwork experience leads to reflections regarding how the 'world of drugs' is largely perceived as alien and threatening. He warns against ethnographic methods being used instrumentally to serve control strategies that perpetuate a distorted view of drug users who are, in fact, located within the normal, local and social dynamic.

Bengt Svensson describes, in Chapter 16, a study based on observations, conversations and in-depth interviews, all of which demonstrate that drug use has certain advantages over and beyond what ordinary life offers.

Chapter 17, by Julian Buchanan and Lee Young, is based on a two-year evaluation of a day programme which aimed to reintegrate long-term problem drug users into the wider community. In-depth interviews with 58 participants provide examples of, and commentaries on, drug use and the processes of stigmatisation, marginalisation and social exclusion, which lead to chronically relapsing drug use.

CHAPTER 12

SOCIAL EXCLUSION: AN OVERVIEW

Susanne MacGregor

The concept of social exclusion brings together a number of the themes running through this monograph. In contemporary social science, social exclusion is commonly understood to mean 'the exclusion of individuals and groups from the mainstream activities of that society' (Glennerster et al., 1999, p. 7). The explanation for exclusion is thought to lie in a concentration of risks in individuals, groups and communities. This understanding of social problems in terms of risk reflects the way in which the ideas of the 'new public health' (Peterson and Lupton, 1996) increasingly influence a wide range of social policies.

The complexity indicated by awareness of the multiplicity of risks means that research also has to recognise complexity. One of the main ways in which such complexity can be grasped is through greater use of qualitative research methods. Such methods include consideration of perceptions and meanings and may involve an eclectic use of methods and concepts drawn from a range of disciplines. Similarly, policy interventions need to recognise the way in which problems are linked together. Multiple problems or risks occurring together are better treated holistically, rather than attempting to separate them out and treat each one individually.

If social exclusion is understood as a concentration of risks, then some scrutiny of the concept of risk is required. Epidemiological studies focus on risk at the macrolevel. Sociological and anthropological studies look more at risk management at the group or individual level. They draw attention to the questions of choice and opportunity. It is not a simple matter to avoid risk or to change behaviour. Risk behaviours are socially embedded: behaviours are mediated by social relations, social context, understandings and obligations. Particular risky behaviours can be rational in context. We need to understand these to make interventions and policies meaningful and effective. At the community level, to change established patterns of activity, the cooperation of those communities is needed. Community involvement is critical for the success of interventions, but it is equally as important to change the perceptions of those — the mainstream — who define poor communities as marginal.

When applying qualitative methods and implementing innovative policy, one practical way to deal with the problem of complexity is to focus on a defined geographical area. Qualitative research is often area-based, partly because conventional sampling techniques are not appropriate for such methodologies. This is also justified because it is increasingly found that social exclusion is mirrored by spatial concentration of risk or problems. Thus, the locality or the community becomes the focus of research and policy. This also allows for the recognition of local variation and difference. The argument is that both research and policy have to be responsive to specific local conditions. Critics of these approaches argue, however, that in so doing there is a danger of neglecting important structural processes that lie behind disadvantage and risk. This criticism can be countered by noting that it falls into the trap of the 'either/or' fallacy that has long bedevilled debates around universalism or selectivism in social policy. Within a context of broad universalist policies addressing structural issues, there is a place for specialist targeted policies focusing on detail and difference.

Different meanings of social exclusion

Social exclusion is currently a fashionable concept, heard as much in political and public discussion as in social scientific argument. Why has this concept come so much to the fore and what is new about it? Is it a case of old wine in new bottles or the relabelling of the old problem of poverty? There are various understandings of the concept of social exclusion in current discourse. It can refer to a lack of paid work, or to a concentration of linked problems in distinct areas or neighbourhoods. At times, it can refer to being outside the social insurance system and, at others, it carries within it assumptions about the existence of an 'underclass' (Smith, 1992).

In looking at these different uses of the term, it is worth reminding ourselves that the way in which we define a problem carries implications about causes and explanations and thus also about the appropriateness of different policy solutions. One strength of recent definitions of social exclusion is that they contain a rediscovery of the social: that is, an awareness that individual traits, strengths and weaknesses are not the only explanation for behaviour, and that policy has to focus as much on social relations as on the individual. Related to this are references to the need for greater coordination of policy responses so that they work together, rather than against each other. Policies need to work together to have greater effect and policies may sometimes be as much the cause as the solution of problems.

Looking at the groups upon which the UK Government's Social Exclusion Unit focuses its attention tells us something about implicit explanations of social exclusion in British public policy today.

The priority groups for the unit are the five million people in workless households, the three million on the 1 300 worst council estates, the 150 000 homeless families and the 100 000 children not attending school. Thus, being outside work, being in particularly deprived neighbourhoods, being without a home or outside school are thought to be the main mechanisms which explain social exclusion. People in these situations are outside mainstream society. Policies therefore aim to target the poorest of the poor.

Social exclusion and poverty

Why then, some may ask, do we talk about social exclusion rather than about poverty and the poor? Is there a difference? What is the relation between poverty and social exclusion? Social scientific studies over many years have pointed out that poverty leads to social exclusion. Indeed the definition of poverty as relative deprivation proposed by Townsend (1979) is very relevant here. (It could be argued that his promotion of this understanding has fed directly into European discussions. The concept of social exclusion has grown out of the discourse of the European Commission and was especially encouraged by France during its Presidency of the EU in 1989, which coincided with the 200th anniversary of the French Revolution (1789). These discussions helped to emphasise French notions of citizenship and inclusion within debate on European social policy.)

Townsend's classic definition of poverty reads thus:

> *Individuals, families and groups in the population can be said to be in poverty when they lack the resources to obtain the types of diet, participate in the activities and have the living conditions and amenities which are customary, or at least widely encouraged or approved, in the societies to which they belong. Their resources are so seriously below those commanded by the average individual or family that they are in effect excluded from ordinary living patterns, customs and activities.*
> (Townsend, 1979, p. 31)

A central idea is contained in this quotation — that poverty leads to social exclusion because it leads to an inability to fully participate. The idea of relative deprivation as inability to participate in mainstream or today's society is also there. This recognises that social expectations and demands change over time, from expectations about ways of dressing and cleanliness, for example, to demands for access to a telephone or transportation, or the need for certain educational qualifications in order to obtain paid work. Of course, inability to participate may be the result of processes other than poverty, such as discrimination against people with disabilities, refugees, people of other languages, colour or religion, or people with certain health statuses or criminal records.

Other, older definitions of poverty worth noting are those which paid attention to multiple deprivation and accumulations of disadvantages in some groups and neighbourhoods (Coates and Silburn, 1973). Studies like these pointed to a concentration of problems and disadvantages in certain deprived areas and highlighted the fact that these neighbourhoods were forgotten in the general celebration of the 'never had it so good' society. Poor housing, poor schools, poor transport, and lack of jobs were all linked. Another interesting finding is that such areas also tend to get poor reputations and sometimes these have a very long history, going back centuries in some cases (White, 1986). These stigmas may also have a material base, where facts of geography mean that certain areas have always been less popular because they are environmentally hazardous or cut off and inaccessible.

While these old definitions remind us of continuities in the facts of poverty and in understandings and explanations for it, there are some differences in the current situation to which the term social exclusion is trying to draw attention. What then is new about poverty and inequality today? There is some evidence that the causes of poverty and social exclusion and the manifestation of these problems have changed shape. Factors long associated with poverty and social exclusion do continue to play a part. Cohort studies show the lifelong influences of childhood poverty. Living in a poor neighbourhood, having poor educational experience and achievement, and family disruption have all been shown to be associated with later disadvantage. Added to these are influences such as contact with the police and, working either positively or negatively, parental interest and attitudes.

These influences show up as outcomes or problems in later life, with higher concentrations of certain experiences among those having experienced a disadvantaged childhood. They include young parenthood, extramarital births, having multiple partners and indicators of adult malaise (mental illness, drug or alcohol use, for example). Other associated outcomes include being unemployed, lacking educational qualifications, being in receipt of welfare benefits, on low income and living in social housing. Recent statistics comparing post-war trends have shown that crime, drug taking and road accidents among young people have replaced the threat of early death from infectious diseases as key characteristics in their lives. Added to this are high rates of unemployment among young people living in certain regions and areas.

Some new processes which have exacerbated basic structural divisions of class, race and gender include the arrival of the information society with its demand for a different range and type of skills and abilities. There is now a much greater divide between those with relevant skills and educational qualifications and those without. The now-recognised increase in social inequality reflects a greater divide between work-rich and work-poor households, especially between the dual-wage household and the household where no one earns an income from regular work. Other influential processes impacting on the construction of poverty, inequality and social exclusion include the growth of single adult parenting, largely a reflection of increased divorce rates and the failing attractions of the marriage contract. Also associated with these trends are increased migration, leading to concentrations of refugees, asylum-seekers and economic migrants in certain areas, and a general loss of community and family supports consequent on social and geographical mobility and changed lifestyles.

In the more advanced technological society and economy, other forms of communication — telephone, Internet, transport — have grown in importance, so that exclusion from communication systems can be another reason for being cut off from mainstream activities. For example, this might happen to those who have no car or driving licence and live in an area with poor public transport, or it could result from having no telephone, no TV licence, or no access to a computer.

Another process recognised as leading to exclusion — financial exclusion — comes from living in an increasingly credit-based economy. People may suffer from financial exclusion if they are not deemed creditworthy. They are then at the mercy of loan sharks and other financial predators (Kempson and Whyley, 1999). This links into another feature of contemporary society: the increased importance of material consumption, where individuals feel they should own certain things in order for them to 'belong' — or to be accepted by others as belonging — from the 'right' sport shoes in the school yard to the 'right' kind of car or house.

Other processes within mainstream society that lead to new forms of social exclusion include the fact that society is increasingly based on competition. The use of league tables and performance measures to judge individuals, schools and other groups has increased the gap between those who are judged to be successes and those who are failures. The gap between the mainstream and the excluded has widened. Here lies the contradiction: a society cannot be based on competition, enterprise and merit and not have some members who fail. The fact of social exclusion reflects core values and processes within mainstream society itself.

Thus, social exclusion results from being judged as: not good enough; surplus to requirements; redundant; unwanted; too old; too ugly; too badly behaved; too disruptive; too odd; too different; or not having the right clothes, the right accent, or the right address.

Responses to social exclusion

Attention to social exclusion in recent research has focused not only on the processes leading to exclusion, but also on how individuals and communities respond to these labels (Cattell and Evans, 1999). What coping mechanisms can be observed? What strategies for survival are developed? Attention is paid not only to the vulnerabilities that concentrate in these individuals and areas, but also to features of resilience. This perception argues that more effective policy interventions will be those which build upon existing patterns of resilience, hazard management and harm minimisation. These are more likely to be accepted and therefore more likely to succeed.

Explanations of resilience draw attention to the key role of social networks operating in civil society in mediating between the pressures that bear down on individuals and communities (risk factors) and their responses and the consequent outcomes or effects. Social networks are the 'bounce factor' in community responses — a protective layer that can absorb shocks and divert pressures. They reflect an accumulation of social capital (which can often have a material base or support in the form of meeting places, symbolic spaces, etc.) built up from webs of mutual obligation and exchanges over the years. Different types of excluded group or community can be distinguished. They all share the fact of being separated out, disadvantaged, perceived as different and often stigmatised. But some give way under this pressure while others fight back. There are resilient individuals, communities or groups and there are those which are fragmented and broken.

Fragmented individuals, groups or communities are those where the webs of social ties have been undermined. This undermining may be the result of wider processes and policies, such as the collapse of employment opportunities, wars and migration, housing allocation policies, slum clearance, and residualisation of housing estates. They may also result from crime and drugs (Wilson and Kelling, 1982). Crime and drugs can offend social norms of mutual obligation. A key feature of extreme drug use is the corruption of relationships, where people may steal from their closest friends, neighbours and relatives or behave selfishly or violently. Even though mutual sharing can be observed in some groups (McKeganey and Barnard, 1992), there is other evidence that, after a time, chronic drug use undermines social ties (Dunlap, 1995).

Sociologists have analysed these processes. Merton provided the classic account (Merton, 1938). One response is to reject the society that is doing the excluding: 'I don't want to join a club that does not want me'. Or the response may be one of anger. This anger can be turned outwards in the form of disruption, crime, riot or interpersonal violence. Or it may turn inwards in the form of self-destructive behaviour — suicide, self-harm, excessive drug taking, alcoholism, compulsive behaviour. Another reaction is one of retreat: withdrawal; sitting indoors; watching TV; displaying apathy; cutting off from the wider world.

These issues are particularly relevant in understanding and responding to drug use. The relation between social processes and emotional and personal development is worthy of much closer study. The choice between structural or psychological explanations is a false one. It is not an either/or choice. In debates about social exclusion and patterns of harmful behaviour such as drug use, it is not good enough simply to replace the 1980s/1990s concentration on individual behaviour as the explanation of failure with an equally simplistic stress on structural forces. We need to pay more attention to the way in which structural processes of change, including exclusion, damage emotional and personal development (Rutter and Smith, 1995). Such complex processes cannot be altered overnight; they require long-term and complex interventions.

Thus, the concept 'social exclusion', if it is to add anything to the concept of poverty, has to refer to the *processes* of exclusion which are present in the whole society. To address social exclusion, policies and interventions have to pay attention to these wider processes, especially in work, family and education, and include remedial health and social supports. In this, we need to look at the way in which mainstream institutions and policies play a part in creating social exclusion. Issues of institutional design and the spending patterns of government departments all play a part. Key policy areas include economic, employment and fiscal policy, housing policy, the operation of the criminal justice system and education policy.

Conclusions

The key elements of the concept of social exclusion are that it is a complex and a multidimensional process for which there are therefore no 'quick fix' solutions. We need to recognise that, to improve the situation, we who are doing the excluding need to change, as much as — if not more than — those on the receiving end of these actions.

The concept of participation is the key one, within the wider concept of exclusion. Being excluded from participation in mainstream activities is the essential feature. At the root, therefore, is the issue of power and the ability to take part in decision-making, especially on those matters that affect one's own daily life and opportunities. Exclusion from processes of governance is very clear in most deprived neighbourhoods. The stress on community involvement in current policies stems from this awareness.

The concept of the mainstream also needs to be questioned — the assumption is that there is, on the one hand, a deviant, stigmatised and disadvantaged group and, on the other, mainstream or normal society to which the former are not allowed to belong. This perception underestimates the degree of differentiation or division in 'mainstream' society. However, these processes of differentiation and division, where they concentrate on certain individuals, groups and communities, lead to a situation, as Townsend indicated, where the gap becomes too great to bridge — access to participation becomes impossible. Added elements of difference enter into and exacerbate the situation.

Perhaps the key feature contained in the idea of the mainstream is that these sections of society do not overtly challenge the system. They appear to have signed up to the core values and ways of doing things. They are moving in roughly the same direction and are not seen to be, as the excluded are, a burden on the overall dynamism and direction of the society.

The author is Professor of Social Policy at Middlesex University, London, UK.

References

Cattell, V. and Evans, M. (1999) *Neighbourhood Images in East London,* York: JRF.

Coates, K. and Silburn, R. (1973) *Poverty: the Forgotten Englishmen,* London: Pelican.

Dunlap, E. (1995) 'Inner-city crisis and drug dealing: portrait of a New York drug dealer and his household', in S. MacGregor and A. Lipow (Eds.) *The Other City: People and Politics in New York and London,* New York: Humanity Books, pp. 114–131.

Glennerster, H., Lupton, R., Noden, P. and Power, A. (1999) *Poverty, Social Exclusion and Neighbourhood: Studying the Area Bases of Social Exclusion,* CASE paper 22, London: London School of Economics.

Kempson, E. and Whyley, C. (1999) *Kept Out or Opted Out? Understanding and Combating Financial Exclusion,* West Sussex: Policy Press.

McKeganey, N. and Barnard, M. (1992) *AIDS, Drugs and Sexual Risk,* Buckingham: Open University Press.

Merton, R. K. (1938) 'Social structure and anomie', *American Sociological Review,* 3(5), 672–682.

Peterson, A. and Lupton, D. (1996) *The New Public Health: Health and Self in the Age of Risk,* London: Sage.

Rutter, M. and Smith, D. J. (Eds.) (1995) *Psychosocial Disorders in Young People: Time Trends and their Causes,* Chichester: Wiley.

Smith, D. J. (Ed.) (1992) *Understanding the Underclass,* London: Policy Studies Institute.

Townsend, P. (1979) *Poverty in the United Kingdom,* Harmondsworth: Penguin.

White, J. (1986) *The Worst Street in North London,* London: Routledge and Kegan Paul.

Wilson, J. E. and Kelling, G. (1982) 'Broken windows', *Atlantic Monthly,* March 1982, 249(3), 29–38.

USING QUALITATIVE RESEARCH TO EXAMINE THE NATURE OF DRUG USE AMONG MINORITY ETHNIC COMMUNITIES IN THE UK

Kamlesh Patel

Below are sample statements that have been collected from a range of Asian community and religious 'leaders' and workers in statutory and non-governmental organisations (NGOs) in the drugs field throughout Britain during the past 10 years (Patel, 1993; Patel et al., 1995).

> *'If there are any Asian drug users, they don't use these (drug) services.'*
> *'Asian people don't use drugs.'*
> *'The few that do use will never inject.'*
> *'Religion prohibits drug taking — therefore it is not a problem.'*
> *'It is a white western disease.'*
> *'Our strong religious and cultural values stop us from this behaviour.'*

These statements clearly highlight the dilemma facing agencies, researchers and drug workers in the UK, operating as a series of myths that have acted as barriers to the development and delivery of drug services for Asian minority ethnic groups.

The majority of the drug prevalence surveys (Leitner et al., 1993; Khan et al., 1995; Mott and Mirrlees-Black, 1995; Parker et al., 1995) suggest that South Asians (Asians) are less likely to use illicit drugs than their white counterparts. Although there are both regional and methodological differences between these various studies, which means they are not directly comparable, the uniform trend is nevertheless impressive: Asians have been significantly under-represented among known populations of problem drug users. In contrast, the over-representation of certain minority ethnic groups within the criminal justice and psychiatric settings (in many cases related to drugs) is well documented (McGovern and Cope, 1987; Green, 1991; Hood, 1992; Maden et al., 1992; Clarke et al., 1993; Keith, 1993; Patel, 1993; Burney and Pearson, 1995; Raleigh, 1995; Pearson and Patel, 1998).

There are a number of qualitative and action research projects which clearly indicate the existence and increasing level of drug use among Asian communities (Patel, 1988; Awiah et al., 1992; Gilman, 1993; Shahnaz, 1993; Patel et al., 1995; 1999; Bridge Project, 1996; Patel et al., 1996; Bola and Walpole, 1997; Sherlock et al., 1997). Their findings, which contradict those from the prevalence studies cited above, could be attributed to a number of factors: for example, members of the

Asian community may be suspicious and concerned about drug-related studies; all-white research teams may not have the trust and credibility of the community; and the Asian community may lack understanding of the nature and purpose of the research studies. Such factors result in poor access and poor participation. Within such a climate, it is difficult to examine the nature and extent of drug use amongst these communities, let alone begin to identify how to develop appropriate and culturally sensitive services.

In Britain, there has been clear evidence since the early 1980s that a concentration of the most serious drug-related problems occurs in areas of high unemployment and social deprivation (Haw, 1985; Pearson et al., 1985; Peck and Plant, 1986; Pearson, 1987a; 1987b), where many minority ethnic groups live. Much has been written about the high levels of poverty, deprivation, educational disadvantage and discrimination in the labour force among Britain's minority ethnic communities. The most recent study by the Policy Studies Institute (Jones, 1996) highlights the serious levels of poverty and low economic activity especially among the Pakistani and Bangladeshi communities in Britain.

This chapter draws on examples from several action research projects (Patel, 1988; Patel et al., 1995; 1999; Sherlock et al., 1997) which examined the nature, perceptions and experiences of drug use among Britain's Asian communities, particularly the Pakistani Muslim community. It begins by providing an understanding of the many complex issues in relation to Asian communities, thus setting the context within which research can take place and service responses can be developed. It goes on to explore briefly the key factors which need to be taken into consideration when conducting research among these communities.

The South Asian community in Britain: setting the context

Just over 3 million (5.6 %) of the 55 million people in Britain are from minority ethnic groups. Half the minority ethnic population is Asian (that is, Indian, Pakistani and Bangladeshi), and 30 % are black. The vast majority of Britain's minority ethnic groups (97 %) live in England, mostly in large urban centres. The research studies that will be examined here concentrate mainly on the Pakistani and Bangladeshi communities in the north of England, although information from other parts of England is also alluded to.

Two important factors need further mention in relation to the demographic figures. Firstly, most Asian populations are concentrated in some of the most deprived inner-city areas in England and in these areas they are frequently the majority, not the minority, population. Secondly, many of the Asian community, particularly the Pakistani and Bangladeshi communities, are young (0–15 years). In some areas, it is estimated that the Asian population will double by the year 2011 (Bradford Commission, 1995; Commission for Racial Equality, 1995). This potentially creates an environment where the use of drugs by young people is a reality.

The nature and extent of drug use within any community are difficult to assess accurately, and this becomes even more difficult when examining a minority community. As already stated, the majority of research has failed to recognise drug use among Asians as an issue and members of the community have themselves denied the existence of the problem. In addition, service providers appear to have undertaken only limited consultation with the wider community. Outlined below are the essential factors of which researchers should be aware when conducting research within Asian communities. It is crucial, before beginning any research activity within these communities, that these demographic, religious and cultural features are understood and taken into consideration. Though specific to these communities in Britain, many of the broad principles will apply to work with a range of minority ethnic groups across Europe.

Diversity: the need for cultural and religious sensitivity in research design

Britain's Asian communities are very diverse and not only differ from the host indigenous community, but also from each other. It is important to note, moreover, that the term 'Asian' has many internal complexities and must be examined carefully. What it means to be 'Asian' encompasses a complex mosaic of different language groups, cultures, religious faiths and geographical regions of origin. In addition, Britain's Asian communities now stretch across four generations, with potentially large gulfs of experience and expectation dividing the first Asian settlers from their grandchildren and great-grandchildren.

As discussed earlier, the Asian community itself has posed barriers to service development by denying the problems associated with the use of drugs among its communities. This reaction needs to be understood in the context that, for many Asians, it is a way of protecting their community from yet again being pathologised as deviants or 'drug pushers'. Holding on to cultural values and a strong religious identity is, for the majority of Asians in Britain, a key day-to-day concern. Therefore, many believe that the reinforcement of these religious and cultural values inherent in their community will stop the use of mind-altering substances. It is essential that these issues be taken into account when designing any research strategy. For instance, we have made the mistake of conducting research that has coincided with religious festivals, when very few people have been willing to engage in discussions about sensitive/taboo areas, thus wasting many weeks of valuable fieldwork activity. It should be noted that many young Asian people are aware that their religion forbids the use of drugs, although a significant number are not sure of the reasons (Patel et al., 1996).

The need for researchers to understand that young Asian people use drugs too

As detailed earlier, research has shown that young Asian people do use drugs, and that use is increasing, as it is in the indigenous population. One worrying trend is the growing number of young people who have developed some form of drug dependency as a direct result of involvement in drug dealing — many tending to use heroin as their first drug of choice. Researchers should be aware that they will encounter official bodies and professionals who will simply deny that Asian young people are as much at risk as the 'white' population; researchers must be prepared to challenge those who dogmatically repeat these assumptions.

The need for researchers to recognise particular patterns of Asian drug use

Heroin and cannabis have been found to be the drugs most commonly used by young Asians, particularly Pakistani and Bangladeshi males. Asian women do not feature in any significant numbers in relation to drug use. However, a couple of small studies clearly highlight trends which suggest that this may be changing (Shahnaz, 1993; Bridge Project, 1996).

That many young Asians do not frequent nightclubs has been offered as a reason by some researchers for their low use of drugs such as ecstasy (Greater Manchester Bangladesh Association, 1995). However, this appears to be changing, particularly among Indian groups and those who attend organised Bhangra events, where the heavy use of alcohol and stimulant drugs has featured (Patel et al., 1995). The use of a range of solvents and increasing use of crack cocaine have been evident among some community groups (the latter particularly amongst heavy heroin users).

The drug trafficking routes from South Asian countries — of cannabis and particularly heroin — are another potential factor which cannot be ignored when examining the nature and extent of these drugs in these communities (Pearson and Patel, 1998). Researchers should have relevant knowledge about these substances before entering the field: for example, understanding patterns of drug use, the terms used for these drugs in minority ethnic languages and the possible links with 'home' countries are invaluable for designing culturally sensitive projects.

The problem of lack of knowledge of, and trust in, services

Those aiming to conduct research in this field should be aware of the conflicting messages of the under-representation of Asian drug users at drug services and the media portrayal of deviant drug peddlers (Murji, 1995). One of the first studies focusing on the drug service needs of Asian communities in Britain highlighted a number of gaps in service provision for this group (Patel, 1988). This was reinforced by an extensive action research project exploring the perceptions of young Asian drug users, particularly young Pakistani men, and a parallel focus on young African women (Awiah et al., 1992). This further confirmed what had been suspected: that drug agencies are often seen by minority ethnic people as 'white-run and white-oriented' and that they are not able to meet their needs.

There are several recurrent themes on this issue in the data in recent studies (Awiah et al., 1992; Patel et al., 1995; 1999; Sherlock et al., 1997): a lack of knowledge of services; the importance placed on the issues of trust and confidentiality; the lack of staff from minority ethnic backgrounds; and the ad hoc development of service provision for minority ethnic drug users.

Those interviewed were frequently found to have little knowledge of the existence of local drug services and what such services may have to offer. Many who experienced problems with drug use sought help either from their general practitioner (GP), or, in certain circumstances, from wider family and community networks. This suggests that the role of primary health-care professionals is crucial in determining the take-up and use of services by Asian drug users. Therefore, when contemplating the issue of gaining access to this group, researchers should be aware of the importance of the link with primary care staff, existing agencies and community groups which work with the target group (though not necessarily drug users), and should aim, where possible, to 'dovetail' the research to utilise existing local links.

Overall, within Asian communities, there is a lack of knowledge about most drugs and their effects. Knowledge is patchy and confused, particularly with respect to risk-taking behaviour. Many are not aware of the existence of drug services and those who are are suspicious and their perceptions are usually negative, primarily based on their experiences of discrimination from wider health and welfare agencies. Even where Asian staff are employed in drugs services, issues of confidentiality, especially within a close-knit community where the *izzat* (the honour of a family and wider community) could be placed in jeopardy, are a constant concern.

These issues, if not sensitively handled, will spell doom for research projects. In our studies, we have consistently allowed time to work with communities before commencing research in order to develop trust and understanding of our core aims. This is an important aspect of the research process which must be planned into the schedule at the outset and which should be treated as vital to the success of the study. As researchers, we should be aware of the histories that surround these people and that sometimes the answers given as a first response need to be explored further once trust is established.

The need for researchers to address myths: 'the few that do use will never inject'

Research has not only identified the under-representation of minority ethnic drug users at drug services, but also their low uptake of needle-exchange schemes. Although there are some regional differences for Afro-Caribbean users (Pearson et al., 1993), the data for Asian users are consistent. This, coupled with community beliefs that injecting is an issue for the white community only and that Asian drug users — particularly heroin users — do not inject, further hampers service development in this area. The question has to be asked: 'Why shouldn't they inject?'

An examination of the situation in South Asia can quickly dispel the belief that HIV/AIDS and intravenous drug use are only an issue for the western world. Throughout the 1980s, there has been a rapid growth in both the use and injecting of heroin in many Asian countries, particularly India, Nepal and Pakistan. Heroin users were estimated to number 1.7 million in the last national survey in Pakistan (Ahmed et al., 1993). Places such as Manipur in north-east India were unaware of Asian injecting drug users (IDUs) until a major HIV/AIDS epidemic associated with injecting use hit the area (Wodak et al., 1993). In Pakistan, though HIV/AIDS does not appear to be as prevalent as in India, a recent study in Karachi reported a 28 % increase in IDUs in the city (Parviz, 1996).

Although still under-reported in the UK, injecting is inevitably a major issue where there are Asian heroin users. The lack of culturally available information and the poor uptake of needle-exchange schemes by young Asians suggest that dangerous injecting practices are occurring (Awiah et al., 1992; Patel et al., 1995). This leads to another worrying issue which has been clearly highlighted in several studies (Patel, 1988; Patel et al., 1995; Sherlock et al., 1997). In some cases, young Asian drug users have been sent to Pakistan or Bangladesh in an attempt by the family to 'remove them from western drug-using influences' and 'stop their access to drugs'. Instead, the young people have returned some months later with hugely increased drug habits, due in the main to the availability and cheapness of drugs, particularly heroin, 'back home' (Pearson and Patel, 1998).

Good practice: an example

The following is an example of successful methods utilised in an action research study based in an NGO street drugs agency in a northern English city — Bradford. It used a multidimensional approach to reach Asian drug users, employing a number of different interventions that targeted the Asian community as a whole. In the first instance, comprehensive profiling of the community was undertaken, thus providing an understanding and acknowledgement of the different value and belief systems, practices and histories of the local Asian communities. Local agencies and community groups were contacted and consulted, and potential partnerships with them were developed.

An Asian action research worker with the same cultural and religious background as the target group was employed. The worker used various methods such as 'cold contacts' and snowballing to reach young people on street corners and local haunts, and ran small group sessions in local centres (Gilman, 1992). Young Asians were engaged in discussion on drug-related topics, either individually or in small groups. Partnerships with a range of local agencies and community groups were further established, not only through consultation but also by providing drugs awareness training. This ensured that we did not simply 'parachute' into the community, undertake our research and leave with the data without offering anything in return. Direct referral systems were set up, arrangements were made with a range of Asian GPs, and support was provided for the primary health-care staff. Alongside these fieldwork activities, a range of media were used to highlight the issue to the wider community.

- A phone-in programme on drug issues was launched on the local Asian radio station. This helped to raise awareness of drug-related issues and allowed discussion amongst the wider community — including parents — without fear of stigma.
- Simultaneously, a leaflet campaign was set in motion, using culturally sensitive materials. Leaflets were placed in locations such as Asian video shops and gro-

cery stores which were frequented by a broad spectrum of both young and old people (note that these venues are not the traditional outlets for leaflets, such as youth clubs and community centres).

- Posters were displayed which aimed to raise awareness of drug issues and to publicise the existence and activities of the local drug agency, including clear references to the policy on confidentiality (Patel et al., 1995).

Over a period of time, the worker built up enough trust and credibility to enable those with drug-related problems to approach him. He then referred the individuals to the local drug service, which, by this time, had undertaken a range of measures to be able to respond to this client group. For example, the service had:

- employed a number of Asian workers in generic posts;
- produced a range of culturally sensitive materials;
- consulted widely with the community in its earlier action research study (Awiah et al., 1992); and
- made its environment more culturally sensitive (Patel, 1993).

With respect to wider policy issues, the service had:

- produced a series of policies on race equality and anti-discriminatory practice;
- provided a series of training events for all its staff; and
- developed a long-term strategic plan for implementation and further service development.

The project in question successfully and dramatically increased the number of Asian drug users attending the service, from only a handful a year to several hundred. However, it should be noted that many factors contributed to this success, including the following.

- *Timescale.* The two-year action research study followed a previous study, both of which involved a significant amount of community development and active outreach. The whole process of organisational and cultural change within the agency took over five years.

- *Focused approach.* The project did not try to work with the whole Asian community immediately, but took a focused strategic approach. Early work involved the identification of a client group — young Pakistani and Bengali men — and, as work with this group proved fruitful, various other initiatives were developed.

- *Staff support.* All the Asian workers within the project had access to, and regular support from, an Asian manager who was experienced in this area of work.

- *Commitment.* The organisation as a whole was committed to taking on the challenge.

Without these considerations, many projects have not had the success for which they would have hoped (Patel, 1997a; 1997b).

Conclusions

In conclusion, the majority of projects, such as the example outlined here, cannot offer prevalence estimates of drug use in the Asian community, as they were not designed to do so. However, what they do show is that the pattern of drug consumption among young Asians, particularly with respect to the use of heroin, is an area that needs urgent attention. The issues discussed here in relation to the migrant communities in the UK will be mirrored now — or in the near future — in many European countries.

The author is Director of the Ethnicity and Health Unit, Faculty of Health, University of Central Lancashire, Preston, UK.

References

Ahmed, S., Ali, M. and Rafiq, M. (1993) *National Survey on Drug Abuse in Pakistan,* Islamabad, Pakistan: Narcotics Control Division, Pakistan Institute of Development Economics (PIDE).

Awiah, J., Butt, S., Dorn, N., Patel, K. and Pearson, G. (1992) *Race, Gender and Drug Services,* ISDD Research Monographs 6, London: ISDD.

Bola, M. and Walpole, T. (1997) *Drugs Information and Communication Needs amongst South Asian 11–14 Year Old Boys,* London: Home Office North West London Drugs Prevention Team.

Bradford Commission (1995) *Bradford Commission Report,* London: HMSO.

Bridge Project (1996) *Drugs and Asian Women in Bradford,* Bradford, UK: Bridge Project.

Burney, E. and Pearson, G. (1995) 'Mentally disordered offenders: finding a focus for diversion', *Howard Journal of Criminal Justice,* 34(4), 291–313.

Clarke, P., Harrison, M., Patel, K., Shah, M., Varley, M. and Williams, T. (1993) *Improving Mental Health Practice,* London: The Central Council for Education and Training for Social Work.

Commission for Racial Equality (CRE) (1995) *Census Data.*

Greater Manchester Bangladesh Association (GMBA) (1995) *Drug Research Project 1995 Comic Relief,* Home Office Drugs Prevention Initiative and Greater Manchester Bangladesh Association.

Gilman, M. (1992) *Outreach,* London: ISDD.

Gilman, M. (1993) *An Overview of the Main Findings and Implications of Seven Action Studies into the Nature of Drug Use in Bradford,* Bradford: Home Office Drugs Prevention Team.

Green, P. (1991) *Drug Couriers,* London: Howard League for Penal Reform.

Haw, S. (1985) *Drug Problems in Greater Glasgow,* London: SCODA.

Hood, R. (1992) *Race and Sentencing,* Oxford: Clarendon Press.

Jones, T. (1996) *Britain's Ethnic Minorities,* London: Policy Studies Institute.

Keith, M. (1993) *Race, Riots and Policing: Lore and Disorder in a Multi-Racist Society,* London: UCL Press.

Khan, F., Ditton, J., Hammersley, R. and Short, E. (1995) *Drug Using Attitudes and Behaviour of Young Members of Ethnic Minority Groups in Glasgow,* unpublished report to the Home Office.

Leitner, M., Shapland, J. and Wiles, P. (1993) *Drug Usage and Drug Prevention: the Views and Habits of the General Public,* London: HMSO.

Maden, A., Swinton, M. and Gunn, J. (1992) 'The ethnic origin of women serving a prison sentence', *British Journal of Criminology,* 32, 218–221.

McGovern, D. and Cope, R. V. (1987) 'First psychiatric admission rates of first and second generation Afro-Caribbeans', *Social Psychiatry,* 22, 139–149.

Mott, J. and Mirrlees-Black, C. (1995) *Self-Reported Drug Misuse in England and Wales: Findings from the 1992 British Crime Survey,* Research and Planning Unit Paper No 89, London: Home Office.

Murji, K. (1995) 'Drugs', in P. Neate (Ed.) *Scare in the Community: Britain in a Moral Panic,* London: Community Care Publications.

Parker, H., Measham, F. and Aldridge, J. (1995) *Drug Futures: Changing Patterns of Drug Use Among English Youth,* Institute for the Study of Drug Dependence, Research Monograph 7.

Parviz, S. (1996) *Demographics, Syringe Injecting Behaviour, Abusive Drug Behaviour, Sexual Behaviour and Seroprevalence of HIV Among Street Intravenous Heroin Addicts in Karachi,* Karachi, Pakistan: Aga Khan University.

Patel, K. (1988) 'A preliminary enquiry into the nature, extent and responses to drug problems (if any) within the Asian population of Bradford', *Social Work Education,* 8(1), 39-41.

Patel, K. (1993) 'Ethnic minority access to services', in L. Harrison (Ed.) *Race, Culture and Substance Problems,* Hull: University of Hull, pp. 33-46.

Patel, K. (1997a) *An Evaluation of the Clasp Project — Black Alcohol Project,* Preston: University of Central Lancashire.

Patel, K. (1997b) *An Evaluation of the Ashanti Project — Black Mental Health Project, Luton,* Preston: University of Central Lancashire.

Patel, K., Pearson, G. and Khan, F. (1995) *Outreach Work Among Asian Drug Injectors in Bradford: a Report to the Mental Health Foundation,* London: Goldsmiths College, University of London.

Patel, K. and Sherlock, K. (1997) *Drug Services and Asian Drug Users in England, Scotland and Wales,* Preston: Lancashire Drug Action Team, University of Central Lancashire.

Patel, K., Sherlock, K., Chaudry, M. and Buffin, J. (1999) *Drug Use Amongst Asian Communities in Cheetham Hill,* Manchester: Lifeline.

Patel, N., Bamhrah, C. and Singh, G. (1996) *Drug Use in the Asian Community,* Preston: Lancashire Drug Action Team, University of Central Lancashire.

Pearson, G. (1987a) *The New Heroin Users,* Oxford: Blackwell.

Pearson, G. (1987b) 'Social deprivation, unemployment and patterns of heroin use', in N. Dorn and N. South (Eds.) *A Land Fit For Heroin? Drug Policies, Prevention and Practice,* London: Macmillan.

Pearson, G., Gilman, M. and McIver, S. (1985) *Young People and Heroin: an Examination of Heroin Use in the North of England,* Health Education Council Research Monograph No 8, London/Aldershot: Health Education Council/Gower.

Pearson, G., Mirza, H. S. and Phillips, S. (1993) 'Cocaine in context: findings from a south London inner-city drug survey', in P. Bean (Ed.) *Cocaine and Crack: Supply and Use,* London: Macmillan.

Pearson, G. and Patel, K. (1998) 'Drugs, deprivation and ethnicity: outreach among Asian drug users in a northern English city', special edition of *Journal of Drug Issues* on 'Contemporary issues concerning illicit drug use in the British Isles', 28(1), 199–225.

Peck, D. F. and Plant, M. A. (1986) 'Unemployment and illegal drug use: concordant evidence from a perspective study and national trends', *British Medical Journal,* 293, 929–932.

Raleigh, V. (1995) *Mental Health in Black and Ethnic Minority People: the Fundamental Facts,* London: Mental Health Foundation.

Shahnaz, I. (1993) *Drugs Education and the Black Community in Lothian,* Edinburgh and Lothian Drug Action Team.

Sherlock, K., Patel, K. and Chaudry, M. (1997) *Drugs and Ethnic Health Project Research Report: West Pennine Drug Action Team,* Manchester: Lifeline.

Wodak, A., Crofts, N. and Fisher, R. (1993) 'HIV infection among injecting drug users in Asia: an evolving public health crisis', *AIDS Care,* 5(3), 313–320.

CHAPTER 14

UNDERSTANDING THE SOCIAL EXCLUSION—PROBLEM DRUG USE NEXUS

Aileen O'Gorman

During the 1990s, the use of the term 'social exclusion' became popular in European social policy discourse as an attempt to describe and encapsulate the development of 'new' social problems which were seen to be related to experiences of material deprivation and disadvantage.

Despite some justifiable criticism of the term for its vagueness and its appropriation as a politically expedient 'catch-all' phrase, it has provided researchers with a useful framework for investigation. For example, in the field of poverty research, the adoption of a social exclusion approach encouraged a shift in focus, from counting the poor and measuring the extent of relative deprivation to developing a qualitative understanding of the processes and mechanisms whereby people become marginalised and socially excluded.

The drugs-deprivation connection

Seminal drugs research studies conducted in England and Scotland in the 1980s (Haw, 1985; Peck and Plant, 1986; Pearson et al., 1987; Parker et al., 1988) had linked problem drug use to various indicators of deprivation. Similarly, in Ireland, data such as the annual report on treated drug misuse (O'Hare and O'Brien, 1992; O'Higgins, 1996), capture–recapture studies (Comiskey, 1998) and community studies (O'Kelly et al., 1988) had consistently indicated the spatial overlap between concentrations of problem drug users and concentrations of people experiencing multiple disadvantage in Dublin's inner-city and outer estates.

However, there was a perceived need for additional research to expand on these findings and broaden our understanding of how such experiences of deprivation and drug use were mediated at an individual level, in order to determine how interventions could be most appropriately targeted. A social exclusion approach, with its stress on the dynamic, multidimensional and processual nature of phenomena, provided the framework for conducting such a study. Furthermore, the social exclusion focus on the institutional mechanisms expelling individuals, households and communities from society encouraged the location of the problem drug use phenomenon as a consequence of structural, rather than individual, pathology — a view which was a guiding principle of the research study discussed here.

Designing the research study

The study set out to explore the relationship between heroin use and social exclusion in Dublin by focusing on the dynamic of social processes and structural forces and locating the perspective and experience of the heroin users within the context of the social and economic structures in which they lived and operated.

The ontological basis for this study stemmed from the critical theory perspective of 'reality' shaped by social, political, economic and cultural forces — a reality which was to be explored through an interpretivist methodology. However, in order to develop a research design which would tease out the multiple factors at play in the social exclusion–problem drug use dynamic and which would elicit an understanding of both the micro perspective of individual 'experiences' and 'meanings' and the macro perspective of social 'structures', it was necessary to utilise multiple data sources. Consequently, in order to capture the complexities of the phenomena involved, the research methodology developed along the lines of a 'field strategy that simultaneously combines document analysis, respondent and informant interviewing, direct participation and observation and introspection' (Denzin, 1970, p. 186).

The study's methodology was further influenced by a body of works ranging from those of interactionists such as Becker (1963) and Lindesmith (1947) on the social processes of drug use, to the sociologists of the Chicago school (e.g. Shaw and MacKay, 1942), who had combined analyses of area statistics with ethnographic studies to explore 'deviant' lifestyles, and also to the work of critical ethnographers such as Willis (1977), Westwood (1984) and Bourgois (1995), who had located qualitative evidence within a critical framework. Subsequently, the final research design focused on data collected from the following sources (O'Gorman, 1999):

- an initial round of 'information' interviews with statutory and voluntary workers in the drugs and related fields in the Dublin area;
- a series of in-depth, loosely structured interviews with heroin users;
- ethnographic studies of neighbourhoods with visible drug scenes (incorporating informal interviews with heroin users, residents and relevant service providers in the area);
- an analysis of existing indicators on drug use, disadvantage and social exclusion; and
- a review of related social and economic policy.

The in-depth interviews and ethnographic studies

The methodological focus on how structures are understood and meanings are interpreted and reproduced, and how both constrain and enable social action, was operationalised in the in-depth interviews through an interview schedule which set out to capture the disparate elements identified as belonging to the social exclusion dynamic.

For example, Ryan (1998) had placed the location of social exclusion in the break-down of socially integrative mechanisms such as the labour market (jobs and income), the State system (access to education, health, housing and social services) and the family and community system (social networks).

Geddes (1995) had identified social exclusion as the inability to fully exercise social, cultural and political rights to employment, health and education, or to secure a minimum level of income. Consequently, the interview schedule was drawn up to reflect on topics concerning neighbourhood, family, social networks, employment, and education and training, as well as drug-using behaviour and the development of a heroin career.

While data from in-depth, flexible interviews impart a degree of 'ethnographic con-text' (Schwartz and Jacobs, 1979), this context was further expanded in the ethno-graphic studies of neighbourhoods with prominent heroin scenes. In these studies, long-term relationships were established with both heroin- and non-heroin-using residents, which allowed the informal ethnographic interviews and the in-depth interviews to mutually inform each other over space and time. In turn, both these data sources mutually informed the (mostly quantitative) data on social exclusion, drug prevalence and related policy.

Multiple data sources

The use of such multiple data sources is not without methodological complications. Triangulating data from different sources is, for example, viewed by Silverman (1985) as a methodological contradiction for research conducted within an inter-pretivist paradigm, in that it implies that partial views can simply be added together to produce a complete picture and is thus based on the (positivist) assumption of multiple mappings of a single reality.

However, while attempts to adjudicate between accounts/data gathered in different settings may indeed fall into this methodological trap, there is a plausible case to be made for understanding each account in the context in which it was produced, and for such accounts to mutually inform each other.

Using multiple data sources to explore the social exclusion–heroin use nexus was additionally useful in ensuring that the relationship between individual lives and social structure was not sidelined (Brückner, 1995) and that respondents' meanings and experiences were located within social processes and structural forces. Without such multiple sources, the study ran the risk that its focus on 'the underclass' would reinforce 'the received wisdom that it is in such groups that the "problem" is to be found' (Hartnoll, 1992, p. 16).

Conclusions

A key 'sensitising concept' (Blumer, 1969) leading the research study concerned the 'tangle of pathology' (Rainwater, 1967) that arose in neighbourhoods, largely through ill-judged planning, housing, economic and social policies and decisions about the distribution of resources. An analysis of both policies and indicators of spatialised social exclusion ([1]) helped elucidate how urban environments reached a process of 'critical mass' (Fischer, 1980), whereby a sufficiently large population of similarly situated individuals generated a set of social conditions over and above the sum total of individual deprivation.

In such settings, individual drug-using careers were seen to develop in a more dysfunctional way, with the ensuing local prevalence of problem drug use further exacerbating conditions for all residents and resulting in a powerful, mutually reinforcing, dynamic of the social exclusion–problem drug use phenomenon. Such findings have clear policy implications by adding empirical support to existing calls for drugs policy to:

- be more cognisant of the environmental context of drug misuse (Advisory Council on the Misuse of Drugs, 1998);
- note the interplay between individual behaviours and the context which helps shape them (Stimson, 1995); and
- focus more on rectifying the failures of society and institutions rather than implementing corrective measures aimed at the individual (MacGregor, 1996).

The author is an independent research consultant based in Dublin, Ireland.

Acknowledgements

This study was funded by the Health Research Board, Ireland. The views expressed are those of the author and do not necessarily reflect the views of the Board.

([1]) The local indicators analysed included: residents' age profile; levels of educational attainment; concentration of public housing; proportions of people in the labour force, in employment and unemployed (all three being necessary to get a 'truer' picture of local employment); as well as the nature of local employment (skilled, semi-skilled, unskilled).

References

Advisory Council on the Misuse of Drugs (ACMD) (1998) *Drug Misuse and the Environment,* London: HMSO.

Becker, H. S. (1963) *Outsiders: Studies in the Sociology of Deviance,* New York: Free Press.

Blumer, M. (1969) *Symbolic Interactionism,* Englewood Cliffs, NJ: Prentice-Hall.

Bourgois, P. (1995) *In Search of Respect: Selling Crack in El Barrio,* Cambridge, UK: Cambridge University Press.

Brückner, H. (1995) 'Research on the dynamics of poverty in Germany', *Journal of European Social Policy* 5(4), 317–322.

Comiskey, C. (1998) *Estimating the Prevalence, Demography and Geographical Distribution of Opiate Use in Dublin,* Dublin: Department of Health.

Denzin, N. (1970) *The Research Act in Sociology,* London: Butterworth.

Fischer, C. (1980) 'Theories of urbanism', in G. Gmelch and W. P. Zenner (Eds.) *Urban Life,* New York: St Martin's Press.

Geddes, M. (1995) *Poverty, Excluded Communities and Local Democracy,* Research Report No 9, London: Commission for Local Democracies.

Hartnoll, R. (1992) 'Overview of existing research methods', in H. F. L. Garretsen et al. (Eds.) *Illegal Drug Use: Research Methods in Hidden Populations,* Rotterdam: Netherlands Institute of Alcohol and Drugs.

Haw, S. (1985) *Drug Problems in Greater Glasgow,* London: SCODA.

Lindesmith, A. (1947) *Opiate Addiction,* Indiana: Principia Press.

MacGregor, S. (1996) *Drugs Policy, Community and the City,* Middlesex University.

O'Gorman, A. (1999) 'Responding to contingencies in the field', in T. Rhodes (Ed.) *Qualitative Methods in Drugs Research,* London: Sage.

O'Hare, A. and O'Brien, M. (1992) *Treated Drug Misuse in the Greater Dublin Area 1990,* Dublin: Health Research Board.

O'Higgins, K. (1996) *Treated Drug Misuse in the Greater Dublin Area: a Review of Five Years 1990–1994,* Dublin: Health Research Board.

O'Kelly, F. D., Bury, G., Cullen, B. and Dean, G. (1988) 'The rise and fall of heroin use in an inner-city area of Dublin', *Irish Journal of Medical Science,* 157(2), 35–38.

Parker, H., et al. (1987) 'The new heroin users: prevalence and characteristics in Wirral, Merseyside', *British Journal of Addiction,* 82(2), 147–157.

Parker, H., Bakx, K. and Newcombe, R. (1988) *Living with Heroin: the Impact of a Drugs Epidemic on an English Community,* Milton Keynes: Open University Press.

Pearson, G., Gilman, M. and MacIver, S. (1987) *Young People and Heroin: an Examination of Heroin Use in the North of England,* Aldershot: Gower.

Peck, D. F. and Plant, M. A. (1986) 'Unemployment and illegal drug use: concordant evidence from a prospective study and from national trends', *British Medical Journal,* 293(6552), 929–932.

Rainwater, L. (1967) 'The city poor', *New Society,* 23, November.

Ryan, L. (1998) 'Poverty studies', in K. MacKeogh (Ed.) *Social Inequality and Intergroup Relations,* Dublin: Oscail, Dublin City University.

Schwartz, H. and Jacobs, J. (1979) *Qualitative Sociology: a Method to the Madness,* New York: Free Press.

Shaw, C. R. and MacKay, H. D. (1942) *Juvenile Delinquency and Urban Areas,* Chicago: University of Chicago Press.

Silverman, D. (1985) *Qualitative Methodology and Sociology,* Aldershot: Gower.

Stimson, G. V. (1995) 'An environmental approach to reducing drug-related harm', in J. W. T. Dickerson and G. V. Stimson (Eds.) *Health in the Inner City: Drugs in the City,* London: Royal Society of Health.

Westwood, S. (1984) *All Day Every Day: Factory and Family in the Making of Women's Lives,* London: Pluto.

Willis, P. (1977) *Learning to Labour,* Westmead: Saxon House.

Further reading

Dean, G., et al. (1984) *Characteristics of Heroin and Non-Heroin Users in a North-Central Dublin Area,* Dublin: Medico-Social Research Board.

Edwards, G. (1995) 'Drugs in the human environment', in J. W. T. Dickerson and G. V. Stimson (Eds.) *Health in the Inner City: Drugs in the City,* London: Royal Society of Health.

European Commission (1994) 'Towards a Europe of solidarity: combating social exclusion', *Social Europe,* Supplement 4/93, Luxembourg: Office for Official Publications of the European Communities.

Rodgers, G., Gore, C. and Figueiredo, J. B. (1995) *Social Exclusion: Rhetoric, Reality, Responses,* Geneva: International Institute for Labour Studies/United Nations Development Programme.

Room, G. (1992) *Observatory on National Policies to Combat Social Exclusion,* second annual report, Brussels: European Commission.

Yeates, N. (1998) 'New thinking on poverty and social exclusion', in K. MacKeogh (Ed.) *Social Inequality and Intergroup Relations,* Dublin: Oscail, Dublin City University.

CHAPTER 15

SOCIAL PERIPHERIES AND DRUGS: AN ETHNOGRAPHIC STUDY IN PSYCHOTROPIC TERRITORIES

Luís Fernandes

In the social sciences, it is now commonplace to say of any subject that it is 'complex'. The topic of this chapter — drugs and social exclusion — brings together two subjects which are complex enough separately. Each of them is a lasting social problem and a source of riddles for the analytical perspective of the human sciences. Moreover, both subjects intersect at some point in the course of the development of social processes in western societies: if we look at drugs, we come upon social exclusion; when we look at social exclusion, we are forced to take drugs into consideration.

The starting-point for our ethnographic research was the description of illegal drug use in an urban-industrial context. At first, we had not even thought about relating this issue to social exclusion: our crucial interest lay in drugs and their use as symbolic features of youth behaviour. In this chapter, the following topics are discussed:

- the way in which, almost involuntarily, ethnographic research 'forced' us to analyse drugs and social exclusion together;
- the relationship between illegal drug use and social exclusion from the standpoint rendered possible by the ethnographic method; and
- the way in which fieldwork made us question drugs, social exclusion and the ethnographic method itself.

Building an ethnographic project

> *I believe that the real evolution of research ideas is not in accordance with the formal descriptions we read about research methods. Ideas are born, in part, from our immersion in the data and in the process of living ... Only by accumulating a series of reports on how a study is really conducted will we be able to go beyond the logical-intellectual image and learn how to describe the research process.* (Whyte, 1955)

The ethnographic research we have been developing is part of a set of investigations carried out, since 1983, by the Centro de Ciências do Comportamento Desviante (Centre for the Study of Deviant Behaviour — CCCD) at the Faculty of Psychology and Educational Sciences at the University of Oporto. These research projects have been guided by an attempt to understand deviant behaviour as bio-psycho-social phenomena: studies have ranged from laboratory work in psycho-physiology to street ethnography concerned with social ecology.

'You don't get into drugs without getting out on the street'

Our experiences as drugs researchers began in a drug treatment unit. The excessive focus on a psycho-pathological approach, and the differences in speech we noticed between the users while inside and outside the institution, quickly led us to become critical of the clinical approach. In 1985, when we joined the CCCD, we were searching for a different way of looking at drug use — a naturalistic look. Our preferred method was in accordance with the research director's aim: the creation of a multidisciplinary research team able to conduct research ranging from experimental to ethnographic methods, from the laboratory to the field, from the biological to the social-cultural approach. In a sentence, he summarised the role of the latter: 'You can't get into drugs without getting out on the street.' The naturalistic look would study the phenomenon of drugs in its daily manifestations, in the actual places where its logic constitutes itself and interacts with the logic of social life, far from clinical and juridical reductionism.

'Extremes touch'

Initially, we produced a history of the drug use of young people in Portugal, so as to contextualise practices revolving around forbidden products and the meanings these had for the groups involved. In this way, we established a trajectory of youth psychotropism based on drug users' life histories.

To summarise very briefly, before the revolution of 1974 — which restored democracy in Portugal — drugs had very little social visibility. During this period, drugs were found only in cultural elites influenced by Anglo-Saxon pop-rock imagery. We named it the 'lysergic period in a restricted circle'. The drugs used were LSD and marijuana.

After April 1974, there are two clear-cut periods. The first lasted until 1980, when drug use was part of behavioural and symbolic constellations associated with youth subcultures (the hashish smoker 'freak' is the main character here). Adolescent drug use expanded and the social-political construction of the 'drug problem' began (see Agra, 1993, for an analysis of the construction of juridical instruments and care structures related to the 'fight on drugs'). The second period began around 1980 and was characterised by the progressive establishment of a 'hard' drugs market: heroin and the junkie become the protagonists. Although drug use had increased during the 'freak' period, in the junkie period 'harder' drugs began to be used and there was the progressive involvement of the socially less favoured.

When we first 'got out on the street', we chose to study an old historical neighbourhood in the centre of the town of Oporto which popular rumour then associated with drug users. Our aim was to produce an ethnography of drugs in youth subcultures. However, the year was 1985, subcultures were less and less important as initiation contexts in the drugs scene, and we were obliged to change our focus. Other contexts and social actors turned urban peripheries into the scenarios for the new elements of urban insecurity: the junkie, the dealer and the drugs markets. In a period of 20 years, drugs had moved from restricted middle- and upper-class groups to the socially less favoured, until they reached the working class, socially excluded groups living in the town's social-spatial periphery. If, as according to a popular saying, 'extremes touch', then we can say that drugs had now touched both extremes of the social scale.

The 'drugs problem', previously approached as a youth management political issue (drug use prevention), a clinical issue (care and treatment) and a juridical issue ('war on drugs'), shows great adaptability to strategies aimed at its destruction. Ironically, confirming the popular 'virus' metaphor, the drugs epidemic invades the social groups and urban areas which are resistant to social control techniques. It is in the context of this deep change that social exclusion emerges as an analytical topic, and the evolution of the phenomenon led us to the main topic of our next ethnographic research: an urban periphery associated with social exclusion.

Psychotropic territories

Since 1990, we have been focusing our research on council estates, some of which are persistently called 'drugs hypermarkets' by the media. Between October 1992 and the summer of 1993, we lived in one of those estates, so as to maximise research opportunities and to immerse ourselves as much as possible in the context. What follows is a short summary of the issues developed on the basis of fieldwork data.

The drugs estates

The images of social exclusion are concentrated in these areas. The primary consequence is the increase of isolation foreshadowed by the estates' topographic position in relation to the town. They are places where the town is interrupted: our fieldwork data describe in detail the features of this spatial and social fracture. The analysis of daily life there allows us to look at these zones as parallel social spaces, often represented by their own inhabitants as territories 'under siege'.

Drugs in the estates

The two main social actors in these territories are the dealer (usually also a drug addict) and the junkie (addicted to hard drugs). They are the main characters in the drugs street scene, and their activities develop as interstices of space and time. We also focused on socialisation processes in these contexts: that is, on how one learns to live in psychotropic territories.

At a later stage, when reassembling the data — the 'writing-up' phase, which involves a degree of construction above that of the 'writing down' (Atkinson, 1990) — the hypothesis was developed that the present eco-social configuration of drugs is an adaptive response to its juridical-moral status. Such an adaptive response allows it to survive, and even expand, despite the numerous measures developed by the machine devoted to fighting drugs. It has at least three axes.

- *Economic adaptation.* Council estates associated with the drugs business are sites of economic fragility, and their inhabitants are either poor or vulnerable to poverty. Economic and labour marginalisation makes it much more likely that they will become involved in street drug dealing than inhabitants of other parts of the town. It might be asked why this does not occur in any poor or vulnerable site: it is because space needs to fulfil some conditions — it must favour ecological adaptation.

- *Ecological adaptation.* 'War on drugs' strategies have generated defensive reactions on the part of the street markets and the places where drug consumers congregate. Both moved to sites which repressive forces find more difficult to access. The drugs council estate is in morpho-topological discontinuity with its urban environment, making it possible for territories over which effective vigilance can be maintained to be constructed.

- *Psychological adaptation.* According to Wirth (1928), 'the ghetto is not only a physical place but a state of mind'. The 'state of mind' offered by heroin is anaesthesia which, in a site kept away by the town — the 'ghetto' — allows one to be kept away.

The 'drugs hypermarket' is, then, organised as a territory. We have called it 'psychotropic territory', and, according to the environmental psychology notion of behaviour setting, defined it as 'a place of concentration of social actors with a role in the drugs business ... It attracts people sharing an interest in a lifestyle in which drugs play a major role — it is ... a spatial matrix of a junkie street subculture ... Its main communicational feature is minimal interaction and it is structured as an interstice of space and time' (Fernandes, 1998).

Conclusions

To carry out ethnographic research is a personal experience that leads to much reflection, particularly when it concerns those in an area on the margin of the normative town. In this final section, we discuss what that experience has led us to question.

The 'world of drugs' is a faraway entity that brings on feelings of fear and threat. At the social-political level this translates as the 'war' on a 'plague' or 'epidemic'. Daily contact with this quasi-virus forced us to question these images, not in order to deny the social seriousness of some of its manifestations, but to look at the drugs world as a normal phenomenon in our societies. It is normal because the mechanisms of its production are not located outside social dynamics, because it is repetitive and recurrent, and because it is established in the concrete practices of the concrete town.

The ethnographer's role in the phenomenon of drugs may then be that of helping its re-naturalisation. The voluntary alteration of the state of the mind through the use of psychoactive substances was turned into a strange, pathological and criminogenic behaviour during the western process of medicalisation and juridification; it is necessary to reinsert it in the social practices from where it emerged. After the attempt to silence it — the first aim of the 'war on drugs' — it is now time to let it speak: about our social mechanisms, particularly those that produce social exclusion.

Our aim here has been to discuss the potentialities and limitations of ethnography. As potentialities, we stress its openness and adequation. As limits, we stress its instrumentalisation.

Openness refers to the ability of ethnography to generate relations with other objects from the initial research object. In our case, drugs led us first to youth subcultures, and later to social exclusion and urban insecurity. We were also stimulated to analyse social-spatial peripheries of the town.

Adequation means that ethnography is useful to reach and observe layers of reality inaccessible to almost every other research method: those of the 'hidden populations' (Adler, 1990) whose social practices are developed 'backstage' (Goffman, 1961).

Instrumentalisation is to be avoided. It occurs when the ethnographer is used as an 'undercover agent' who may serve invasive control strategies. Ethnography might join a strategy that replaces a policed society with a 'softer' surveillance machine made up of social scientists.

The author is Professor at the Faculdade de Psicologia e Ciências da Educação da Universidade do Porto, Portugal, and a researcher at the Centro de Ciências do Comportamento Desviante at the same university.

References

Adler, P. (1990) *Ethnographic Research on Hidden Populations: Penetrating the Drug World,* National Institute on Drug Abuse Research, Monograph Series.

Agra, C. da (Ed.) (1993) *Dizer a Droga, Ouvir as Drogas,* Oporto: Radicário.

Atkinson, P. (1990) *The Ethnographic Imagination: Textual Construction of Reality,* London: Routledge.

Fernandes, L. (1998) *O Sítio das Drogas,* Lisbon: Notícias.

Goffman, E. (1961) *Asylums: Essays on the Social Situation of Mental Patients and Other Inmates,* Garden City, NY: Doubleday Books.

Whyte, W. F. (1955) *Street Corner Society: the Social Structure of an Italian Slum,* Chicago: University of Chicago Press.

Wirth, L. (1928) *The Ghetto,* Chicago: University of Chicago Press.

CHAPTER 16

SPEED FREAKS, JUNKIES AND OTHERS —
WITH DRUGS AS COMPANIONS

Bengt Svensson

This chapter describes the everyday life of a group of drug users in Malmö, southern Sweden. At the same time, it addresses why they continue to lead an addict's lifestyle and what advantages this lifestyle has for them compared with life in 'ordinary' society.

The data, which were collected through ethnographic fieldwork between 1989 and 1995, are based on observations, conversations and in-depth interviews. The study, which included drug users with different drug-using patterns, different social backgrounds and lifestyles, focused on a group of 10 key informants — 8 men and 2 women. Besides the core group of 10, 20 more drug users were interviewed and observed between 1 and 10 times. In total, there were more than 500 personal meetings.

The study lies within the symbolic-interactionist tradition of sociology. It rests on the premise that people actively construct and maintain their reality and act in terms of the symbolic meanings they attribute to it. As people are best understood in their own environment, it is therefore essential for researchers to take part in this milieu in order to understand how those they are studying interpret their social worlds (Blumer, 1969). From interactionists such as Shibutani (1955), Strauss (1978) and Biernacki (1986), concepts such as social worlds, organising perspective and social identity were employed in the study. Drug users have their own social worlds and express corresponding social identities: their acts are guided by their organising perspective, which is derived from the drug users' subculture.

Everyday life

The study examines everyday life from the action aspect — that is, questions concerning work and leisure, how life is structured and how different drugs are used. Also considered is the belonging aspect, which includes questions about where a person 'hangs out', the people with whom he/she is in contact and the culture to which he/she belongs. Finally examined is the expression aspect — that is, how the drug addicts view themselves and how others view them and the lifestyles they follow.

The highly varied lives led by the informants — how periods of intensive drug use alternate with periods of abstention, and attempts to leave the world of the drug addict — are also studied. The addict's relationship to drugs is examined utilising the metaphor of a love affair, but one that takes many different forms. The first meeting can be a 'one-night stand' only, or it can mean love at first sight and the start of an affair. It is forbidden love with special attractions and dangers. A decision will follow to live separately and meet regularly or to live together. In the latter case, the relationship is gradually established as a marital relationship, characterised by security, habits and routines, moments when passion flares up again, periods of doubt, and possibly a decision to break up. A break-up can lead to divorce, but the relationship can also be resumed after a period of separation. If the divorce is lasting, this can lead to the person living singly for the rest of his/her life (that is, without drugs). The result can also be that they start a new relationship, replacing the drug with a new one such as alcohol: even then, there is a risk of infidelity, which can happen when they return temporarily to the old love object.

The analysis examines the environment to which the drug user belongs as a special social world in which the user has also developed a social identity as a drug addict. Since the world of drugs is separated from ordinary society, chiefly as a consequence of narcotics legislation, it is characterised, as Shibutani (1955) says, by a special organisation, systems of communication, rules, a status system and an argot. Life in the drug world is shaped by a special culture — a subculture. It is from this that the drug addicts take their organising perspectives, the cultural matrix that governs their everyday lives.

An important element of the subculture is its view of different drugs. A literature review shows that those ethnographic researchers who have tried to understand drug addicts on their own terms differ from them in their view of the effects and the place of the drugs in the subculture. These researchers, who often adopt a symbolic-interactionist outlook, point out that the effects of the drug are, to a large extent, socially constructed. They put emphasis on the attractions of the lifestyle rather than the drug. For drug addicts, on the other hand, the effects of the drug are absolute, ascribed to the pharmacology of the substances. If the effects are not as they expect, it is because the quality of the drugs is poor, not that the setting is wrong. Their main reason for leading a life as a drug user is the drug, not the lifestyle (for example, Becker, 1963; Goldberg, 1971; Rettig et al., 1977; Hills and Santiago, 1992; Taylor, 1993; Faithfull, 1994).

The study began with the assumption by the author that there was a solidarity among drug addicts and that this was one of the main attractions of the lifestyle, but this viewpoint changed to one which concluded that there is, in fact, extensive sociality, but without solidarity. There is outward solidarity vis-à-vis outsiders and authorities of various kinds: the primary expression of this is not to 'snitch' (inform the police or the authorities of illegal activities). There is no inward solidarity, however. Informants constantly emphasise this: in this world it is 'every man for himself'. No one does anything for anyone else without the ulterior motive of benefiting from it in the future. They let others down, trick their friends, steal from others in the group, expose others to risk, ignore pleas for help, and so on. The lack of solidarity is due to them all doing business with each other, such as selling drugs, committing burglaries and sharing the profits, receiving and selling stolen goods, exchanging goods for drugs, treating someone to a dose of drugs and expecting one in return, charging people who use their flat as a 'crash-pad', arranging contacts with dealers, and selling drugs on a commission basis for a dealer. Thus, relations between the actors in the drug world are generally permeated with economics, which can be a strain on any relationship. In addition, these relations are also enacted in an atmosphere which requires a literal struggle for survival.

Unsuccessful attempts to break out

Lack of solidarity was identified as the main reason why the sample wanted to leave drugs behind: only one informant never talked about giving up drugs. He was a former sailor and had retired early after an accident that left him unable to use his left arm. For him, life on amphetamines was the best conceivable. He could live like a king for a day: he allowed himself the right to steal food and commit burglaries when he had no money; he could buy sex directly from a prostitute or indirectly by letting a woman live with him for a while; he had a large circle of acquaintances; and he described his regular prison sentences almost as a holiday. It can be assumed that 'retirement' from this life would be too uneventful for him.

Discussions with other informants about their attempts to break out — or to break into 'normal society', as one could also say — demonstrated some of the difficulties involved. As experienced drug addicts, with a large network of drug-using contacts and a short planning perspective, being used to seeing money run quickly through their fingers, they come to a world where these skills have little value and in which it is essential to be able to plan one's finances. Even if they move to a new town, they can still come into contact with drug users: their experience of prisons and treatment facilities, and, sometimes, their physical appearance give them access to a recognisable underground network, consisting of people with a similar history.

For many years, the drug has been a source of strength, pleasure and consolation, an object around which they assembled with others and the acquiring of which structured their whole day. In 'normal society' it is a criminal offence to have anything to do with the drug. They have to find a sense of belonging in new social worlds, develop new social identities and build up new relationships. The old relationships had their obvious limitations, giving sociality with no solidarity, but they were still characterised by the security of familiarity, by what Scheff (1994) calls 'attunement'. Their encounters with people in the addicts' world are often characterised by pride, the meeting of one professional with another, whereas without drugs they have to find their bearings in new settings. This means meetings with other people are sometimes painful and embarrassing, accompanied by a sense of mutual alienation. These encounters are occasions of shame.

Scheff's concept of attunement can also help in understanding the decision to give up drugs. Once again, the love affair metaphor can be used. Ever since the first meeting, expectations of a positive experience have been built up, but, if the 'meeting' with a drug is also laden with other feelings such as guilt about doing something illegal, unhealthy and far too expensive, then it can bring a sense of guilt and shame. Getting high on a drug leads to a lack of attunement. If several encounters with the drug give the same negative result, the user questions his/her ties to it. This can be the start of an attempt to break out. However, if the relationship to the drug is durable, love can blossom again.

Conclusions

In the study, the traditional question 'Why do drug addicts not give up drugs?' was reversed to ask instead 'Why do they continue to live as drug addicts?'. To contribute to an answer, users' everyday lives were examined, rather than their pathology or the defects or merits of the care system. This revealed that there are reasonable explanations for why they remain in the addicts' world, without resorting to the use of psychological terms labelling them as impulsive, self-destructive, or suffering from an early derangement.

The study demonstrated the relative advantages that a life of addiction can have, and the disadvantages that the alternative, 'ordinary' life often entails for them. It is not that addicts simply 'make do' with a marginal existence of poverty and solitude: their everyday lives are not always wretched and cheerless. Reasons given for staying in the addicts' world show that, although it means misery, being let down, a lack of solidarity, illness, suffering and death, it also has other features — the sociality, eventfulness, the short perspectives, the 'everything will work out fine' attitude, the sense of competence, having something to do (in the form of criminal ways of making a living) and the artificial pleasure of the drugs. This can be contrasted with the alternatives: solitude, unemployment, poverty, idleness and the sense of being superfluous. Despite these difficulties, many of the informants made constant attempts to break into 'normal' life. This can be seen as an expression of their having the same basic goals in life as people in general: to live a 'normal life' and be respected by 'normal people'.

The author is Assistant Professor at the School of Social Work, University of Lund, Sweden.

References

Becker, H. S. (1963) *Outsiders,* Toronto: The Free Press.

Biernacki, P. (1986) *Pathways from Heroin Addiction,* Philadelphia: Temple University Press.

Blumer, H. (1969) *Symbolic Interactionism,* Englewood Cliffs: Prentice-Hall.

Faithfull, M. (1994) *Faithful,* London: Penguin.

Goldberg, T. (1971) *Haschare,* Stockholm: Aldus.

Hills, S. and Santiago, R. (1992) *Tragic Magic,* Chicago: Nelson Hall.

Rettig, R., Torres, M. and Garrett, G. (1977) *Manny: a Criminal-Addict´s Story,* Boston: Houghton Mifflin.

Scheff, T. (1994) *Microsociology,* Chicago: The University of Chicago Press.

Shibutani, T. (1955) 'Reference groups as perspectives', *American Journal of Sociology,* 60, 522–529.

Strauss, A. (1978) 'A social world perspective', *Studies in Symbolic Interaction,* 1, 119–128.

Svensson, B. (1996) *Pundare, jonkare och andra,* Stockholm: Carlssons.

Taylor, A. (1993) *Women Drug Users,* Oxford: Clarendon Press.

PROBLEM DRUG USE, SOCIAL EXCLUSION AND SOCIAL REINTEGRATION: THE CLIENT SPEAKS

Julian Buchanan and Lee Young

This chapter is based on a two-year evaluation (1996–98) of 'Second Chance' (since renamed 'Transit'), a structured day programme (SDP) located in Liverpool, UK, which aims to reintegrate long-term problem drug users into the wider community.

SDPs are a relatively new and important addition to the existing range of services available to recovering drug users. Second Chance embraces a harm-reduction approach and therefore accepts those who continue to use illegal drugs and/or those who are maintained on methadone, so long as they are working towards gaining more control over their lives. The programme operates for 12 weeks and incorporates educational components, social and vocational skills training and opportunities for leisure pursuits.

The researchers set out to elicit the experiences and opinions of the drug users attending Second Chance, where the staff refer to them as 'students'. This is a deliberate strategy to remove the 'addict' label and display respect towards those participating in the programme. The perspective underpinning the study is that service users are in a unique position to make judgments about the effectiveness and impact of drug services.

The data are taken from in-depth interviews with 58 students who completed the 12-week programme. Each student was tracked and interviewed on four separate occasions over a 12-month period, with six key areas selected for assessment: relationships, confidence/self-esteem, offending, drug use, health and aspirations.

While this provided rich data regarding the effectiveness of the SDP, it crucially demonstrated a strong relationship between problem drug use and social exclusion.

Drug use and social exclusion

A significant finding of the study was that, regardless of individual motivation to achieve change and move away from a drug-centred lifestyle, students described a process of stigmatisation, marginalisation and social exclusion. This was a recurring theme in all six assessment areas.

Relationships

Questions regarding relationships powerfully illustrated the sense of public disapproval of drug use that has been internalised by this sample of students. Of considerable concern should be the deep and intrusive impact that moral, social and political disapproval of 'drug addicts' has had upon them.

When asked how other people view them, student comments illustrated a strong sense of social dislocation.

> *'They look down on me as scum of the earth and as someone not to be associated with.'*
> *'They see me as a drug addict, a smackhead, and they think I'd rob them.'*
> *'I feel the odd one out. I've nothing in common with them. I start to get paranoid.'*
> *'I used to avoid them like the plague. I used to be scared of what they might think.'*
> *'I feel nervous in case I slip up, I know they would look at me in disgust.'*

Acutely aware of strong social disapproval from the wider community, students speak of anxiety and unease when operating in any environment other than a drug-using milieu.

> *'I'd feel vulnerable, even answering the phone.'*
> *'I used to stay by myself and I didn't trust people.'*
> *'I had drug associates and only one friend really.'*
> *'I was living life in a bubble, wasting my life drugged up.'*
> *'I lost all my confidence.'*
> *'I never really mixed with people who have never taken drugs.'*

Comments such as those reproduced so far illustrate the dominant impact of drugs upon the lives of many drug users. In this life, they have little or no relationships that they would describe as friendships; instead they refer to acquaintances with drug associates. This is a point emphasised by many of the students, who felt it was important to distinguish between the two.

This harsh, isolated life had a negative impact upon the internal well-being of most of the students, many of whom lacked confidence and self-esteem. This undermined their ability to form relationships and tended to reinforce their social isolation and subsequent dislocation.

Confidence/self-esteem

Students differentiated between friendships in the 'normal' world, and acquaintances in the 'drug culture'. A similar division emerged in relation to confidence. They acknowledged that they lacked 'real' confidence, but a large number masked this deficit by using drugs.

> *'I'd use drugs to give me confidence.'*
> *'When I was on drugs I had confidence.'*
> *'I wish I was more confident. It was okay when I had diazepam. One week I have it and I'm okay and the next I run out and I'm bad.'*
> *'One of the reasons I use is that I get confidence but it's a false confidence.'*

Unless issues of confidence, self-esteem and relationships are understood as they impact on problem drug users, intervention strategies are unlikely to be fully effective.

Offending

A considerable amount of attention is given by the media to drug-related crime. Drug users are often portrayed as callous criminals who have no regard for others and are likely to commit crime whether or not they take drugs. However, the research indicated that many of these students committed crime only to support their drug addiction. Therefore, if they were not dependent on drugs, they would be less likely to be involved in criminal activity, and many wished they were not.

> *'I'm not a thief, I'm not a robber, it's because of the drugs and my situation.'*
> *'I was using street drugs and I had to find money to support my habit.'*
> *'All my offending is directly related to the drug use, either to support my habit or to replace money I have spent on drugs.'*
> *'The only reason I offended was due to drugs.'*
> *'I would only commit a crime for drugs.'*

Indeed, some students had managed to remove themselves from the criminal scene. It does appear that drug-related crime may be reduced through the rehabilitation and reintegration of people who have problems with drugs.

> *'Now that I'm on a script I'm not offending, it was only ever to support my habit.'*
> *'Now I'm not using, so I don't need to find money.'*
> *'I'm not offending, I'm not taking drugs.'*
> *'I've too much to lose. I'm doing NVQ2 [a vocational qualification] in computers and Spanish and I'm going to do Japanese, so there's no way I'd offend again.'*

Drug use

Although some drug users have reasons for continuing with drugs, the research indicated that many became tired and frustrated, trapped within a monotonous pattern of life. Many wanted change.

> *'Drugs take over your life, you can't get on as normal. You wake up and have to take something to feel normal.'*
> *'I hate it, I hate methadone, it's horrible. It switches half your body off.'*
> *'I want to get off the methadone.'*

A life centred around drugs causes isolation and marginalisation. Many students just wanted to be reconnected with wider society and had begun to do something about it.

> *'I'm sick of it. I see people with their own houses, family and friends. I'd like friends who don't use.'*
> *'I am trying to stop — as I explain to my parents, it's gradual. I've come down from 90 ml [methadone] to 45 ml, it's gradual.'*
> *'I've been wanting to change for five years.'*
> *'I want to be drug free, get a job and live a normal life.'*
> *'It is difficult — you feel divorced from the mainstream. I want to get back into it.'*

Health

The research sought to identify the impact of problem drug use upon diet, weight, fitness and sleeping patterns. Prior to attending the SDP, many had developed a routine of sleeping during the early part of the day and staying awake during some or all of the early hours of the morning.

> *'I couldn't sleep, I was tossing and turning all night, sweating and waking up at 4 a.m.'*
> *'Before methadone I couldn't sleep until dawn. I was so tired it was terrible, my mind would be whirring round. I just wanted to turn it off.'*
> *'I go to bed at 10.30 p.m. and can wake at 3 a.m. and not get back. It can happen at least two times a week — I'm fucked and it pisses me off.'*

The routine, stimulation, activity and regular eating pattern that occurred when students attended Second Chance have no doubt assisted many to develop a healthier sleeping pattern.

> *'It's got better [sleeping pattern] as my health has improved.'*
> *'... since I've been coming here, you get into a routine.'*

Aspirations

Six months prior to starting at the SDP, the vast majority of students had very low expectations of what they might be able to achieve in life.

'No prospects for someone like me, I gave up years ago thinking I could get a job, I might as well reach for the moon.'
'I'm getting up and coming down here, joining the world, but I don't hold much hope for the future after this course.'
'Not very high, there's a lack of opportunity.'

Many students not only became optimistic and displayed an increased confidence and self-esteem as the programme progressed, but perhaps most importantly many developed specific and realistic individualised plans of how they hoped to progress.

This is illustrated by the comments from one student interviewed over a six-month period.

'I'm hoping that I achieve what I've come here to do. I've some doubt, things could go wrong, but I'm determined.' (Interview 1).
'My confidence has increased, I've lots of outside contacts now, I feel very optimistic now.' (Interview 2).
'I want to be a sound technician — they [Second Chance] are helping. They're starting sound and music in here, I'm really encouraged to get on with what I want to do.' (Interview 3).

In particular, students valued the respect shown to them by staff at the SDP, which was contrary to their everyday experience, and they appreciated being treated as an equal.

It seems that this process, more than anything else, helped develop their self-confidence, and purposeful activity gave them a sense of achievement.

'It's done an awful lot. It's helped me that they trust me. If people trust me then I can help them. They've shown me that there's a nice person inside who can commit to a course. They've helped me with my self-esteem.'
'The respect we were shown, we were treated as an equal — not as a drug user.'
'It'll help me to meet people and definitely give me encouragement. The staff listen to you and are concerned. It's helping me get back into a routine. It's helping me express myself, which I've always found hard in the past.'

Strategies for inclusion

This research indicates how problem drug users experience social and economic exclusion. 'Steps to reintegration' (Figure 1) outlines the phases and difficulties that they encounter in their attempts to reintegrate into the wider non-drug-using community.

Importantly, it also shows the role and importance of structured day programmes like Second Chance. The figure shows the steps to reintegration.

- *Chaotic*: the person has little insight and no real desire to change his/her pattern of drug taking.

- *Ambivalent*: the person sometimes expresses some motivation to change his/her pattern of drug taking but quickly relapses to 'old' habits and thoughts.

- *Action*: the person is clear about his/her future direction and makes a determined and positive effort to do something about his/her drug use.

- *Control*: the person becomes stable and in control of his/her drug taking. He/she may even stop taking illegal drugs completely.

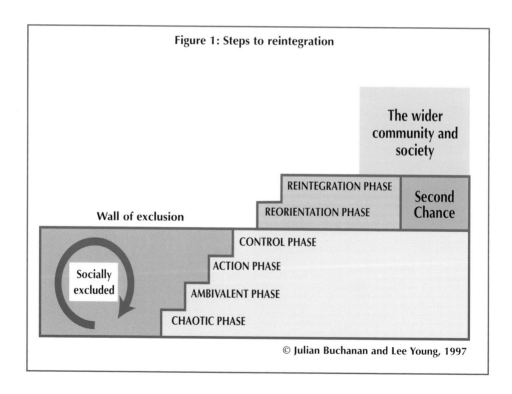

Figure 1: Steps to reintegration

The wider community and society

REINTEGRATION PHASE

REORIENTATION PHASE

Second Chance

Wall of exclusion

CONTROL PHASE

ACTION PHASE

AMBIVALENT PHASE

CHAOTIC PHASE

Socially excluded

© Julian Buchanan and Lee Young, 1997

This process of recovery can take many years, with relapse occurring frequently. Once the 'control phase' has been reached, recovering drug users who seek social reintegration are frequently prevented from gaining access to non-drug-using social networks and are subtly denied opportunities that are available to others, such as voluntary work, educational courses, employment and housing.

This process of structural discrimination we describe as a 'wall of exclusion'. The strong and pervasive stereotype of the 'hopeless addict' has also become an internalised identity that leads to lack of confidence, low self-esteem, low expectations and a lack of marketable skills.

Structured day programmes can provide an empowering environment that supports students through the difficult and challenging 'reorientation phase'. Many Second Chance students appreciated the opportunity to rediscover social relationships. Their social network had previously been dominated by so-called 'acquaintances', whose only real interest was in the drug rather than the person. This rediscovery of social relationships sometimes involved facing up to emotions, recognising responsibilities, becoming accountable and learning to trust and be trusted.

Conclusions

The majority of students who took part in this research have been socially excluded for most of their lives. It could be argued that, for many of those attending Second Chance, it was for them a 'first chance', an opportunity to prove their capability to themselves, their families and the wider community.

The important contribution of structured day programmes should not, therefore, be understated: they play an important part in enabling marginalised groups such as problem drug users to take advantage of educational, training and employment opportunities. Without such programmes, many of these people will be unable to break through the 'wall of exclusion' and will remain trapped within a life dominated by chronically relapsing drug use.

Julian Buchanan is Senior Lecturer and course leader for the MA in Substance Misuse at the University of Central Lancashire, UK. Lee Young is a lecturer at Liverpool University, UK.

Acknowledgements

This chapter is based on Buchanan, J. and Young, L. (1998) *The Impact of the Second Chance Structured Day Programme for Recovering Drug Users: a Student Perspective,* Liverpool: Social Partnership, Transit. Available from Amazon books.

DRUG MARKETS

PART VI

INTRODUCTION

*T*he first chapter of this section, Chapter 18, summarises a review drawn up by the EMCDDA workgroup on the relationship between drugs and crime. This review focused on the past, present and future role of qualitative research in exploring the extent and nature of the drugs–crime relationship. The chapter highlights the paucity of studies on the drugs–crime relationship and addresses the problems of collecting such data. It then identifies the themes and contributions already apparent in various EU countries and concludes that community-wide collaborative studies are now being funded to explore the real differences in the way the drug problem is defined and responded to, both between and within Member States.

On the basis of data derived from the Rotterdam Drug Monitoring System (DMS), Chapter 19, by Peter Blanken, Cas Barendregt and Linda Zuidmulder, describes some aspects of retail-level drug dealing in Rotterdam in the market of marginalised (almost) daily users of heroin and cocaine. The authors describe how retail-level drug dealers, operating from 'house-dealing addresses', have reacted to changes in local drug enforcement policies and analyse the retail-level illegal drug market in terms of business economy concepts. The chapter also addresses the feasibility of regulating the local drug market, taking into account the views of police officers, drug users and retail dealers, non-drug users and health outreach workers. In this way, the authors demonstrate how qualitative community-based research can contribute to understanding the development of the retail supply side of the illegal drug market.

In Chapter 20, Michel Schiray describes an experimental project in three cities and in the 'techno dance' scene which combined indirect methods, such as court records, with direct interviews. The project confirmed that French organised crime is involved in the French drug market, side by side with the individual chains established by young people and immigrant populations. He concludes that applying qualitative research and more traditional indirect methods to all the drug markets in France, and at European level, would result in a better understanding of the drug distribution market and trafficking between countries.

In Chapter 21, Letizia Paoli shows how qualitative methodologies can be fruitfully employed to evaluate police reports and judicial documents concerning the higher levels of the drug supply system. She argues that, by interpreting law enforcement data through the lenses of scientifically sound hypotheses, it is possible to reach conclusions which contrast with official theories and dogmas. In particular, the information provided by pentiti (literally 'penitent' prosecution witnesses) has provided knowledge about the phenomenon of the Mafia and organised crime in Italy, which has reached a level previously inconceivable. She concludes that, although judicial and police statistics and reports are only a second-best source of information, they are too important to be left solely to moral entrepreneurs.

Karen Ellen Spannow's ethnographic study of an illegal drug market in a Danish town provides the focus of Chapter 22. This study was undertaken to examine the effect of police control strategies that aimed to reduce the supply of illegal drugs and the various criminal activities which financed their use. Spannow presents findings which demonstrate that qualitative research has the potential for deconstructing some of the myths that haunt the discussion on illegal drugs and, consequently, for inspiring more rational responses to illegal drug use. She describes a market in which the majority of drug users obtain drugs from a private address and only the most desperate were forced to buy on the open market.

In Chapter 23, Mark Gilman describes how the closed markets of 15 years ago in a north-western English city (resembling those described by Spannow in Denmark) have changed. He argues that policing methods have played a part in shaping the impersonal and dangerous modern market in Manchester today, where heroin distribution has become centralised in open street markets in the inner city which are difficult to police. New dealers are now in the business simply to make money and the prison experience has become more commonplace and normative in many working-class areas. Gilman concludes that the police can become real partners in multi-agency drug work by setting modest, but achievable, goals of disrupting the heroin business rather than unachievable goals of eradicating drugs.

CHAPTER 18

EXPLORING RELATIONSHIPS BETWEEN ILLICIT DRUGS AND CRIME: QUALITATIVE RESEARCH ACROSS THE EUROPEAN UNION

Howard Parker, Jane Fountain, Peter Blanken, Uwe Kemmesies, Letizia Paoli and Karen Ellen Spannow

The review of qualitative social and criminological research on the drugs–crime relationship, compiled by the EMCDDA drugs–crime workgroup, is one component of a longer-term strategy to explore the significance and potential of qualitative social and criminological research in describing relationships between illicit drugs and crime.

This project is, in turn, part of a broader EMCDDA mission to consolidate knowledge and develop new collaborative initiatives across the EU with respect to drugs research generally. The workgroup's review focuses on the past, present and future role of qualitative research in exploring the extent and nature of the drugs–crime relationship. It builds on a literature search already undertaken, with additional data from a network of qualitative researchers across the EU, which was identified as part of two projects: 'Inventory, bibliography and synthesis of qualitative research in the European Union' and 'Coordination of working groups of qualitative researchers to analyse different drug use patterns and the implications for public health strategies and prevention' (Fountain and Griffiths, 1997; 1998; 1999).

This chapter summarises the workgroup's review of the extent of qualitative research into the drugs–crime relationship and the problems of collecting such data, and highlights the themes and contributions already apparent in various EU member countries.

Methods

There is no easy way of effectively collecting and synthesising current knowledge about the drugs–crime relationship across 15 countries. Much has been gained by electronic literature and citation index searches and regular contact with experts in each country, but, with research reported in many languages and with diverse traditions regarding dissemination, such searches have their limitations. The key example of this is the 'grey' literature, such as reports to organisations that have commissioned research in a region or city. Such publications are traditionally for internal consumption only or have a limited circulation, and are written in one language. They must be obtained through international networking if our goal is to produce a comprehensive and sophisticated analysis that sets these research findings in a cultural, political and conceptual context. Without this sophistication, we are unlikely to have a realistic view of what can be achieved through future attempts at collaboration.

The workgroup's review involved six researchers networking over several months in order to identify the relevant qualitative research. By producing reviews for all EU countries and then attempting to produce a synthesis, we have, hopefully, effectively described the current situation and begun to assess both the pitfalls and the potential for extending research into drugs–crime issues with the assistance of qualitative research methods.

Drugs and crime: the research disparity

Our ability to describe the nature and extent of research into the drugs–crime relationship has developed rapidly in the past few years, given the impetus of the EMCDDA both as a funder and ongoing collector of secondary data. The EMCDDA's annual reports on the state of the drugs problem in the European Union (e.g. EMCDDA, 1998), based on information gathered by national focal points using standard templates for data collection and collation of results from across the Union, provide an acid test of data availability.

It is thus salutary that, whilst enormous progress has been made in some areas in collation, attempts to collect and collate findings on drug use and crime have not been able to produce a satisfactory data set and consequently a knowledge base covering the EU (beyond official statistics). This is due to both the absence of research results from several Member States and the diversity of approaches and formats of those who do offer data.

Although new ventures are rapidly improving the situation (e.g. European Forum for Urban Security, 1998), a picture of unevenness and of a lack of systematic or thematic research into the drugs–crime issue has also been found in the most recent and most focused European networking research ventures. At best, an overall audit would capture studies of the following topics, as listed by Bless et al. (EMCDDA, 1996):

- patterns of offences/offenders in drug law violations (e.g. possession, supply);
- criminal behaviour in specific groups of drug users (e.g. known heroin addicts);
- drug use amongst identified groups of criminals;
- the temporal and causal relationship between drugs and crime in some groups;
- local illicit drug markets (distribution, economics);
- open drug scenes and public nuisance;
- the relationship of drug markets to local licit economies and criminal markets;
- lifestyles and 'careers' of (selected) illegal drug users;

- description of police enforcement policies; and
- impact of public health interventions (e.g. methadone treatment) on criminality.

The study by Bless et al. of drug-related urban petty crime and the responses to it also offers many insights into the difficulties and dilemmas involved in collaborative network research, whether its aim is to collate and synthesise available knowledge or to set about commissioning collaborative, comparative, inter-country research programmes.

We are warned of the difficulties and pitfalls encountered in defining and capturing the meaning of terms across languages (e.g. 'petty', 'delinquency'). We are advised that there is a lack of connection within Member States between local research data collection/project development and evaluation, on the one hand, and the national and international academic social science–criminology–addictions literature, on the other.

Attempting to access grey literature from 'outside', as described above, is problematic. The converse is also true in that, in most Member States, local policy-makers and the criminal justice system have little easy access to the international academic literature, such as the effect of methadone treatment on crime or the consequences of dispersing open drugs scenes.

This disjunction is particularly obvious when we move away from quantitative research and towards qualitative endeavours. An associated observation made by previous networkers is that those drug-related 'problems' which have the highest political and public perception priority are not necessarily the best researched.

> *The availability of information in the cities is inversely related to the extent to which different categories of drug-related crimes are perceived as important policy priorities. Whilst data on offences against the drug laws are commonly available, data on street dealing, public nuisance and drug-related property crimes are fewer and usually of poor quality.* (EMCDDA, 1996)

A more comprehensive picture of research, particularly qualitative inquiry into drugs–crime relationships, is provided by ongoing search and monitoring work commissioned by the EMCDDA, which backs up this finding. For example, of 551 references involving drugs research with a qualitative component, only 43 were focused on a crime dimension. Moreover, of 89 projects with a qualitative component currently being undertaken, only 10 were concerned with aspects of crime and even these included studies of drug users in prison (Fountain and Griffiths, 1999).

In summary, although the networking strategies discussed above have had distinctive primary goals, they shared one common objective — collating research into the drugs–crime issue. Despite considerable resources and effort, it is significant that they reached the same conclusions: there is only a small amount of literature on the issue, most of which is quantitative; this literature is unevenly spread across member countries; and it is disparate in its nature. Furthermore, it would be unwise to detach such research findings from their temporal and political context, in that we need to understand them in terms of their objectives and functions within the societies where they were conducted.

The workgroup's review: a summary

The workgroup's review reports on qualitative research in five areas.

Supply, distribution and local drug markets

As collective interest in drug market and drugs tourism grows (e.g. European Forum for Urban Security, 1998), and the complexity of their development and maintenance becomes clearer, there will — or should — be far more collaborative research effort. Much of this will be quantitative, but the need for qualitative inquiry is unequivocal. Some recent research has been driven by public concern about the visibility and nuisance attached to open markets (e.g. in Germany and the Netherlands). In addition, with the creation of a single Community market with fewer restrictions on migration and travel across the EU, we are becoming more aware of links between nationality, organised crime and drug markets (Dorn et al., 1998) and a dynamic relationship between countries which supply drugs and those where they are consumed.

In short, as globalisation continues, the likelihood of any Member State protecting itself from drugs availability or associated problems through unilateral action diminishes. However, it is quite clear that solutions are not easy to come by: we are only beginning to understand the unintended consequences that flow from closing down specific drug markets.

Drug users' lifestyles and careers

Little qualitative research has been undertaken focusing on the lifestyles and careers of drug users within the EU, yet, where it has (e.g. the Netherlands and the United Kingdom), much insight has been gained. With problem drug use and social exclusion being clearly linked in so many Member States, and with addicts and junkies being so despised and stigmatised across the Union, the need to better understand and humanise these lifestyles seems self-evident.

Drugs–crime relationships

As Figure 1 illustrates, by far the most research effort has gone into exploring the relationship between drugs and crime, primarily at the user level. It is abundantly clear from the review that, where this is carefully undertaken, numerous different relationships are found and the picture becomes complicated, far more so than the politicians' view that 'all drug use leads to further crime'.

Figure 1: A simplified overview of qualitative research activity on the drugs–crime relationship across the EU

Topic	Belgium	Denmark	Germany	Greece	Spain	France	Ireland	Italy	Luxembourg	Netherlands	Austria	Portugal	Finland	Sweden	UK
Supply, distribution and local drug markets	–	•	•	–	•	•	–	•	–	•	•	–	•	–	•
Drug users' lifestyles and careers	–	–	•	–	•	–	–	–	–	•	–	–	–	•	•
Drugs–crime relationships	•	•	•	•	•	•	•	•	•	–	•	•	–	•	•
Enforcement and criminal justice	–	•	•	–	•	•	–	•	–	•	–	•	–	•	–
Treatment and welfare responses	–	•	•	–	–	–	–	–	–	•	–	–	–	–	•
Strong qualitative tradition?			✓		✓	✓		✓							✓

Figure 2 outlines the range of different relationships — and indeed non-relationships — which European research has identified. We should note, for instance, that there is little evidence of a crime consequence (beyond possession/use infraction) from the enormous recreational drugs scene across Europe (relationship (a)). Alternatively, there is an almost universally identified connection between 'hard' dependent drug use, poverty and acquisitive crime (relationship (e)) and at the level of organised supply and trafficking (relationship (c)). There is still very little research on the impact of drug intoxication on offending (relationship (d)). Significantly, studies in most EU countries have identified the complexities around the relationship between criminal careers which merely involve — rather than are driven by — dependent drug use (relationship (b)).

Figure 2: The crime–drugs/drugs–crime matrix

Crime	Key connections	Drugs
Offenders who never/occasionally take drugs	(a) → None ←	Drug users (recreational and dependent) who rarely/never break the law (other than by using illicit substances)
'Lifestyle' offenders, mainly young adults, whose crime is about sustaining a lifestyle which includes drug use	(b) → Unclear ←	Drugs are primarily part of a crime lifestyle; rates of use are determined by available resources
'Strategic' offenders who supply drugs for illegal financial gain	(c) → Strong ←	Drug dealers/suppliers who are primarily involved in financial/illegal gain
Offenders, not regular drug users, who under the influence of a psychoactive drug commit 'out of character' offences	(d) → Occasional ←	Drug users who under the influence of a psychoactive drug commit 'out of character' offences
Offenders prior to heavy drug use, which produced, accelerated and aggravated crime–drugs careers	(e) → Strong ←	Drug users whose dependency moved them beyond legitimate financing into crime and often complex drugs–crime careers

Enforcement and criminal justice

Qualitative research activity varies greatly across countries with respect to exploring the role of the police, courts and prison in defining, containing and managing 'drug' offenders. This topic reminds us that the stimulus for particular research styles and themes is often embedded in a particular society's cultural and intellectual traditions.

In France, for instance, such research is borne of a 'liberal' concern with stigma and even deviance with respect to State intervention, whereas the stimulus in modern Germany is somewhat different: research into policing repeatedly shows that, of the whole drugs distribution industry, it is low-level visible drug dealers and user-dealers, often 'migrants', who receive the most scrutiny and are the most prosecuted and punished. The question must be asked whether these operations are the appropriate target for such a high proportion of enforcement time and resources. Qualitative 'underdog' investigations have a tendency to pose such politically awkward questions.

Treatment and welfare responses

Most research on treatment uses quantitative methods, but a qualitative approach is important when we are dealing with hard-to-reach problem drug users. As the development of multi-professional initiatives to intervene in the lives of problem drug users continues, the kinds of studies undertaken in the Netherlands and the UK, which focus on the perceptions and impacts on users, will also be far more valued. Currently, however, a robust research literature has developed only in evaluations of methadone programmes.

Conclusions

We do not claim to have produced a comprehensive review of all the qualitative research conducted on drugs–crime relationships in the EU, for the reasons discussed earlier. Nonetheless, we hope to have provided a useful template and a first attempt at an overview of qualitative research activity with a drugs–crime focus.

In the EU as a whole, there is a dearth of studies on drugs–crime relationships in general, yet many aspects of this relationship cannot realistically be undertaken without utilising ethnographic and qualitative techniques. As shown by Figure 1, the qualitative tradition has an intrinsic role in social research in only five Member States (Germany, France, Italy, the Netherlands and the UK) and is almost totally absent in the same number. The topics which have attracted qualitative research also vary considerably.

We have noted how the qualitative technique has either been neglected or has played only a minor part in the research traditions of some Member States. Aside from the academic debates about the validity of qualitative methods, one of the key reasons for this is that such studies tend to produce politically difficult and uncomfortable conclusions: the qualitative approach, when applied to analysing facets of the 'drugs problem', will sometimes challenge current wisdom and public and political analyses.

Such studies often find that official policy and practice are ineffective because they are based on misconceptions and oversimplifications. Moreover, by creating new knowledge, qualitative studies sometimes expose contradictions in official responses: they can show that certain assumptions and everyday interventions lead to stereotyping and injustice. However, as the EU matures and confronts issues of racism and discrimination against 'migrants', and recognises that the actions of one Member State impact on others (e.g. drug tourism), its ability to deal with complexity and contradiction is increasing. This is already being witnessed in the funding of Community-wide collaborative studies and a willingness to explore the real differences in the way the 'drugs problem' is defined and responded to, both between and within Member States.

The authors are members of the EMCDDA workgroup on the drugs–crime relationship (1997–98). This chapter is taken from their review of the qualitative research in this area, the full version of which includes profiles for each EU Member State and can be found on http://www.qed.org.uk.

References

Dorn, N., Oette, L. and White, S. (1998) 'Drugs importation and the bifurcation of risk: capitalisation, cut outs and organised crime', *British Journal of Criminology*, 38, 537–560.

EMCDDA (1996) *Pilot Project on Drug-Related Urban Petty Crime*, Lisbon: EMCDDA.

EMCDDA (1998) *Annual Report on the State of the Drugs Problem in the European Union*, Lisbon: EMCDDA.

European Forum for Urban Security (1998) *Drug-Related Cross-Border Traffic Patterns*, Paris: European Forum for Urban Security.

Fountain, J. and Griffiths, P. (Eds.) (1997) *Inventory, Bibliography, and Synthesis of Qualitative Research in the European Union*, Lisbon/London: EMCDDA/NAC.

Fountain, J. and Griffiths, P. (Eds.) (1998) *Coordination of Working Groups of Qualitative Researchers to Analyse Different Drug Use Patterns and the Implications for Public Health Strategies and Prevention*, Lisbon/London: EMCDDA/NAC.

Fountain, J. and Griffiths, P. (Eds.) (1999) 'Synthesis of qualitative research on drug use in the European Union: report on an EMCDDA project', *European Addiction Research*, 5, 4–20.

RETAIL-LEVEL DRUG DEALING IN ROTTERDAM

Peter Blanken, Cas Barendregt and Linda Zuidmulder

Over recent decades, the vast majority of drug research has been directed at studying the prevalence of drug use, the characteristics of drug users, the possible causes and consequences of drug use and the effectiveness of prevention and treatment programmes.

Comparatively little is known about the way in which illicit drugs are sold. Of course, there are some exceptions, mostly from the US (e.g. Adler, 1985; Williams, 1989; Bourgois, 1995). In the Netherlands, Korf and Verbraeck (1993) used data from ethnographic fieldwork and interviews to demonstrate that dealers operating at the 'middle' level of the drug markets, distributing cannabis, cocaine, amphetamines or ecstasy, strongly reacted and pro-acted to developments in local drug-enforcement tactics. As far as drug dealing at the consumer or retail level is concerned, some studies have addressed street dealing (Mieczkowski, 1986; MacCoun and Reuter, 1992; Berg and Andersen, 1993).

Less is known about the effects of policy measures on the drug market. Prices and quality of drugs at the retail or consumption level are assumed to be related to the influx of illegal drugs into the market. It is assumed that, in times of shortage, prices might rise and quality might drop, while in times of abundance the opposite occurs. A recent longitudinal study in Australia, however, could not show any significant relationship between the amount of heroin seized, the price and quality at the retail level, and the perceived availability of heroin among drug users entering treatment (Weatherburn and Lind, 1997).

This chapter describes some aspects of retail-level drug dealing in Rotterdam in the market of marginalised (almost) daily users of heroin and cocaine. The first section describes how retail-level drug dealers, operating from 'house-dealing addresses', have reacted to changes in local drug-enforcement policies. In the second section, some results are presented on a closed meeting in which the feasibility of regulating the local drug market was discussed. The third section summarises an analysis of the retail-level illegal drug market in terms of business economy concepts.

The majority of the data are derived from the Rotterdam drug monitoring system (DMS), which combines qualitative and quantitative research methods to study drug users outside the treatment system in their natural habitat. Information is collected from a network of key contact persons (such as drug users and dealers, health outreach workers and police officers), yearly small random sample surveys among marginalised (almost) daily heroin and cocaine users, and the cornerstone of the DMS, community fieldworkers (see Chapter 36).

Retail-level drug dealers' responses to police enforcement

Over the years, a line of qualitative field research has been established in Rotterdam in which the supply side of the illegal — mainly heroin and cocaine — market has been described (e.g. Blanken and Adriaans, 1993; Grund, 1993; Blanken et al., 1996; Barendregt et al., 1998) and developments in this market have been monitored (Blanken and Barendregt, 1998). Data collected by the Rotterdam DMS showed the effects of a more repressive police enforcement operation (code-named 'Victor'). Dealers operating at the retail level from house-dealing addresses responded to the Victor operation by changing the conditions under which they were selling heroin and (base-) cocaine (Blanken and Barendregt, 1998).

One result of Victor was that the majority of dealers raised the minimum unit of sale of heroin and cocaine base. Thus, for instance, instead of selling small amounts of 0.1 gram of heroin for NLG 10 (EUR 4.5), they sold in quantities of no less than a quarter of a gram for NLG 25 (EUR 11.3). They had at least two reasons for doing so. Firstly, it reduced the number of customers and secondly — and simultaneously — the number of movements in and out of the house was reduced.

Parallel to the increase in the units of sale, the dealers limited the amount of time drug users were allowed to stay at the address to consume their drugs. Alternatively, they no longer allowed customers to use drugs on the premises. Finally, these house-dealing addresses changed the cocaine product they sold from cocaine-hydrochloride to smokable cocaine base or crack cocaine. Although this was partly in response to drug users' preferences (Blanken et al., 1996), it also contributed to the policy of reducing the time buyers were allowed to stay at the dealing address. By selling ready-to-smoke cocaine base, it was no longer necessary for drug users to prepare it themselves [1].

Blanken and Barendregt (1998) concluded that increased police repression of a local drug market is followed by a reorganisation of drug-dealing practices that is aimed at the 'self-protection' of the dealers and that might be at the expense of drug users' interests.

Feasibility of 'regulating' retail-level drug dealing

A DMS-related project (Blanken and Hendriks, 1996) addressed the feasibility of regulating the supply side of the illegal drug market. In a closed meeting, representatives from different parties affected by the undesired side-effects of drug dealing under prohibition discussed the potential ways in which drug dealing could contribute to — as formulated by the participants in the discussion — 'the general well-being of both drug-using and non-drug-using citizens'.

---

[1] It should be emphasised that, for many years, smoking heroin from tinfoil (i.e. chasing the dragon) and basing cocaine out of a small — often self-made — base-pipe have been the predominant routes of drug taking for the majority of marginalised (almost) daily heroin and cocaine users.

Local neighbourhood police officers, non-drug-using citizens, drug users, retail-level drug dealers, and community health outreach workers — all speaking in confidence and on their own behalf — started to formulate domains of interest and sets of demands as to how they could imagine retail-level drug dealing might be regulated (see Figure 1).

Figure 1: Domains of interest and sets of demands with respect to the feasibility of regulating drug-dealing addresses

	Drug users	Local residents	Neighbour-hood police	Drug dealers	Treatment/ health outreach workers
Make-up and situation of dealing address					
Own entry			•		
Away from street scene			•		
Distributed over the city		•			
Accessibility	•				•
Separate rooms (e.g. to inject)	•				•
Dealer and personnel					
Attitude towards, and reputation among, drug users	•		•	•	•
No record of convictions; low profile		•	•		
Social responsibility				•	•
Managerial responsibility: inside and outside				•	
Sales and profit				•	
Customers of dealing address					
Steady group of customers		•	•		
Small-scale	•	•	•		
From street scene			•		
Drug supply and other services offered					
Quality and price of substances	•				
(Free) drug use paraphernalia	•				•
Meals	•				
Diversity (take-away/opening hours)	•		•		
Stimulating drug treatment contact					•
House rules and regulations					
Behavioural code: both indoors and outdoors	•	•			
Length of stay (minimum/maximum duration)	•		•		
Number of in- and outgoing movements		•	•		
No hanging around outside; tidy up outdoors		•			
Be properly dressed		•			
Drug sale only indoors		•			
Payment in cash (no goods)		•	•		
Control of regulation process					
Procedure for complaints		•	•	•	
Contact between dealer, consumers, police, local residents and health outreach workers			•	•	

For instance, it was agreed that dealing addresses should only serve a limited number of customers, and only those who had roots in the specific neighbourhood. It was also agreed that they should have preset opening hours, provide drug users with the necessary drug paraphernalia, and operate in an atmosphere that promoted controlled patterns of drug use and reduced drug-related harm.

It was concluded that there was some agreement between the different parties in defining the domains of interest and sets of demands that could possibly contribute to a regulation of dealing addresses in order to arrive at a more controllable situation. However, given local differences, it was questionable whether one general blueprint could be defined: it was argued that, within the domains of interest, sets of demands should ideally be defined to match each new situation. Finally, it was suggested that initiatives should, as much as possible, make use of existing situations and, for instance, seek cooperation with drug dealers who had been operating in a certain neighbourhood for some time without causing nuisance and who had no other criminal involvement (Blanken and Hendriks, 1996).

Drug dealing in the light of business economy concepts

Based on qualitative DMS field observations, three different forms of retail-level drug dealing in the market of marginalised heroin and cocaine users have been described in terms of the business economy concepts of 'corporate objectives' and 'marketing mix' (Barendregt et al., 1998). The first was a regular house-dealing address located in the apartment of a dependent drug user, run by Zappa. The second were two dealing addresses, called 'the basements', run by two men and financially facilitated and supervised by a representative of a foundation affiliated with the Paulus Church (²). The third was a group of young men who were primarily dealing cocaine base in a street 'copping' (buying illicit drugs) area.

There appeared to be large differences between the three different dealing practices with respect to the corporate objectives the dealers pursued. While the basements primarily aimed at continuation, the emphasis for the others was much more on short-term profit. These corporate activities materialised in the way the dealers positioned their merchandise on the market. The way in which the actual selling of heroin and cocaine was organised included measures taken by the dealer to control nuisance for the non-drug-using community (see Figure 2).

An illustration of these differences can be seen in the selection of customers — the regular house-dealing address, aiming at short-term profit, went to great lengths to

---

(²) The Paulus Church and its pastor, Hans Visser, have a long tradition of standing up for the most marginalised members of society. Since the early 1980s, the Paulus Church has been closely collaborating with Nico Adriaans and the Rotterdam Junkie Union. This has led to — among other things — a night shelter, the provision of warm meals, medical care for the uninsured, and the establishment of drug-using rooms (one of which was *Perron Nul* or Platform Zero). The experiences of the Paulus Church with drug-using rooms has underlined the potential importance of drug dealers in the process of controlling drug use patterns and its consequences (Visser, 1996).

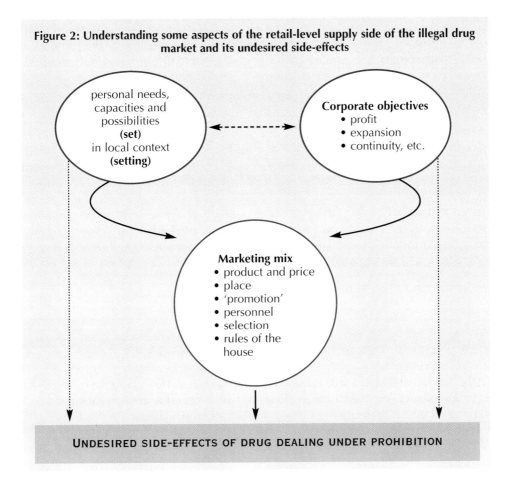

Figure 2: Understanding some aspects of the retail-level supply side of the illegal drug market and its undesired side-effects

attract as many customers as possible, in spite of the undesired nuisance consequences.

> *Meanwhile a tough competitive struggle over customers is going on between Zappa and another dealer, Jan. Zappa knows what's what with respect to dealing. In a few days he has managed to build quite a list of customers. He is snatching Jan's customers by calling them in before they arrive at Jan's address. Because of this Jan is furious ... [Later] when I arrived at Leo's apartment, the place where Zappa is dealing, Jan was there. He was drunk and stoned and swaying with a chopping-knife. The only reaction he elicited from Zappa was that Zappa picked up the phone and asked Jan to look outside. In front of the address was a car with a couple of guys showing Jan their guns. Having seen that, Jan returned home, heavily cursing. (Field note: October 1997)*

In contrast, the basements tried to control the size of their customer group, which contributed to a relatively tranquil atmosphere at the address and little nuisance for the neighbours.

> By the time we are leaving, two customers move from the smoking area towards the counter. A white man in his late 20s asks Pedro, the dealer, if his friend can get a 'membership card' (become one of Pedro's customers): 'He is okay, just like me. We are working together.' He sings the praises of his friend with the moustache. Pedro replies that the basement is full and that his friend should try at the other basement address. Without further discussion the two of them leave the premises. Rasta Peter, the doorkeeper, follows them and closes the door. (Field note: December 1997)

For the young men selling cocaine base in the street 'copping' area, the actual selling seemed to be of secondary importance. Gaining a 'reputation' by engaging in bravado behaviour appeared to be more important than striving for financial economic goals.

> Dealer Larry talks about the tension among the street dealers. Because the many dealers have too few customers to serve and too little space to work, some sort of boredom comes up. Therefore, the dealers start to provoke customers or whoever happens to pass by. The dealers do whatever they want to, it might even be to someone from 'their own' group, as long as it results in sensation and a thrill. A little later Uli, another street dealer, left his apartment and was curious what we were talking about and joined the group. He admitted that everything was just meant to be 'a big joke, a laugh', and he added: 'I am a dirty bastard and everybody that trusts me is stupid.' I did not deny that. (Field note: October 1997)

Barendregt et al. (1998) conclude that the extent of self-regulation among retail-level drug dealers is closely related to their corporate objectives. The more dealers aim at continuity, the more inclined they are to organise their dealing practices in ways that consider the interests of non-drug-using residents. The basement addresses have succeeded the most in reducing nuisance and creating an atmosphere of tranquillity and respect. The core ingredients of this 'success' are situated in the fact that the basements and their personnel have grown from within the drug scene and that the basements are small-scale operations. However, small-scale operating dealing

Figure 3: Drug dealing categorisation along a 'mobile/location-bound' dimension

Mobile drug dealing		Location-bound drug dealing	
+	Mobility		–
Street dealing	Dealing by mobile phone	House-dealing address	Facilitated

addresses have small-scale financial margins and perhaps, as Barendregt et al. state, it is necessary that they somehow are supported in order to survive financially.

The financial aspects of retail-level drug dealing were further studied in a DMS-related research project in which 17 'active' (i.e. not incarcerated) drug dealers were interviewed (Ponsioen et al., 1999). Results showed that, for many respondents, financing their own drug use was their primary motive for dealing. Categorised along a 'mobile/location-bound' dimension (see Figure 3), the mobile — primarily street — dealers were able to finance their own heroin and cocaine use, and earned approximately NLG 75 (EUR 34) a day. In order to achieve this, they worked long hours and served around 15 customers. The location-bound dealers (at the house-dealing addresses and the facilitated dealers of the Paulus Church and the basements) had a larger clientele — around 35 drug users — and worked well over eight hours per day. Given their higher costs (rent, electricity, personnel such as a doorman, and additional services provided to the drug users), however, they did not earn large amounts of money either. At the end of the day they had covered their own drug use and earned approximately NLG 130 (EUR 59) each in cash.

Conclusions

The Rotterdam drug control policy is in a continuous process of development and refinement. Over the past few years, more extreme policy measures have been discussed in order to address the drugs–health and the drugs–crime and nuisance relationship. These drug policy measures range from compulsory treatment of (dependent) drug users who have been in repeated contact with police, via the development of drug use rooms, to discussions on the possibility of regulating some forms of drug dealing.

As has been briefly sketched in the foregoing paragraphs, qualitative community-based research can contribute to understanding the development of the retail-level supply side of the illegal drug market. Although it is recognised that the results cannot be generalised to other Dutch cities — let alone to other European countries — some of the mechanisms that seem to operate at the retail level of drug dealing may also have validity in other settings.

Retail-level drug dealers organise their business according to their personal capacities and possibilities in a specific local context. They decide upon their corporate objectives, in which short-term (large) profits and continuity (combined with smaller profits) seem to compete. Implicitly or explicitly, they settle upon a 'marketing mixture'. This complex system of personal, setting and marketing mix characteristics might determine the extent to which drug dealing contributes to, or reduces, the undesired side-effects of drug dealing under prohibition.

Compulsive and harmful drug consumption patterns can be considered as an undesired side-effect of drug use that might be related to specific forms of drug dealing as well. It has been argued elsewhere that the setting in which drugs are used may support drug users' strategies to self-regulate consumption patterns (Grund, 1993;

Blanken et al., 1997). Another aspect of the undesired side-effects of drug dealing is nuisance, as experienced by non-drug-using neighbouring residents. A number of reports have documented that drug dealing can be organised in such a way that nuisance is reduced (Blanken and Adriaans, 1993; Barendregt et al., 1998).

It might thus be a challenge for future qualitative research to contribute to unravelling the relationships between drug dealing and the undesired side-effects of drug dealing under prohibition for drug-using and non-drug-using residents.

Peter Blanken was Senior Researcher at the Addiction Research Institute, Rotterdam (IVO), and is now on the Central Committee on the Treatment of Heroin Addicts (CCBH), Utrecht, the Netherlands. Cas Barendregt is Coordinator of Community Fieldwork at IVO. Linda Zuidmulder is a community fieldworker at IVO.

References

Adler, P. A. (1985) *Wheeling and Dealing: an Ethnography of an Upper-Level Drug Dealing and Smuggling Community*, New York: Columbia University Press.

Barendregt, C., Blanken, P. and Zuidmulder, L. J. (1998) *Drugshandel en overlast in Rotterdam (Drug Dealing and Nuisance in Rotterdam)*, Rotterdam: Instituut voor Verslavingsonderzoek (IVO)/Erasmus Universiteit Rotterdam.

Berg, J. E. and Andersen, S. (1993) 'Street sale of heroin: a profitable way of making a living?', *Drug and Alcohol Dependence*, 32, 287–291.

Blanken, P. and Adriaans, N. F. P. (1993) *ECHOs van een mespuntje fantasie, (ECHOs of a Knife Tip of Fantasy)*, Rotterdam: Instituut voor Verslavingsonderzoek (IVO)/Erasmus Universiteit Rotterdam.

Blanken, P. and Barendregt, C. (1998) 'De illegale drugsmarkt in Rotterdam: Enkele resultaten van het Rotterdams Drug Monitoring Systeem 1995–1997', *Tijdschrift voor de Politie*, 60(4), 14–19.

Blanken, P., Barendregt, C. and Hendriks, V. (1997) *Een onderzoek naar het roken van cocaïne-base en zelf-controle mechanismen: Op is op. Niets is voor altijd! (A Study of Smoking Cocaine-Base and Mechanisms of Self-Regulation)* (IVO series 14), Rotterdam: Erasmus Universiteit Rotterdam/Instituut voor Verslavingsonderzoek (IVO).

Blanken, P., Barendregt, C., Vollemans, L. and Hendriks, V. (1996) *Druggebruikers in Feijenoord: een onderzoek naar hun situatie en behoeften met betrekking tot het kopen en gebruiken van drugs, huisvesting, inkomsten en tijdsbesteding* (IVO series 9), Rotterdam: Erasmus Universiteit Rotterdam/Instituut voor Verslavingsonderzoek (IVO).

Blanken, P. and Hendriks, V. (1996) 'Mogelijkheden tot regulering van de aanbodzijde van de illegale drugsmarkt ter beheersing van de ongewenste neven-effecten van druggebruik en -handel', in T. Quadt (Ed.) *Verantwoord Schoon in Rotterdam: Een aanzet tot een discussie over interventies op de aanbodzijde van de gebruikersmarkt in Rotterdam*, Rotterdam: Gemeentelijke Gezondheidsdienst voor Rotterdam/Projectbureau Verslavingszaken.

Bourgois, P. (1995) *In Search of Respect: Selling Crack in El Barrio*, Cambridge: Cambridge University Press.

Grund, J.-P. C. (1993) *Drug Use as a Social Ritual: Functionality, Symbolism and Determinants of Self-Regulation* (dissertation) (IVO series 4), Rotterdam: Addiction Research Institute (IVO)/Erasmus University Rotterdam.

Korf, D. and Verbraeck, H. (1993) *Dealers en dienders (Dealers and Policemen)*, Amsterdam: Universiteit van Amsterdam/Criminologisch Instituut 'Bonger'.

MacCoun, R. and Reuter, P. (1992) 'Are the wages of sin $30 an hour? Economic aspects of street-level drug dealing', special issue of *Drugs and Crime, Crime & Delinquency*, 38(4), 477–491.

Mieczkowski, T. (1986) 'Geeking up and throwing down: heroin street life in Detroit', Criminology, 24(4), 645–666.

Ponsioen, A., Blanken, P. and Barendregt, C. (1999) *Een onderzoek naar de economie van de drughandel op detailhandelsniveau: Mag 't een grammetje minder zijn? (A Study of the Economics of Drug Dealing at the Retail Level: Can It Be a Gram Less?)* (IVO series 19), Rotterdam: Erasmus Universiteit Rotterdam/Instituut voor Verslavingsonderzoek (IVO).

Visser, H. (1996) *Perron Nul: Opgang en ondergang (Platform Zero: Rise and Fall),* Zoetermeer: Meinema.

Weatherburn, D. and Lind, B. (1997) 'The impact of law enforcement activity on a heroin market', *Addiction,* 92(5), 557–569.

Williams, T. (1989) *The Cocaine Kids: the Inside Story of a Teenage Drug Ring,* Reading, MA: Addison-Wesley.

CHAPTER 20

ILLICIT DRUG DISTRIBUTION ORGANISATION IN FRANCE: METHODOLOGICAL EXPERIMENTATION AT THREE LEVELS OF RESEARCH

Michel Schiray

For an economist, quantification at micro level and, particularly, at macro level is a prime preoccupation, but in the area of illegal drug trafficking there is a dearth of quantitative tools. Data from systematic administrative records and/or general surveys that are carried out on a regular basis are required, but these are usually available only in a fragmented form in a few countries. These quantitative data are also incomplete, unreliable and circumstantial, or else they are biased by political considerations or by more direct operational factors at national and international level. Data are also susceptible to various types of methodological or political manipulation, which considerably hinders scientific investigation. The experience of the Centre National de la Recherche Scientifique (CNRS) suggests that more research is called for in this field than in those such as economics and social affairs, which are more visible than illegal drug trafficking and easier to monitor on a regular basis. The approach should be based on qualitative methods, in order to confirm the quantitative exercises, which can be performed by any economist using the basic databases available and formulating hypotheses of differing detail and scope.

Choosing a method

The ability to gradually refine hypotheses directly depends on the production and processing of new information. To achieve this aim, there are two main options: direct or indirect methods.

Direct methods, which are employed mostly by ethnologists or sociologists, involve obtaining information from those involved in — or close to — drug trafficking (drug traffickers and users, their family and friends, neighbours, and persons physically present in the area in which the trafficking takes place, such as caretakers and supermarket staff). The aims of such research obviously vary according to the scientific and social disciplines concerned: the ethnological approach concentrates on a tiny section of the market, while the economic approach seeks to understand the organisation and dynamics of the system as a whole. The more simple surveys, carried out using questionnaires, often provide conventional, incomplete and superficial answers, and this demonstrates the highly segmented nature of the information, typical of an opaque, strictly-divided and closed market.

The direct approach therefore calls for a complex, multi-level interview methodology to be devised, fulfilling at least three basic needs:

- a range of interviews to enable a logical chain of information to be followed and gradually reconstructed;
- continuous verification by cross-checking the information through additional interviews; and
- repetition of the interviews over time, thereby strengthening the relationship of trust with interviewees.

This methodology is therefore both very detailed in its design and execution, and highly time-consuming.

Indirect methods are based on knowledge which is essentially gathered and processed by bodies specialising in drug-related matters. In France, the institutions which deal most with the drugs issue are the police, gendarmerie and customs, as well as the courts.

Without going into detail here, it should be pointed out that, in drug treatment centres and in institutions fostering social development (in particular those involved with young people), those in charge take pains not to get involved with data collection by the criminal justice system. This is due to their desire not to compromise their role and, in particular, to shield themselves from any knowledge of their clients' involvement in drug distribution and trafficking. This clearly demonstrates the conflict existing between policies of repression and those of rehabilitation and of prevention and integration. It also shows the difficulties involved in combining issues that should be grouped together under a single policy, in particular at local level. In the case of France, the modest results achieved by Conseils Communaux de Prévention de la Délinquance (CCPD) would appear to bear witness to this.

Experience accrued from several years of work in this field shows that, despite the creativity and enthusiasm of researchers, the lack of funding by research institutions and those responsible for dealing with drug and drug addiction problems makes it hard to avoid working in cooperation with bodies involved in repression (the police and the courts) if a methodological basis for information about drug markets is to be attempted.

The means of investigation — and therefore of knowledge — of the police and other legal bodies are disproportionate to those available for social science researchers. Researchers have to recognise their comparative limits and to be modest about their capacity to produce a large, fresh knowledge base. They have to learn to take advantage of police information and knowledge by reinterpreting and building on it according to their own specific goals.

Information produced and disseminated by the police is limited to the statistical figures for arrests relating to the use, trafficking and seizures of drugs. The Office Central pour la Répression du Trafic Illicite de Stupéfiants (OCRTIS) collates all the data gathered by the police, gendarmerie and customs. This provides routine, basic and tailored data that do nothing to highlight the phenomena of drug networks and organisation, nor market dynamics. Nevertheless, the data reveal the main routes and geographical entry points of substances coming into the country, and the location of the main national markets. These institutions are wary of producing information, however, despite the potential pool of knowledge existing within them. Consequently, the knowledge is diffuse, under-exploited, fragmented and currently reserved for operational purposes only. The scientific challenge is to ascertain how to share this public asset for different purposes, with the overall objective of gaining knowledge about the realities and growth of an undeniably important economic and social phenomenon.

Three phases of research in France

The research detailed in this chapter started at the end of 1993. It was based on an experimental project on disadvantaged districts undertaken for the Conseil National des Villes. It was gradually extended to cover wider areas in order to obtain a clearer picture and understanding of the organisation of drug trafficking at national level and its international links.

Phase 1

The first initiative, which lasted three to six months, was experimental in nature. It aimed at testing, from a methodological perspective, the quality and relevance of any sources of information that might be used for gaining knowledge about the phenomenon in a short period of time. In six districts within three cities (Marseilles, Paris and Lille), the sources which could be used to gather the necessary information were tested in great detail by four specialised research teams [1]. Of the large cross-section of indirect and direct methods employed, this research showed that court records, since they included police inquiries, continued to be one of the most stable and accessible starting-points, although they gave an incomplete picture. Direct methods, using regular questionnaire- or interview-based surveys carried out with drug users, their friends and family, and with individuals and institutions responsible for their medical and social care, confirmed the patchy nature of police knowledge. This led to a methodology being devised that was based on court records and police information. Direct methods can then be used to expand these findings, as research on drug dealers requires more detailed and long-term investigations.

---

[1] This research led to the publication by the Conseil National des Villes of *L'economie souterraine de la drogue,* Paris, 1994. Coordinated at the Maison des Sciences de l'Homme by Michel Schiray, it brought together four research teams: Le Groupe de Recherche et d'Analyse du Social et de la Sociabilité (GRASS/CNRS) led by Michel Joubert and Monique Weinburger; the Lastrée-IFRESI/CNRS led by Dominique Duprez; the Clinique Liberté led by Anne Coppel; and the Centre International de Recherche sur l'Environnement et le Développement, CIRED/EHESS/CNRS, led by Michel Schiray.

At the beginning of the 1990s, attention in France focused on the volume of drug trafficking taking place in some disadvantaged districts in the suburbs of large towns. The enquiries, whilst recognising the strong impact of such activities on social life in the district — in particular on young people — did not assess the impact at the economic level, in particular with regard to the distribution of income, the circulation of money and local investment. Two main organisational models were shown to exist. The first was local markets, with the coexistence of small groups of dealers sharing points of sale and regrouping themselves in the wake of police repression, and comprising, for the most part, young people who were well settled in the area. There was no sign of a trend towards mergers or the emergence of dominant, structured organisations. Links with the outside were fragmented and there was no strong tendency for these groups to be taken over by larger criminal organisations. The model seems to be fairly typical of drug trafficking organised by young people. Although it was noted that these dealers show a strong tendency towards professionalisation in their field, there was no sign of them becoming integrated in local economic life through investment. That this model is widespread would seem to confirm the theory that local markets are open and competitive.

The second, frequently-observed, model is that of more integrated groups formed along ethnic, family or community lines. This model is more stable in nature and, moreover, tends to produce local monopolies. It is more structured and exploits with greater ease a dependent, external workforce consisting mainly of illegal immigrants recruited in their home communities. This model is more obviously geared towards economic reward than the first. However, it was observed from the surveys undertaken in districts in both Lille and Marseilles that this accumulation of wealth does not remain in the districts where the dealers are operating, but is sent to their home countries. The model reflects, therefore, the typical strategies and organisations of immigrants who want to return to their home countries in the short or medium term.

With the open and competitive model of young people in a district, violence may be used as a means of gaining a foothold in a market, but surveys in several places have shown that, in districts and suburbs of France, this violence, in its extreme forms (in particular, murder), is often spasmodic and of short duration.

Some scope for agreement and even cooperation between groups of dealers may exist in certain districts. This is understandable, given their common background and that these young people are acquainted. The most representative example studied concerns the heroin 'supermarket' in the Bagneux district in the southern suburbs of Paris. The last big conflict — between heroin and cannabis dealers — dates back to the beginning of the 1990s. The coexistence of this model with that of ethnic minority groups in this district is certainly more likely to lead to conflict: sometimes the conditions of competition change, in particular by a reduction in prices brought about by a shortening of the distribution chain, or at the expense of the quality of the product.

The surveys which were initially conducted in six districts and then extended to a wider area of the suburbs of the three cities (2) did not reveal the involvement of traditional criminal (i.e. not drug-related) organisations in the local drugs markets. Local distribution networks seemed to be relatively distinct from them, and seemed to be more fragmented and poorly structured. Although it appeared that some of the more 'traditional' criminals were turning to the drugs trade, they were apparently acting on an individual, rather than an organised, basis. These findings led, notably in Paris and Marseilles, to a rethink of accepted theories concerning the role of the suburbs in city drug markets and the position of the various networks in the distribution chains.

Phase 2

A second research phase set about extending the local approach to drug trafficking in the suburbs to the whole city. This was piloted in Paris, taking court records as a starting-point (3). It is at the heart of the capital that the biggest drug-market business and criminal organisation networks have been found. This trade is characterised by its extraordinary internationalisation. Drug dealers of 47 different nationalities were tried in court in one year alone: one third from 'national' networks comprising various nationalities and two thirds from 'mixed' networks consisting of several different nationalities, but with the majority being French. In Paris, there is much more emphasis on commercial links with the outside world than is the case in the suburbs. The scale of transactions and the size of drugs seizures is often higher, suggesting that the city centre plays a larger role in intermediary distribution than the suburbs. Various cases show how the 'underworld' and traditional organised crime are involved in the large-scale distribution of drugs in the city and its suburbs, and that it is an international redistribution centre for drugs from producer countries to other European and North American markets. These are the cases which lead to money laundering: investments in real estate in France and abroad; investments in currencies and banking; and, above all, investment in businesses, not only gaming and entertainment, but also in traditional industries. It is this kind of offence that those in charge of combating money laundering at the Ministry of Economy and Finance are endeavouring to uncover.

---

(2) Following the previous experimental research, this second phase of research was carried out with the Conseil National des Villes and with the support of the DGLDT (Délégation Générale à la Lutte contre la Drogue et la Toxicomanie). Coordinated by Michel Schiray at the Maison des Sciences de l'Homme, it brought together five research teams: the GRASS/CNRS, led by Michel Joubert and Monique Weinburger; the Lastrée-IFRESI/CNRS, led by Dominique Duprez and Michel Kokoreff; the Centre d'Ethnologie de Recherches Méditerannéennes/CNRS, led by Jean Marc Mariottini; the Institut de Recherche en Epidémiologie de la Pharmacologie (IREP), led by Rodolphe Ingold and Mohamed Toussirt; and the CIRED/EHESS/CNRS, led by Michel Schiray with Nacer Lalam. This piece of research was not completed due to interinstitutional relations. It was the subject, however, of five unpublished reports which may be consulted at the MILDT (ex-DGLDT), at the OFDT, at the Conseil National des Villes or the Maison des Sciences de l'Homme, in Paris.

(3) This was undertaken as part of the research on L'organisation du trafic et des marchés de drogues illicites et leur liaison avec les économies officielles et non-officielles: Rapport sur l'état de la recherche, CIRED/Maison de l'Homme, Ministère de l'Enseignement Superieur et de la Recherche, Paris, December 1998. This research was led by Michel Schiray, and was carried out with Nacer Lalam, with the participation of Chokri Bensalem.

Phase 3

A third phase of research, which was not focused on any given territory, enabled information on coexistence, competition and intermingling between different networks to be gathered. This research, which was carried out recently ([4]), based its approach to the organisation of the drugs trade on the new social phenomenon of 'techno' dance music. This has led to new distribution networks that are based as much around music and musical events as around the users themselves.

A number of direct cross-border distribution chains and networks have been clearly identified in the ecstasy sector of the drugs market. These involve new dealers, who are young for the most part and who go straight to the source — mainly the Netherlands, but also Spain — in order to ensure their supplies. Other products are channelled via specialised distribution chains and networks connected with the techno dance movement.

The most important finding of this research is that it has shown how more strictly criminal organisations, originating from the traditional underworld criminal scene in French cities (usually named *les milieux,* particularly in the south of France), have grown up around these new and marginal chains and networks. Currently, in numerous regions, these traditional criminal groups seem to dominate the markets, not only for ecstasy, but also for a large proportion of the other drugs consumed at dance events, particularly cannabis and cocaine. This might be explained by the greater presence of the techno dance scene in discotheques and night clubs, more often than not run by the 'underworld', rather than in the more irregularly held 'rave parties' organised by those involved in the scene.

Conclusions

This is a new and important research finding in France. It confirms that French organised crime is also involved in the French drug market, side-by-side with the individual chains established by young people and immigrant populations. However, the authorities specialising in such matters have difficulty acknowledging this. The methodology used to reach this finding combined direct and indirect techniques, and could usefully be applied more widely to all of the drugs markets in France. This would result in a better understanding of the relationships between the various types of networks sharing the drug distribution market: mainly local networks of young people, ethnic immigrant networks and organised criminal networks. Extending this research to the European level would also show differences in the patterns of drug trafficking between countries.

The author is an economist and researcher at the Centre National de la Recherche Scientifique (CNRS), École des Hautes Études en Sciences Sociales (EHESS), France.

([4]) *Étude des filières de produits psychotropes à partir du mouvement techno,* CIRED/Maison des Sciences de l'Homme/Observatoire Français des Drogues et des Toxicomanie (OFDT), Paris, February 1999. This research was conducted by Thierry Colombie and Nacer Lalam, under the scientific direction of Michel Schiray.

CHAPTER 21

QUALITATIVE METHODOLOGY AT THE EDGE: ASSESSING ITALIAN MAFIA GROUPS' INVOLVEMENT IN DRUG TRAFFICKING

Letizia Paoli

Although this chapter may provoke some qualitative researchers, its aim is to show how qualitative methodologies can be fruitfully employed to evaluate data sources that many orthodox ethnographers regard as unreliable and essentially misleading: police reports and judicial documents concerning the higher levels of the drug supply system. The following pages do not claim that these sources are objective and can always be taken at face value. Rather, they are inspired by the conviction that there are certain aspects of the drug phenomenon that are difficult to study using traditional ethnographic methods, yet are too relevant to be documented exclusively by the mass media and law enforcement agencies.

Some ethnographic studies of upper-level drug dealing do exist: for example, the inquiry carried out by Patricia Adler (1985) in the late 1970s. The loose nature of this network of distributors and the low level of secrecy enforced by some of their members allowed direct observation of high-level drug transactions. However, in the case of more structured criminal groups and, specifically, of the Italian Mafia consortia, this has so far proved practically impossible.

The only known exception is represented by the two years of direct contact that the American anthropologist Francis Ianni had with a New York-based Italian-American crime family in the early 1970s (Ianni, 1972). Even in this case, the observation was only partial, since Ianni was totally excluded from taking part in the planning and accomplishment of any illegal activity: indeed, the scarcity of information on illegal businesses has been indicated as the main weakness of his study (Reuter, 1983).

Where direct access is not allowed, police and judicial sources often represent the only source of knowledge, and the aim of this chapter is to show how they can be independently assessed by researchers adopting qualitative methodologies. Interpreting law enforcement data through the lenses of scientifically sound hypotheses, it is possible to reach conclusions that contrast with official theories and dogmas.

Methodological precautions

To attain such a goal, methodological precautions are necessary: reliance on judicial and police documents cannot be unconditional. Firstly, the discrepancy between judiciary records and the events in the 'real world' must be addressed. It is important to keep in mind that:

> ... the judiciary optic necessarily tends to privilege those aspects of real phenomena which assume a greater relevance under the juridical-formal profile, so that the facts reported in the trial papers are not truly such (so to say) in their factual totality, but are selected and ordered as a function of their normative qualification. (Fiandaca and Costantino, 1990, p. 87; see also Sbriccoli, 1988)

Secondly, it is important to classify law-enforcement sources according to their reliability. Reports of drug seizures and wiretappings, for example, have a relatively high degree of objectivity, certainly higher than most intelligence and judicial reports. As far as the Italian Mafia groups are concerned, another relatively reliable source of information has become available since the early 1980s. Following the example of Tommaso Buscetta, the first contemporary Mafia boss to become a *pentito* (i.e. a prosecution witness), hundreds of Mafia adherents and gangsters started to 'cooperate with Justice' — that is, to report their crimes and experiences in the underworld to police officers and judges. According to the data published by the Ministry of the Interior, which is responsible for protecting collaborators, 1 177 had done so by 30 June 1996 (Ministero dell'Interno, 1996).

These *pentiti* (literally 'penitents', former Mafia affiliates now cooperating with police and judicial authorities), as they are popularly called, represent the best possible substitute for participant observation in a world that hardly tolerates independent observers, and over the last 15 years they have provided insiders' accounts that have proved to be highly valuable to researchers. This information has provided knowledge about the phenomenon of Mafia and organised crime in Italy that has, in the last 15 years, reached a level that was previously inconceivable.

The revelations of *pentiti* are, however, a double-edged data source and a great amount of critical prudence is necessary in dealing with them in order to avoid the risk of reproducing the worn-out tenets of Mafia ideology, or of legitimating false-hoods which may give a defendant some advantage. To allay this concern, it is worth remembering that the police officials and the prosecutors, who are the first to gather and check the collaborators' confessions, conduct an initial screening which is subsequently double-checked by the courts. Even so, the social scientist should attempt to support these controls with an independent assessment of the reliability and coherence of the statements. Of course, from a theoretical point of view one cannot rule out the possibility of a collective 'conspiracy' by the *pentiti* to give a distorted vision of the Mafia or to achieve some other goal. Yet there are several phenomena that justify the positive — though not unconditional — appeal of these sources. Foremost, there is the multiplicity and dissimilarity of informants.

Then, there is the high number of law enforcement officials and independent observers who have gathered their confessions, as well as the diversity of historical moments during which similar accounts have been put forward. In addition, there are surprising analogies between contemporary judicial reports and descriptions of Mafia associations provided by law enforcement officials and independent observers, dating as far back as the last century. Instead of assuming that contemporary *pentiti* might have carefully read the 19th-century criminological literature (Catanzaro, 1991), these analogies can be regarded as a proof of long-term continuities. Finally, it must be remembered that the information disclosed by justice collaborators has also found confirmation in what is still regarded by some as the only source of objective information: the wiretappings of conversations among the *Mafiosi* themselves (Paoli, 1997).

With these basic precautions in mind, the analysis of police and judicial sources can begin. If it is carried out accurately, such an enterprise may even find proof for hypotheses that are far removed from official assessments and media reports, as the following examples will show.

Mafia groups' share of the illicit drug trade

Italian and European public discourse tends to assume that the higher levels of the illicit drug distribution system are controlled by powerful criminal organisations, among which Italian Mafia groups play a central role. Once these organisations are defeated, the reasoning goes, markets will dry up and drug consumption will be strongly discouraged.

As far as the Italian Mafia groups and drug markets are concerned, however, it is hard to find evidence of such an assumption, even in police and judicial data. A major investigation carried out in the mid-1980s in Sicily — the so-called Palermitan *maxiprocesso* — revealed the Sicilian Mafia groups' involvement in transcontinental heroin smuggling in the late 1970s and early 1980s. Morphine was imported from some Middle and Far Eastern countries, transformed into heroin in Sicilian laboratories and then shipped to the United States (TrPA, 1986). The turnover of the overall business was impressive: it has been estimated that between four and five tons of pure heroin were produced by Sicilian laboratories each year in the late 1970s. This quantity, largely exported to the United States, represented some 30 % of the total demand of that country. Subtracting the costs of production and transport, this gave a net profit of approximately ITL 700 000–800 000 billion (EUR 350–400 million) (Arlacchi, 1988). Subsequent investigations revealed the growing involvement of other southern Italian Mafia groups, in particular the Calabrian 'Ndrangheta. In March 1994, 5 490 kilos of cocaine were seized on the outskirts of Turin, which allegedly constituted the last of eight similar shipments financed by a coalition of seven Calabrian Mafia families (TrTO, 1994).

Notwithstanding the huge quantities occasionally dealt with, there is no evidence that Sicilian and Calabrian Mafia organisations ever controlled the Italian drug market, much less the European one (Becchi, 1996). Law-enforcement activities and some city-level ethnographic studies show that drug markets are hardly ever supplied by one single wholesale drug distributor (Arlacchi and Lewis, 1990a; 1990b; Ruggiero, 1992; Becchi and Turvani, 1993; Ruggiero and South, 1995). Instead, there is a plurality of drug suppliers, each relying on their own distributors. Judicial investigations additionally show that *Cosa Nostra* members have been progressively marginalised from wholesale heroin and cocaine trafficking (Ministero dell'Interno, 1993; 1994; 1995) and that even 'Ndrangheta families, who up to a few years ago benefited from their influence in northern Italy, are now increasingly feeling the competition from a variety of foreign suppliers.

Drug laboratories in southern Italy

Up until the early 1990s, it was widely assumed among the general public and the law-enforcement community that heroin refineries still existed in Sicily and that new heroin and cocaine laboratories had been established in several southern Italian regions. However, this was not supported by law-enforcement activities. Since the mid-1980s, no professional drug laboratory has been discovered in Sicily, nor in any other regions of the Italian Mezzogiorno. Theoretically, of course, this does not completely rule out their existence. Nonetheless, it seems more reasonable to assume that a process highlighted by Roger Lewis in the mid-1980s is under way.

> As with other markets, the production of heroin (finished goods), morphine and heroin base (semi-finished goods), as well as the raw material (opium), increasingly takes place in the periphery to take advantage of minimal production and labour costs. (Lewis, 1985, p. 15)

Such a hypothesis is also suggested by the American Drug Enforcement Administration today (NNICC, 1995).

Business patterns

During the 1990s, organised crime suddenly became a 'hot topic' in public discourse. In such a debate, which frequently assumed the tones of a moral panic, drawing an analogy between criminal organisations and multinational corporations became fashionable and was simplistically pursued by a number of scholars. For example:

> Transnational criminal organisations, particularly drug-trafficking organisations, operate unrestricted across international borders. They are very similar in kind to legitimate transnational corporations in structure, strength, size, geographical range and scope of their operations. (Williams and Florez, 1994)

Law enforcement activities can provide substantial evidence to refute this analogy. An example is the Sicilian Mafia groups' transcontinental trade in heroin of the early 1980s. As several inquiries have shown, approximately 100 Sicilian Mafia families are associated in a consortium known as the *Cosa Nostra*. In the late 1950s, some of these groups set up a superordinate body of coordination — the so-called Commission for the Palermo Province — and in the mid-1970s a homologous institution at the regional level followed suit (Paoli, 1997; see also Paoli, 1999). Nonetheless, a careful reading of the *maxiprocesso* acts, including the separation of facts from interpretations, reveals no evidence of a centralised management of the drug trade. Indeed, the different phases of the trade were run by several independent units largely — but not exclusively — composed of *Cosa Nostra* members, who sold the substances to one another. Far from considering themselves part of a larger enterprise, importers and exporters were very jealous of their foreign contacts (TrPA, 1986, Volume IX).

In short, there is today no doubt that some large-scale southern Italian Mafia organisations exist, but they do not operate in the manner of a multinational corporation. Whenever their affiliates enter illegal markets, they are subject to the same constraints, deriving from the illegal status of the products, that plague all illegal entrepreneurs. Due to these constraints, much of the activity is 'disorganised crime' (Reuter, 1983) and within drug markets there is no imminent tendency towards the development of large-scale criminal enterprises (Paoli, 1999).

Conclusions

Judicial and police statistics and reports are only a second-best source of information and, whenever possible, they need to be complemented with the results of empirical studies carried out by independent researchers. The higher levels of the narcotics distribution system, however, cannot be directly observed by academic scholars but occupy an important place in public debate, and assumptions concerning them strongly influence national and international drug control policies. There is no doubt that, due to the scarcity of secondary sources and the obstacles to empirical inquiry, it is particularly irksome and tiring to study these topics. They are, however, too important to be left only to moral entrepreneurs.

The author is a researcher at the Criminology Research Unit of the Max-Planck Institute for Foreign and International Criminal Law in Freiburg, Germany.

References

Adler, P. A. (1985) *Wheeling and Dealing: an Ethnography of an Upper-level Drug Dealing and Smuggling Community,* New York: Columbia University Press.

Arlacchi, P. (1988) *Mafia Business: the Mafia Ethic and the Spirit of Capitalism,* Oxford: Oxford University Press.

Arlacchi, P. and Lewis, R. (1990a) 'Droga e criminalità a Bologna', *Micromega,* 4, 183–221.

Arlacchi, P. and Lewis, R. (1990b) *Imprenditorialità illecita e droga. Il mercato dell'eroina a Verona,* Bologna: Il Mulino.

Becchi, A. (1996) 'Italy: Mafia-dominated drug market?', in N. Dorn, J. Jepsen and E. Savona (Eds.) *European Drug Policies and Enforcement,* London: Macmillan, pp. 119–130.

Becchi, A. and Turvani, M. (1993) *Proibito? Il mercato mondiale della droga,* Roma: Donzelli.

Catanzaro, R. (1991) *Il delitto come impresa: Storia sociale della mafia,* Milano: Rizzoli.

Fiandaca, G. and Costantino, S. (1990) 'La mafia negli anni '80: Il fenomeno mafioso tra vecchi e nuovi paradigmi', *Sociologia del diritto,* 3, 75–96.

Ianni, F. (1972) *A Family Business: Kinship and Social Control in Organized Crime,* New York: Russel Sage Foundation.

Lewis, R. (1985) 'Serious business: the global heroin economy', in A. Henman, R. Lewis and T. Malyon (Eds.) *Big Deal: the Politics of the Illicit Drug Business,* London: Pluto Press, pp. 5–49.

Ministero dell'Interno (1993) *Rapporto annuale sul fenomeno della criminalità organizzata per il 1992,* Roma.

Ministero dell'Interno (1994) *Rapporto annuale sul fenomeno della criminalità organizzata per il 1993,* Roma: Camera dei Deputati, doc. XXXVIII-bis, 1, XII legislatura.

Ministero dell'Interno (1995) *Rapporto annuale sul fenomeno della criminalità organizzata per il 1994,* Roma.

Ministero dell'Interno (1996) *Relazione sui programmi di protezione, sulla loro efficacia e sulle modalità generali di applicazione per coloro che collaborano alla giustizia: I semestre 1996,* Roma: Senato della Repubblica, doc. XCI, 1, XIII legislatura.

NNICC (National Narcotics Intelligence Consumers Committee) (1995) *The NNICC 1994: the Supply of Illicit Drugs to the United States,* Washington, DC.

Paoli, L. (1997) *The Pledge to Secrecy: Culture, Structure and Action of Mafia Associations* (dissertation), Firenze: European University Institute.

Paoli, L. (1998) 'Droga-traffici', in P. Pezzino (Ed.) *Mafia, Enciclopedia elettronica,* Torino: Cliomedia.

Paoli, L. (1999) *Fratelli di mafia: Cosa Nostra siciliana e la 'Ndrangheta calabrese,* Bologna: Il Mulino.

Reuter, P. (1983) *Disorganized Crime: the Economics of the Visible Hand,* Cambridge: MIT Press.

Ruggiero, V. (1992) *La roba, economie e culture dell'eroina,* Parma: Pratiche editrice.

Ruggiero, V. and South, N. (1995) *Eurodrugs: Drug Use, Markets and Trafficking in Europe,* London: Routledge.

Sbriccoli, M. (1988) 'Fonti giudiziarie e fonti giuridiche: Riflessioni sulla fase attuale degli studi di storia del crimine', *Studi storici,* 29(2), 491–501.

TrPA, Tribunale di Palermo, Ufficio Istruzione Processi Penali (1986) *Ordinanza-sentenza di rinvio a giudizio nei confronti* by G. Abbate et al., novembre.

TrTO, Tribunale di Torino, Ufficio del Giudice per le Indagini Preliminari (1994) *Ordinanza di custodia cautelare in carcere nei confronti* by S. Belfiore et al., 23 giugno.

Williams, P. and Florez, C. (1994) 'Transnational criminal organizations and drug trafficking', *Bulletin on Narcotics,* 46(2), 9–24.

CHAPTER 22

WELFARE, CRIME AND NETWORKING:
FINANCING A DRUG HABIT

Karen Ellen Spannow

Over a two-year period from August 1993 to August 1995, researchers from the Centre for Alcohol and Drug Research at the University of Åarhus conducted an ethnographic study of the illegal drug market in Åarhus, which is the second largest city in Denmark (Spannow, 1997). The study was primarily undertaken to throw light on the effects of police control strategies. The main aims of these strategies are to reduce the supply of illegal drugs and the various criminal activities to finance their use. As most of the resources used to address problems which are seen as related to the use of illegal drugs is spent by the police and the criminal justice system, it is important to explore whether these stated objectives are reached.

Police control strategies

The control strategy of the police turns on the belief that drug dealing takes place within hierarchical relationships, implying that a few individuals at the top are making enormous profits while leaving the drudgery and dirty work to lower-level associates. For this reason the special Danish drug police force has increasingly been occupied with taking measures against international drug trafficking. Street control is left to a plain-clothes squad, which, due to rapid rotation of staff, cannot develop a work culture with a more subtle understanding of the drug problem. The result is that most of those arrested for drug offences are users only or small-scale dealers: only a small minority of the criminal court cases concerning drug dealing involve significant sums of money (Storgaard, 1992). While this state of affairs could be used to modify the hierarchical model, it has instead been used so far to confirm the assumption that those at the top are hard to expose, and to support police claims that the arrests of users and small-scale dealers may serve as a lead to higher level distributors.

How the value of drugs is assessed at all levels of distribution

Against this background, one of the main research questions of the study was 'Is there any truth in the hierarchical representation of drug dealing given by police as the legitimisation for their work?' In addition, the study examined the amount of money users spend on drugs. Whenever the police make a seizure of illegal drugs, the value of the goods is appraised on the basis of the highest street price. If the drugs are seized at the border, police further multiply this price, assuming that the drugs will be diluted before reaching the market. This practice, which might imply that the value of seizures is set too high and, subsequently, that criminal activities for financing drug use are overestimated, prompted the research team to collect data relating to prices at different distribution levels and to ask questions about how widespread dilution was.

Use of qualitative methodology

Quantitative methodology would be of limited use in answering these questions, mostly for practical reasons: it is difficult to identify those involved in the distribution of illegal drugs and this is best accomplished by seeking them out personally. Even then, it still might not be feasible to ask them to fill in a questionnaire asking sensitive questions about their illegal business. Qualitative methodology, including conversational interviews, in combination with observation of key informants, is much more likely to yield results.

By hanging out at places where heroin users were known to meet, members of the research team made a number of contacts with users of illegal drugs. After some time, these contacts had enough confidence in the researchers to refer them to dealers who were not moving openly amongst groups of drug users but were nevertheless central for the groups' regular supplies of heroin. In this way, the research team gained access to first-hand information about heroin trafficking, distribution, prices at different distribution levels and dilution. By interviewing a number of 'recreational' drug users, using the same snowball methodology, the team also gained insight into the distribution of drugs other than heroin (i.e. cannabis, amphetamines, cocaine, ecstasy).

Distribution patterns

The researchers found a marked difference in distribution patterns according to the drug in question. Cannabis and amphetamines were, to some extent, under the control of organised biker clubs, who, although they maintained that they were not criminal organisations, had a number of 'supporters' who helped with distribution. However, cannabis and amphetamines were also sold by individuals, and on the basis of information from users it was estimated that the bikers may have no more than a 50 % share of the market: the use of cannabis is especially widespread in Denmark [1] and often distributed on a non-profit (but cost-covering) basis among people who know each other [2].

---

[1] Lifetime prevalence of cannabis use is around 30 % (Laursen and Sabroe, 1996).

[2] A questionnaire was sent to 120 schoolchildren in the age bracket 14–17. More than 50 % said they had been offered cannabis for sale. Only 13 % said they had used it.

A different pattern was found regarding distribution of heroin. Possibly because of the provincial and limited size of the market in Åarhus, it was not possible to identify any high-level distributors who were not dependent on the drug themselves. Rather, the market was supplied by relatively few user-dealers (who will be referred to as wholesalers) who smuggled heroin into Denmark by raising around USD 10 000 (EUR 9 500) to buy around 250 grams of heroin from other European cities (mainly Amsterdam). They would set part of the drugs aside for their own use, and then sell the rest to a regular group of seven or eight smaller-scale dealers (henceforth identified as retailers).

As a rule, the wholesalers avoided selling on the open market themselves, not wanting to attract police attention. The retailers picked up the heroin at the wholesalers' private residences and other drug users were kept away to reduce the number of visitors. The retailers, as a rule, also had regular customers who came to their homes to buy heroin. In turn, some of these customers could be found at the open market, selling small packets of drugs of varying quality. In general, all actors in the illegal trade in drugs estimated that something between 10 and 15 % of the drugs consumed in Åarhus were sold on the open market.

The question of dilution

The price of heroin increased at each distribution level, and at the time of the study the heroin for which the wholesalers had paid USD 40 (EUR 38) per gram was sold to retailers at USD 120 (EUR 114) per gram, and realised a final 'street price' as high as USD 400 (EUR 380) per gram. Retailers used the same strategy as the wholesalers — setting aside some of the drug for themselves and doubling up the price for their customers. As a rule, dilution did not take place, except among those selling on the open market.

This was confirmed by a study of the quality of heroin seized partly at the border and partly directly from the open market in Åarhus (Kaa and Bowmann, 1997). The police claim that drugs are diluted at each level, but profits gained in this way could not be confirmed. Dealers explained that, since they had regular customers, they would be in trouble and eventually out of business if they sold low-quality drugs; to maintain customer loyalty, they also tried to do business with the same suppliers abroad, in order to ensure drugs of predictable, uniform quality.

Thus, rather than finding a distribution pyramid, with a drug-free 'drugs baron' at the top, what was found was a number of steady networks where all those involved were dependent on the drug they were selling.

In relation to the question of financing drug use, it was found that much smaller sums were spent than was assumed by the police. The majority of users managed to get the drug at less than half the price charged on the open markets. Only the most desperate addicts tried to sell diluted heroin at street level in an effort to reduce the cost of their own supply.

In addition, it was found that most addicts never got as much heroin as they would have liked, and the majority kept withdrawal symptoms at bay with the help of other drugs and alcohol.

By interviewing two retailers who each had seven or eight regular customers, it was found that their customers spent varying amounts on heroin each month. Furthermore, the trade in illegal drugs was much brisker at the beginning of the month, when buyers received their social benefits from the welfare office.

This may partly be explained by the fact that addicts in methadone treatment increase their use of drugs in addition to those prescribed when they have money, but it also related to some heroin users not receiving any drug substitution treatment.

Conclusions

To sum up, the study disclosed a much more varied pattern of drug distribution and financing of drug use than is implied by police strategy and explanations for it. The money required to maintain a heroin habit is, in reality, much lower than police estimates, and therefore the crimes committed to finance use may be smaller than they suggest. In addition, state benefits were found to play an important role in financing illegal drug use.

In deciding appropriate and effective resource allocation, one should also consider the main target of police control work: to reduce the consumption of illegal drugs. All drug addicts interviewed in the study were asked whether their drug intake was influenced by police control, and all denied that that was the case (unless they had been arrested and unable to obtain drugs). The majority obtained drugs from a private address and only the most desperate were forced to buy in the open market. It can be concluded that myths about the urgency of drug dependence are playing a powerful role in maintaining the police attitude towards drug addicts.

The study demonstrated that qualitative research has the potential for deconstructing some of the myths that haunt the discussion of illegal drugs. The assumption that heroin addicts need to have heroin every few hours, at any cost, was not found to be the case.

The assumption that every addict is paying the highest street price for heroin was also shown to be wrong. General estimates about the scale of criminality necessary to keep up a heroin habit were found to be far too high. Finally, it was not possible to confirm the perception that distribution of heroin is organised as a hierarchical structure, with a non-using profit-maker at the top.

In an ideal world, the results of this study and others confirming its results (Kaa and Bowmann, 1997; Vangsgaard, forthcoming) would be used to change both the rhetoric and police strategies surrounding heroin use and distribution. However, whilst qualitative research has the power to reveal a more accurate and detailed picture of aspects of drug use, it does not necessarily follow that it has political influence and the impact to bring about real change in resource allocation and responses.

Looking at drug policy, treatment and prevention strategies in Denmark, it is obvious that interventions are not based on existing knowledge and research. Rather, research findings are used somewhat selectively and often only the data that confirms established beliefs and traditions are implemented in interventions. A major challenge is to build up more respect for qualitative research posing critical questions; this has the potential of inspiring more rational responses to illegal drug use.

The author is an anthropologist employed as Assistant Research Professor at the Centre for Alcohol and Drug Research, Åarhus University, Denmark.

References

Kaa, E. and Bowmann, H. (1997) *Det illegale stofmarked i Århus (The Illegal Drug Market in Aarhus)*, Århus Universitetsforlag.

Laursen, L. and Sabroe, K.-E. (1996) *Alkoholbrug og Alkoholpolitik (Use of Alcohol and Alcohol Policy)*, Århus Universitetsforlag.

Spannow, K. E. (1997) *Narkotikamiljøer i Århus: en etnografisk analyse (Drug Circles in Aarhus: an Ethnographic Analysis)*, Centre for Alcohol and Drug Research.

Storgaard, A. (1992) *Straf for narkotikahandel (Penalties for Drug Dealing)*, Canfaus skrifter, 1.

Vangsgaard, P. (forthcoming) *Politiets Narkotikakontrolindsats (Drug Control Efforts by the Police)*, dissertation.

CHAPTER 23

A QUALITATIVE VIEW OF DRUGS POLICING:
HEROIN MARKETS
IN GREATER MANCHESTER, UK

Mark Gilman

Over the last 15 years (1984–99) many aspects of the 'heroin scenes' in the north-west of England have changed. Those concerned with the prevention and treatment of heroin use have seen three paradigm shifts in that time.

In the early to mid-1980s, the dominant paradigm was a focus on the health of the individual heroin user. The arrival of HIV saw a paradigm shift towards public health. Primary prevention and treatment for abstinence fell into the shadow of harm reduction. Needle exchanges were established and methadone began to flow in the name of public health. The current paradigm shift is towards crime preven-tion and community safety. In this paradigm, the methadone flow could be increased to serve crime prevention and community safety.

The key shift within this paradigm is the recognition of the role of the police serv-ice as full partners in prevention and treatment efforts geared towards community safety. Drawing on data derived from a variety of qualitative methods over these 15 years — interviews, focus groups, participant observation and covert, informal observation — this chapter will examine the role played by policing in shaping the markets for heroin in the Greater Manchester area of the United Kingdom. The chapter will also suggest how policing might be imaginatively used in the age of compulsory treatment and community safety.

There are several different illegal drugs markets serving different groupings of drug users in Greater Manchester. The most obvious market distinction is between those that operate to serve 'recreational' drugs users and those serving those 'addicted' to heroin and, albeit to a lesser extent, crack cocaine (Gilman, 1992a). This chapter focuses on the development of heroin markets in the city. It should be noted that crack cocaine is increasingly also sold in many of these markets.

Like many other parts of the UK, Greater Manchester experienced its first ever hero-in epidemic in the early 1980s. Heroin became available in cheap and plentiful sup-ply in many towns and cities where it had previously been quite unknown (Pearson et al., 1985; Pearson, 1987; Parker et al., 1988). The Lifeline Project maintains an ethnographic connection with heroin markets, and the 'recreational' counterparts, to inform the project's commercial production of targeted harm-reduction educational materials (Gilman, 1992b; 1993). Over the last 15 years there have been several key developments in the heroin markets of Greater Manchester.

'Closed' market distribution of heroin

Fifteen years ago most people who used heroin in the city bought it in the area in which they lived. They usually bought it from someone who was also a user (a 'user-dealer'). These user-dealerships characterised a 'closed' market system centred around domestic dwellings. When visiting the user-dealer's home, the customer might be allowed to inject or smoke some of the heroin there and might even be offered a cup of tea. These closed heroin distribution networks were quite relaxed from the customer's point of view, and their primary purpose was to fund the user-dealers' heroin use.

Closed markets made it difficult for new recruits to get involved in heroin use as new users needed to be introduced to the user-dealer by one of their close-knit circle of customers. Potential new, and especially younger, customers were refused service for reasons of business economics, market positioning and morals. However, the primary reason for refusal was that the user-dealer was not in the business to make 'pure money'. User-dealers just wanted to be able to make money to buy their own heroin and to 'keep things sweet' for themselves and their small customer base.

With the benefit of hindsight, senior police officers and the user-dealers they locked up agree that these closed markets were easy to police. The user-dealer spent much of the day in a state of intoxication and was therefore less than vigilant in the organisation of counter-surveillance measures. The local community often provided a wealth of good quality information about local user-dealers to the police. When the police acted against these small user-dealers, the courts cast them as 'Mr Bigs' and handed out some very heavy sentences.

Every time a small user-dealer was imprisoned, they left behind all their customers. These customers were addicted to heroin. They held to a pharmacological determinist view of their own heroin use: they had to have the heroin. They felt that they had no real choice, as the need for heroin was driving their lives. A few individuals were able to 'buy some time' by finding a doctor to prescribe another opiate, such as methadone. The rest carried on committing acquisitive crimes to buy street heroin from those dealers who managed to evade the efforts of the police.

Centralisation of heroin distribution

This process saw heroin distribution become ever more centralised in 'open' street markets in inner-city Manchester. Moreover, it became centralised in parts of the inner city that were, and still are, the most difficult to police.

The reasons why these inner-city areas were so difficult to police are complex, but one of the key reasons is that they contained significant numbers of black people who remembered the troubles between the police and black communities in 1980–81. During that period, many of England's cities had seen 'rioting' or 'uprisings' (depending on the political viewpoint). These manifested themselves as battles between youth — predominantly, but not exclusively, Afro-Caribbean — and the police. Moss Side in Manchester was one area were black youth rose up against what they saw as police racism. This was a time when the police operated a practice of 'stop and search'. Black youth felt that this practice — sometimes referred to as the 'SUS' laws (stopped on SUSpicion of a crime) — were inherently racist. The police claimed that they did not receive the same quality of information about heroin dealers operating in black areas as they had received in traditional white working-class communities.

Once heroin distribution became centralised, the cosy relationship between user and user-dealer was gone. The new dealers were in business to make 'pure money'. Predominantly white users now bought their heroin from black strangers. These strangers did not use heroin; they did not like heroin and saw it as a 'dirty' drug that was used by 'dirty' white junkies who had no self-respect and therefore deserved no respect. Heroin users were seen by these new dealers in the same way many prostitutes see their clients: with contempt. Open street markets were impersonal and dangerous. Heroin users were abused by the new dealers in all manner of ways: they were subject to violent street robberies and were sexually harassed and abused. Sometimes the abuse was much more subtle. They were simply made to wait. A lasting image of this period is of a young heroin-addicted mother with a baby in a pushchair, waiting in heavy winter rain to score a GBP 10 bag of heroin, whilst the dealers sheltered in a café, openly laughing at her plight. Why did the dealers abuse the addicts in this way? The answer is depressingly simple: because they could. Many of these dealers were young black men who had very little power in mainstream white society. Here, however, on these streets where the heroin trade was plied, they did have power. Even if this power could only be exercised over weak, defenceless addicts, it was still power, and so it was used.

The depth of self-loathing that addicts experienced when this happened was such that one enterprising firm of young white criminals from another part of the city set up in the heroin business. They prided themselves on user-friendly heroin marketing. As one of these young white men said, 'OK so they're junkies and bagheads but they are still people ... they want to be treated with a bit of respect ... that's what we give 'em ... they'd much rather come to us than some black kid that's younger than some of their kids and treats 'em like shit.'

A predominantly white police force found undercover police work much more difficult and potentially much more dangerous in black areas. They also found it much harder to act against those dealers, like the one quoted above, who did not use heroin and who were much more vigilant in their counter-surveillance measures. Firearms became a regular feature of these inner-city heroin markets. Dealers started to engage in territorial disputes. These disputes resulted in violence and even death for some of them. The drug-related violence escalated and led to some tragic incidents and accidents.

The new heroin dealing structure made it much easier for new recruits to get involved in heroin use. The new dealers did not care to whom they sold heroin in their search to maximise profits. Introductions were not necessary, as the dealing was done in the public arena of the streets. Media reports ensured that everyone knew where to go for heroin in Manchester and other areas of the north-west. Taxis, private cars and public transport brought the bedraggled army of heroin addicts to open inner-city street markets. They brought with them the cash they had made from selling goods stolen in their own areas. The heroin markets flourished.

Young men who were growing up in inner-city areas that were host to these open street markets looked to the drugs trade as a source of income — a job. They would begin apprenticeships by acting as a 'tout', 'steerer' or 'courier'. These open street markets seemed a long way away from the old-fashioned, almost quaint, very British closed heroin markets and began to take on a distinctly North American feel (Bourgois, 1995; Simon and Burns, 1998).

When it became clear what was happening (around 1986–87), the black communities of inner-city Manchester began asking some very serious questions about the policing of their area: 'Why is the sale of heroin being allowed to remain in this area?' 'Why is nothing being done about it?' 'Are you allowing these markets to operate from here because we are black?' This was a sentiment expressed at many public meetings. At one such meeting, a black resident said that they felt that the police were letting the heroin market flourish in their areas as a covert policy of confinement. This argument became known as 'keeping the lid on the dustbin'. It was proffered by people who saw the police as an institutionally racist organisation only too happy to let black communities suffer the debilitating consequences of having to live alongside open street markets selling heroin and crack cocaine.

However, these were not the only voices to be heard in these areas. Other voices, whilst recognising heroin and crack cocaine dealing as a negative influence in their community, were so suspicious of the police that they were reluctant to help them. Their experiences of policing actions were so negative that they claimed to be more afraid of the police than the dealers. In October 1998, the Chief Constable of Greater Manchester Police announced that his force was institutionally racist. The debate around policing and race is very live in the UK at the time of writing, and feeds into debates around heroin markets and appropriate policing methods.

The centralisation of heroin dealing in open street markets remains a major problem for the police. Surveillance is relatively easy at the various sites of dealing. However, without good inside information and people who are willing to have video cameras sited in their properties or to appear as witnesses, little progress can be made. This further frustrates those in the local community who feel that they are being abandoned and that nothing is being done to disrupt and dismantle open street markets in their areas. These feelings of abandonment are not confined to black communities but are shared by white working-class communities. One white working-class woman living in an area that is home to an open street market for heroin commented: 'How long would this kind of thing [open heroin markets] be allowed to happen if their [the police's] kids had to walk past people selling heroin on their way to school?'

Young impressionable men in these areas see that the dealers are 'getting away with it'. They have nice clothes, nice cars, nice girls and lots of money. They are successful. They have status. They matter. Consequently they become role models. The community's morale declines accordingly. Despair and fear set in.

Policing and the modern market

In more recent years, the mobile telephone and pager system has supplemented, and in some cases replaced, open street markets. Dealers operate a heroin delivery system that resembles a pizza delivery service. Orders are placed by calling a mobile phone number and the heroin is delivered by couriers to pre-arranged sites. Heroin users will often have a list of these numbers: the streets of cities like Manchester are home to highly visible, homeless heroin addicts who are willing to pass on these numbers to new users for a small commission. Dealers operating these delivery systems are trying to build up a regular customer base. Deals are made secretly and swiftly, often using coded language, and the pre-arranged sites can easily be changed.

In these markets, it is much easier to apprehend the buyer than the dealer. Arresting heroin addicts is like shooting fish in a barrel, but it is not high status in policing terms, and runs the risk of attracting criticism from some of those concerned with the welfare of drug addicts. However, actions against dealers seem to have limited results and make a large charge on the public purse. Despite the difficulties, the police have mounted successful operations against heroin dealing, but the result is that they have merely moved the problem around within the same area. A small number of dealers occasionally get long prison sentences. One of the most reliable sources of good information comes from people who want to see rival dealers locked up so that they can have their business. Competitive, commercial dealers are delighted when their business rivals are arrested: they can improve their market share overnight. When this has happened, those who have stepped in have tended to be younger and more cavalier. These young dealers are often teenage males who feel compelled to make public displays of their propensity for violence.

The threat of long prison sentences does not deter certain young men in inner-city areas from getting involved in selling heroin. In any case, they face a much more real threat from within their criminal fraternities: the death penalty has not been abolished in the criminal world. Yet this does not act as a deterrent. The rewards are simply too great for enforcement and criminal justice alone to have a lasting impact on those involved in the dealing of heroin and crack cocaine for 'pure money'.

Over the last 15 years, the prison experience has become more commonplace and normative in many working-class areas of Greater Manchester. However, the 7- to

10-year sentences that are handed out to heroin dealers are too much for all but the most desperate young men. Unfortunately, the impoverished urban areas of Greater Manchester are producing suitably desperate young men who are prepared to take the risks 'in search of respect' (Bourgois, 1995).

Conclusions

Policing has played some part in shaping the modern markets for heroin and crack. The user-dealers of yesterday have disappeared under the weight of their long prison sentences. The open street markets emerged as a response. The mobile telephone has supplemented the open street market.

By adopting a zero tolerance approach to heroin in an area, the police could arrest and harass heroin addicts and known dealers. This would send a clear message to all those involved in heroin. The net effect would be to displace the problem: like standing on a balloon filled with water, it would just pop up somewhere else. Zero tolerance of heroin could then be applied to that area. This approach would satisfy the majority of the community not involved with heroin and would interrupt the business of commercial dealers and their customers. Some police officers have realised that approaching the heroin problem as a business to be disrupted can have real impact.

In 1998, the BBC screened a television series called *Cops,* which was set in Manchester and deliberately blurred the edges between drama and documentary. In one episode, a very experienced policeman apprehends a small-scale drug dealer. Having searched the dealer, the policeman takes the drugs and sets the dealer free. The dealer remonstrates with the policeman, asking to be arrested. The policeman refuses to arrest him. The policeman knows that the dealer is working for a bigger dealer and that this bigger dealer will demand the money for the drugs. If the small-scale dealer cannot deliver the money, return the drugs or show that he has been arrested, the bigger dealer will automatically believe he has been cheated. This will breed suspicion within the heroin business. Suspicion of one's partners is bad for business. The net effect will be disruption of the heroin business.

Compulsory treatment and testing orders are set to be implemented in the United Kingdom. Perhaps the police could focus their efforts on the heroin addict buyers rather than the sellers and divert them into 'early retirement' (Gilman and Pearson, 1991).

Once the addicts are captured and contained within treatment settings, we know that considerable reductions are made in acquisitive crime rates (Gossop et al., 1998). The contemporary paradigm of crime prevention and community safety allows for local solutions to be devised for the local problems associated with heroin.

Imaginative use of policing could play a major part in multi-agency partnerships that are designed to reduce heroin-related harm to addicts, their families and the wider community who suffer from the acquisitive crimes committed to raise money for street heroin. By setting modest but achievable goals of zero-tolerance style disruption of the heroin business, rather than grand, unachievable goals of eradicating drugs, the police can become real partners in multi-agency drugs work.

The author was formerly Director of Research at the Lifeline Project, Manchester, UK.

References

Bourgois, P. (1995) *In Search of Respect,* Cambridge: Cambridge University Press.

Gilman, M. (1992a) 'No more junkie heroes', *Druglink,* May–June.

Gilman, M. (1992b) 'Smack in the eye', in P. A. O'Hare et al. (Eds.) *The Reduction of Drug Related Harm,* Routledge.

Gilman, M. (1993) 'Smack in the eye, peanut Pete and the new puritans', *International Journal of Drug Policy,* 4(1).

Gilman, M. and Pearson, G. (1991) 'Lifestyles and law enforcement', in D. K. Whynes et al. (Eds.) *Policing and Prescribing,* Macmillan.

Gossop, M., Marsden, J. and Stewart, D. (1998) *NTORS at one year. The National Treatment Outcome Research Study: Changes in Substance Use, Health and Criminal Behaviour One Year after Intake,* London: Department of Health.

Parker, H., Bakx, K. and Newcombe, R. (1988) *Living With Heroin: the Impact of a Drugs 'Epidemic' on an English Community,* Milton Keynes: Open University Press.

Pearson, G. (1987) *The New Heroin Users,* Oxford: Blackwell.

Pearson, G., Gilman, M. and McIver, S. (1985) *Young People and Heroin: an Examination of Heroin Use in the North of England,* Health Education Council Research Monograph No 8, London/Aldershot: Health Education Council/Gower.

Simon, D. and Burns, E. (1998) *The Corner: a Year in the Life of an Inner-city Neighbourhood,* New York: Broadway Books.

DRUG SERVICES EVALUATION

PART VII

INTRODUCTION

*T*he evaluation of drug services is the theme of this section, which opens with Chapter 24, by Neil Hunt, demonstrating how qualitative process evaluation affected the development of a drug prevention project in the UK. The section continues with chapters by researchers who have evaluated a range of services provided for a variety of problem drug users.

Anna Rodés and Catherine Pérez demonstrate in Chapter 25 how the perceptions and opinions of injecting drug users are important for both evaluating services and for facilitating the peer-education model of service provision.

Justin Kenrick's work with drug-using prostitutes/sex workers in Scotland is described in Chapter 26. This work shifted the research funder's focus away from evaluating service provision towards an understanding of how the women themselves interpreted their experiences of sex work/prostitution. Kenrick's work revealed the opposing ways women made sense of their experience and highlighted that both choice and pain were present in the women's experiences. With this deeper understanding, services planners could provide for apparently contradictory needs.

In Chapter 27, Mats Hilte also demonstrates that, when women drug users are given the opportunity to reveal their own perspectives, they are more successful in overcoming their drug problems.

Sam Wright and Hilary Klee conducted an evaluation of treatment services in the UK for amphetamine users. In Chapter 28, they demonstrate the value of qualitative research by revealing that the outcome measures of improvement — as defined by the Department of Health — could damage critically important interpersonal relationships in a way that could jeopardise a client's chances of success and lead to relapse.

Janusz Sierosławski completes the section, with Chapter 29, by looking at a qualitative approach to needs assessment in the Polish city of Poznań where services for problem drug users are less well developed than in western Europe.

ZEBRA WATCHING IN RURAL ENGLAND: THE CONTRIBUTION OF A QUALITATIVE PROCESS EVALUATION TO A NEW DRUG PREVENTION PROJECT TARGETING YOUNG PEOPLE

Neil Hunt

This chapter describes aspects of the evaluation of a rural drug prevention project — the Grey Zebra (Hunt and Hart, 1998). The project name was chosen to signify that drug use is not a black-and-white issue, and originated out of concern within the county of Kent that young people in rural areas had especially poor access to drug services of any kind. Although there was strong general feeling that 'something should be done', it was less clear exactly how it should be done.

West Kent Health Authority, with additional support from the Safer Kent Committee and Maidstone Rotary Club, provided project funding to a local non-statutory service — the Kenward Trust. This paid for a full-time project worker who, alongside two existing outreach staff and occasional volunteers, worked from a caravan in different localities on weekday evenings. The workers visited a series of different villages for one evening a week over periods of up to 10 weeks. Operating within a harm-reduction model, the work involved:

- engaging young people;
- discussing their drug use (legal and illicit) and identifying any related concerns; and
- providing information about drug-related harm and risk reduction through both informal conversation and a range of more structured activities.

The evaluation took place over a period of one year and was commissioned to assist in understanding how the project could best develop and what outcomes it might produce.

Close attention was paid to the advice given by Dorn and Murji (1992, pp. 38–39), who found that the research evidence for interventions that successfully prevent drug use — the aim of the project as described in its original proposal — was poor. Consequently, they recommended that careful process evaluations should be conducted before proceeding to evaluate outcomes. These conclusions led directly to the adoption of a qualitative process evaluation, which could provide the detailed descriptive information that would inform a subsequent outcome evaluation.

Evaluation methodology

The data collection involved field notes, interviews and focus-group data collected whilst the project was working with young people. A careful balance was necessary between collecting close-up data on what actually happened when the work was going on and minimising interference with the workers or intruding on the young people.

Alongside understanding how the project operated in the field, the evaluation also examined the organisational context of the work. As a multi-agency project involving a wide range of bodies, it was important to understand what the different stakeholders [1] wanted, and how systems could best be developed to steer it effectively. Thus, data were also collected from the following sources:

- observational data at meetings of the steering group, the management team and project workers' team meetings;
- documentary analysis of minutes and operational policies devised during the year; and
- interviews with stakeholders.

Learning from the evaluation

The learning from the evaluation can be summarised with reference to some of the basic questions that surround most innovative projects: What is the project trying to do? How can the project best do it? Who is the project targeting? How will we know if it has worked? A qualitative approach to the evaluation was very useful in answering each of these questions.

What is the project trying to do?

An early task of the evaluators was to work with the project staff to specify more clearly the aims and objectives of the project. In order to evaluate any programme, it is necessary to have clear, measurable objectives. Although the original proposal identified an aim and several objectives, it became clear, after talking with the project staff, that these did not encapsulate all the actual intentions of the project.

Drawing on documentary evidence relating to the project proposal and observational data at steering group meetings, and in conjunction with the project workers,

---

[1] The term 'stakeholder' refers to any person or agency with an interest in the aims and objectives of the project. Altogether, these include the target population itself, other community members, project workers, funders and other public sector agencies on the steering group, such as youth services, drug services and the police.

the evaluators were able to assist the project team in specifying more easily evaluated aims and objectives. For example, discussion with the project workers showed that they expected the project to leave some lasting effect after its visits, which were typically over 6 to 10 weeks in each village. However, the mechanism by which this might happen was not explicit. In drawing attention to this point, the evaluators enabled the project workers to clarify that they expected some community change to occur. This was then reflected in an additional objective — to identify and act on opportunities for involving community members in relevant ongoing activities. Clarifying the objective appeared to increase this emphasis in the subsequent work.

How can the project best do it?

Although the initial clarification of aims and objectives assisted with specifying the intentions of the project, field observations and interviews provided useful data concerning ways in which they could be achieved. The involvement of the evaluators meant that a culture of experimentation was adopted, rather than a premature commitment to a single mode of working. The immediate feedback this provided also allowed the work to develop in a way that was highly responsive to the views of the people targeted by the project. The limitations of the published evidence-base for such work meant that, in many respects, the best evidence for 'what works' was collected in the field, through qualitative evaluation.

How to 'get the culture right'?

From the outset, the project aimed to differentiate itself culturally from other local services for young people by promoting a high level of ownership of the space within and around the caravan. This was achieved by encouraging visitors to bring their own music to play on a tape player in the caravan, to help themselves to the tea, coffee and soft drinks provided, and by minimising imposed rules. Since the caravan went to the places where the young people 'hung out', bad language was tolerated and the workers did not attempt to impose rules about tobacco smoking, other than within the caravan itself. In practice, it was largely racist and homophobic remarks that caused the workers to ask whether more formal rules were necessary.

The interviews with young people consistently produced animated feedback about how they felt respected by the workers because they were permitted to act in a less rule-bound, more authentic way. The project was spontaneously contrasted very positively with other statutory services that were perceived as 'adultist' — i.e. failing to appreciate the young person's point of view. Consequently, the milieu meant that drug prevention information materials and activities within the project appeared to have far higher source-credibility than might otherwise have been the case. This was valuable information as, to some extent, the project workers initially lacked confidence about whether they were adopting the right approach, and there was also a risk that a service that tolerated such behaviour would attract criticism from statutory services.

How to identify effective activities?

In much the same way, the data collection helped identify activities that seemed most worth persisting with or developing. For example, one project worker was especially imaginative at adapting mainstream children's games in ways that enabled them to be used for drug education. A logic game was adapted to 'Guess the drug' by a series of yes/no questions about its attributes. Questions used in another game involving moral judgments were replaced by those about drug decisions, enabling values to be explored in more detail.

How to clarify the role of ex-users?

Since one project worker and one volunteer were ex-drug users, the evaluation was able to provide immediate feedback and clarification regarding how best to draw upon such experience. One session in which the workers described their experience of bad trips with LSD had a high impact on the group of 13- to 14-year-old boys with whom this was discussed. When describing this to the evaluators later, they were emphatic that this had changed their view of LSD and they were now resolved not to take it.

Such apparently effective work was also contrasted by the young people with their experiences elsewhere of ex-users being involved in drug prevention. One group described how someone had talked to them about his experience as a drug user but how he talked a lot about how much he used to use and deal and how he knew various 'hard men'. This person was dismissed as 'a bit of a wanker really. He was just showing off to us.' The evaluation revealed that experience of drug use does not guarantee high source-credibility: the manner of relating to young people and drawing on the experience is the key to its effectiveness.

Who is the project targeting?

The workers were initially uncertain whether they should each work generically across the population using the project, or whether they should specialise. By feeding back observations on the particular skills of different workers, greater role definition and specialisation evolved. Although rigid demarcation was resisted, the evaluation promoted an understanding of individual project workers' special skills, so that, for instance, a young child with suspected family problems might be channelled towards one particular worker. Similarly, working with older recreational users became more the province of another, who took greater responsibility for engaging the older group that were sometimes hanging around at the edges of the project. Yet another worker took lead responsibility for organising the more structured activities within the caravan. At the end of the year, it had become clearer that 14- to 17-year-olds were the main group that the project could expect to influence.

In the course of this process, a rather unexpected function of the evaluators seemed to be to fulfil something of a supportive, supervisory role. Although supervision arrangements were made from the outset, the absence of any obvious, local, specialised, professional reference group who would undertake detached, rural drug prevention work meant that the workers still had a number of concerns about whether they were doing the job correctly. Being able to give feedback about the evaluators' observations of good practice for each worker, supported by feedback from the young people themselves, appeared to be greatly valued by the project workers.

How will we know if it has worked?

Drawing on the data collection across the project, the final evaluation report summarised evaluable, intermediate and end outcomes. Following Pawson and Tilley (1997), the likely mechanisms by which the project could achieve each outcome were described. The use of a qualitative approach had enabled these to be clarified during the evaluation.

Had an outcome evaluation been attempted from the outset, it would have been disadvantaged by working from a poorly informed understanding of how the project operated. This changed somewhat over the course of the year. Some outcomes, such as enhanced inter-agency practice, community change and identification of the need for service developments, would also largely have been overlooked. In this project, a qualitative process evaluation was valuable for defining both the scope of outcomes and how these might best be evaluated.

Conclusions

The evaluation was valuable in providing immediate feedback from the target population, thus helping to shape the way that the work was delivered. It also helped sustain an experimental working environment in which different approaches could be tried, and adopted or rejected according to their success. Without this emphasis, it is likely that the project team would have felt it necessary to pay more attention to quantitative performance measures, such as contact rate. The initial qualitative process evaluation helped ensure that an eventual outcome evaluation would be more meaningful. It also enabled the different statutory stakeholders' wants and needs to influence the project, alongside the voices of members of the community in which it was working and, most importantly, of the young people themselves.

The author is Research Manager for Invicta Community Care NHS Trust in Maidstone, Kent, UK.

Acknowledgements

Thanks are due to: my co-evaluator Laura Hart (a woman with a real talent for engaging children); the young people of rural Maidstone for talking so freely to us; the project workers — Alison Swan, Denise Hayward and Craig Lindsay — for being so stimulating to work with; the project management team from the Kenward Trust and Cornerstone; and the various members of the steering group for their openness. Finally, thanks to Ann Palmer and Helen Medlock of West Kent Health Authority — two people who understand the importance of qualitative evaluation.

References

Dorn, N. and Murji, K. (1992) *Drug Prevention: a Review of the English Language Literature*, London: ISDD.

Hunt, N. and Hart, L. (1998) *The Grey Zebra: Evaluation of a Young Person's Mobile Drug Project*, Maidstone: Invicta Community Care NHS Trust.

Pawson, R. and Tilley, N. (1997) *Realistic Evaluation*, London: Sage.

CHAPTER 25

Clients' perceptions of the structure and operational characteristics of Southern European syringe-exchange programmes: Pesesud-1

Anna Rodés, Catherine Pérez and the Pesesud-1 (Programas Échange Seringues Europa Sud) working group [1]

Southern European countries are the most affected by the AIDS epidemic among injecting drug users (IDUs), their sexual partners and their children. Of the cumulative AIDS cases diagnosed in Europe up to the end of 1995, 43 % were related to injecting drug use. Of these cases, 93 % were IDUs, 6.2 % were heterosexual partners of IDUs and 1.4 % were children whose mothers were IDUs. More than 90 % of the cumulative AIDS cases associated with injecting drug use were concentrated in south-western Europe.

The cumulative incidence rate of AIDS cases in IDUs in southern Europe was 58.6 cases per million inhabitants (124 cases per million inhabitants in Spain, 63 in Italy and 23 in France), in contrast with 3.7 cases per million inhabitants observed in north-eastern Europe [2]. Furthermore, AIDS cases attributable to heterosexual transmission in Europe have increased, especially in the countries that show the highest AIDS incidence rates among IDUs. Thus, up to the end of 1995 in Spain, heterosexual transmission of HIV reached an incidence rate of 22.9 cases per million inhabitants — 2.4 times greater than the average for other European countries — which since 1994 has accounted for the second most frequent transmission route [3].

Since the beginning of 1990, several strategies to prevent HIV infection associated with injecting drug use have been adopted, and a harm-reduction approach to the problems derived from injecting drug use has emerged. All harm-reduction interventions consider injecting drug use as a phenomenon causing considerable health

---

[1] The Pesesud-1 working group consisted of: Anna Rodés, Catherine Pérez, Albert Moncada, Mireia Alberni and Jordi Casabona (Ceescat, Badalona, Spain); Suzanne Cagliero and Alain Edwige (*Medécins du Monde*, Paris, France); and Alessia Sabbatini and Alfredo Nicolosi (*Consiglio Nazionale delle Ricerche*, Milan, Italy).

[2] European Centre for the Epidemiological Monitoring of AIDS, *HIV/AIDS surveillance in Europe*, quarterly report, 1996, 30 June.

[3] Secretaría del Plan Nacional sobre el SIDA, Instituto de Salud Carlos III (1997), *Epidemiología del Sida en España 1996*, Madrid: Ministerio de Sanidad y Consumo.

problems for both individuals and for society. The slow but progressive implementation of substitution programmes with opiates (methadone or buprenorphine) and syringe-exchange programmes (SEPs) are the result of this emerging approach.

In 1996, the Pesesud working group was launched, financed by the European Commission. Its objective was to assess the rate of SEP development in Spain, France and Italy, and to describe their structural and operational characteristics. In the first phase of this project, a quantitative study was supported by a qualitative study to complete and clarify data obtained from the quantitative research. The quantitative study included a postal survey of all identified SEPs, with an overall response rate of 84 %; information about more than 200 programmes and 500 distribution points from the three participating countries was collected.

For the qualitative study, four programmes in each country were selected according to their type, size and geographical location and site visits to each were conducted. Following semi-structured interview guidelines, project members interviewed a total of 79 individuals, including 41 SEP directors and staff, 12 public health officials and 28 SEP clients. The areas investigated were related to the background, structural and operating rules of the programmes, their integration into the community, and clients' perceptions of the SEP.

This chapter describes the clients' perceptions of the SEP they attend, the extent to which their needs have been met by it, and their patterns of drug use. Owing to significant differences between the countries and SEPs selected, an overall description cannot be provided. Thus, in this chapter, one programme from each country is described. These were selected to represent different types of SEP: the first combines different types of exchange points, the second is a fixed location SEP and the third is a mobile SEP.

Programme d'Échange de Seringues de Médecins du Monde, Marseilles, France

This SEP was started in 1994 following a pilot street-work phase to evaluate the needs of IDUs and the ways in which they obtained sterile injecting equipment. The programme combined several types of exchange points: a bus stopping in different areas of the city; a street-outreach team; and two syringe exchange machines. In 1996, the bus made more than 2 881 exchanges, contacted at least 579 users and distributed more than 40 000 sterile syringes.

Four individual in-depth interviews with clients of the bus were held (three 28-year-old men and one 24-year-old woman). Buprenorphine was the primary injected drug of all four participants; one occasionally injected heroin, and one of the two who used cocaine injected it. All individuals injected between one and four times a day. Three individuals reported not reusing syringes more than twice, but one reported reusing them many times when he could not obtain new ones. Although all participants reported using their own syringes, one individual shared the prepared drug.

All participants knew of the existence of other SEPs in the city, but only one attended them more than three times a week. One individual attended the bus three times a week and another only once a week. One person reported using an exchange machine regularly and also purchasing anti-AIDS kits (Steribox) in pharmacies. Another participant reported using an exchange machine occasionally. The location of the bus stops was convenient for three of the participants because they lived in the same neighbourhood. The opening hours of the bus were convenient: one person remarked that Sunday was an especially convenient time for users who worked, since pharmacies were closed then. The same person suggested later opening times on Sunday (currently 15.00 to 19.00 hours) to give those users who got up late and bought the drug before getting syringes more time to acquire sterile injecting equipment.

Participants knew about the bus because they had read information about its location in the anti-AIDS kits provided by pharmacists and exchange machines and through information from their peers. Before these programmes had come into operation, they had purchased the Steribox, costing EUR 0.75 to EUR 1 in pharmacies. However, three participants reported feeling uncomfortable about the way in which the pharmacist treated them and sometimes feeling discriminated against. Three participants reported calculating the number of syringes they needed before going to the SEP, but one individual reported obtaining only one syringe at a time because he was living with his parents and did not know where to hide them.

With respect to the physical characteristics of the bus, one person said 'c'est impeccable' (it's impeccable). The atmosphere in the bus was praised, and they felt able to talk with staff when they had a problem.

The quality and the number of syringes (in bags of 10) provided on demand by the staff was greatly appreciated. One person thought the SEP should also provide cotton filters and cookers for injectors to prepare the drug mixture. Although condoms were also available, one person reported never asking for them.

When participants were asked about the risk-reduction messages provided by the SEP staff, they reported feeling well-informed. They were also asked about the help received from staff in getting social or medical care and entering into drug treatment if they so wished. None of the participants had requested drug treatment programmes, although one person reported occasionally going to a 'sleep-in' centre in the city and also periodically receiving financial aid from the state.

Programa de Intercambio de Jeringuillas, SAPS, Barcelona, Spain

This SEP was started in 1993 as an emergency social centre for the marginalised drug addict population. The project's premises are situated in a wing of an emergency health centre and entered via the fire escape. The service operates every night from 22.00 to 06.00 hours. In 1996, the service made more than 21 235 exchanges, contacted more than 2 200 users and distributed approximately 100 000 sterile syringes.

A focus group was held with four clients (one 37-year-old man, another 26-year-old man, a 26-year-old woman and a 33-year-old transvestite). Heroin was the primary injecting drug for the three participants who injected it on a daily basis. Two participants injected cocaine occasionally, one of whom was in a methadone programme, and another smoked brown heroin. The female participant reported sharing her syringe with her husband, another reported accepting used syringes 'once in a while' if his own syringe was broken or if he was 'without works but with drugs'. Two individuals did not accept used syringes.

Two participants knew about the SEP through friends, whilst another participant was informed by a neighbour. Three individuals had attended the service for six months, and one had attended since its opening. All but one knew about other SEPs in the same area and had occasionally used them, particularly those based in pharmacies.

'Syringe street markets' were reported by one person. The location of the service was convenient for all the participants, since they lived in the same area. The opening hours were convenient for one person, but a second reported preferring daytime opening hours because the night timetable was inconvenient for those who lived with their families or spouses.

One person complained about the small space from which the service operated. Participants assessed the exchange service very positively, because they were able to obtain as many syringes as they needed. The person in methadone substitution treatment attended the service mainly for food and only occasionally took syringes. One person complained about the quality of the syringes distributed, remarking on their uselessness for injecting cocaine.

Participants generally expressed positive opinions about the SEP ('life-saving', the only link they have with reliable information, etc.), and particularly about the SEP staff. They emphasised the respectful way in which they were treated, the 'family' atmosphere, and the good company. One commented: *estoy muy contenta, como en família, te hablan, te escuchan, te ayudan* (I'm very satisfied, like in a family, they talk to you, they listen to you, they help you).

With respect to risk-reduction messages provided by the SEP staff, three participants reported learning specific techniques besides the importance of using sterile syringes, such as how to clean skin before injecting, how to select a vein, and how to avoid air entering the syringe. One person reported having enough information.

Participants were also asked about the help received from staff in getting social or medical care and entering into drug treatment if they so wished. One noted that he had entered a methadone programme because of the help received from the staff. All participants appreciated the existence of regular meetings between the SEP staff and clients.

Unità di Strada in Turin, Italy

This SEP was started in 1994. Contact with users was established in an area known as 'the biggest drug market in Turin', which is frequented by people from many regions. The mobile unit works from Tuesday to Sunday between 11.00 and 15.00 hours, a timetable chosen because it covers the time that pharmacies are closed and because it coincides with the beginning of the daily consumption routine. In 1996, the programme made more than 42 000 exchanges, made contact with approximately 1 800 users and distributed approximately 90 000 sterile syringes.

A focus group interview was held with four SEP clients (three men of 33, 29 and 25 and one 21-year-old woman). Heroin was the primary injecting drug for three participants and cocaine for the other. They all injected daily, but the frequency was dependent on their personal finances. One participant did not use syringes more than once, two participants reused a syringe at least twice and another participant up to five or six times. Two participants reported accepting used syringes very occasionally. Condom use was reported by one participant, but the other two males never used them.

Two participants knew about the SEP from their peers and one person because he had seen the mobile unit. Only one participant knew about another SEP in the city.

All individuals had contacted the SEP for the first time more than six months previously; one of them visited it daily and a second participant a couple of times a week. Before the opening of the SEP, they all used to purchase syringes in pharmacies. The location of the different stops of the unit were considered quite convenient by all the participants, although one individual complained about the distance from where he usually hung out and the location where the vehicle stopped on Tuesdays.

Two participants preferred the injection material in kits and the other two preferred individual syringes. Two participants took one to two syringes at a time while another participant took five or more.

Participants expressed positive opinions about the SEP staff and one of them placed considerable emphasis on the respectful way in which he was treated. One participant reported being helped by the staff twice when he had overdosed. Two participants remarked that, aside from the practical aids provided by the staff, the people they met there were also important to them. One commented: *'a volte ti trovi da solo come un cane e invece vieni qui e parli tranquillamente se hai un problema'* (sometimes you find yourself alone like a dog but now you can come here and talk calmly if you have a problem).

Conclusions

The inclusion of qualitative methods into the study allowed the completion and interpretation of some of the findings from the quantitative part. In this study, IDUs' perceptions and opinions are of particular interest, since this group is the target population of SEPs: the findings not only influenced the way in which the SEP was run, in order to better meet their needs, but also facilitated the adoption of a peer education/community organising model of service provision.

Anna Rodés is a research associate at the Centre for Epidemiological Studies on AIDS (Ceescat) in Barcelona, Spain. Catherine Pérez is a research psychologist at Ceescat.

CHAPTER 26

USING QUALITATIVE RESEARCH TO INFORM SOCIAL POLICY ON SERVICES FOR DRUG-USING PROSTITUTES/SEX WORKERS

Justin Kenrick

The research presented here was conducted over four months in 1997 as 'An evaluation of the provision of a health care, outreach, education and HIV prevention service for females in the sex industry in Lothian' for Lothian Health Board under the guidance of Roger Lewis, at that time Director of the Centre for HIV/AIDS and Drugs Studies (CHADS). The purpose of the evaluation was to reassess the service needs of the client group and assess whether the current service provider, ScotPep, was meeting those needs.

Research methods

The methodology of the evaluation involved participant observation, in-depth interviews and some statistical analysis. Participant observation was achieved through becoming a part of the women's working lives by spending many evenings and nights on the streets of Leith, in Edinburgh, Scotland, while they sought 'punters', and in the drop-in centre there. The research also involved interviewing women selling sex in flats and saunas. ScotPep staff were interviewed, and the researcher also participated in their work.

To gain a broader perspective, interviews were conducted with police, health services, policy makers, and also with workers and users of Shiva, an alternative service provider which had previously been funded by Lothian Health Board before they switched their funding to ScotPep. As Shiva had before them, ScotPep primarily ran its outreach work by contacting women on the streets and in saunas, and by providing a drop-in centre (which included a medical clinic) for sex workers near to the women's 'beat'. Conflict and bad feeling existed between ScotPep and Shiva during the research period, and service provision by Shiva gradually ceased, partly due to lack of funding.

227

Research findings

Women's experience of sex work/prostitution

It quickly became apparent that, in order to evaluate service provision, the research had to focus on women's experiences of service provision relative to their needs, and that understanding their needs required an understanding of how they experienced sex work/prostitution.

By shifting from the research funder's focus on evaluating service provision to a focus on understanding how the women themselves interpreted their experience of sex work/prostitution, the conflict between the two different service providers (ScotPep and Shiva) was able to be seen as reflecting the opposing ways in which the women themselves made sense of their own experience. Those funding research are often doing so in order to find answers to questions which are not explicitly stated in the researcher's remit, and, in this context, the funder wanted to understand which (if any) service provider should be funded.

ScotPep's philosophy tended towards seeing the women as choosing to engage in sex work from a limited range of economic options, whilst Shiva's was that prostitution was a result of previous or current abusive relationships: ScotPep stressed the role of choice, Shiva stressed the role of pain in women's experience. One of the fundamental findings of the research was that the women themselves described their experience in both of these ways: moving between asserting at one moment that their work was a rational choice, and at another disclosing the pain and abuse involved. It proved virtually impossible for any of the women, the service providers, the media or the research funders to consistently remain aware that both choice and pain were present in the women's experience.

Commercial transaction or inherently degrading?

Whilst, on the one hand, women described sex work as being 'just another job', they also often talked emphatically about their disgust at the interaction, sometimes directing this at the punters and sometimes at themselves. ScotPep focused on supporting women doing 'just another job', although the reality of their service provision was that it made space for both the ways in which women experienced their situation. The following incident highlights the contradiction, and is also an example of the way in which process-oriented participant observation can enable researchers to use their own emotional responses to remain continuously (albeit peripherally) involved and open to the complexity of the situation.

> At a ScotPep meeting one woman (D) spoke of a journalist asking her *'Does ScotPep encourage you to work?'* and replying *'No, and if you can give me the sort of money I can get on the street then I'll stop.'* Later she turned to me and said *'You're a prostitute, you get paid at the end of the month or week.'* I was a bit taken aback by my work being equated with prostitution. *'But do you enjoy it?'* I replied, quite feebly, it

being the only aspect of my work I felt might distinguish it from prosti-tution. 'No, I bloody hate it. But when I went to the Social [welfare agency] I could get only 89 quid [pounds] [EUR 54] for me and my bairns [children]. Now, I get into a car, and get 30 quid [EUR 18] for spreading my legs in the back of the car. I hate it, punters crawling all over me, it's disgusting. I feel dirty, filthy. I scrub myself when I get home, really scrub myself. I clean everything, under the bed, you could eat off my floor it's so clean. Some nymphomaniacs enjoy it, but I don't, I hate it.' D went on to say that you can't be in a relationship and do this work — she said she stopped working when she got into a rela-tionship. Later, I was told that her relationship broke up because her partner said she was treating him like a punter. (Field note)

This incident highlights the difference between the assertion of many women that prostitution is 'just a job', and the emotional reality of their experience. Doubtless both levels of experience exist simultaneously. For example, several women inter-viewed used, or have used, sex work to finance a college course in the hope that they would then be able to find better paid work. Such choices may be rational on one level, but that does not necessarily change what may be a repulsive experience. A woman might speak in detail about the process of being abused and pimped which led to her becoming a prostitute, and yet will assert that 'I don't have a prob-lem with being a prostitute' once she has stepped into her 'working' role. Here, again, there appear to be two levels of experience.

The split self

Perhaps the key finding of this research was that outreach and medical provision in this area is vital: not just because of the perceived health and safety risks, but because almost all women working in this area are living split lives. Thus, their access to routine services such as a GP (general practitioner), a GUM (genito-urinary medicine) clinic, or a drugs service is limited, because their work, and often the accompanying drug use, dominates their lives, or because, in attempting to keep a sharp divide between the private self and the working self, they will not access the services they need when they are not working.

Throughout the study, many women described living a double life as intensely dis-tressing, indicating that the emotional costs of this work are extremely high. Other comments showed that sex in exchange for money is not sex as intimate contact, but sex as a physical act requiring the sex worker's emotional absence, and that, for the person offering sexual services to be emotionally present, money has to be absent.

How the service is used

The key finding of the research in terms of service provision involved an under-standing of how the experience of the split self informed women's use of ScotPep's needle exchange, drop-in centre and clinic.

The needle exchange

ScotPep's harm-reduction approach to safeguarding women's health as sex workers also applied to their drug use. Women could talk with a ScotPep worker in a side room in the drop-in and address issues around their drug use, including using the needle exchange there. The result of this easy access to a needle exchange, coupled with the services offered for sex workers, led to an increase in the use of the needle exchange, rising from 12 clients (May 1996–January 1997) to 43 (January 1997–September 1997). This is a high number for any drugs project in Lothian, let alone one whose main focus is not drugs. Whilst around half the increase in clients was due to an influx of women from Glasgow, the rest was due to the increased use of heroin by women in Edinburgh. An additional success was that half those who used the needle exchange in 1996 were no longer injecting by September 1997.

The drop-in centre

The drop-in centre was used very differently, depending on the degree to which the women allowed their whole self or only their 'working' self to be present:

> For 99 % of women working [as sex workers], nobody knows they're working. You're having to lie to people, having to hide a part of yourself in your other life. There's mental health issues there. You have value and respect in the drop-in centre space where you can be yourself.
> (U, a ScotPep worker)

The women used the facility for very different reasons. Visits were often hasty, with women using the place functionally, wanting their personal selves to remain hidden. They came to use the toilet, to change clothes, get warm, obtain supplies of condoms, or use the needle exchange. Others were in a hurry to see the doctor, exchange safety information concerning dangerous men in the area, or have a brief one-to-one session with a drop-in worker or counsellor about a pressing problem.

However, when an incident or problem occurred and they found that there was support for them as individuals, then the relationship to the space could change: they might pause for a cup of tea or coffee, a chat rather than just rushing through, and perhaps the risk would be taken to mention their children or something else from their 'non-working' lives. Just by its existence, the drop-in centre enabled women to make threadlike connections back and forth across the divided aspects of their lives.

The clinic

The different medical approaches of the previous (Shiva) and current (ScotPep) service providers not only reflected their different philosophies, but also the different ways in which the women themselves made sense of the territory. ScotPep's approach, which respects the women's 'choice' to be sex workers and seeks to support them in taking care of themselves in this role, is reflected in the type of medical service provided by their GUM doctors: focusing on the risks inherent in the women's role as sex workers, rather than on broader medical and social needs. As one ScotPep doctor put it:

> We're not GP trained doctors so we shouldn't provide general stuff. [Running the clinic is] a hell of a lot of hassle for the returns, but for every working woman you treat, you are covering a very large number of sexual contacts. One woman is equal to 50 general contacts.

This focus on sexual health means that some GUM staff appear to believe that women arrive at the clinic through conscious choice, and assume that they will use the clinic, whoever is operating it, and whether or not it is working alongside a drop-in centre providing additional services. However, sometimes, women who had first attended with a relatively minor problem were persuaded by other clients to seek help to deal with larger issues: the notion of sex workers always being able to make conscious decisions about seeking medical or counselling help would therefore seem to be incorrect. Most of the women were either chaotic drug users and/or wanted to keep their sex work secret, which meant that they were reluctant to see their family GP or attend other GUM clinics. As a consequence, the clinic was of vital importance and clearly needed to be alongside a drop-in centre, in order that the women's wider personal, social and health issues could also be addressed.

Conclusions

This chapter has demonstrated the way in which qualitative research can begin to challenge the assumptions of practitioners — in this case health professionals — not directly under evaluation, and can thereby inform policy decisions, such as the context required for a medical clinic to be effective.

Although funding for ScotPep's (and, previously, Shiva's) outreach work through their drop-in centres and clinics was originally justified on the grounds of providing a bridge between service providers and a marginalised group with severe health and safety risks, providing a bridge between normally opposing aspects of a person's life can be an equally important task.

Even from the purely medical point of view, the clinic is only made accessible to those who need it most because it is located at the drop-in centre, which itself provides a bridge both between opposing aspects of a woman's life and to services which otherwise might remain out of reach. The very nature of a drop-in centre, which welcomes stories about, for example, the women's children, supports and encourages them to bring the divided personal and work parts of their split selves together. For the women, negotiating this internal meeting would appear to be the prerequisite for making free choices in the face of both aspects of their lives.

The usefulness of this research to policy-makers lay in conveying an inclusive understanding of service provision in the field of sex work/prostitution, an understanding which the media, policy-makers and service providers can easily lose sight of given the highly emotive nature of the territory.

In very practical terms, the research pinpointed the way in which medical outreach, the drop-in centre and women's needs interacted. It recommended that Lothian Health Board should not attempt to merge ScotPep and Shiva's organisations, since their approaches were mutually exclusive. ScotPep's harm-reduction approach was seen as the most valuable, since their approach was less threatening to the women themselves. The major failing of the service — that it might not address the painful issues that brought women into prostitution and kept them there — could be redressed by providing trained counsellors. Consequently, the research recommended that securing permanent premises for ScotPep's drop-in centre was extremely important, not only to enable the effective continuation of health and safety provision, but to facilitate the support women can provide for each other, and the changes they can negotiate for themselves.

The author is an Honorary Fellow in the Department of Social Anthropology, University of Edinburgh, Scotland, UK.

CHAPTER 27

NARRATIVES OF RECOVERY FROM CLIENTS AND STAFF IN TREATMENT ORGANISATIONS

Mats Hilte

The recovery process has been studied both as part of treatment settings and as a natural process: Winick (1962) describes it as a matter of 'maturing out' of drug abuse, and Stall and Biernacki (1986) refer to the same process as being natural and spontaneous. Stall and Biernacki describe the factors involved in the recovery process in terms of 'pushes' and 'pulls', where deteriorating health and negative social consequences push people out of drug use, and stable economic and social living conditions pull them out.

Another vocabulary is used within treatment settings: Frankel (1989) depicts the treatment process as a transformation of identities. In our current research project, we are studying how the client speaks about the process of recovery. Are the recovery tales told differently depending upon the type of treatment programme? Who are the main characters in the recovery plot and what are the basic activities in the stories told?

Research aims

The main purpose of this research project is to study women who abuse psychoactive substances and how their path to recovery is negotiated and narrated in the context of a specific treatment programme. Four different programmes and 28 women are participating. The main aims are to document:

- the women's backgrounds (education, work experience, drug-using patterns, former rehabilitation attempts, etc.);
- how the women describe their problems and their recovery process; and
- how the women's problems and their recovery process is described by members of the staff in the treatment programme.

Methods

Sample and data collection

The research project is designed as a qualitative case study based on tape-recorded, in-depth interviews. The group of women participating in the study were interviewed on four different occasions: at the beginning, middle, and end of the treatment process and one year after treatment was terminated. The participating treatment centres were chosen to represent as varied and broad a range as possible, including both in-patient and out-patient treatment, short-term and long-term programmes, voluntary and compulsory programmes, and unisex and mixed institutions. Between them, these institutions used a variety of treatment ideologies: the Hazelden model, the therapeutic community and solution-focused therapy.

Analysis

The interviews with the women and the staff members were analysed with the help of narrative theory, which understands the women's narratives of recovery as situationally and socially constructed accounts characterised by a certain type of experience: in our study, the women talk about their experiences of substance abuse and treatment. Denzin (1989) calls these types of narratives 'self-stories'. These stories are not the product of an independent and autonomous individual, but rather are part of socially accepted ways of accounting for individual experiences.

The telling of a story is an important part of human beings' ways of making sense of their life experiences. By way of this sense-making process, the individual is constructing and reproducing identity and subjectivity. Alasuutari (1992) contends that the reproduced subjectivity is collective in nature and that it provides the individual 'with lenses through which concrete phenomena or events are perceived and interpreted' (p. 67). Putnam et al. (1996) have pointed out that narratives are produced and reproduced in organisations, as members make sense of events and their significance for the organisation. In this respect, the narratives are vehicles through which values and beliefs are produced and transformed, and are, therefore, an important factor in the socialisation of newcomers.

According to Propp (1968), narratives can be analysed and classified by focusing on the morphological form of the story: i.e. who the main characters in the plot are and what basic actions they perform that have significance for the subsequent course of action. The basic actions can be ordered according to such principles as chronology and causality.

Alasuutari (1992) maintains that every story consists of stative events (sentences describing a state of affairs) and active events (which change the state of affairs). Gergen (1997) has identified three elementary narratives: the progressive, the stable and the regressive tale. In the progressive narrative, actions and events are linked together to reinforce a development. The progressive narrative depicts a positive and cumulative process of change. It could be represented by the statement 'I am really learning how to deal with my drug dependence and I am making progress every day.' In the regressive narrative, the opposite occurs. The actions in the story are interpreted as part of an ongoing downward slide, where conditions are constantly getting worse, and this is characterised by statements such as 'I am really losing control over my drug use and the negative consequences of that are growing every day.'

Findings

The narratives of members of staff within the separate treatment programmes have much in common. In three of the four programmes, the main character is the victimised client. In the recovery plot, the victimised client must go through changes in order to be rehabilitated. She must gain an understanding of why she is addicted to psychoactive drugs. That understanding will, at the same time, pave the way for an identity transformation.

The Hazelden programme describes the client as the victim of an illness and presupposes that she must reach some kind of understanding about that state of affairs in order to become drug-free. The active event in this narrative is the giving up of a state of denial and the acceptance of an identity as a recovering drug user or sober alcoholic. The client is gradually transformed from the victimised to the responsible individual.

Within the therapeutic community, the client is portrayed as the victim of negative emotional experiences and the oppression of women. The active event in the plot is the development of insights into the client's emotional life and a growing awareness of the oppression of women and their dependence upon men. In this kind of narrative, the victimised client is transformed into a self-confident and self-conscious client.

The victimised client is also the main character in the recovery plot told by staff members working in compulsory institutional care. Here, the client is the victim of a self-destructive lifestyle and identity. The active event in the integrity narrative is the transformation from self-destructiveness to a greater sense of integrity of self. The main character in the integrity narrative changes from a victimised to a constructive-minded client.

In the narrative of staff members working with solution-focused therapy, the main character is the competent client, where the active event is new perspectives on, and new solutions to, old problems. Another feature that distinguishes the solution narrative from the rest is that the plot does not say anything about the clients' past or their problems. The narrative is oriented towards the future and the solutions to problems identified only by the client themselves. Another difference is that the main character is not undergoing any identity transformations, as in the other recovery plots.

Our analysis of the clients' narratives has not yet been completed, but some preliminary remarks can be made. The way the women describe their problems and recovery process does not always tally with the dominant story-line of staff from the treatment programme in which they are participating. Instead, they develop an individual style in their narrative accounts, picking out certain parts of the plot and using different kinds of 'selves' as the main character. One interesting result is that the success of the clients' recovery process is not necessarily dependent upon the reproduction of the dominant story-line from the treatment programme. There are women who stick to the dominant story-line in their narrative accounts but have relapsed, and there are women who have developed their own individual story-line and have succeeded in ceasing to use drugs.

Another observation we have made is that the women's self-stories are not neutral accounts. Rather, they are embedded in dominant gendered stories that are important in maintaining the social construction of femininity in contemporary society. The role as mother and wife is an important ingredient in the stories told by the women, but, due to their drug use, many of them have not been able to live up to conventional expectations and have as a consequence suffered feelings of shame and guilt. The social construction of the guilty woman is a recurrent theme in many of the self-stories.

Conclusions

Two important conclusions can be drawn from these preliminary results. Firstly, clients do not have to reproduce organisational values and beliefs in their self-stories in order to be successful in the recovery process. The treatment staff, as well as the researcher, need to be more open to multiple narratives with multiple meanings. The treatment ideology, with its dominant story-line, can otherwise limit the clients' actions and force them into straitjacket identities. If clients are pushed into identities that do not fit their own experiences and values, there is a greater risk of relapse into drug misuse after the treatment programme is completed. Secondly, women should be given the opportunity to 're-story' their lives in relation to alternative meaning systems. The dominant cultural stories about women tend to be sexualised and subjugated stories. When women are given the opportunity to re-story their lives, they develop self-reliance and self-knowledge, which makes them more prepared and able to cope with problems and conflicts in everyday life without the help of drugs.

The author is Associate Professor at the School of Social Work, Lund University, Sweden.

References

Alasuutari, P. (1992) A Cultural Theory of Alcoholism, New York: State University of New York Press.

Denzin, N. K. (1989) *Interpretative Biography,* Qualitative Research Methods, Vol. 17, August 1989, London: Sage.

Frankel, B. (1989) *Transforming Identities,* New York: Peter Lang.

Gergen, K. J. (1997) *Realities and Relationships,* Cambridge: Harvard University Press.

Propp, V. (1968) *Morphology of the Folktale,* Austin: University of Texas Press.

Putnam, L., Phillips, N. and Chapman, P. (1996) 'Metaphors of communication and organization, in S. Clegg, C. Hardy and W. R. Nord (Eds.) *Handbook of Organization Studies,* London: Sage, pp. 375–409.

Stall, R. and Biernacki, P. (1986) 'Spontaneous remission from the problematic use of substances', *International Journal of the Addictions,* 21, 1–23.

Winick, C. (1962) 'Maturing-out of narcotic addiction', *Bulletin on Narcotics,* 14, 1–7.

CHAPTER 28

TREATMENT SERVICES
FOR AMPHETAMINE USERS

Sam Wright and Hilary Klee

A wide variety of research exists within the scope of qualitative work. One definition, which seeks to encompass the whole spectrum, describes qualitative research as 'a particular tradition in social science that fundamentally depends on watching people in their own territory' (Kirk and Miller, 1986, p. 9).

Illicit drug use and its treatment lends itself well to the design and methods of qualitative research for four main reasons. First, due to the largely covert nature of drug use, the majority of drug users are a 'hidden population' and research which is designed to locate individuals in their own environment will be more effective at identifying drug users and investigating aspects of their lives. Second, there are many areas within the study of drug use and its treatment which remain under-researched and undocumented, so that qualitative enquiry, which encourages the discovery of new behaviours and perceptions, will make a significant contribution to knowledge about drug use. Third, because of the illegal nature of drug use, the development of trust between researcher and participant is essential, and this can more easily be achieved face-to-face in an environment where the participant feels most at ease. Finally, many aspects of drug use behaviours involve a variety of risks for the individual which appear counter-intuitive to concepts of health protection and general harm minimisation. Only through in-depth qualitative work can these behaviours be unravelled and understood.

The Centre for Social Research into Health and Substance Abuse (SRHSA) in the UK has a long history of combining qualitative and quantitative research in the investigation of a variety of aspects of illicit drug use. This mixture of methods has been found to produce a richer understanding of drug users' actions, experiences and attitudes, and has often revealed aspects of drug-using behaviour which warrant further investigation.

This case study reports on the qualitative aspects of one research project conducted by SRHSA between 1995 and 1997 (Klee and Wright, 1999a; 1999b). The research was designed to investigate the effectiveness of treatment services for amphetamine users in the north-west of England. There were three main aims: to reveal amphetamine users' attitudes towards treatment services; to record their experiences of service provision; and to monitor any changes in health, drug or social factors during treatment.

The main elements for evaluating treatment outcomes were defined by the Department of Health Task Force (1996), focusing on abstinence or reduction of drug use and injecting, improving physical and psychological health and enhancing drug users' social functioning and their life context. Our amphetamine project recorded these data over a period of 6 to 10 months, contrasting the experiences of amphetamine users who were seeking drug treatment with a matched-case control group of amphetamine users who were not in contact with treatment services. This case study will describe some of the contributions that the qualitative research made to our understanding of the effectiveness of drug services for amphetamine users, particularly regarding the contradictions inherent in the process of attempting to abstain from amphetamine use.

Qualitative research with amphetamine users

Despite being the second most prevalent illicit drug in the UK, amphetamine use has received relatively little attention until recently (Klee, 1992). The research that has been conducted in treatment settings has generally been small-scale clinical trials focusing on the prescribing of dexamphetamine to clients and monitoring their subsequent use of street amphetamine. The research reported here was the first matched-case control study of clients in treatments, and it employed researchers independent of treatment services to encourage clients to freely disclose behaviours which they may have kept secret from drug workers.

In order to ensure comprehensive views of the effectiveness of services, a variety of perspectives were sought, including the views of current amphetamine clients, ex-clients and amphetamine users who had never approached services. The majority of amphetamine users were interviewed in their homes, and this frequently resulted in family members becoming involved in discussions and contributing further information to the interviews. In addition, focus groups and individual interviews were held with health professionals working with drug users in the region, in order to gather the experiences and beliefs of service providers.

The research with amphetamine users consisted of a series of in-depth, semi-structured interviews, which were tape-recorded (for further details see Wright et al., 1998). The researchers were trained to probe for great detail in the interviews and to check for inconsistencies in participants' accounts. Immediately before the second, third and fourth interviews, the researchers re-read the previous interview to identify missing or ambiguous information. This enabled them to question any discrepancies in information and to encourage interviewees to discuss such issues more fully, which allowed greater clarity and understanding of behaviour patterns to develop over time. It also enabled the researchers to identify recent changes in behaviour, and to probe for motivations and experiences associated with the change.

The interviews combined open and closed questions, the former to collect data that were rich in detail. Much of this additional information was coded for quantitative analyses, but it was also important in revealing and validating emergent themes. Interview participants were encouraged to talk openly about their attitudes towards drug use, their experiences of drug services and their experiences in trying to reduce or stop their amphetamine use. They were asked to reflect on their motives for taking amphetamines, to describe any problems arising from their drug use and to identify the events which precipitated their decision to abstain from amphetamines and seek treatment. The research included not only details regarding the defined treatment outcomes, but also wider issues such as the social context and lifestyles of the individuals interviewed. As interviews were mainly conducted in participants' homes, observations were made regarding their domestic arrangements and interpersonal relationships. These were recorded in field notes and were used to inform the subsequent analyses and interpretations.

A wider understanding of service evaluation

The statistical data regarding the outcome measures defined by the Department of Health Task Force were collected and analysed, with the results indicating that drug service clients made significant progress in reducing amphetamine use, particularly during the first few months of receiving treatment. However, one important feature of qualitative research is that it questions the taken-for-granted or 'common-sense' definitions of the social world and seeks to identify and make problematic the associated cultural assumptions (Silverman, 1993). In the amphetamine research, the qualitative data provided us with a richer understanding of the contradictions inherent in attempting to evaluate the effectiveness of drug services. It helped us to identify the competing motivations of amphetamine users who were seeking treatment, and the social context within which their drug use and their attempts at abstinence occurred.

First, there were the difficulties that individuals faced in identifying that their drug use was problematic, and in overcoming the barriers to seeking treatment (Wright et al., 1999). It can be very difficult to contemplate abstention until quite severe problems have developed, particularly for stimulant users whose drug use can temporarily give them a confident and motivated persona which is valued by society. The stigma of being classified as a problem drug user made many amphetamine users reluctant to seek treatment, and commonly held negative stereotypes about opiate users resulted in a desire not to be treated as a drug addict. Treatment services were perceived by drug users and staff alike as being strongly opiate-oriented, and the belief that little help was available for amphetamine users was also a barrier to presenting for treatment. Many amphetamine users presented to services initially but never returned (Wright and Klee, forthcoming), indicating that access to drug treatment and client retention rates should be factors in evaluating service effectiveness.

For those who pursued treatment and attempted to abstain, the lethargy, depression and psychological distress associated with ceasing amphetamine consumption made them question their reasons for ceasing drug use. In-depth interviews revealed the unanticipated difficulties faced by those trying to stop long-term, heavy amphetamine use. This meant that, whilst clients may make substantial improvements in the short term, outcomes for the longer term were more variable. As with many types of behavioural change, there can develop over time a degree of ambivalence towards sustained abstention from drugs. Motivations for change can be questioned and, particularly where clients believe that they are stopping drug use for the sake of their family as opposed to their own personal desire to stop, the incentive to remain drug-free may be lost.

Whilst it is recognised that family support, and particularly having a drug-free partner, is important in enhancing the effectiveness of drug treatment, the amphetamine project uncovered a degree of ambivalence within some relationships concerning drug reduction or abstention. Some partners of clients in treatment reported relationship problems due to the psycho-social effects of withdrawal that their partners were experiencing. Some non-drug-using partners admitted that they would have preferred the clients to continue with controlled amphetamine use, which enabled them to be more confident, dynamic and happy. Other partners were equally disturbed by changes in their relationships: some were impatient for clients to 'recover' and interpreted even reduced drug use as failure, and others felt that the client's success in achieving abstinence and becoming more self-reliant meant that they were not needed, and that their role in the relationship was questioned.

Problems were also experienced within other close interpersonal relationships. Individuals who had kept the extent of their drug use hidden from their family and close friends faced difficulties in explaining their depressed and lethargic behaviour as they stopped using amphetamines. Clients' children often found it hard to understand why their previously gregarious and energetic parents were suddenly irritable and moody.

Becoming a non-drug user also had implications for clients' wider social networks, particularly for those whose social circles were comprised mainly of drug users. Many clients had to end friendships with other drug users, either to try to minimise temptations to use, or because patterns of socialising changed once amphetamines were no longer used. For some clients, the significant changes in their socialising were experienced as a heavy loss, and many expressed the need to develop new support networks as a crucial element in maintaining their attempts at abstinence. Thus, whilst one outcome (reduction of drug use) was welcome, it could have a negative impact on several other aspects of their lives, which could in turn diminish their likelihood of continued abstention.

Conclusions

This brief case study can only illustrate some of the contributions that qualitative methods and analyses made to the amphetamine research. Qualitative research in this project involved more than simply supplementing quantitative analyses with some extra validation and providing interesting quotes to illustrate key points: the data give rise to new insights that are not self-evident from numerical comparisons alone, and that often act as a catalyst for further exploration. Qualitative analyses were extremely valuable in the amphetamine research, revealing that, whilst some of the outcome measures defined by the Department of Health indicated improvement, this could be at the cost of damaging critically important interpersonal relationships in a way that could jeopardise clients' chances of success and lead to relapse.

Sam Wright was formerly a research fellow at the Centre for Social Research into Health and Substance Abuse (SRHSA), in the Department of Psychology and Speech Pathology, Manchester Metropolitan University, Manchester, UK. Hilary Klee is the Research Director at SRHSA.

References

Department of Health Task Force to Review Services for Drug Misusers (1996) *Report of an Independent Review of Drug Treatment Services in England,* London: Department of Health.

Kirk, J. and Miller, M. (1986) 'Reliability and validity in qualitative research', *Qualitative Research Methods,* series 1, London: Sage.

Klee, H. (1992) 'A new target for behavioural research: amphetamine misuse', *British Journal of Addiction,* 87(3), 439–446.

Klee, H. and Wright, S. (1999a) *Amphetamine Use and Treatment: a Study of the Impediments to Effective Service Delivery: Part 1. Access to Drug Treatment Services,* Manchester: SRHSA, Manchester Metropolitan University.

Klee, H. and Wright, S. (1999b) *Amphetamine Use and Treatment: a Study of the Impediments to Effective Service Delivery: Part 2. Treatment and Its Outcomes,* Manchester: SRHSA, Manchester Metropolitan University.

Silverman, D. (1993) *Interpreting Qualitative Data,* London: Sage.

Wright, S. and Klee, H. (forthcoming) 'A profile of amphetamine users who present to treatment services and do not return', *Drugs: Education, Prevention and Policy.*

Wright, S., Klee, H. and Reid, P. (1998) 'Interviewing illicit drug users: observations from the field', *Addiction Research,* 6(6), 517–535.

Wright, S., Klee, H. and Reid, P. (1999) 'Attitudes of amphetamine users toward treatment services', *Drugs: Education, Prevention and Policy,* 6(1).

PROBLEM DRUG USE IN POZNAŃ, POLAND: A QUALITATIVE APPROACH TO NEEDS ASSESSMENT

Janusz Sierosławski

A growing trend in drug use has been observed in Poland since the beginning of the 1990s. Quantitative changes are accompanied by changes in the character of the phenomenon, and the drug scene in Poland has started to resemble the west European scene.

Reactions to the drug problem at local level also began to play a more significant role, and response to the subsequent social problems was, to a significant degree, delegated to the local level. This created a demand for research providing information that can be used in forming a local preventive strategy. An example of such endeavour is the research requested by the city of Poznań in 1998. The project was based on the methodology developed by the Multi-City Study project, implemented by the Pompidou Group, Council of Europe (Hartnoll, 1994a), utilising the experiences of a project in Warsaw (Sierosławski et al., 1997).

The project in Poznań used a variety of methods: statistical data and the results of preceding studies were collected and analysed; research on the first treatment demand was initiated according to the protocol of the Pompidou Group (Hartnoll, 1994b; Stauffacher, 1999); and interviews with the drug-using street population, selected by snowball sampling, were conducted. This chapter presents the results of the study, together with conclusions and recommendations regarding the local preventive strategy.

The city of Poznań, with a population of 580 000, is the fourth largest city in Poland, located in the west of the country. According to previous research, Poznań does not differ much from the country's overall average regarding the prevalence of the occasional use of drugs. The percentages of users of specific drugs are somewhat higher than average, but significantly lower than Warsaw, for example. The indicators of treatment demand in Poznań are slightly higher than average but significantly lower than in regions of high prevalence, such as Warsaw, Szczecin or Katowice. The indicators of drug-related criminality suggest that the rates for Poznań are low, being almost half the country's average.

Drug treatment in the city is limited to one outpatient clinic — a counselling centre run by an NGO ('Monar'). Additionally, drug users may receive assistance in outpatient psychiatric clinics and a psychiatric hospital. There is also a detoxification unit in the psychiatric hospital in the city of Gniezno, near Poznań. There are rehabilitation centres located across the entire country, although not in the Poznań area. Very limited harm-reduction activities are conducted, mainly by NGOs, but these have not developed into a coherent programme. In sum, the assistance offered to drug users in Poznań is poorer than in other big cities. Information about drug users in the city is also poor: therefore, there is a clear role for qualitative research.

Method

The study of drug users was carried out using in-depth interviews focusing on drug histories, present life circumstances (health, family situation, source of income, housing, and so on), lifestyles, experiences regarding adjustment to being members of a drug-using group, and problems. Respondents were also asked for information necessary for planning interventions: that is, their readiness to utilise various services; their expectations concerning the shape and scope of assistance; and the conditions under which they would cooperate. The second area of interest was an assessment of the attitudes of the city residents towards drug addiction and drug users. Assessing these dominant attitudes is useful for defining the conditions of the implementation of intervention strategies, and can also be utilised to formulate the aims of public education campaigns.

Although the interviews with drug users were unstructured, the scope of information to be collected was strictly defined. The sequence of subjects to be discussed was decided by the interviewers, making it possible for them to return to issues if later information shed new light on them. The answers were noted in detail by the interviewer, in a strictly defined format, including recording comments verbatim, with the aim of limiting misinterpretation.

The selection of respondents was based on the snowball scheme (Hartnoll et al., 1995; Korf, 1997). Individuals were identified by interviewers in locations where drug users meet, and respondents were selected randomly from the list of nominees (see Chapter 32 in this monograph).

Information for quantitative analysis was recorded on another questionnaire, which aimed to assess the number of drug users in the city. The 'benchmark' method (Taylor, 1997) was utilised to perform this assessment. Other quantitative data collected for the study were gender, age, drugs used, treatment episodes in in-patient clinics, police records and HIV status.

Results

In the course of the study, 47 regular drug users displaying drug-related problems were interviewed. There were 32 males (68 %) and 15 females (32 %), with an age range of 18 to 45 (mean 25, median 23). The education of respondents varied from elementary school leavers to current university students. Most of the respondents were from families of good material standards and high social status. Most were born in Poznań. Their initial contact with drugs was around the age of 14 to 16. They initiated drug use with volatile substances (glue, etc.), sedatives, sleeping drugs or, particularly the younger respondents, marijuana.

The motive for initiation was usually curiosity. Sometimes, the first use was related to 'showing off' to a group, to impress somebody, or to feel part of a drug-using group. Quite frequently, it was difficult to define the motivation: in some cases, initiation was 'accidental', determined by a series of occurrences, without distinguishable intention or reflection (for example, when someone takes marijuana at a party). Large amounts of free time, without adult supervision, contributed to the initiation and continuation of drug use. An important factor appeared to be a lack of understanding in those close to the respondent and an absence of parental love. The second factor seems to play a more significant role in the process of continuing drug use.

Three patterns of drug use can be distinguished from the results of the study.

- The first, the traditional and the most destructive pattern, is the use of home-produced opiates, the so-called 'Polish heroin' (PH), used intravenously. This is sometimes enhanced by other drugs such as sedatives, amphetamines, drugs from the morphine group and cannabis. These substances are usually taken in addition to PH, or sometimes instead of it in times of short supplies. In this pattern of use, PH is always the primary drug and users are almost always strongly dependent on the substance.

- The second pattern combines the use of various drugs, such as amphetamines, hallucinogens, sedative substances, sleeping drugs, cannabis and, less frequently, cocaine or heroin. Usually, it is hard to define the primary drug, and even when this is possible, it is so only for a short period of time. Intravenous administration of drugs is less frequent than in the first pattern, and users are not always dependent.

- Cannabis constitutes the primary substance in the third pattern of use. Sporadically, other substances are added, such as amphetamines or hallucinogens. Marijuana and hashish are used every day or almost every day. This pattern of use does not include injecting.

It should be noted that PH appears exclusively in the first pattern, and its use is the basic criterion of stratification among drug users in Poznań. Two clearly distinct worlds of drug users can be distinguished in the city, and there is no respect or empathy between them. An individual entering the social circle of the PH users immediately drops out of the circle of other drug users, who see PH as a 'dirty drug' and its users as degraded people. There is some truth in statements like this, because PH users are in most cases worse off, in terms of money and health, than individuals using other drugs. However, even when this is not the case, the status of the individual is determined by his/her pattern of drug use.

The group of PH users is most significantly differentiated from the other drug users in respect of age and the length of their drug careers. The group includes older users who started their drug-using careers with homemade opiates in the 1970s and 1980s, and those from the 1990s whose drug careers began by following one of the other two patterns. All the PH users had undergone treatment — in many cases a number of times.

Individuals using drugs according to the new styles (the second and third drug-using patterns identified by the study) are younger, and their first encounters with drugs occurred in the last decade. Some of them, despite the regular use of drugs, are full-time students. The majority of them have never attempted treatment: their main problem is of a financial nature, especially if they use the more expensive substances such as heroin and cocaine.

The respondents had no problems regarding access to drugs: all of them had contacts with dealers. At the same time, they confirmed that purchasing drugs other than from their dealers is difficult. There are no street sellers in Poznań, unlike Warsaw, Krakow or Wroclaw, and dealers are very cautious: to buy drugs one needs to be recommended by an existing customer.

The use of injected drugs frequently involved needle and syringe sharing. This occurred more frequently in the group of PH users. Although respondents were aware of the infection hazards, the issue was meaningless because of the shortage of sterile injecting equipment. Even those who tried to avoid sharing indicated that, when they were intoxicated by the drug and had no control over their injecting equipment, they could not be sure that safety rules were followed. The safety measures undertaken were only using their own equipment and rinsing it in cool water, as hot water decalibrates needles. In the case of the PH group, a frequently used procedure was to warm the drug before injecting, in order to defuse any HIV contained in it. The risk of infection was often unacknowledged or considered an 'occupational hazard'. Frequently respondents were not interested in having HIV tests, either just because they were afraid of tests, or because they preferred to be ignorant rather than face a positive result.

The prevailing income sources of the PH-using group, besides disability pensions and social assistance, were the production of PH, dealing, pick-pocketing, shoplifting, prostitution (males and females) and begging. In most cases, all income was spent on drugs, and, frequently, basic life needs remained unsatisfied. The life circumstances of the majority revealed rejection by families, lack of personal support, homelessness and lack of a stable source of income. The most significant determinant of their situation was the possession of a permanent home.

During periods of homelessness they lived at railway stations, under bridges, or other drug users gave them shelter. These periods coincided with a low point in their material, health and psychiatric condition. Such a situation promoted the initiation of criminal and deviant behaviours, such as prostitution or stealing. The health conditions of the majority of this group were simply catastrophic: the most frequently reported problems were heart disease, kidney disease, liver disease, vein infections and multiple infective jaundice. Depression was the most common psychiatric sickness. These drug users lived on the margins of society and felt totally rejected: they frequently encountered dislike or hostility and were treated much worse than alcoholics. Therefore, the most frequently declared need of these respondents was the understanding of others: in interviews, a longing to preserve some remnant of dignity was often seen.

All respondents were aware of the existing treatment opportunities in Poznań. Most of them, however, were not interested in starting treatment, as they did not feel addicted, or considered themselves incurable. Those who had contacted the counselling centre of Monar (an out-patient clinic) assessed the motivation of the staff highly, but indicated too narrow a range of treatment offered, unsatisfactory accommodation and too few staff. In the majority of cases, their opinions regarding detoxification wards and rehabilitation centres were very critical.

As discussed earlier, one of the study objectives was an assessment of the number of drug addicts in the city, using the 'benchmark' technique (Taylor, 1997), and the range of interventions thus required. In the interviews with drug users, respondents were asked to provide some information on every drug addict known to them. In total, the 47 respondents nominated 239 others. For the purpose of assessment, data (where available) of the nominees' treatment at in-patient clinics were utilised. In 42 instances, the respondents did not know if their nominee had undertaken treatment. Therefore, 197 nominations containing the necessary information were used to perform the assessment. Of these, 57 had been treated and, on this basis, the proportion of treated persons among all drug addicts was calculated at 29 %. Thus the number of all drug addicts in Poznań is 3.5 times higher than the number of those treated. Statistical data from the in-patient clinic revealed that 100 city residents had been treated there because of drug problems. Therefore, the total number of drug addicts in Poznań was assessed at around 350.

Conclusions

The results of the study led us to formulate the following recommendations concerning local preventive strategy.

- The most urgent need seems to be for organised, broad activities on harm reduction. The significant number of cases of those dependent on PH after unsuccessful treatment, and discouraged from further attempts, supports this. The degree of needle and syringe sharing and prostitution means that the hazard of contracting and transmitting infectious diseases (HIV, hepatitis C virus (HCV), etc.) is high. The programme of harm reduction should be addressed, first of all, to PH-dependent individuals.

- The most important element of the programme is methadone substitution, and full access to needles, syringes and disinfectants. The harm-reduction programme should be based on the outreach method (Rhodes, 1996).

- In Poznań, there is a need to extend the existing out-patient treatment services. The counselling centre of Monar should offer a full range of services, including out-patient treatment programmes for users of cannabis, amphetamines or hallucinogens; as shown by the study, these new drug users can progress to PH use. The clinic should also provide post-treatment assistance for individuals after treatment in the in-patient clinics. This target will require more staff and accommodation.

- There is no need to establish — either in the city, or in the district — a rehabilitation centre, nor is there a need to develop other forms of residential treatment. However, the one detoxification ward in the region should not be closed.

These results, conclusions and recommendations were publicly presented at a special meeting of local and regional authorities, organisations involved in responding to the issue of drug use in the city, representatives of the local media and deputies to parliament from Poznań. Making the results of the study public property allowed local authorities to demonstrate their activities in the area of drug use prevention. It also created circumstances prompting further activity to consider the recommendations.

The author is a senior researcher at the Institute of Psychiatry and Neurology, Warsaw, Poland.

References

Hartnoll, R. (1994a) *Multi-City Network on Drug Misuse Trends: Guidelines for City Reports and Annual Updates,* Strasbourg: Council of Europe.

Hartnoll, R. (1994b) *Drug Treatment Reporting Systems and the First Treatment Demand Indicator: Definitive Protocol,* Strasbourg: Council of Europe.

Hartnoll, R., Balsa, C., Griffiths, P., Taylor, C., Hendriks, V., Blanken, P., Nolimal, D., Weber, I., Toussirt, M. and Ingold, R. (1995) *Handbook on Snowball Sampling,* Strasbourg: Pompidou Group, Council of Europe.

Korf, D. J. (1997) 'The tip of the iceberg: snowball sampling and nomination techniques, the experience of Dutch studies', in G. V. Stimson, M. Hickman, A. Quirk, M. Fischer and C. Taylor (Eds.) *Estimating the Prevalence of Problem Drug Use in Europe,* Lisbon: EMCDDA.

Rhodes, T. (1996) *Outreach Work with Drug Users: Principles and Practice,* Strasbourg: Council of Europe.

Sierosławski, J., Zielinski, A., Sierosławska, U. and Szata, W. (1997) 'Warsaw', in *Multi-City Network Eastern Europe,* Strasbourg: Council of Europe.

Stauffacher, M. (1999) *Pompidou Group Project on Treatment Demands: Treated Drug Users in 23 European Cities,* Annual Update 1997, Trends 1992–1997, Strasbourg: Pompidou Group, Council of Europe.

Taylor, C. (1997) 'Estimating the prevalence of drug use using nomination techniques: an overview', in G. V. Stimson, M. Hickman, A. Quirk, M. Fischer and C. Taylor (Eds.) *Estimating the Prevalence of Problem Drug Use in Europe,* Lisbon: EMCDDA.

METHODOLOGICAL ISSUES

PART VIII

INTRODUCTION

*S*ome of the issues surrounding the use of qualitative methods are the subject of this penultimate section.

In Chapter 30, Mike Hough questions the applicability of the 'medical paradigm' of evaluation to drug policy. He suggests that, in circumstances where it is neither ethical nor practical to mount randomised controlled trials (RCTs), evaluative research should be re-conceptualised. He addresses the key issues in evaluative research and provides a set of guiding principles for evaluation.

In Chapter 31, Odd Lindberg issues a warning about the use of computer programs for qualitative data analysis (QDA). He stresses the importance of using theories or conceptual frameworks which are guided, rather than limited, by empirical data.

Uwe Kemmesies describes, in Chapter 32, developments in the snowball sampling technique which is widely used to study hidden populations. A core feature of this method is to provide a level of contrast and quality of reflection that cannot be achieved by quantitative methods alone.

A number of chapters in Part VIII address difficulties in gaining access to target populations. In Chapter 33, Paula Mayock describes the methodological difficulties encountered in a community-based study of drug use among young people aged between 15 and 19 in an inner-city area. She describes the significance of gaining the acceptance and cooperation of one key individual who occupied a central position in the social structure of the group and the importance of this influential development for the research.

Rhidian Hughes addresses methodological difficulties in recruiting injecting drug users in Chapter 34. He points out that it is not the drug use per se that makes recruitment for research purposes difficult. In his small qualitative case study, it was the drug users' position within society, compared to the researcher's, that made them hard to reach.

Tom Decorte reflects on the ethical dilemmas he encountered in Belgium in Chapter 35 and concludes that the principal aim of qualitative research should be to understand drug users better. This should be done by studying drug users from within their culture rather than from outside it and to present their world as they see it.

The final chapter, Chapter 36, is by Peter Blanken, Cas Barendregt and Linda Zuidmulder and it examines the potential role for active drug users to be employed as community fieldworkers on the scientific research team. Such fieldworkers require careful selection, training and, most importantly, support. These are essential to ensure the necessary balance between personal involvement with their drug-using peers and their fieldwork.

CHAPTER 30

EVALUATION: A 'REALISTIC' PERSPECTIVE

Mike Hough

This chapter questions the applicability of the 'medical paradigm' to evaluation of drug policy. I have some experience of evaluation exercises in this field, and have mounted more in the related field of crime control. Little of this work has succeeded in achieving the scientific rigour conventionally expected of evaluation. Some readers will no doubt regard this chapter as a self-serving piece by an incompetent or underfunded methodologist. However, my view is that the 'medical' approach to evaluation in many areas of social policy is actually inappropriate and unhelpful. The ideas here owe a debt to the work of Ray Pawson and Nick Tilley (1997).

The issues discussed in this chapter would not be of central importance to policy if it were not for the enthusiasm with which governments now aspire to 'evidence-based policy'. The British Treasury is increasingly linking its funding of social programmes to evidence of effectiveness. This is a welcome move — unless 'evidence' is defined in a narrowly restrictive way. There is a risk that this will happen as, increasingly, reviews of effective practice tend to assign scores to evaluations on the basis of their apparent methodological rigour. Random control trials (RCTs) score highest. The process as it bears on British drug policy is best exemplified by the effectiveness review (Department of Health, 1996).

Evaluation: the medical paradigm

The preferred approach for medical evaluation is to assemble experimental and control groups who differ only in one respect — their exposure to the treatment under trial. RCTs can be regarded as the gold standard of medical evaluation. It is the random allocation of subjects to the two groups which guarantees that they differ only in exposure to the treatment. However, there are 'second best' approaches that are quasi-experimental in design. Simple time series analysis assumes that subjects are their own controls, the only change over time being exposure to the treatment. A stronger form of design would be a 'before-and-after' approach, involving matched control and experimental groups.

My research unit is currently engaged in a number of evaluative studies ([1]). Some are designed to assess the impact of referral or treatment programmes for problem drug users. Others are concerned with the impact of crime control measures. The

---

([1]) Details of the work and publications of the Criminal Policy Research Unit can be found on South Bank University's website (http://www.sbu.ac.uk).

consensus amongst researchers, funders and end-users of this sort of research is that, in an ideal world, RCTs should be used where possible, and, failing this, the tightest form of quasi-experimental design should be adopted. In practice, neither my own nor other British studies typically follow either path. This is because there are several serious obstacles:

- ethical problems;
- problems of complexity and cost; and
- problems associated with reflexivity.

Ethical problems

The particular state of development of medical knowledge is such that ethical problems in RCT medical evaluations can generally be overcome. Patients are buyers (at first or second hand) of services which, in principle, they desire. All that is needed is for an experimental group to be offered an informed choice whether or not to participate in a trial. Sufficient numbers of both practitioners and patients accept the logic of the RCT methodology to make it viable. There are obviously problems in ensuring that the former offer the latter a choice which is genuinely informed. However, medical RCTs are only rarely compromised by any differential take-up of the offer of participation [2].

By contrast, neither drug workers nor prospective clients of drug programmes are likely to accept the logic of an RCT. Both groups are likely to have clear views and preferences about different interventions and are unlikely to allow the toss of a coin to replace professional decision-making on the one hand, or personal choice on the other. The informed choice on which clients are likely to insist is between the competing treatment options, rather than the choice to participate in an experiment in which the options are randomly allocated. Treatment is negotiated between client and practitioner.

The ethical problems of mounting RCTs in this field become amplified when a criminal justice dimension is introduced. Many problem users are involved in a range of criminal activities related to their drug use — typically, acquisitive offences and drug supply. Their first exposure to treatment agencies may follow arrest, prosecution or conviction. Whilst RCTs have sometimes been mounted in a criminal justice setting, judicial or quasi-judicial decision-makers will generally prove extremely hostile to the prospect of surrendering their authority to the toss of a coin. The randomisation process will be seen as capricious and incompatible with justice.

Problems of complexity and cost

Even if the ethical problems surrounding RCTs for drug treatment services can be overcome, there are daunting practical problems in actually mounting one. Similar (or greater) practical problems relate to quasi-experimental designs.

---

[2] Arguably, the exclusion of risk-averse patients from both groups could lead to partial results.

The treatment regime is likely to be extended over time, and maintaining pro-gramme integrity may be a problem. Clients are often likely to be highly ambivalent towards treatment, and drug dependency is a relapsing condition. Clients are likely to live fairly chaotic lives and an RCT will see substantial attrition from both experi-mental and control groups.

Where the design is quasi-experimental rather than an RCT, the problems are com-pounded by the difficulty of assembling a genuinely comparable comparison group. In any area, the supply of problem users who are eligible and amenable is often lim-ited, and it is often little more than a brave hope that sufficiently large samples can be assembled to serve as experimental and control groups. Indeed, more often than not, we find ourselves struggling to lay our hands on reasonably sized samples of people passing through the experimental treatment — even before worrying about comparison groups.

An alternative strategy is to assign people to experimental and control groups not at an individual level but at an area level. In other words, one aims to find a compari-son area which matches the experimental one in all relevant respects except the treatment under evaluation. The problem here lies in the high degree of variability and volatility in drug problems across an area. The comparison area may allow inferences about causality to be made — but these may also mislead.

Let us assume that all these problems have been overcome and treatments have been delivered, as intended, to two groups — either randomly assigned into experimental and control groups, or purposefully assembled as matched comparison groups. The hapless evaluators still have an uphill struggle ahead of them. Tracking down prob-lem drug users some 6 to 12 months after they enter treatment is hard work. In our studies there has been a heavy attrition rate — sometimes approaching 50 %. Tracing people to re-interview a further 12 months later is equally problematic. We suspect that those who are contactable include a disproportionate number of 'successes'. The 'failures' will probably — but not always — be harder to contact. Follow-up work is also labour-intensive. We have rarely exceeded a contact rate in excess of two respondents a day. This would not be a problem if evaluative research into social pro-grammes were funded as lavishly as pharmaceutical trials. However, it is not.

Even when the respondent has finally been tracked down, there are problems of response bias. One is likely to be reliant on self-reported measures of drug use — though, with adequate funding, urine or hair testing is now a possibility. Where self-reporting is used retrospectively, it places considerable demands on the memories of people who may have been in a state of chaos at the relevant time. Many will exag-gerate both the extent of problems 'before', and the progress that they have made 'after'. It is easier to admit to illicit and anti-social behaviour in the distant, rather than the immediate, past.

Problems associated with reflexivity

Within limits, medical knowledge is objective. Empirical evidence can provide the basis for a consensus that one particular cancer treatment outperforms another, for example. Our knowledge about social processes is of a different order. Our understanding of social processes actually affects the way these processes operate. This reflexivity — to use sociologists' jargon — poses some difficulties for the project ensuring 'evidence-based practice' in fields where knowledge is especially likely to be reflexive.

This point is best developed by offering an example. Cognitive behavioural programmes are in vogue in many fields, including work with problem drug users. They are in vogue because they have been widely evaluated and have emerged relatively well from evaluation. I would argue that their current effectiveness lies precisely in the way in which the helping professions currently conceptualise problems such as drug dependency and offending. An approach which addresses such problems in terms of cognitive, rather than moral, failure allows them to address questions about social responsibility in a technical, morally neutral way. This is probably very helpful at this precise point in our social and cultural history. In 25 years' time, it probably will not be. Solutions to medical problems are superceded, but for different reasons: they are supplanted by more effective remedies. Whilst their relative effectiveness may have changed, their impact on the organism has not.

The key point here is that our understanding of social processes is, at least in part, constitutive of the way in which these processes operate. Our reactions to psychotropic drugs are at least in part socially determined. What 'works' and what doesn't in tackling problem drug use is likely to be temporally and culturally specific. Simply trying to establish whether a treatment programme works betrays a crudity of thought about the interaction between problem, treatment and cultural context.

Conclusions

The upshot is that much work within the field of illicit drug use falls far short of the standards by which the medical world, at least, is used to assessing research evidence. Indeed, the largest and most costly evaluation of drug services in Britain, the National Treatment Outcome Research Study (NTORS), is a follow-up study allowing only for internal comparisons between treatment modalities (Department of Health, 1997). There is no pretence at experimental rigour approaching the RCT paradigm.

As for our own work, we have similarly taken a 'before-and-after' approach, carrying out time series analysis only on those who have been exposed to particular interventions ([3]). We have typically found substantial reductions in problem drug use and in drug-related offending. However, against the gold standard of random controlled trials, our research design is weak.

It is questionable whether one should apologise for these shortcomings. In circumstances where it is neither ethical nor practical to mount RCTs, it is probably worth

---

([3]) See http://www.sbu.ac.uk/cpru for references and copies of reports.

trying to reconceptualise how best to set about evaluative research. Below are some principles to guide evaluative research in settings characterised by complexity, reflexivity and hostility towards random allocation.

- The aim of such evaluation should not be to identify whether or not something 'works'.
- Evaluation should aim to identify the contexts in which an approach works or fails to work.
- It is as important to identify the mechanisms by which measures achieve their effect as it is to identify the presence or absence of positive outcomes.
- It is unrealistic to aim to assemble in a single study experimental and comparison groups which are identical in all relevant aspects except exposure to treatment.
- It makes sense to rely on multiple comparisons within the study, and between the study and other similar ones.
- This maximises the chances of identifying the contexts in which programmes achieve an impact, and the mechanisms by which they do so.
- Whilst any such study will rely on quantitative measures of outcome (e.g. self-reported drug use), qualitative data will be crucial in forming an understanding of how any impact was achieved.
- Results are unlikely to be definitive, and are very likely to be subject to interpretation and speculation.

The author is Professor of Social Policy at South Bank University, and Director of the Criminal Policy Research Unit, London, UK.

References

Department of Health (1996) *The Task Force to Review: Services for Drug Misusers,* report of an independent review of drug treatment services in England, London: Department of Health.

Department of Health (1997) *NTORS: the National Treatment Outcome Research Study,* second bulletin, London: Department of Health.

Pawson, R. and Tilley, N. (1997) *Realistic Evaluation,* London: Sage.

GROUNDED THEORY AND COMPUTER-ASSISTED ANALYSIS OF QUALITATIVE DATA: SOME PROPOSALS FOR THE PRACTICE OF QUALITATIVE RESEARCH

Odd Lindberg

The purpose of this chapter is to identify and discuss some issues related to qualitative research and the use of computer programs for qualitative data analysis (QDA). The development of specific programs for QDA, and the number of their users, have increased rapidly in recent years (Weitzman and Miles, 1995; Bruhn and Lindberg, 1996). The danger is that the software makes it so easy to code text to categories, search the data, and restructure and edit text that the whole process can easily be dominated by an empirical approach and technical concerns. The theoretical reflections that should be dominating qualitative analysis seem to have been put aside in favour of a more empirical approach by many of the programs' users. It is therefore of great importance to stress the need for a live and constructive discussion about methodological and theoretical approaches and research processes in relation to qualitative research and the use of qualitative computer programs.

Most of the QDA software on the market is constructed out of a theoretical and methodological approach that is deeply rooted in empirical findings, a perspective that could be called 'close to data' or 'data-near' (grounded theory, phenomenology, ethnomethodology, etc.). A new version of such software is N'Vivo. The name implies data-near: *in vivo* categories are those found directly in the data as statements by respondents. Derek Layder comments on the data-near approach:

> *Social analysis (or science understood in an amended sense) must be defended as a species of explanation, especially in the face of recent attempts to decompose and dissolve it into mere reportage and/or descriptions of 'local narratives' — the voices of those people studied.* (1998, p. 3)

The problem discussed in this chapter is the trend towards many qualitative researchers (and many who use QDA) using an approach which, as Layder (1998, p. 2) stresses, 'cuts itself off from a sense of tradition and continuity in social analysis'. Such a data-near approach could be provocatively termed 'naive inductivism'.

Qualitative research and grounded theory

Many qualitative researchers are inspired by grounded theory, the overall approach of which is inductive, rather than deductive, verification of theory (Glaser and Strauss, 1967; Glaser, 1978; 1992; 1994; Strauss, 1987; Strauss and Corbin, 1990). Above all, an inductive approach means that researchers should start by making intensive studies of empirical phenomena and gradually develop theories that are grounded in the data. Theories should also fit the data and not the other way around. The conceptual categories that are developed should thus closely represent the significant meaning of the data, which presupposes that the researcher would not adjust the data to pre-prepared categories: the data should be approached with an unbiased and open mind.

On the one hand, Glaser and Strauss are arguing for a research that allow data to 'speak for themselves'.

> An effective strategy is, at first, literally to ignore the literature of theory and fact on the area under study, in order to assure that the emergence of categories will not be contaminated by concepts more suited to different areas. Similarities and convergences with the literature can be established after the analytic core of categories has emerged. (1967, p. 37)

On the other hand, they argue that reading social science literature gives the researcher knowledge of conceivable concepts which contribute to the theoretical sensitivity which is a necessary resource in the process of interpreting data.

Even if the grounded theory approach included reading literature, it is the inductive approach that is its dominating feature (Layder, 1993). Yet what can occur when a data-near or N'Vivo approach is employed is that the theory or the concepts that are developed have a strong resemblance to our everyday language, and, thus, a low level of abstraction.

Many researchers are 'name-dropping' and inventing 'new' concepts for everyday, well-known phenomena. In many research reports, the research is reduced to a short-sighted, common-sense emphasis of name-giving and sorting of data. For example, recently, in a question about coding procedures on the Internet, a qualitative researcher revealed: 'basically I stayed very close to the data often using the actual words the participant used such as "asking for help" and "seeking information".' These very descriptive data-near studies can, of course, be valuable, but there is a risk that the concepts become superficial empirical categories and that researchers present new names for combinations of characteristics/qualities. Thus, the paradox is that, although grounded theory was presented as an alternative to the positivistic-orientated social science, the approach actually involves an empiricist ontology that, generally, is the sign of positivism.

The limitations of grounded theory, and thus of much qualitative research, is as follows (see also Danemark et al., 1997).

- The approach considers established theories and concepts as obstacles rather than resources, by stressing that concepts should emerge from data through an unbiased process of coding.

- There is a strong tendency to tie the development of theories to immediate impressions of the empirical reality in a quite obvious way. This way of working will impede knowledge about more basic social structures.

- The approach has not considered the meaning and consequences of the problematic relation between everyday understanding and scientific abstractions.

- Concepts that describe basic social structures and mechanisms will always exceed and complicate people's everyday experiences.

The result is that, if researchers use only software to categorise their data and work according to a data-near approach, qualitative research and analysis will not contribute to an accumulation of knowledge within social science. We will not be able to explain social phenomena — the essence of social science. It is not the software in itself that is the problem, but rather the methodological and theoretical considerations of the researcher before the research process starts and during the continuing process of analysing the data.

Reality seen as differentiated

Reality can be viewed as differentiated, and this approach introduces a critical realist research strategy (Sayer, 1992; Layder, 1993; Bhaskar, 1997). Figure 1 shows three different domains of reality (from Bhaskar, 1997, p. 13). The basis is the domain of 'real'. Here, we can find the mechanisms that produce events, and they exist whether the event occurs or not. When the mechanisms produce an actual event, whether we observe it or not, it falls into the domain of 'actual'. When such an event is experienced it becomes an empirical fact and falls into the domain of 'empirical' (Bhaskar, 1997).

Figure 1: Domains of reality

	Domain of empirical	Domain of actual	Domain of real
Experiences	X	X	X
Events		X	X
Mechanisms			X

Another way of expressing this is that empirical phenomena are a part of the actual, which, in turn, is a part of the real. It is important not to mix abstract concepts with empirical categories. Our abstract concepts separate different mechanisms, while empirical categories divide reality into different types of events or phenomena. A science focusing on the social reality can therefore not be reduced to empirical events, nor to the domain of the empirical. If only that is done, the result is a narrow view of science in which reality will come out as flat as a pancake, without ontological depth. The causal mechanisms we seek in social science should be sought on the social level: social phenomena are produced by social forces.

To conduct research from a critical realist approach means identifying the social relations and structures which hold causal mechanisms which, in turn, have the ability to produce observable empirical effects. It should be noted, though, that causal mechanisms do not always produce observable empirical effects. Often, different mechanisms cooperate to produce a certain result, but sometimes they counteract each other.

That the expected result from the force from a certain causal mechanism fails to appear does not mean that it has ceased to exist. The force is still there but does not lead to visible effects, because the counteractive effect from other forces is stronger. An example of this is when an individual, in spite of a strong feeling of solidarity with a trade union, chooses not to be a member because of strong opposition from the employer. We could say that the relation between the mechanisms and their effects are occasional. Different occasional releasing factors for producing the effects are needed. Causal forces have to be analysed as latent, as tendencies with intrinsic force, to produce different events. The causal forces are not observable in themselves: empirical observation is only the result. We have to use social theory and abstractions to 'reach' the causal mechanisms, the social relations and the structures from which they emanate. In other words, 'Scientifically significant generality does not lie on the face of the world but in the hidden essence of things' (Bhaskar, 1997, p. 227).

Conclusions

Below are some suggestions for the future direction of qualitative research.

- We can understand, analyse or categorise social reality only through a theoretical language of concepts.
- These concepts are continuously being developed.
- The theoretical language always contains an interpretation of the social reality.
- The definition of qualitative research should include theories which are guided by, rather than simply limited by, empirical data. Such theories attempt to depict structural features of social life which may be difficult to observe in an immediate way. As Layder (1998, p. 47) puts it, 'the grounded theory approach represents a waste of good theory'.
- Social science should be explanatory and cumulative.
- Our theories or conceptual framework should not be limiting our research but opening it up. They should not be used to classify reality from an advanced

given system, but rather to guide the analysis and interpretation of the social reality. During the analytic process, we can then use networks of associated concepts to continuously open up the data and build theories.

• If we can use established theories and concepts in an open way, in order to reach behind the scenes of activity and the immediate empirical world, a combination of qualitative research and use of the software can offer us fantastic opportunities to analyse qualitative data. We can then use the data in a deeper and more theoretical and analytical sense.

The author is a senior lecturer in the Department of Social Science, University of Orebro, Sweden.

References

Bhaskar, R. (1997) *A Realist Theory of Science,* London: Verso Classics.

Bruhn, A. and Lindberg, O. (1996) 'Kvalitativ metod och datateknologi', in P. Svensson and B. Starrin (Eds.) *Kvalitativa studier i teori och praktik,* Lund: Studentlitteratur.

Danemark, E. E., Jacobsen, J. and Karlsson, J. (1997) *Att forklara samhallet,* Lund: Studentlitteratur.

Glaser, B. (1978) *Theoretical Sensitivity: Advances in the Methodology of Grounded Theory,* Mill Valey: Sociology Press.

Glaser, B. (1992) *Basics of Grounded Theory Analysis,* Mill Valey: Sociology Press.

Glaser, B. (1994) *Emergence versus Forcing: Basics of Grounded Theory Analysis,* San Francisco: Sociology Press.

Glaser, B. and Strauss, A. (1967) *The Discovery of Grounded Theory,* Chicago: Aldine.

Layder, D. (1993) *New Strategies in Social Research,* London: Polity Press.

Layder, D. (1998) *Sociological Practice: Linking Theory and Social Research,* London: Sage.

Sayer, A. (1992) *Method in Social Science,* London: Routledge.

Strauss, A. (1987) *Qualitative Analysis for Social Scientists,* Cambridge: Cambridge University Press.

Strauss, A. and Corbin, J. (1990) *Basics of Qualitative Research: Grounded Theory Procedures and Techniques,* London: Sage.

Weitzman, E. and Miles, M. (1995) *Computer Programs for Qualitative Data Analysis,* London: Sage.

CHAPTER 32

HOW TO REACH THE UNKNOWN:
THE SNOWBALL SAMPLING TECHNIQUE

Uwe Kemmesies

> *Who knows if fish kiss?*
> *Above the water they don't do it;*
> *under water you can't see it.* (Author unknown)

This German saying serves as an appropriate introduction to research into drug-using behaviour, as it illustrates the nature of one of the most speculative research fields and one of the basic problems of ethnography: how hidden populations are accessed.

In the social sciences, the snowball sampling technique is widely used to study hidden populations and sensitive topics, and has been implemented in a range of drug research projects worldwide (e.g. Zinberg, 1984; Erickson et al., 1987; Mugford and Cohen, 1989; Díaz et al., 1992). This technique facilitates sampling by making it possible to obtain a wider range of research contacts within the culture of a particular group, in order to provide an account of meanings and activities from inside the unknown. The core features of the method are 'the selection of samples utilising "insider knowledge" and referral chains among subjects who possess common traits that are of research interest' (Kaplan et al., 1987).

Snowball sampling: a definition and methodological profile

> *Snowball sampling ... is a method for recruiting new cases through a process of onward referral from known cases. Sampling starts with one or more individuals who are known to meet the given criteria (e.g. 'current cocaine user').* (Hartnoll et al., 1997, p. 7)

Hartnoll et al. provide the core definition of this sampling technique, although methods vary depending on the research interest (e.g. whether the aim of a project is to focus on the whole group of drug users of a given local area, or on the diversity of using patterns within a subgroup of current users).

Use of the snowball sampling technique is generally motivated by two purposes.

- To achieve broad and heterogeneous samples. Samples recruited in institutions related to the use of illicit drugs (e.g. treatment centres, prisons) are biased and lead inevitably to findings with limited generalisability. Quantitative survey methods also provide a restricted view of the phenomenon.

- To focus on aspects of the phenomenon which cannot be reached by other methods. Use of indirect indicators (e.g. drug deaths, arrests, seizures) or statistical projections (e.g. the capture–recapture method) does not provide qualitative information on drug-using networks or individuals.

The following methodological profile (see Hartnoll et al., 1997) of the snowball technique can be presented. The technique has the following advantages.

- It avoids the need for large samples. Purposive sampling avoids the need for the large samples required in general population surveys, and the relatively small interviewed sample provides a basic profile of a much larger number of nominees. For example, a household survey carried out in 1987 in Amsterdam was based on a sample of 4 445 interviewees, which reported that just 17 people had used cocaine in the past month and 57 had used it in the past year. However, a snowball study in Amsterdam (Cohen and Sas, 1993) reported on 160 interviews with cocaine users and provided basic data on 750 cocaine users known to those 160 individuals.

- It provides a broader sample than indirect indicators. If the phenomenon is examined by means of indirect indicators only (e.g. overdoses, arrests, drug deaths, etc.), the analyses inevitably reflect only the problematic consequences of the drug-using phenomenon. This does not represent the phenomenological horizon of the use of illicit drugs.

- It gives qualitative information on social networks as well as individuals. When reflecting on the chain referrals guided by the question 'who, out of which social milieu, refers to whom, belonging to which social milieu?', snowball sampling provides qualitative information about the social networks related to drug use.

How it works: methodological problems and limitations, and how to handle them

Although the basis of snowball sampling is the recruitment of new interviewees through referrals from earlier respondents, the technique is more complex than its name suggests. Five distinguishable phases seem to be imperative to ensure a controlled sampling procedure. Figure 1 shows these successive stages, integrating the concepts of the technique described by Hartnoll et al. (1997), Korf (1995) and Watters and Biernacki (1989).

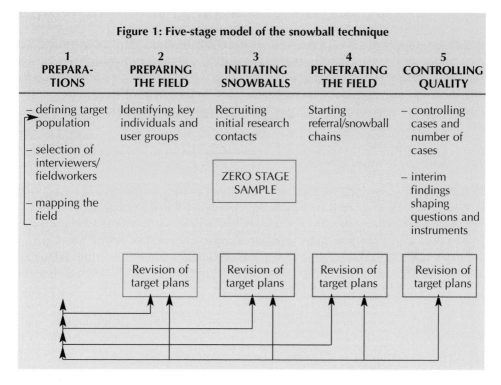

Figure 1: Five-stage model of the snowball technique

1 PREPARA-TIONS	2 PREPARING THE FIELD	3 INITIATING SNOWBALLS	4 PENETRATING THE FIELD	5 CONTROLLING QUALITY
– defining target population	Identifying key individuals and user groups	Recruiting initial research contacts	Starting referral/snowball chains	– controlling cases and number of cases
– selection of interviewers/ fieldworkers		ZERO STAGE SAMPLE		– interim findings shaping questions and instruments
– mapping the field				
	Revision of target plans	Revision of target plans	Revision of target plans	Revision of target plans

Stage 1: Preparations

First the target population is tentatively defined according to the research focus. For example, if the aim of the project is to study controlled drug use, an operational-isation of the core criteria which define controlled drug use is important. From that definition, the sampling criteria of the target population ('controlled drug users') can be derived.

When the target population is defined, the fieldworkers who will contact them and gather the data are selected and trained. To facilitate access, it is important that the researchers be familiar with the geographical and social research sites, and with the population to be studied.

The more hidden the target population, the more complex the process of 'mapping the field'. The potential research sites where the target population is expected to be reached have to be explored by observation and other qualitative techniques, such as interviews with key players in the field. Exploring these sites ('ethnographic map-ping') is guided by the question: 'where are the geographic and social boundaries of the target population located, or does the phenomenon of interest spread nation-wide, over all milieus, without any significant regional and social differences?' Defining the target population and mapping the field is also based 'on the available knowledge of the research team, indicators of various institutions (police, treatment, hospitals), previous studies, and information disseminated through popular mass and underground media' (Hartnoll et al., 1997, p. 20).

Stage 2: Preparing the field

In this phase, the first contacts with the research field and potential respondents take place. Key individuals and interest groups are identified and informed about the study's purposes. The fieldworkers become more acquainted with the groups to be focused upon, a process which facilitates access to the different subgroups. During this process, potential respondents are 'verified' to ensure that they are members of the target population.

Stage 3: Initiating snowballs

In order to achieve a far-reaching representative sample, the selection of the initial research contacts (the 'zero stage sample') is important and should be randomised. It is doubtful whether this special research field allows recruitment of a representative sample in a statistical sense, because of extensive formal and informal social control. However, it is possible to achieve a comparable representative sample, in a qualitative sense: a sample which illustrates the phenomenon's diversity and complexity, and which represents the variety of drug-using behaviours and subgroups.

If a strategy is devised which is based on theoretical assumptions and previous studies, a random selection of places, times and, finally, respondents should be made. However, this procedure is an ideal-typical one and is often not feasible — mainly due to limited knowledge about the hidden aspects of the phenomenon. More practically, initial contacts are randomly selected out of the list of potential respondents gained from key informants in the previous phase of the snowball process.

Stage 4: Penetrating the field

After having established the first contacts in the target population, snowball chains can be started. The selection of respondents from the group of nominees from the zero stage sample should be randomised.

As Cohen (1990, p. 64) says, 'It does not guarantee a random sample, but seems to be the best available way to select a cross-section of users who are as representative as possible.' This selection process is the methodological mechanism to prevent the central potential disadvantage of snowballing: that, considering that drug use is highly stigmatised behaviour, it is to be expected that respondents will nominate the drug users they know best, which is likely to result in snowball chains moving in a circle within one homogeneous subgroup. Thus, not randomising at the stage of initiating snowballs and penetrating the field can result in a sample which only restrictively represents the phenomenon.

A step from one respondent to the next in the chain is called a 'wave'. Normally, the sampling process follows only 'linear' chains: only one respondent is selected out of the list of potential interviewees provided by the foregoing respondent. Of course, 'bilinear' or 'multilinear' chains are also possible, but a decision to use these options should be well founded: if it is the aim of the project to recruit all the drug users in a particular location, it should be attempted to recruit all those nominated within all the referral chains.

There are no systematic research efforts into the reasons why, for example, initial contacts could not be made or why chains could not start. A better knowledge base of factors influencing chain referrals would be useful to improve the snowball technique. Nevertheless, the work that has been done so far allows three plausible assumptions on this issue to be made.

- *Quality of field exploration.* The number of zero stages and consecutive waves is affected by the quality of the fieldwork conducted at the second stage of the snowball process. The more familiar the fieldworkers are with the field, the easier the process of obtaining access to the target population.

- *Quality of fieldworkers.* The importance of having sensitive fieldworkers should not be underestimated. The more they are able to make potential respondents trust in the anonymity of the research, the more the latter are likely to believe that it will have no negative consequences and to agree to participate.

- *Policy.* The more rigorous and repressive the formal and informal control mechanisms concerning the behaviour under study are, the less likely the target population is to take part in the study.

Stage 5: Controlling quality

At this stage of the sampling process, the chain referrals are monitored. 'On the basis of regular intermediate analyses, it is decided whether or not to extend chains, and ideas are developed about other networks which may be thought to exist within the population but have not yet been located' (Korf, 1995, p. 125).

Ongoing revision of target plans

This model is an ideal one: in practice, there are no clear-cut stages. As shown by the arrows in Figure 1, snowball sampling is a dynamic process. Revision of the target plans and of the definition of the target population has to be taken into consideration at all stages of the process: if, for example, information gained during 'mapping the field' leads to a revision of the definition of the target population; or if, during the stage of 'penetrating the field', no snowball chains can be started because, for instance, the initial contacts are not willing to nominate new respondents. Furthermore, the sampling process should be accompanied by intermediate reflections, especially concerning those individuals and subgroups who could not be accessed. Reflecting upon the reasons for refusal to participate is a useful strategy to gain deeper insight in the more hidden areas of the field. The reasons for non-participation often touch on core characteristics of the phenomenon and provide useful information with which to better judge the study's findings.

Conclusions

The controversial question of the representativeness of snowball samples and their usefulness in estimating prevalence has been omitted from this chapter. The respective underlying mathematical models and foundations (which are thoroughly described and discussed by Taylor and Griffiths, 1997) have not been discussed for three reasons.

- The aim here is to present snowball sampling in its original form, as an ethnographic technique for obtaining access to the field of interest.
- The underlying mathematical models and respective assumptions need to be better investigated and thus developed: they are still largely speculative.
- Representativeness will be hard to estimate as long as social control and the consequent stigmatisation exist in this field.

To confront drug research's main problem, that of representativeness, snowball samples should be guaranteed to start from as many independent zero stages and to step through as many waves in each snowball as possible. Nevertheless, the uncertainty about representativeness remains, although it is not confined to snowball sampling.

As Sandwijk et al. (1995, p. 101) wrote, 'Any empirical "evidence" resulting from measurements even if using such large-scale instruments as ... [population] survey[s] must be regarded as a pale shadow of the real world.' The aim of snowballing is to give this shadow more contrast, and more quality of reflection, than is achieved by using quantitative approaches only.

The author is a social scientist at Göthe-University, Frankfurt (Main), Germany.

References

Cohen, P. (1990) *Drugs as a Social Construct,* Elinkwijk: Utrecht.

Cohen, P. and Sas, A. (1993) *Ten Years of Cocaine,* Amsterdam: Department of Human Geography, University of Amsterdam.

Díaz, A., Barruti, M. and Doncel, C. (1992) *The Lines of Success? A Study on the Nature and Extent of Cocaine Use in Barcelona,* Barcelona: Laboratori de Sociologica.

Erickson, P., Adlaf, E. M., Murray, G. F. and Smart, R. G. (1987) *The Steel Drug: Cocaine in Perspective,* Toronto: Lexington Books.

Hartnoll, R., Griffiths, P., Taylor, C., Hendriks, V., Blanken, P., Nolimal, D., Weber, I., Toussirt, M. and Ingold, R. (1997) *Handbook on Snowball Sampling,* Strasbourg: Council of Europe.

Kaplan, C. D., Korf, D. J. and Sterk, C. (1987) 'Temporal and social contexts of heroin-using populations: an illustration of the snowball sampling technique', *The Journal of Nervous and Mental Disease,* 9, 566–574.

Korf, D. J. (1995) *Dutch Treat: Formal Control and Illicit Drug Use in the Netherlands,* Amsterdam: Thesis Publishers.

Mugford, S. and Cohen, P. (1989) *Drug Use, Social Relations and Commodity Consumption: a Study of Recreational Cocaine Users in Sydney, Canberra and Melbourne,* Sydney: Department of Sociology.

Sandwijk, J. P., Cohen, P. D. A., Musterd, S. and Langemeijer, M. P. S. (1995) *Licit and Illicit Drug Use in Amsterdam II,* Amsterdam: Instituut voor Sociale Geografie.

Taylor, C. and Griffiths, P. (1997) 'Snowball sampling: methodology', in R. Hartnoll, C. Balsa, P. Griffiths, C. Taylor, V. Hendriks, P. Blanken, D. Nolimal, I. Weber, M. Toussirt and R. Ingold (1997) *Handbook on Snowball Sampling,* Strasbourg: Pompidou Group, Council of Europe.

Watters, J. K. and Biernacki, P. (1989) 'Targeted sampling: options for the study of hidden populations', *Social Problems,* 4, 416–430.

Zinberg, N. E. (1984) *Drug, Set and Setting: the Basis for Controlled Intoxicant Use,* New Haven/London: Yale University Press.

CHAPTER 33

ENGAGING 'DIFFICULT-TO-REACH' YOUNG PEOPLE IN A STUDY OF INNER-CITY DRUG USE

Paula Mayock

Opiate use in Ireland is located mainly in a number of Dublin's inner-city and sub-urban communities. With no visible signs of the heroin problem abating, concern for young people is high, particularly for those living in areas where heroin use is concentrated. The study forming the focus of this chapter undertook to examine drug use by young people aged between 15 and 19 in one such locality. The research site is an area considered to have one of the most serious drug problems in the state and has been designated for inclusion in the government's Local Drug Task Force initiative.

The difficulties researchers face when attempting to collect reliable and valid quan-titative data on adolescent drug use within the general population are well docu-mented (e.g. Marsh et al., 1989; Davies and Coggans, 1991). The current study, with its emphasis on exploring subjective meanings and perceptions, presented different challenges to those associated with gathering quantitative data on young people's drug-taking history and behaviour. Unique methodological considerations arise when undertaking a study which seeks the participation of minors (Hill et al., 1996; Hill, 1998). Furthermore, the illegality of drug use places a fundamental constraint on the disclosure of details of what is usually a private and hidden activity. From the outset of the study, access was a major consideration, one which altered variously in magnitude throughout the course of the fieldwork.

The main body of the data was collected using individual in-depth interviews, and focus groups were used to investigate broader issues pertaining to young people's perception of drug use within their community. A total of 57 young people were interviewed individually and a further 24 took part in focus group discussions.

The recruitment process

The practical difficulties of making contact with a large number of young people from within a community (as distinct from a more formal setting, such as a school) were exacerbated by the sensitive nature of the topic under investigation. Numerous ethical issues, particularly those relating to confidentiality and consent, had to be addressed prior to entering the field. This chapter will document some of the main features of the recruitment process and will then focus on a specific problem of access, namely that of securing the cooperation of a group of young people referred to here as 'difficult to reach'.

Interviewing young people from within a community setting about intimate aspects of their lives is better viewed as a process, rather than as a single isolated occurrence arranged following consent. Access routes are not clearly marked and the identification of relevant 'gatekeepers' was an essential first step. Educating others about the purpose and nature of the research (Shaffir, 1991) was critical to winning approval, acceptance and personal support from professionals who were in regular contact with prospective research participants.

Initially, the essential 'gatekeepers' consisted of youth and community workers and local drug counsellors. However, as knowledge of the social terrain expanded and additional support and acceptance were secured, this group of adult contacts was extended to include local community members who had reliable knowledge of peer networks and/or 'hunches' about the activities of certain groups. Adult informants were instrumental in making introductions to young people: their detailed knowledge of community events and local culture informed many important procedural decisions relating to access and provided short cuts to contacting a range of prospective participants.

Introductions to young people by trusted adults were vital, but were not adequate in themselves to secure cooperation. The establishment of trust and rapport was a necessary precursor to gaining the acceptance of those being studied (Wax, 1980; Fontana and Frey, 1994). Therefore, the initial task of 'getting in' was followed by the more complex research requirement of achieving status with the group. This was a dynamic process which demanded time, patience and perseverance. Active participation on the part of the researcher within a range of settings was central to what is best described as an incremental process of gaining credibility. Regular contact and involvement with various groups of young people allowed natural points of contact to emerge and assisted in the creation of contexts for non-intrusive interaction with the group. The establishment of complementary relationships (Agar, 1977), whereby the researcher played a subordinate role compared to that of prospective participants in the formation of relationships, was essential to the establishment of authentic communication patterns.

Initiative was required when it came to approaching young people directly regarding the issue of participation. In general, this interchange was somewhat more deliberate and structured than that which typified the day-to-day interactions between the researcher and the young people. This was also the stage at which greater detail about the study was communicated and when assurances regarding confidentiality were provided. The reputation of the researcher was critical to the process of recruitment, and the endorsements and affirmations of previous interviewees were influential in securing the cooperation of more resistant participants. As the fieldwork entered later phases, snowballing, whereby the sample of informants was generated by the young people themselves (Robson, 1993), played an increasingly significant role in the recruitment process.

The amount of time invested in the participants' social milieu meant that the study embodied many ethnographic qualities. It took weeks, and in some cases months, of participation within particular settings to gain the acceptance of many informants. Involvement, observation and interaction were essential to the process of recruitment and played a pivotal role in the selection process. As the researcher learned more about the young people within the selected research locality, relevant distinctions between various types of drug user emerged and specific individuals were targeted for interview. This process of targeted selection involved constant assessments of the 'cast' of possible participants, with the recruitment of particular young people taking precedence over others during different phases of the study. This technique of judgmental sampling (Fetterman, 1991) is one upon which many fieldworkers rely. Of the range of groups targeted for participation, one was particularly challenging and time-consuming. This is the group referred to here as 'difficult to reach'.

The 'difficult to reach'

Current and ex-opiate users were considered to be an important component of the sample. Some young people were accessible through drug treatment and counselling services, from a methadone maintenance programme, and through the local community drug team and satellite clinics. In these settings, the researcher was vouched for by staff and these interviews were conducted with relative ease. However, those who had not sought treatment and who were largely unknown to drug agencies or other services presented quite a different challenge.

The difficulty of gaining access to young people who are deeply immersed in the drug scene, particularly those involved in the early stages of heroin use, has been noted previously by other researchers (Pearson et al., 1985; Pearson, 1987). The reasons for this are complex. Serious drug involvement (particularly with heroin) is a highly stigmatised activity and the fear of being judged or punished creates a powerful barrier to disclosure. Young people go to considerable lengths to conceal their drug status from both adults and peers and are unlikely to want to disclose details of their activities to anyone, particularly a stranger.

Knowledge acquired during the course of conducting fieldwork lent considerable weight to the belief that a sizeable number of young people aged between 15 and 17 were more deeply involved in drug use than might be expected. Initially, this information was based on anecdotal evidence, but it gained greater credence as time progressed and as adult informants conveyed their suspicions about the drug activities of particular groups. Finally, and importantly, those interviewed previously were instrumental in transforming these unsubstantiated suggestions into more definite and reliable data. The cooperation of a number of young informants proved to be vital in providing access routes to this group of drug takers who were undoubtedly the most elusive of all interviewees. This task of recruitment was firmly located within the community and therefore the researcher could not benefit from the security and back-up of adults known to the targeted population (Power, 1994). Moreover, the majority of these young people were unlikely to want to make their drug-taking behaviour known to the study's gatekeepers.

A combination of strategies led to some eventual success in engaging a number of young heroin users, despite the rather prohibitive nature of this avenue of enquiry. The main contact point in achieving this was the street, which is probably the most difficult contact situation (Farrant and Marchant, 1971). Frequent visits were paid to a small number of carefully selected outdoor locations in the hope of meeting one of a number of young people with whom the researcher had previously established a trusting relationship. Much of this work was located in one large local-authority housing complex which has a large population of heroin users and has gained considerable notoriety as a 'drugs supermarket'.

Over a period of several weeks, a number of contacts were made with young heroin users and the role of the researcher was made known to them. Given that immediate acceptance could not be expected, a process of literally 'hanging around' became part of the researcher's daily routine. Frequent visits were paid to specific locations, with the regularity and quality of contact being far more significant than the duration of any one meeting aimed at enhancing relationships.

During this period, it was both unnecessary and unhelpful to provide the young people with constant reminders of the research and more productive to seek out ways of developing meaningful modes of communication. This was achieved largely by following their conversational lead and not appearing overly anxious to gain acceptance. Knowledge and understanding of the local drug culture was also important in breaking down traditional barriers to open communication.

The most influential development was that of gaining the acceptance and cooperation of one individual who occupied a central position in the social structure of the group (Fine, 1980). This high-status group member was able to allay feelings of scepticism and suspicion on the part of more hostile group members. The relationships established, although fragile initially, proved to be the researcher's most reliable means of accessing a world characterised by secrecy and concealment. Much of the success in securing some interviews hinged on a readiness to create and exploit opportunities for contact whenever possible. Knowledge and understanding of the behavioural and social norms of the group were important prerequisites to responding appropriately to individuals in a fluid situation. Having established an identity with the group, the researcher's task was undoubtedly aided by these frequently bored adolescents being intrigued by the interest of an outsider. The researcher's level of engagement with the group yielded valuable insights into the mechanisms which influence and guide young people's drug use, as well as the range of techniques they employ to conceal their behaviour from the outside world.

Conclusions

In a community-based study of this kind, access is not a one-off event. It is a social process which has to be negotiated and re-negotiated throughout the entire course of the fieldwork (Burgess, 1991). Efforts to establish contact with young people do not cease until the researcher is satisfied that every possible avenue has been explored with respect to accessing suitable participants. This involves searching through networks of friends, sympathetic acquaintances, and sometimes, complete strangers, for possible routes of access (Werner and Schoepfle, 1987). Upon entering the field, the researcher is likely to face various forms of resistance and this cannot be planned for in advance. Such unforeseen developments can be instrumental in reshaping the course of data collection, and definite plans to collect data within a specific time-span can be disrupted. Irrespective of the level of preparation, research techniques must be developed in response to emerging developments.

Given the nature of the enquiry, it was hardly surprising that difficulties arose during the course of recruiting participants for the study. More surprising, perhaps, was the number of young people who willingly agreed to participate. It must be said that the effort required to complete the interview was not insignificant. The decisions of others not to participate must also be respected. The greatest challenge will be that of representing the personal details entrusted by young people in a manner which does justice to those who gave so generously of their time and commitment.

The author is Research Fellow at the Children's Research Centre, Trinity College, Dublin, Ireland.

References

Agar, M. (1977) 'Ethnography in the streets and in the joint', in R. Weppner (Ed.) *Street Ethnography: Selected Studies of Crime and Drug Use in Natural Settings,* London: Sage Publications.

Burgess, R. G. (1991) 'Sponsors, gatekeepers, members and friends: access in educational settings', in W. B. Shaffir and R. A. Stebbins (Eds.) *Experiencing Fieldwork: an Inside View of Qualitative Research,* Sage Publications.

Davies, J. and Coggans, N. (1991) *The Facts About Adolescent Drug Abuse,* London: Cassell.

Farrant, M. R. and Marchant, H. J. (1971) *Making Contact with Unreached Youth,* Manchester: Youth Development Trust.

Fetterman, D. M. (1991) 'A walk through the wilderness: learning to find your way', in W. B. Shaffir and R. A. Stebbins (Eds.) *Experiencing Fieldwork: an Inside View of Qualitative Research,* Sage Publications.

Fine, G. A. (1980) 'Cracking diamonds: observer role in little league baseball settings and the acquisition of social competence', in W. B. Shaffir, R. A. Stebbins and A. Turowetz (Eds.) *Fieldwork Experience: Qualitative Approaches to Social Research,* New York: St. Martin's Press.

Fontana, A. and Frey, J. H. (1994) 'Interviewing: the art of science', in N. K. Denzin and Y. S. Lincoln (Eds.) *Handbook of Qualitative Research,* Sage Publications.

Hill, M. (1998) 'Ethical issues in qualitative methodology with children', in D. Hogan and R. Gilligan (Eds.) *Researching Children's Experiences: Qualitative Approaches,* Dublin: The Children's Research Centre, Trinity College.

Hill, M., Laybourn, A. and Borland, M. (1996) 'Engaging with primary-aged children about their emotions and well-being: methodological considerations', *Children and Society,* 10, 129–144.

Marsh, A., Dobbs, J. and White, A. (1989) *Adolescent Drinking,* London: HMSO.

Pearson, G. (1987) *The New Heroin Users,* Basil Blackwell.

Pearson, G., Gilman, M. and McIver, S. (1985) *Young People and Heroin: an Examination of Heroin Use in the North of England,* Research Report No 8, Health Education Council.

Power, R. (1994) 'Some methodological and practical implications of employing drug users as indigenous fieldworkers', in M. Boulton (Ed.) *Challenge and Innovation: Methodological Advances in Social Research on HIV/AIDS,* London: Taylor and Francis.

Robson, C. (1993) *Real World Research: a Resource for Social Scientists and Practitioner-Researchers,* Oxford: Blackwell.

Shaffir, W. B. (1991) 'Managing a convincing self-presentation: some personal reflections on entering the field', in W. B. Shaffir and R. A. Stebbins (Eds.) *Experiencing Fieldwork: an Inside View of Qualitative Research,* Sage Publications.

Wax, M. L. (1980) 'Paradoxes of "consent" to the practice of fieldwork', *Social Problems,* 27(3), 272–283.

Werner, O. and Schoepfle, G. M. (1987) *Systematic Fieldwork: Foundations of Ethnography and Interviewing,* Vol. 1, Sage Publications.

CHAPTER 34

RECRUITING INJECTING DRUG USERS

Rhidian Hughes

Some, but by no means all, of the activities in which drug users engage could be regarded as potentially 'sensitive' (Lee, 1993) or 'unrespectable' (Dean and Barrett, 1996) research topics. This can make drug users a particularly difficult group to contact and recruit for research.

Hammersley and Atkinson (1995) point out that making contact with any study group involves a subtle and reflexive process of negotiation. Access often has to be continually negotiated and re-negotiated over time (Lee, 1993). Typically, negotiations involve individuals and organisations that have a particular relationship with groups of drug users. Contacts established from these sources can then enable researchers to extend their contacts to other groups, sometimes as part of a 'snowball' sampling strategy (Biernacki and Waldorf, 1981; see Chapter 32 in this monograph). Ethnographic studies have used these approaches with, for example, drug agencies (Power, 1989); a pharmacy (McKeganey and Barnard, 1992); and a detached drug worker (Taylor, 1993).

In addition, drug users themselves can perform a number of roles to help contact and recruit others for research. These roles range from introducing and guiding researchers through drug-using groups, assisting in the accessing and recruitment of participants for research, and acting as fieldworkers, to observing drug-using patterns and conducting interviews (Power, 1995).

A case study

The substantive focus of this chapter draws on material collected during a small qualitative study that aimed to explore drug injectors' perceptions of HIV-related risk behaviours inside and outside prison. The research was conducted in the community in two cities in the north of England. The study generated data from 17 one-to-one in-depth interviews with a vignette, three small groups comprising respectively five, three and two participants, and diary field notes.

This case study focuses on two sections. The first section identifies the ways in which access was negotiated with services in contact with drug injectors. The second section explores some of the methods used to contact and recruit the drug injectors themselves. The sampling strategy aimed to recruit a wide range of drug injectors with prison experience, including roughly equal proportions of men and women. These aspects of the research process were mixed, but are separated here for analysis and discussion. As Stanley and Wise (1993) argue, there are a number of myths surrounding the presentation of research methods and it is important that they are not presented in an inaccurate 'hygienic' form to suit prevailing norms.

Negotiating access with services in contact with drug injectors

The starting-point for the fieldwork was to contact a range of services. Those approached included needle- and syringe-exchange schemes, drug-counselling services, young people's projects, residential drug treatment centres, probation services and various types of hostels. A series of letters, telephone calls and face-to-face meetings established contact with key members of staff within these services.

The purposes of these contacts were twofold:

- first, to ask professionals for their advice and input into the research — this included inviting feedback on the research instruments, especially when developing the vignette (Hughes, 1998a), and discussing strategies to recruit drug injectors with prison experience; and

- second, to ask whether they could help recruit participants.

Research involving the cooperation of services demands a number of important considerations (Power, 1989). At the outset, it is important to note that the majority of services contacted over the course of this study responded positively to the research, most agreeing to cooperate. However, an important factor influencing readiness to cooperate was the extent to which the research would take up time and resources. Refusal to help was usually due to the conflicting pressures facing staff and the services. For example, in one case:

> The manager listened to what I had to say then politely refused. He had a number of reasons. These include a 90 % occupancy rate; staff pressures including one member of staff on long-term sick leave and new staff joining; a number of academic and other researchers visiting, including prison officers on placement; and a concern that he did not want to turn [the residential drug treatment centre] into a 'zoo'. (Field note)

This example illustrates the range of conflicting priorities that many services face. In addition, one exceptional case for refusal involved a manager remarking that the research would not be relevant or of interest to the residents in the hostel.

> Spoke with [the manager] of [the hostel] today. Having outlined what I was doing she replied that 'none of the residents would be interested in that'. (Field note)

The use of gatekeepers such as these managers raises a number of important ethical and practical considerations (Homan, 1991). As illustrated above, they can make decisions about who will or will not take part in the research and this has important implications for sampling and the ways in which research findings are interpreted, notably that the sample characteristics may limit the generalisability of the data (Schofield, 1993).

Contacting and recruiting drug injectors

Having been granted access to recruit via services, the next stage of the project was to make contact with eligible drug injectors and invite them to participate. To highlight awareness of the study and the researcher, three complementary strategies were used.

- First, introductory letters with attached pre-paid envelopes were distributed within services. In some locations, letters were placed in communal areas and in others they were given out by staff.
- Second, posters were put up in services.
- Third, over a number of weeks an advertisement was placed in *The Big Issue*, a magazine sold by homeless people in the UK.

These briefly outlined the purposes of the research and invited those eligible to contact the researcher. These strategies were complementary in the sense that drug injectors would often know about the research from a number of sources, highlighting that access points often overlap.

Some, although relatively few, contacts were made directly through these awareness-raising strategies [1]. The most successful technique for contacting and recruiting drug injectors into the study was to spend time with them. In this respect, meeting people in low-threshold services such as drop-in centres or in the common rooms of hostels enabled the researcher and potential participants to get to know each other, thus building up confidence in the research relationship. However, it is important not to underestimate the value of the awareness strategies, which facilitated contact with people. By reference to the advertisements, conversations about the research could quickly be sparked. These could help the researcher to ascertain whether individuals were eligible to be invited to participate. In other cases, injectors would identify themselves as being eligible when the research was mentioned to them. For example:

> A new resident at the hostel let me in today. She asked me who I was.
> As soon as I had explained who I was and what I was doing she said
> 'I'll do that'. (Field note)

In some services, communal areas enabled the researcher to spend time informally meeting with potential participants. Recruitment from other services was facilitated

---

[1] Similarly, in Australia, Spooner et al. (1997) found that an advertised 'phone-in' was unsuccessful in recruiting rural drug injectors, noting that 'outreach' and 'street-intercept' yielded the highest response rates.

by staff, acting as gatekeepers, who introduced participants to the researcher. In addition, snowball sampling techniques and time spent getting to know people outside these service settings, typically and literally on the street, helped to reach those not in touch with services. The awareness strategies also helped when meeting people in these ways. For example, when purchasing *The Big Issue* magazine a mention of the study could help to make contact with drug injectors.

> *I bought* The Big Issue *and whilst starting to look to see if the advertisement had been placed I mentioned the research. The vendor said 'So you're the one looking for injectors.' He went on to say how he knew a couple of people who 'might be interested in that'.* (Field note)

An integral component of contacting and recruiting drug injectors is maximising opportunities as and when they arise. After an agreement to participate, an in-depth interview or small group discussion was arranged as soon as possible. However, some declined invitations to participate because they were not available at the time of contact (Hughes, 1998b). In these cases, handing out copies of the introductory letter provided people with an opportunity to make contact with the researcher at a time more convenient to them. Some were also encouraged to pass on the letter to others who might be interested in, and eligible for, the study.

A difficulty regularly encountered during the fieldwork concerned the recruiting of women. Some, although not a great many, contacts were made with women inside and outside service settings, and they generally responded positively to the research. Yet it remained difficult to recruit women. Drug injectors may not participate in research because of their other concerns and priorities (Hughes, 1998b). For women in particular, the responsibility of childcare can be an important consideration. For example:

> *I met Debbie and her child at the drop-in centre today. We agreed a time at which to meet up again but she did point out that an interview is 'a long time with a child to consider' ... [Later] Debbie missed the appointment.* (Field note)

To help deal with these problems, the end of the fieldwork period focused solely on recruiting women. It involved spending more time in settings such as hostels which housed women and in services with 'women only' sessions [2]. Such strategies helped to recruit some additional women into the study. Ultimately, however, the extent to which special groups can be contacted and recruited for research relies heavily on the timing and resource constraints of the study (Lee, 1993). In this study, fewer women than was hoped or expected participated. This may reflect, for example, fewer numbers of women drug injectors than men, especially within drug services (Vogt, 1998). It could also reflect some of the issues raised when men interview women (Owen, 1996).

---

[2] As a man, I was unable to spend time in the 'women only' sessions. However, some women would arrive early and this could provide an opportunity to meet.

Drug injectors, researchers and relationships: some closing observations

To help understand the difficulties that arise during recruitment, it is important to recognise the relational dynamics of research. Individual researchers have a particular relationship with participants, characterised by differing degrees of social distance. The ubiquity of drug use, and therefore drug users, indicates that it is not these individuals themselves who are difficult to access. Rather, being 'hard to reach' is the product of a particular relationship researchers have with participants. In the present study, drug injectors' lives were often characterised by disadvantage and, therefore, it is their position within society compared to that of researchers which can make them hard to reach, rather than their drug use per se.

Trust and confidence in the relationship with the researcher was one reported reason why injectors agreed to take part in the present study (Hughes, 1998b). Goto (1996) also found that trusting behaviours are more likely to occur in situations where there is little uncertainty and where those involved are socially close. Participation in research is often a new and potentially uncertain activity, typically requiring contact with researchers who are not well known to participants. Thus, in the research setting, trust may be inhibited. This can help to explain some of the difficulties of recruitment — notably of female drug injectors in the present study.

Conclusions

This chapter has reflected on some of the issues that arose when contacting and recruiting drug injectors in one qualitative study. As Mills (1959) has argued, it is essential that researchers are innovative and imaginative in the ways in which they undertake such tasks. This, together with the need to reflect on research practice (Shakespeare et al., 1993), is central when developing qualitative research strategies with drug users.

The author is based in the Department of Social Policy and Social Work at the University of York, UK.

References

Biernacki, P. and Waldorf, D. (1981) 'Snowball sampling: problems and techniques of chain referral sampling', *Sociological Methods and Research*, 10(2), 141–163.

Dean, H. and Barrett, D. (1996) 'Unrespectable research and researching the unrespectable', in H. Dean (Ed.) *Ethics and Social Policy Research*, Luton: University of Luton Press and Social Policy Association.

Goto, S. G. (1996) 'To trust or not to trust: situational and dispositional determinants', *Social Behaviour and Personality*, 24(2), 119–132.

Hammersley, M. and Atkinson, P. (1995) *Ethnography: Principles in Practice*, London: Routledge.

Homan, R. (1991) *The Ethics of Social Research*, Essex: Longman.

Hughes, R. (1998a) 'Considering the vignette technique and its application to a study of drug injecting and HIV risk and safer behaviour', *Sociology of Health and Illness,* 20(3), 381–400.

Hughes, R. (1998b) 'Why do people agree to participate in social research? The case of drug injectors', *International Journal of Social Research Methodology,* 1(4), 315–324.

Lee, R. M. (1993) *Doing Research on Sensitive Topics,* London: Sage.

McKeganey, N. and Barnard. M. (1992) *AIDS, Drugs and Sexual Risk: Lives in the Balance,* Buckingham: Open University Press.

Mills, C. W. (1959) *The Sociological Imagination,* Oxford: Oxford University Press.

Owen, D. (1996) 'Men, emotions and the research process: the role of interviews in sensitive areas', in K. Carter and S. Delamont (Eds.) *Qualitative Research: the Emotional Dimension,* Aldershot: Avebury.

Power, R. (1989) 'Participant observation and its place in the study of illicit drug abuse', *British Journal of Addiction,* 84(1), 43–52.

Power, R. (1995) 'A model for qualitative action research amongst illicit drug users', *Addiction Research,* 3(3), 165–181.

Schofield, J. W. (1993) 'Increasing the generalisability of qualitative research', in M. Hammersley (Ed.) *Social Research: Philosophy, Politics and Practice,* London: Sage and Open University Press.

Shakespeare, P., Atkinson, D. and French, S. (Eds.) (1993) *Reflecting on Research Practice: Issues in Health and Social Welfare,* Buckingham: Open University Press.

Spooner, C., Bishop, J. and Parr, J. (1997) 'Research methods for studying injecting drug users in a rural centre', *Drug and Alcohol Review,* 16(4), 349–355.

Stanley, L. and Wise, S. (1993) *Breaking Out Again: Feminist Ontology and Epistemology,* new edition, London: Routledge.

Taylor, A. (1993) *Women Drug Users: an Ethnography of a Female Injecting Community,* Oxford: Oxford University Press.

Vogt, I. (1998) 'Gender and drug treatment systems', in H. Klingemann and G. Hunt (Eds.) *Drug Treatment Systems in an International Perspective: Drugs, Demons and Delinquents,* London: Sage.

A QUALITATIVE STUDY OF COCAINE AND CRACK USE IN ANTWERP, BELGIUM: SOME ETHICAL ISSUES

Tom Decorte

A qualitative study of cocaine and crack use in Antwerp in Belgium was conducted between January 1996 and December 1998. The goals of the study were:

- to locate a minimum of 100 experienced cocaine users, preferably from non-institutionalised populations;
- to gather epidemiological data in order to contribute to the fragmented knowledge on the nature and extent of cocaine use in Belgium; and
- to provide an in-depth description of social rituals and rules (informal control mechanisms) and the processes through which these are transmitted.

Traditionally, epidemiological research in the field of drug use has been confronted with the problem of the low social visibility of the target group. The present study used the snowball sampling technique, participant observation and a double interview (a semi-structured questionnaire and an open biographical interview) to gain access to a variety of different networks of drug users, to nurture relationships of trust so that new introductions would be forthcoming, and to gain an insider's view of a group of cocaine users.

Through the establishment of relationships with high-status individuals on the nightlife scene, we finally obtained 25 different entrance points and a sample of 111 experienced users. The purpose of this chapter is to provide a description of some ethical problems that emerged in the course of the study.

Ethical problems

Gaining access

Functioning within a framework of illegality, potential prosecution and social unacceptability, the cocaine users had often achieved a delicate balance — involving a variety of behaviours and rituals, rules and languages (argots) — in their everyday lives between maintaining access to cocaine, protecting their identity and exercising control over use of the drug or its undesired side-effects.

In gaining and maintaining access to this world, none of the fieldworkers' activities should be threatening to this balance. We spent much time and energy in informing key individuals about the study. They were given basic information on its aims, the executing organisation and its personnel, the research methods, the role of the interviewer and the role of the respondent. It was particularly emphasised that there was no relationship between the researcher and law-enforcement agencies or treatment institutions.

Since illicit drug users are regarded as outsiders by the rest of society, and since the repressive climate probably stimulates them to regard the rest of society as outsiders, we had a substantial barrier to overcome before we found people willing to participate in the study.

Although we were often welcomed with sympathy and genuine interest, many cocaine users refused to participate because, for example, they feared arrest, did not trust the researcher, did not appreciate the purpose of a scientific study, saw their cocaine use as a strictly private matter, or because of rumours that the researcher was being followed by undercover police officers.

Setting a date and place

When a respondent agreed to participate in the study, an appropriate date and place had to be fixed for the interviews. Usually, telephone numbers were exchanged but sometimes a housemate or a member of the family answered when we telephoned to arrange the interview. If they wanted to know what our call was about, it was essential to be discreet. In a few cases, we had to go to great lengths to conceal their participation from their partner or other family members: we were asked not to contact them, but to wait for them to take the initiative.

Physical dangers

Although conflicts between the researcher and respondents are not inconceivable, no such incidents occurred. However, during the fieldwork we became acquainted with some professional dealers. Although we did not deal ourselves, we participated in many of their activities, attending social gatherings, travelling with them, and watching them plan their business activities. The highly illegal nature of their occupation makes drug dealers and smugglers secretive, deceitful, mistrustful and paranoid. There were occasions when we felt threatened, but as we developed trust with some high-status members, these minor crises could be averted.

Participating, observing or both?

In order to study cocaine users effectively as they engage in their habit in their natural setting, researchers must make moral decisions about law-breaking. Researchers need not be full participants, yet they witness or are told about illegal acts and are trusted not to report them to the police.

During the fieldwork, we were frequently asked whether we had ever used cocaine ourselves. It was often said that a non-cocaine-using researcher would always be an outsider and so would be unable to understand some vital aspects of using the drug. It can be tempting for researchers to say that they have had experience with cocaine (or other drugs) in order to gain the confidence of respondents. We have been offered cocaine on several occasions; such invitations could have been an indication of trust and friendship or a test of whether we were researchers rather than agents of social control.

Role confusion

Enduring relationships developed with a few of the study participants and these could lead the researcher into difficult situations. People often revealed very intimate details about themselves and about their relationships with others who were also known to the researcher. Gossip was frequent. For example, several respondents gave their opinion about the nature and extent of the cocaine use of others, and one respondent revealed to us her affair with the partner of another respondent. A researcher witnesses the positive and negative elements of people but must resist the temptation to offer opinions.

We were sometimes called upon to leave the role of participant observer and get involved. On several occasions we were confronted with questions about the possible effects of cocaine, for instance: 'I only use one or two grams in a weekend. That means I can control my cocaine consumption, don't you think? It can't do any harm, can it?'. Another time a woman came to ask us to accompany her friend to a treatment agency, 'because she's really got problems with ecstasy and speed, and I don't wanna go there'. Once or twice, respondents called us at night 'because they needed someone to talk to'. Thus we were sometimes pulled between our observer role (not to influence the natural setting) and our participant role (to offer friendly help or advice).

Interview effects

We discovered that the combined use of a semi-structured questionnaire and an open interview prompted reactions from many respondents. Firstly, it appeared that the interviews stimulated many of them to reflect about their own cocaine use. Secondly, when asked to report on their experience of 91 possible adverse effects of cocaine, several participants realised their lack of knowledge about the drug they used: 'I didn't know cocaine could cause so many effects!' or 'Jeezes, did I really experience all these adverse effects?' or 'I never really realised that my heartbeat increased when using coke.' Thirdly, certain questions actually encouraged some respondents to experiment; for example, when asked if they had ever applied cocaine to their genitals, some respondents reacted along the lines of: 'I didn't know that was possible. I should try it once.' And fourth, after two hours of intense conversation, some participants said: 'All this talking about cocaine makes me wanna do it again.'

Privacy of the researcher

Observing drug users in their natural habitat means the researcher has to keep unusual hours and penetrate previously unknown territory. We worked at night and slept during the day because that is what many of the people we studied did. Our commitments to partners, family, friends and colleagues suffered from the irregular working hours, nights out, fatigue and irritability associated with intensive fieldwork. In this situation, a lack of psychological and emotional support may lead to a feeling of isolation and we sometimes felt we were swinging back and forth between two worlds: our own and that of the respondents.

Sometimes we felt that we did not or could not function properly in either world. In addition to developing support networks amongst friends, family and colleagues, a remedy is to withdraw temporarily from the field. However, in a study such as this, one cannot stay away too long because of the risk of losing contacts, concrete data on events in the field and the confidence of the respondents.

Privacy of the participants

Another source of concern for us was the police. We worried about local police or drug agents discovering the nature of our study and confiscating our tapes and field notes, or following us to see where and with whom we interacted. In order to protect ourselves and our data in the case of arrest, we informed the Office of the Public Prosecutor of Antwerp about the study. The police themselves were not informed, and we only had an oral agreement with the public prosecutor that our data would not be confiscated if the researcher was arrested when in the company of respondents. We were therefore in a vulnerable position, as we had 'guilty knowledge' about respondents' involvement in illegal money racket systems, the arms and drug trade, theft, etc. In order to maintain respondents' confidentiality, all data were coded, all transcribed tapes were destroyed, and none of the data was kept at our homes or in the office. We shifted the tapes and transcriptions between different hiding places and finally transferred the data into an uninvolved person's possession.

Telling the 'truth'

There is no single 'truth' about drug use or addiction. Explanations drug users give for their drug use make sense not so much as facts, but as primarily functional statements shaped by a climate of moral and legal censure. One implication of using institutionalised drug users in drug research is that they may retaliate in some way. Participants who feel that they are being manipulated or forced to comply with a researcher may lie, or purposely distort their answers to a questionnaire, or give any answer that seems convenient. There is no doubt that some of our respondents lied to us about the quantity or the frequency of their cocaine use, their criminal activities and certain aspects of their health, such as seropositivity. However, verification of their accounts was accomplished, when possible, through members of their peer group and through direct observation. During interviews, respondents would often recount the experiences of others; this information was used as an additional source of verification.

Effect of drugs on data gathering

On occasion, respondents were under the influence of cannabis, cocaine, ampheta-mines or other drugs during an interview. Attempting to interview them whilst they were affected by cannabis or heroin did not prove effective, as they became either confused or sleepy. Cocaine and amphetamines, in contrast, proved to be a research aid, rendering respondents talkative and sociable.

Conclusions

In this chapter, we have described some of the ethical problems which we encoun-tered during fieldwork. Some of the difficulties of using snowball sampling, partici-pant observation and interviews are inherent in the method itself and are likely to emerge in research projects in a wide range of substantive areas. Many of the prob-lems recounted here, however, result from this study's focus: a deviant phenomenon that is surrounded by moral, legal or social sensitivities.

The problems presented above illustrate some of the ethical questions to consider when beginning a qualitative study such as ours: What are the beneficial conse-quences of the study? How can informed consent of the participating subjects be obtained? How can the confidentiality of the interview subjects be protected? What are the consequences of the study for participating subjects? How will the researcher's role affect the study? There are no easy answers to these questions, although ethical guidelines produced by methodologists may give some direction, and participating in research communities may provide additional concrete back-ground knowledge for making ethical decisions.

Traditionally, most studies of illicit drug use (especially in Belgium) only produce a partial picture, because they are based on the best-known, most visible, most easily accessible and probably most marginalised subgroups of drug users. Observing or interviewing respondents with the intention of affecting their lives in any way (help-ing, treating or controlling them) biases the research findings. We believe the prin-cipal aim of qualitative drug research should be simply to understand users better: to learn from them what they do and why, trying to describe their behaviour, not from our point of view but from theirs. We should seek to study drug users from within their culture rather than from outside it and to present their world as they see it. In general, we should try to withhold judgments about the appropriateness or inappropriateness of drug-using behaviours.

The author is Senior Assistant in the Department of Penal Law and Criminology, Faculty of Law, University of Ghent, Belgium.

Further reading

Adair, E. B., Craddock, S. G., Miller, H. G. and Turner, C. F. (1995) 'Assessing consistency of responses to questions on cocaine use', *Addiction,* 90, 1497–1502.

Biernacki, P. and Waldorf, D. (1981) 'Snowball sampling problems and techniques of chain referral sampling', *Sociological Methods and Research,* 10, 141–163.

Davies, J. B. (1997) *Drugspeak: the Analysis of Drug Discourse,* Amsterdam: Harwood Academic Publishers.

Dunlap, E., Johnson, B. et al. (1990) 'Studying crack users and their criminal careers: the scientific and artistic aspects of locating hard-to-reach subjects and interviewing them about sensitive topics', *Contemporary Drug Problems,* 17, Part 2, 121–145.

Griffiths, P., Gossop, M., Powis, B. and Strang, J. (1993) 'Reaching hidden populations of drug users by privileged access interviewers: methodological and practical issues', *Addiction,* 88, 1617–1626.

Hendriks, V. M., Blanken, P. and Adriaans, N. F. P. (1992) *Snowball Sampling: a Pilot Study on Cocaine Use,* series 32, Rotterdam: Instituut voor Verslavingsonderzoek (IVO), Erasmus Universiteit.

Hser, Y. (1993) 'Data sources: problems and issues', *Journal of Drug Issues,* 23, 217–228.

Power, R. (1989) 'Participant observation and its place in the study of illicit drug abuse', *British Journal of Addiction,* 84, 43–52.

Rouse, B. A., Kozel, N. J. and Richards, L. G. (Eds.) (1985) *Self-Report Methods of Estimating Drug Use: Meeting Current Challenges to Validity,* Washington: NIDA.

Turner, C. F., Lessler, J. T. and Gfroerer, J. C. (1992) *Survey Measurement of Drug Use: Methodological Studies,* Washington: Department of Health and Human Services.

CHAPTER 36

COMMUNITY FIELDWORK: BRINGING DRUG USERS INTO RESEARCH ACTION

Peter Blanken, Cas Barendregt and Linda Zuidmulder

Studies focusing on 'known' drug users such as those in treatment or in the criminal justice system bypass all those whose consumption patterns do not result in health or social problems. Locating and studying this 'hidden' population of drug users in their natural context has resulted in a number of creative research methodologies (see, for instance, Biernacki and Waldorf, 1981; Kaplan et al., 1987; Watters and Biernacki, 1989; Hendriks et al., 1992; Broadhead et al., 1995; Hartnoll et al., 1997).

A core feature of drug research projects is that drug users are the subjects of research: seldom do they participate in its development and implementation. An important characteristic of much of the research into illegal drug use conducted by the Addiction Research Institute Rotterdam (IVO) is the concept of community fieldwork, which is based on the 'added value' of experiential knowledge. The community fieldworker is an active drug user who is therefore familiar with the behaviours, the specific rules and rituals and the social networks of drug users. Importantly, they have easy access to the natural context in which most drug use takes place and are trusted by drug users.

Community fieldwork

The main task of community fieldworkers is to establish and maintain contact with key contact persons, such as drug users and dealers, in and around drug scenes. In order to achieve this, 'being in the community' is a crucial element of their work. As a result of this 'free-floating' community fieldwork, they will observe and be informed about developments taking place; for instance:

- the appearance of new groups of users in specific drug-using populations;
- the emergence of 'new' drugs;
- the re-emergence of 'old' psychoactive substances; and
- shifts in drug administration rituals.

These changes must then be communicated by the community fieldworker to the research team — for example, in the form of field notes. Conversely, the community fieldworker can also inform the community about results of studies, such as methods by which HIV is transmitted or strategies to self-regulate cocaine consumption. Ultimately, the successful community fieldworker can establish a research alliance between the community and academia.

Figure 1: Ethnographic research and community fieldwork	
Interview with an ethnographic researcher studying 'fringe group youth' (P. Giesen, *de Volkskrant*, 5 April 1993)	**'Would be' interview with a community fieldworker studying 'fringe group youth'** (adaptation of Giesen, 1995, by Peter Blanken)
The ethnographic researcher lives in two different worlds.	The community fieldworker lives in two different worlds.
One part of the week he/she sits behind a desk and a computer. The remaining hours he/she hangs around with youngsters in the shopping mall or around the railway station.	One part of the week he/she hangs around with youngsters in the shopping mall or around the railway station. The remaining time he/she sits behind a desk and a computer.
The ethnographic scientist is, and will always be, a strange presence on the scene — an old geezer.	The community fieldworker is, and will always be, a strange presence in academia — an oddball.
However, in general he/she manages to gain confidence: 'Often you are made a fool of, but in the end many youngsters trust you and consider it to be kind of a distraction.'	However, in general he/she manages to gain confidence: 'Often you are not taken seriously, but in the end many scientists trust you and do appreciate the added value.'

Participation in all phases of the research

Community fieldworkers can contribute to the design and methodology of a study. Whether they are full members of a research team or work on a freelance basis, the outcome of their free-floating fieldwork activity is knowledge of developments that are taking place in different drug scenes. They can thereby:

- suggest topics for research;
- assist in preparing research proposals;
- comment on research questions;
- give valuable input to, and feedback on, the selection of research instruments; and
- aid in defining study populations and the development of sampling strategies.

When a study is implemented, community fieldworkers inform the community about the project, and prepare and conduct fieldwork. Their role means they have up-to-date knowledge on when and where networks of drug users can be located. Community fieldworkers who are full members of the research team will subsequently contribute to data analysis and preparation of the research report. They can often point out possible meaningful relationships between data, assist in interpreting results and shed new light on explaining unexpected findings.

Such cooperation with drug users in research is not unique. Several studies and health outreach projects have employed them either to contact drug users in their natural habitat and/or for the collection of research data (see, for instance, Froner and Rowniak, 1989; Broadhead and Fox, 1990; Griffiths et al., 1993; Grund, 1993; Barendregt et al., 1995; Blanken et al., 1995; Kuebler and Hausser, 1997). These projects have used different terms to describe the drug users' function, such as community fieldworker, community health outreach worker, jobist, peer or privileged access interviewer. No matter what term is used, all researchers and health prevention workers expect more or less the same added value, as outlined above, and also expect to benefit from the networks and knowledge of the active drug users they employ as fieldworkers.

Some implications and practical consequences

Recruitment and selection

Community fieldworkers can be recruited through a wide variety of channels. For example, we have contacted active drug users through our own ethnographic fieldwork and with the assistance of drug-related services (such as drop-in centres, methadone programmes, drug user interest groups or 'junky unions') and health outreach schemes. In these cases, we gave intermediaries a profile of the drug users we would like to work with and asked them to introduce us to those who might be suitable candidates.

Every potential community fieldworker is given a 'job interview'. It seldom happens that candidates are rejected at an early stage: a process of self-selection starts during the training period and continues during the free-floating and interviewing phases of the community fieldwork. In some of our research projects, the drop-out rate reached 50 %. It is thus no luxury to recruit more drug users at the start of a project than the number actually needed.

Community fieldworkers leave the research team for a variety of reasons. For instance, they can be arrested or find a more lucrative job (such as dealing). Sometimes, it transpires that community fieldworkers do not have enough useful contacts, or that they are afraid of losing control over their drug use because of their close contact with the drug scene. In addition, being engaged in community fieldwork is not always an exciting activity and they may simply lose interest in the study.

Training

Before community fieldworkers start ethnographic fieldwork or the collection of data in the context of a survey, training sessions are held in order to:

- establish a relationship of respect and trust, both among the community fieldworkers and between them and the researcher(s);
- inform them about practical and organisational aspects of the study;
- explain the aim and the framework of the research;
- explain, discuss and rehearse the research instrument, such as an observational scheme, a field-note format or an interview (as a result of this, the instrument is often adjusted);
- explain, discuss and rehearse the procedure for collecting information (for instance, what behaviour to observe, which situations to describe or how to randomly recruit respondents); and
- develop and practise strategies on how to present themselves as community fieldworkers who are part of a research team.

The duration of this training course depends on the complexity of the research project, the data-collection instruments that are used and the aptitude of the community fieldworkers. On average, training courses are held for five three-hour sessions. All training sessions begin with a simple meal in order to socialise and gain mutual trust. After data collection begins, a 'booster' training session is often held.

Community fieldworkers' incentives

Money is often assumed to be the primary incentive for drug users' willingness to cooperate in research as community fieldworkers. Other incentives, such as feeling recognised as a valuable person, or increasing status, may be thought of as of secondary importance. Of course, money is an important incentive but, in itself, is not sufficient to commit an individual to the research project. The so-called secondary incentives have proved to be at least as valuable. We noticed that the community fieldworkers need and appreciate close monitoring of their work, not as a form of control, but specifically as an expression of support and appreciation, and as a motivating factor to continue the job. Another factor contributing to their commitment is the degree of difficulty of the tasks they have to perform: it seems that the more concrete and structured a task is, the higher the community fieldworkers' commitment.

Respondents' rewards

Respondents always receive compensation for the time they invest in answering our questions, and as a token of appreciation for contributing to our research. In some studies, we have given them a small gift, chosen in line with the goal of the study and the lifestyle of the target group (for instance, a personal drug injecting paraphernalia kit, a lighter, a small hashish pipe and cigarettes). The decision to compensate respondents with such items instead of money was made on the assumption that, if community fieldworkers were given cash with which to pay respondents, the temptation to spend it themselves and falsify data might be too great. However, in some studies, respondents did receive financial compensation (about EUR 6.50), and community fieldworkers were provided with between EUR 13 and EUR 19.50

in sealed envelopes in order to pay two or three respondents. The community field-workers endeavoured to be regarded as trustworthy members of the research team, and this system proved unproblematic.

Conclusions

One of the tasks of researchers studying drug users is to find ways of reaching those who are not institutionalised. Among these there is a large pool of talented individuals who are capable of, and interested in, contributing to scientific research. As described here, incorporating active drug users into a research team as community fieldworkers means that they must be identified, selected, trained and — most importantly — supported. In addition, researchers are faced with the challenging task of maintaining the interest of community fieldworkers, who may be confronted with various motivating and demotivating factors, some of which have been mentioned in the preceding paragraphs. The core dilemma confronting community fieldworkers is finding a balance between personal involvement with their drug-using peers and their fieldwork: between community engagement and keeping a scientific distance.

Peter Blanken, formerly Senior Researcher at the Addiction Research Institute Rotterdam (IVO), is now employed at the Central Committee on the Treatment of Heroin Addicts (CCBH), Utrecht, the Netherlands. Cas Barendregt is Coordinator of Community Fieldwork at IVO. Linda Zuidmulder is a community fieldworker at IVO.

Acknowledgements

This chapter is dedicated to Nico Adiaans, co-constructor of the community fieldworker methodology at the Rotterdam Addiction Research Institute, and all community fieldworkers who have followed him.

References

Barendregt, C., Blanken, P. and Christiaanse, R. (1995) *De achterkant van drugsoverlast,* Rotterdam: Stichting Odyssee/Deelgemeente Delfshaven.

Biernacki, P. and Waldorf, D. (1981) 'Snowball sampling: problems and techniques of chain referral sampling', *Sociological Methods and Research,* 10(2), 141–163.

Blanken, P., Vollemans, L., Verveen, J., Hendriks, V. and Adriaans, N. (1995) *Perron Nul en de bezoekers die er kwamen: Het Rotterdams Drug Monitoring Systeem, 1994,* series 7, Rotterdam: Addiction Research Institute (IVO)/Erasmus University Rotterdam.

Broadhead, R. S. and Fox, K. J. (1990) 'Takin' it to the streets: AIDS outreach as ethnography', *Journal of Contemporary Ethnography,* 19(3), 322–348.

Broadhead, R. S., Heckathorn, D. D., Grund, J.-P. C., Stern, L. S. and Anthony, D. L. (1995) 'Drug users versus outreach workers in combating AIDS: preliminary results of a peer-driven intervention', *Journal of Drug Issues,* 25(3), 531–564.

Froner, G. and Rowniak, S. (1989) 'The health outreach team: taking AIDS education and health care to the streets', *AIDS Education and Prevention,* 1(2), 105–118.

Griffiths, P., Gossop, M., Powis, B. and Strang, J. (1993) 'Reaching hidden populations of drug users by privileged access interviewers: methodological and practical issues', *Addiction,* 88, 1617–1626.

Grund, J.-P. C. (1993) *Drug Use as a Social Ritual: Functionality, Symbolism and Determinants of Self-Regulation,* series 4, Rotterdam: Addiction Research Institute (IVO)/Erasmus University Rotterdam.

Hartnoll, R., Griffiths, P., Taylor, C., Hendriks, V., Blanken, P., Nolimal, D., Weber, I., Toussirt, M. and Ingold, R. (1997) *Handbook on Snowball Sampling,* Strasbourg: Council of Europe, Pompidou Group.

Hendriks, V. M., Blanken, P. and Adriaans, N. F. P. (1992) *Snowball Sampling: a Pilot Study on Cocaine Use,* series 2, Rotterdam: Addiction Research Institute (IVO)/Erasmus University Rotterdam.

Kaplan, C. D., Korf, D. and Sterk, C. (1987) 'Temporal and social contexts of heroin-using populations: an illustration of the snowball sampling technique', *Journal of Nervous and Mental Disease,* 175(9), 566–574.

Kuebler, D. and Hausser, D. (1997) 'The Swiss hidden population study: practical and methodological aspects of data collection by privileged access interviewers', *Addiction,* 92(3), 325–334.

Watters, J. K. and Biernacki, P. (1989) 'Targeted sampling: options for the study of hidden populations', *Social Problems,* 36(4), 416–427.

QUALITATIVE RESEARCH WITHIN A GLOBAL RESEARCH AGENDA

PART IX

INTRODUCTION

*T*he final section of this monograph is devoted to qualitative research on drug use in the context of a global research agenda. In Chapter 37, Jane Fountain, Paul Griffiths and Richard Hartnoll look at the European Union and highlight the fact that the scale of qualitative drug research conducted in the EU varies greatly between countries. They also point out that high-quality work of this type is rarely published in drug-specific scientific journals.

In Chapter 38, John Fitzgerald comments on the relationship between qualitative research and drug policy in Australia. He documents the challenge of influencing drug policy when politicians will only support policies that can be 'sold' by talk-back radio hosts to their over-50s listeners.

Zili Sloboda provides a history of the contributions made by qualitative research to the study of drug use in the USA. In Chapter 39, she highlights the debate between those wishing to render qualitative approaches more scientific and those wishing to preserve the 'purity' of the ethnographic approach.

Finally, in Chapter 40, Michael Stauffacher, Dagmar Hedrich, Paul Griffiths and Janusz Sierosławski summarise the situation in central and eastern Europe. They conclude that a comprehensive approach should include training individual experts and research teams and exchanging experiences between researchers across and beyond Europe.

QUALITATIVE RESEARCH ON DRUG USE
IN THE EUROPEAN UNION ([1])

Jane Fountain, Paul Griffiths and Richard Hartnoll

The European Monitoring Centre for Drugs and Drug Addiction (EMCDDA) is increasingly focusing attention on developing comparable methodologies in qualitative research across the European Union (EU) and supporting the development of networks to further this. Until recently, such activity has tended to concentrate on quantitative methodologies, such as the harmonisation of survey data sets and treatment reporting systems.

This work is critical to the ability to monitor the use of illicit drugs and to provide policy-makers with a sound basis for identifying appropriate responses. However, developing an understanding of patterns of drug consumption and their relationship to health and social problems is a complex process. This understanding is only possible if informed by data collected using a diverse set of methodological techniques. Quantitative data is never likely to be sufficient unless informed and supported by qualitative inquiry, but, in terms of EU networking, qualitative research remains a relatively neglected area.

To some extent, this may be due to issues inherent in the methodology itself, since the techniques designed to produce a detailed understanding of behaviour in specific contexts do not easily lend themselves to methodological standardisation. Nevertheless, there is much to be gained by disseminating insights gained through qualitative studies — particularly amongst policy-makers — and by developing networks of those engaged in this kind of endeavour. In addition, methodological and theoretical advances are most likely to be achieved if supported by an active research community where good communication links exist between researchers investigating similar topics within their own countries.

Two EMCDDA projects (Fountain and Griffiths, 1997; 1998), therefore, centred on producing a comprehensive picture of qualitative research on drug use in the EU, with the focus on publications from the last 10 years, studies currently in progress and researchers using qualitative methods. The projects also aimed to highlight the areas likely to be fruitful for future activity, both within each country and on a collaborative, EU-wide basis. This chapter offers an overview of the issues raised by an examination of the data that had been collected and synthesised, and by two sem-

---

([1]) This chapter is based on Fountain and Griffiths (1997; 1998; 1999).

inars held in the context of the projects (the website set up as part of the projects can be found on http://www.qed.org.uk).

Towards a definition of qualitative research

The issue of defining qualitative research has been the subject of much debate (see, for example, Denzin and Lincoln, 1994; Lambert et al., 1995). The definition of what constitutes qualitative research in a European context is complicated by many studies having employed a combination of qualitative and quantitative methods. The two EMCDDA projects have made significant progress in the development of a model of identification by summarising publications according to, for example, sample generation and key findings. Such a strategy will allow a clearer debate on what constitutes the boundaries of qualitative inquiry.

Development of qualitative research in the EU

Some general comments on the extent of qualitative inquiry in the EU can be made from the data collected by the two EMCDDA projects. Firstly, the scale of qualitative drug research varies greatly between countries. In some — notably Spain, France, the Netherlands and the UK — there appears to be a relatively high level of activity, whilst elsewhere — Greece, Luxembourg and Portugal, for example — very little relevant qualitative research could be identified. This observation must be placed into the following context:

- the scale of research into drug use varies greatly across the EU, regardless of the methodology used;
- some countries have very little tradition of conducting qualitative as opposed to quantitative research in any topic area;
- the scale of drug use varies greatly across the EU, and in some countries has only recently begun to be seen as a priority area for research investment; and
- some countries do not have a strong social science tradition, meaning that, historically, central government funding has not been available for research activities.

Throughout the European Union — as elsewhere — qualitative methods have not been embraced by researchers and funding bodies wholeheartedly. On the other hand, the pace of development of significant qualitative research into drug use across the EU has varied immensely from country to country. In some countries, this can be partly explained by a paucity of any research into drug use, whatever the methodology. For example, the UK has had a strong tradition in this respect, whilst research into drug use in Ireland has begun only relatively recently, and in Greece is in the early stages of development. In the past decade (the focus of the EMCDDA projects), however, it can be said that, overall, there has been a greater receptivity to the use of qualitative methods in the EU.

There is no overall body defining research priorities in any EU country, so the topics that attract funding vary. However, a significant factor in the development of qualitative research in many countries — notably Germany, Spain and the UK — was the public health imperative to reduce HIV infection associated with drug use, as discussed in the introduction to this monograph. This emphasised the need for research methods capable of understanding the social context and meaning of risk behaviours among hidden or 'hard-to-reach' populations. The impact of HIV infection and AIDS on the research agenda in the last 10 years, and on the focus of qualitative research in particular, should therefore not be underestimated. More recently, in some EU countries, this focus has been widened to include other drug-using risk behaviours such as hepatitis C virus (HCV) transmission and co-morbidity.

Research themes

The bibliography of publications and 'grey' literature (unpublished reports, etc.) collected for the project currently contains over 700 items. Over 100 recent and current relevant qualitative projects have also been identified. Entries in both these databases (see http://www.qed.org.uk) were thematically analysed, revealing both historical and geographical differences in the topics of qualitative inquiry conducted across the EU. Whilst health risks associated with injecting populations — particularly HIV risk behaviour — probably accounted for a large proportion of qualitative research activity in the late 1980s and early 1990s, more recently studies of new drug trends and drug use by young people have become increasingly popular. In the Netherlands, for example, there is a considerable body of work reflecting that country's relatively sophisticated system for qualitative monitoring of patterns of illicit drug use. It is likely that more studies will investigate issues surrounding injecting in the future, as researchers address the challenge of explaining HCV infection rates among drug injectors.

The bulk of current qualitative research activity identified by the EMCDDA projects is either concerned with patterns of drug use or addresses some aspect of intervention. In some countries, however — particularly Greece, Italy, Luxembourg, Austria, Portugal, Finland and Sweden — few or no current qualitative research projects could be located.

In the last decade, by far the greatest number of publications and grey literature have addressed issues associated with patterns of drug use, which includes drug use by young people and new drug trends. Risk behaviour and health also constitutes a major topic of study. Much of the literature addressed interventions, these being largely qualitative evaluations of treatment. In Germany, Spain and the UK, this theme was particularly evident: around half of all the German qualitative research addressed some aspect of treatment or other interventions.

Two areas where fewer publications were detected were those focusing directly on qualitative methodology and policy issues. However, it should not be assumed that studies are not relevant to policy, but rather that few qualitative studies make policy-making itself the topic of inquiry. The shortage of papers addressing methodological issues is perhaps of greater concern. Researching patterns of illicit drug use is a complex topic requiring both sophisticated and rigorous methodological procedures. Given that qualitative methodology is poorly developed in some countries in the EU, methodological texts would represent a valuable resource that would enable researchers to discuss and to develop qualitative methodological approaches.

Current qualitative research funding in the EU

An examination of the funding sources of current qualitative research projects on drug use reveals that, although these vary between countries, on the whole, government departments and health authorities appear to be the biggest investors. It should be noted, however, that the projects could locate little or no current qualitative research activity on drug use in almost half of the 15 EU countries (Greece, Italy, Luxembourg, Austria, Portugal, Finland and Sweden).

Considerable funds are allocated to research on drug use in some countries and the particular focus of funders influences not only which aspects of the phenomenon are investigated, but also the methodology of those investigations. If, for example, a funding body sees drug use as largely of a medical or a prevalence-measurement concern, then the projects funded will reflect that viewpoint and use quantitative methods. However, the contributions made by qualitative research to the understanding of HIV infection amongst injecting drug users (IDUs) has meant that there is a growing acceptance of a multi-method approach to data collection and analysis. The majority of current projects which incorporate qualitative methods are investigating patterns of drug use and some aspect of intervention, traditionally the domains of quantitative researchers.

No EU country has a central funding body for research into drug use, but, in some, various initiatives have outlined research priorities and/or have made funds available to projects with a qualitative element. Examples include the Home Office Drug Prevention Initiative in the UK; the government's Science and Technology against Drugs Programme in Ireland; and the Framework Programme for Research on Addiction in the Netherlands. It is also encouraging to note that the European Commission has funded several collaborative projects with a qualitative element.

The relevance of qualitative research on drug use for policy-making

The data collected for the EMCDDA projects show clearly that a substantial body of qualitative research and expertise exists in a few countries, whilst, in others, this is a novel approach. It is also clear that there is untapped potential for bringing this knowledge into the policy domain in the EU, which offers a natural laboratory in which drug use can be examined within different social, cultural and policy contexts. Such an examination reveals the limitations of quantitative research. Comparable statistical surveys can be conducted in different countries, but the problem of interpretation remains: what the results mean in the different countries and the implications for policy.

It is here that the data from qualitative research are invaluable, as they reveal the links between the different actors, and their contexts, and allow efficient and relevant interactions and interventions to be developed. However, the process that begins with a drug-related problem and ends with decision-making aimed at solving that problem is not straightforward. A fruitful working relationship between researchers and policy-makers is often hindered by misunderstandings: policy-makers may often ask questions to which they have already found political answers, and researchers may give scientific answers to political questions. There are numerous situations where researchers are best able to enter and explore an aspect of drug use using qualitative methods, yet very often it is a high-profile, politicised 'problem' they are funded to investigate, and, as such, the research results will affect policy and intervention.

The issue of the relationship between research and policy is critical if research is to have any impact on policy and public health. For instance, HIV, AIDS and HCV amongst drug users remains a substantial problem in many countries, and the responses to it — from both a research and policy formulation point of view — vary considerably from one country to another. In some, such as parts of Germany, there are considerable problems in promoting harm-reduction approaches. In others, such as the Netherlands, harm reduction is the principal response to the problems of HIV and other health risks amongst drug users.

Ultimately, though, however 'good' the qualitative research, its influence on policy will also be related to many other factors: the political moment; the role of the media; the relationship between the researchers and the policy-makers; the ways in which findings are managed in their dissemination; and whether data are converted into ideas and interventions which others can easily use in further developing policy and practice.

It is encouraging that, in a number of countries, research activity into drug use seems to be increasing. In some respects, this can be seen as corresponding to drug use moving up the agenda of policy-makers' concerns. This, coupled with the realisation that simply relying on statistical data sets is not sufficient to understand the phenomenon, has prompted the development and funding of qualitative projects in a number of countries.

Increasing the impact of qualitative research on the policy agenda

One of the problems faced by researchers, regardless of their methodological orientation, is how to make their research relevant to, and influential on, the policy agenda. Research can only be of use to policy-makers if it addresses those questions that are driving policy formulation in a timely fashion. Historically, qualitative research has often been characterised by intensive, long-term and detailed studies of specific subcultural groups, but the time-consuming nature of this kind of enterprise is not always compatible with the demands of today's health-care agenda.

Qualitative research has the potential to develop the necessary rapid reporting systems demanded by policy-makers: the quick accumulation of focused data on specific topic areas. There has been some fruitful collaboration between qualitative and quantitative researchers who have employed a mixture of their methods (such as capture–recapture, network sampling, site sampling, snowball sampling and benchmark calculation techniques) to produce some innovative studies of drug prevalence.

Qualitative research is also only likely to be influential if it has credibility with policy-makers. In some respects, the situation has improved recently, and there is evidence to suggest that policy-makers have become more sophisticated in their understanding of the importance of different types of data in developing an over-view of complex issues.

The EMCDDA projects have demonstrated how much high-quality qualitative research is available across the EU. However, many of the studies they identified are available only in report form or in national publications of limited circulation. Thus, the benefits are not available for exchange and information or for identifying which aspects of drug use are specific to a locality and which cut across local and national boundaries.

Regardless of their methodology, studies are likely to be most influential if they are available in the public domain. The scientific scrutiny that such material receives also helps to maintain quality: if qualitative research studies are not seen as method-ologically rigorous, they are unlikely to be credible or influential. Evidence col-lected during the course of the projects suggests that qualitative researchers often experience considerable difficulty getting their work published in drug-specific scientific journals. Although many drugs journals have recently been more ready to consider qualitative reports than previously, a forum dedicated to publishing such material is overdue.

It is hoped that the projects' website (http://www.qed.org.uk) will provide a useful resource for those wishing to learn more about the range of qualitative studies that have been conducted across the European Union. The continuing support of the EMCDDA provides an opportunity for qualitative research to reach a wider audi-ence, including those designing policy, prevention or legislative inventions aimed at reducing the problems associated with drug consumption.

Jane Fountain is a research sociologist at the National Addiction Centre (NAC), London, UK. Paul Griffiths was a senior research officer at the NAC at the time of writing and now works at the United Nations International Drug Control Programme (UNDCP), Vienna, Austria. Richard Hartnoll is the head of the Department of Epidemiology, EMCDDA, Lisbon, Portugal.

References

Denzin, N. K. and Lincoln, Y. S. (1994) *Handbook of Qualitative Research,* Thousand Oaks, CA/London/New Delhi: Sage.

Fountain, J. and Griffiths, P. (Eds.) (1997) *Inventory, Bibliography, and Synthesis of Qualitative Research in the European Union,* Lisbon/London: EMCDDA/NAC (updated version available on http://www.qed.org.uk).

Fountain, J. and Griffiths, P. (Eds.) (1998) *Coordination of Working Groups of Qualitative Researchers to Analyse Different Drug Use Patterns and the Implication for Public Health Strategies and Prevention,* project report, Lisbon/London: EMCDDA/NAC.

Fountain, J. and Griffiths, P. (Eds.) (1999) 'Synthesis of qualitative research on drug use in the European Union: report on an EMCDDA project', *European Addiction Research,* 5(4), 4–20.

Lambert, E. Y., Ashery, R. S. and Needle, R. H. (1995) *Qualitative Methods in Drug Abuse and HIV Research,* Monograph 157, Rockville, MD: NIDA.

CHAPTER 38

SELLING STORIES TO THE MASSES: QUALITATIVE RESEARCH AND AUSTRALIAN DRUG POLICY

John Fitzgerald

What follows is a short summary of recent qualitative drug research in Australia and its role in drug policy. This chapter, however, is not a wide-ranging review of Australian qualitative research. Rather, it is a strategic commentary on the dynamic relationship between qualitative drug research and the drug policy agenda. Of particular interest is the capacity of qualitative work to produce research stories — stories about drug users, about research into drug use and about the governance of drug users. The chapter finishes with some stories to illustrate how the profile of Australian qualitative drug research may be changing into a more strategic and more politicised field of research and policy practice.

The focus on drug-using social fields

For the last 20 years, qualitative drug research in Australia has been dominated by North American 1960s and 1970s sociology. This is now changing, not because of any emerging academic tradition, but rather because of a generally greater politicisation of drug research in Australia, following the federal government's veto of a prescribed heroin trial after the most exhaustive feasibility study in the country's drug history.

In the past, Australian qualitative drug research has focused on drug-using social fields, particularly the work of:

- Phil Dance (1990; 1991; 1999; Dance and Mugford, 1992) on enthusiast groups of heroin users;
- David Moore on punks (1990) and recreational users of amphetamines and ecstasy (1992a; 1992b; 1993a; 1993b);
- myself and colleagues on the use of ecstasy and hallucinogens (Fitzgerald and Hamilton, 1994) and street heroin markets (Fitzgerald et al., 1999a; 1999b);
- Barb Denton on women drug traffickers in and out of prison (Denton, 1998); and

- Lisa Maher on the use of heroin by south-east Asian heroin users, which has highlighted the relationships between social and cultural structures and illegal drug use (Maher et al., 1997; 1998).

The focus of the most recent Australian qualitative drug research has been on how drug use fits into specific social contexts, rather than on other levels of analysis. This has made it possible to target specific social fields for interventions. Perhaps as a result, there have been various interventions aimed at some of these drug-using social worlds.

A small-scale example of this was our work on khat (qat) use by east-African immigrants to Australia (Stevenson et al., 1996). In a short piece of contract qualitative research examining the health and social effects of khat, we recommended that east-African immigrants be allowed to import it for use in community settings. Some years later, in 1998, regulations prohibiting importation of khat were changed to allow members of east-African communities to import limited quantities. For most of us, it was strange that a piece of qualitative research could actually produce a result in the form of changed drug policy. More importantly, for me, it symbolised a specific role that qualitative drug research has had in Australia: it has provided in-depth understanding of particular social fields — often those regarded as exotic, difficult to access or too hard to understand using quantitative methods.

The focus of Australian qualitative drug research on the social field (rather than the individual) as a unit of analysis is a curious one that perhaps reflects a particular characteristic in the Australian qualitative research tradition. I use the word 'tradition' with caution, because I believe Australia probably has no central qualitative research tradition. It would be more accurate to say that Australian qualitative drug research is a disparate network of disciplinary interests centred in 1960s and 1970s North American structuralist deviance sociology and symbolic interactionism. It is only in recent times that qualitative drug research, based in more contemporary social theory, has emerged (although this is not peculiar to Australia — see Manderson, 1995).

As a consequence of this rather static theoretical orientation, I believe we have inadequate explanations of the relationships between broader drug policy discourse, specific social fields and individual practices. This is not the fault of the researchers, but has come about as a result of the position of qualitative research more generally in Australia. The pragmatism of harm reduction, linked with the individualist orientation of addiction discourse, has limited the sorts of questions that can be explored using qualitative methods. Over the past 10 years, funding bodies have often supported 'patterns-of-drug-use' research in exotic drug-using social worlds, rather than qualitative research that looks explicitly at the relationships between broader drug policies and individual drug-using practices.

Concern has been raised over the poor appreciation of qualitative research by health funding bodies at a national level: the National Health and Medical Research Council (NHMRC) commissioned a study into the attitudes of project grant assessors towards qualitative research, as a result of poor funding support (Chapman et al., forthcoming). The NHMRC (1994) has also produced a special guide for institutional ethics committees because of poor institutional understanding of what qualitative research methods actually are. It is no surprise, therefore, that the research that is supported tends to be based on older, more conservative theoretical frameworks and uses more conservative methods. For example, ethnography — when it is used — is used mostly when other options have been exhausted.

In the early 1990s, when the rest of the world was focusing on individual risk behaviours, Australian qualitative research tended to continue its focus on subcultures and social worlds. Quantitative drug research certainly followed the international tendency to focus on individual risk behaviours (asking how many times injecting equipment was shared and with whom, etc.). However, ironically, missing the focus on individual drug-using behaviours may have been fortuitous, as it allowed a few qualitative researchers to study the more social/structural determinants of health, rather than becoming embedded in the rational choice theories that dominated the public health agenda of the late 1980s and early 1990s.

Understanding risk behaviours

Not all Australian qualitative research looked at subcultural/cultural structures and social fields, however. The focus on injecting risk behaviours during the 1980s and 1990s was most apparent in the work of Wendy Loxley. Loxley has continued to produce qualitative/quantitative work into the late 1990s (Loxley, 1997; Loxley and Davidson, 1998), more recently looking at opioid overdose. This work has been central in continuing to define risk in terms of individual behaviours. Some recent work on overdose has suggested that environmental and cultural factors may be as important in shaping heroin overdose as user behaviour (Fitzgerald et al., 1999a). This range of approaches can only enhance our understanding of the complexities around overdose in public settings.

Refining interventions

Some qualitative work has been important in the refinement of interventions in specific social contexts. The National Centre in HIV Social Research has been influential in bringing qualitative research on drug use into sexualised cultural settings. Although much of this research has been quantitative, the work of Erica Southgate (Southgate and Hopwood, 1998) and Kate Ireland (1998) on drug use in gay settings has been an important shift in focus for qualitative drug research. The most notorious piece of work on drug use in explicitly sexualised social contexts was that of Kim Benton (1994) — the Piss, Powders and Pleasure project. This project, explicitly targeted at the gay male dance culture, was maligned in national parliament and removed from circulation because of its explicit safe drug use message. Most agreed that this was a fabulous outcome for the project, prompting widespread debate about safe-using initiatives (that were not just about injecting) not only among the gay male dance culture, but also among the wider community.

Research as policy process

Looking at the small proportion of grants going to qualitative drug research, it could appear that traditional academic qualitative research in Australia occupies a small role in the drug research and policy agenda. However, if a wider codification of what constitutes 'qualitative' research is used, there has been a significant role for qualitative work in shaping that agenda. This distinction between qualitative research and qualitative work is made because I believe some of the most significant Australian drug research is packaged for public consumption using qualitative tools through the creation of research stories. It is these research stories that are sold to the broader public, to the political process and to the drug research and policy community.

It is this shift to a greater appreciation of the research story that has been responsible for a heightened sensitivity to the necessity of drug research being more tightly linked to the political process. More specifically, there appears to be a greater appreciation by researchers that it does not matter how good the research is; if the story from the research cannot be sold to 'the masses', it will not be sold to the politicians, and if it cannot be sold to the politicians, then it will have little direct effect. The lesson here comes from the recent failure of a feasibility study into heroin prescribing to convince federal politicians to support a trial of prescribed heroin (Bammer, 1995). Whilst the feasibility study has had an enormous impact in terms of shifting the policy agenda, the rational argument for clinical trials of prescribed heroin did not succeed.

Australian drug research is just emerging from an intense drug debate following this exhaustive five-year study into the feasibility of a prescribed heroin trial in the Australian Capital Territory (ACT). In 1998, Australia's Prime Minister, John Howard, vetoed the trial in the face of a convincing rational argument. The research (a mix of qualitative and quantitative) put out a research story that a clinical trial of prescribed heroin would reduce crime and alleviate harm to the community, producing a rational argument for the medical control of a health problem. Unfortunately, although receiving significant public support, this rational argument did not receive support from our conservative federal government.

The apparent failure of research to produce a workable outcome in this case based on rational argument sent a clear message to Australian drug researchers more generally: drug research has to have a strong political story for it to achieve outcomes, and such stories cannot simply be scientistic rational stories; they must be connected to a political process. In the case of the heroin trial, strategies such as organising self-help groups of parents of drug users to advocate on behalf of the research, television forums and public debates were all part of the research process. Creating a story for research is a qualitative technique, although it was never named as such, and other researchers watched closely as it became a significant part of the policy process. The degree of policy thinking in Gabriel Bammer's research work has thus set a new standard for drug research in Australia. The research was significant in rewriting the country's research and policy agenda. It seems that, more than ever, drug research now watches the political climate as much as the academic journals when it comes to considering the next grant application.

An example of a piece of qualitative work that produced a range of outcomes with a strong political focus was the recent work of Lisa Maher (Maher et al., 1997; 1998). Her fieldwork and interview-based research with south-east Asian heroin users in south-west Sydney spawned several repackaged research stories. There was a national radio documentary, television news coverage, an in-depth investigative television documentary and a photographic exhibition. All of these produced very personal accounts of the role and effects of heroin in the lives of drug users and were perfect for mass consumption. They had all the qualities of a human interest story: misadventure, suffering, evil, struggle against the odds and, sometimes, redemption. The qualitative work that went on as part of the research process made the research accessible and was essential to its success in influencing drug policy.

Conclusions

As a result of the recent overt politicisation of Australian drug research, there appears to be an opportunity for several new strands of qualitative drug research to emerge. The first strand would focus on the 'how?' questions: how qualitative drug research shapes the drug policy process and vice versa. Certainly, the work of Virginia Berridge has been insightful in the development of drug policy in the United Kingdom (Berridge, 1994; see also Chapter 2 in this monograph). A crucial question for Australia may well be 'how did the feasibility study into prescribed heroin fail to bring about change?'. This may seem to be an academic question, but it needs to be answered for some very practical reasons. Rational argument has failed to produce changes in drug policy. Other ways to argue, sway opinion and create research stories that have policy effects need investigation.

A second strand of qualitative drug research may be work that is focused more on the creation of strategic research stories. In Australia, there have been a number of epiphanic moments (or moments of transformation) for some very public figures when thinking through drug policy. Professor David Pennington, when reporting on the findings of his inquiry into drugs in the Australian community in 1996, often said that he had been profoundly affected by the stories that he had heard. The history of heroin use in former Prime Minister Bob Hawke's own family was apparently instrumental in gaining his support for the National Campaign Against Drug Abuse in 1986. Police commissioner Neil Comrie's recent disclosure of a friend's son's death from heroin overdose was influential in his supporting progressive policing policies in Victoria. State premier of New South Wales Bob Carr's resistance to harm reduction is apparently linked to his brother's death from drug overdose some time ago. Qualitative work might focus on which kinds of stories will be influential in this kind of political field. The personal transformation story seems to be a powerful story for political purposes, and we need to ask what the limits of this kind of account are, and what kind of link this can have to qualitative research.

As an illustration, I will conclude this chapter with a short story about efforts in Australia to link qualitative research to the federal policy process. The context for this story is that, immediately following the Prime Minister's veto of the heroin trial in 1998, it appeared from several sources that he was heavily influenced by opinions on tabloid talk-back radio. It was an election year: the over-50s demographic that listens to talk-back radio was not supportive of a heroin trial, and the Prime Minister was explicitly targeting his policies to appease this electoral sector. Utterly dissatisfied with the conservative side of the government's drug policies, an academic colleague and myself approached one of the more progressive federal opposition Labour politicians, offering assistance in establishing some drug policy positions. Before we could outline any particular policy position or research story, the federal politician advised us that he would only support a drug policy that could be 'sold' by the talk-back radio hosts to their over-50s listeners. In other words, any new drug policy story would need to be targeted at this audience for it to receive support from the federal opposition. This has had a profound effect on my thinking about the links between qualitative research and drug policy. It is a saleable story that matters, not rational argument.

We know that the stories that have been most successful in changing practices on the ground have been personal transformation stories — those of senior police and politicians. Surely this has to say something to qualitative drug researchers about the power of story to effect change and the need to produce research stories that can have some impact? Maybe, in the future, qualitative researchers will look more closely at the political field, and at linking their research stories with the policy agendas of the times. Then, when politicians look for advice on how to sell research stories to the masses, they may look to qualitative research for the answers.

The qualitative drug research field in Australia faces some significant challenges. With a conservative government in place, and abstinence-oriented politicians continuing to favour law-and-order drug strategies, there is plenty of work ahead to produce research stories that can have some impact on drug policy.

The author is Senior Research Fellow, Department of Criminology, University of Melbourne, Australia.

References

Bammer, G. (1995) *Report and Recommendations of Stage 2: Feasibility Research into the Controlled Availability of Opioids,* National Centre for Epidemiology and Population Research.

Benton, K. W. (1994) *Piss, Powders and Pleasure: an Education Resource Addressing the Interaction of Alcohol, Drugs and Sex,* Canberra: Commonwealth Department of Health, Housing, Local Government and Community Services.

Berridge, V. (1994) 'The relationship between research and policy: case studies from the post-war history of drugs and alcohol', *Contemporary Drug Problems,* 21(4), 599–629.

Chapman, S., Gifford, S., Dugdale, P. and O'Brien, M. (forthcoming) *Final Report of a Review of the Reception of Qualitative Research Proposals by the Public Health Research and Development Committee,* Australia.

Dance, P. (1990) 'Befriending friends: methodological and ethnographic aspects of a study of a Canberra group of illicit drug users', *The International Journal on Drug Policy,* 2, 34–36.

Dance, P. (1991) 'A study of twenty recreational intravenous drug users in Canberra', in G. Wardlaw (Ed.) *Epidemiology of Illegal Drug Use in Australia 1990,* Canberra: National Campaign Against Drug Abuse.

Dance, P. (1999) *Scene Changes, Experienced Changes: a Longitudinal and Comparative Study of Canberrans who Use Illegal Drugs,* doctoral thesis, Australian National University.

Dance, P. and Mugford, S. (1992) 'The St. Oswald's day celebrations: "carnival" versus "sobriety" in an Australian drug enthusiast group', *Journal of Drug Issues,* 22(3), 591–606.

Denton, B. (1998) *Women's Business: Working in the Drug Economy,* doctoral thesis, Latrobe University, Melbourne.

Fitzgerald, J. L. and Hamilton, M. (1994) *An Exploratory Study of Hallucinogen Use in Melbourne,* Melbourne: Department of Public Health and Community Medicine, University of Melbourne.

Fitzgerald, J. L., Broad, S. and Dare, A. (1999a) *Regulating the Street Heroin Market in Fitzroy/Collingwood,* Melbourne: Victorian Health Promotion Foundation.

Fitzgerald, J. L., Hope, A. and O'Brien, M. (1999b) *A Day in the Life: Health and Support Requirements of the Young Injecting Drug User Population in Melbourne's CBD,* Melbourne: University of Melbourne.

Ireland, K. (1998) '"Pretty boys", "queer boys" and "fag hags": mapping queer youth drugs fields', paper presented to the Fifth HIV/AIDS and Society Conference, National Centre in HIV Social Research, Macquarie University.

Loxley, W. (1997) *At Risk and Unprotected: Findings from the Youth, AIDS and Drugs (YAD) Study,* National Centre for Research into the Prevention of Drug Abuse, Curtin University of Technology.

Loxley, W. and Davidson, P. (1998) *Forgetting to Breathe: Opioid Overdose and Young Injecting Drug Users in Perth,* National Centre for Research into the Prevention of Drug Abuse, Curtin University of Technology.

Maher, L., Dixon, D., Lynskey, M. and Hall, W. (1998) *Running the Risks: Heroin, Health and Harm in South West Sydney,* National Drug and Alcohol Research Centre, Monograph No 38, Sydney: National Drug and Alcohol Research Centre.

Maher, L., Dixon, D., Swift, W. and Nguyen, T. (1997) *Anh hai: Young Asian Background People's Perception and Experiences of Policing,* research monograph series, Sydney: University of New South Wales.

Manderson, D. (1995) 'Metamorphoses: clashing symbols in the social construction of drugs', *Journal of Drug Issues,* 25, 799–816.

Moore, D. (1990) 'Drinking: the construction of ethnic identity and social process in a western Australian youth subculture', *British Journal Addictions,* 85(10), 1265–1278.

Moore, D. (1992a) *Recreational Drug Use, with Particular Reference to Amphetamines, Ecstasy and LSD, Amongst a Social Network of Young People in Perth, Western Australia,* National Centre for Research into the Prevention of Drug Abuse, Curtin University of Technology.

Moore, D. (1992b) 'Deconstructing "dependence": an ethnographic critique of an influential concept', *Contemporary Drug Problems,* 19(3), 459–490.

Moore, D. (1993a) 'Ethnography and illicit drug use: dispatches from an anthropologist in the "field"', *Addiction Research,* 1, 11–25.

Moore, D. (1993b) 'Beyond Zinberg's "social setting": a processual view of illicit drug use', *Drug and Alcohol Review,* 12, 413–422.

National Health and Medical Research Council (1994) *Ethical Aspects of Qualitative Methods in Health Research: an Information Paper for Institutional Ethics Committees,* Canberra: National Health and Medical Research Council.

Southgate, E. and Hopwood, M. (1998) 'The social construction of risk and control among Sydney gay men who inject drugs', paper presented to the Fifth HIV/AIDS and Society Conference, National Centre in HIV Social Research, Macquarie University.

Stevenson, M., Fitzgerald, J. L. and Banwell, C. (1996) 'Chewing as a social act: cultural displacement and khat consumption in the east African communities of Melbourne', *Drug and Alcohol Review,* 15(1), 73–82.

CHAPTER 39

QUALITATIVE RESEARCH ON DRUG ABUSE IN THE USA

Zili Sloboda

Traditionally, US researchers have used a variety of approaches to investigate relevant questions about drug abuse, such as who is most affected by it, and how best to intervene. The challenge to these researchers has been the stigma associated with the use of substances that are deemed illegal, and the attendant range of negative legal and social sanctions.

This situation has forced drug users to lie about their consumption and, in many instances, to seek anonymity. Furthermore, drug abuse leads users into a life of poverty and ill-health, making them marginal to the wider society and difficult for researchers to access. For these reasons, studies of drug users have included qualitative as well as quantitative methods.

The term 'qualitative', as used here, is broad, and suggests less control over who is being studied, more openness as to what is being studied and/or closer involvement of researchers with their study subjects. Qualitative research, then, includes the use of secondary data sets, focus group approaches, and the use of 'convenience samples', as well as participant observation.

Evolution of theories of addiction

Qualitative research is recognised as having contributed greatly to our understanding of the phenomenon of drug abuse in the United States. Feldman and Aldrich (1990) have summarised these contributions up to the 1990s, beginning with the work *Opium Addiction in Chicago* by Bingham Dai (1937). Dai describes opiate users in Chicago prior to the enactment of the Harrison Act of 1914, which was designed to control the sale and prescription of narcotics.

Ten years later, *The Nature of Opiate Addiction* (1947), by Alfred Lindesmith, was published. This book was influential in changing contemporary views about addiction. Based on his interviews with street opiate addicts, Lindesmith developed his theory of addiction, in which he states that addiction occurs because the drug user connects the diminution of withdrawal symptoms with the resumption of drug use. It is this cycle of use, withdrawal and use again that Lindesmith believes underlies addiction and not the psychoactive 'high' associated with the drug (Lindesmith, 1980). His work at the time ran counter to existing policy, which treated addiction as a crime and addicts as criminals. Lindesmith's position was that drug abuse was a disease and should be treated as such. Although this debate did not begin with Lindesmith, his research supported it and was important, as it supplemented the biological research that was being conducted at the Public Health Service Hospital located in Lexington, Kentucky, where narcotic addicts were being treated and studied.

Lifestyle and career frameworks

Interest in the next two decades moved from asking the 'why?' of addiction to the 'how?' Becker (1963) and Finestone (1957) described the lifestyle and careers of drug users. These frameworks of lifestyle and career continued to be used throughout the 1960s and into the 1990s. Various ethnographers, including Waldorf (1973), along with more quantitative researchers such as Nurco et al. (1981), tried to identify the diversity of careers and lifestyles to develop taxonomies — or groupings — of drug users. Although there continues to be interest in lifestyle, the generalisability and practicalities of these taxonomies have yet to be demonstrated.

Greater funding for research as illicit drug use increased

The growing tolerance of the public towards drug use, and the increased availability of drugs other than heroin during the 1960s, introduced new populations to drug abuse, which included youth from middle- and upper-income families. Drugs touched many households. The Monitoring the Future survey was initiated in 1975, surveying 9 400 high-school seniors in a sample of public and private schools. The data showed that over 55 % reported having tried at least one illicit drug at least once in their lives. This percentage increased to 65.6 % in 1981 and then gradually declined to a low of 40.7 % in 1992 (National Institute on Drug Abuse, 1999). Since then, the percentage has begun to rise again but has not yet surpassed the 1975–81 figures. In the late 1970s, concern about the introduction of so many young people to drugs caused politicians to increase funding for drug abuse programmes and for research.

Significant qualitative research during the 1960s and 1970s included studies of specific populations such as low-income urban heroin users (Preble and Casey, 1969), poolroom hustlers (Polsky, 1967), amphetamine users (Cary and Mandel, 1968), hippies (Cavan, 1972), methadone patients (Soloway, 1974), cocaine users in Miami (Cleckner, 1977), prostitutes (James, 1976), phencyclidine (PCP) users (Feldman et al., 1979), and women heroin injectors (Rosenbaum, 1981). In addition, studies of the everyday life of drug users and their coping and 'copping' provided insights into the drug user as a human being (Hughes et al., 1971; Agar, 1973; Stephens and McBride, 1976). Many of these researchers combined quantitative with qualitative techniques, in most cases using structured interviews along with more open-ended sampling and data-collection procedures. An interest in the economy of drug abuse, trafficking and associated violence also emerged around this time.

Works by Johnson et al. (1985), Fields (1984) and Goldstein (1985) have not only studied the dynamics of the drug user's life on the street, but have also shown that many users have never been in treatment. These observations, in addition to the evolution of urban field stations, led to more in-depth community studies of drug users, such as the work by Hanson et al. (1985), Biernacki (1986) and Bourgois (1995). This foundation of knowledge and methods proved to have even greater significance with the advent of HIV and AIDS within the drug-user communities. Of particular importance was emphasising the social context of drug-using risk behaviours.

New qualitative research techniques

During the 1970s and 1980s, a number of new qualitative research techniques were developed to estimate prevalence in order to study specific drug-abusing populations. These techniques had important implications for the future and include: snowball and other nomination sampling methods (Biernacki and Waldorf, 1981; Watters and Biernacki, 1989); use of official data (Pearson et al., 1976; Sloboda and Kozel, 1999); capture–recapture methods for estimating prevalence (Greenwood, 1971); and network analyses (Trotter et al., 1995). The National Institute on Drug Abuse underscored the importance of these approaches in its publication of a number of monographs on qualitative techniques and findings from supported qualitative studies (Battjes and Pickens, 1988; Lambert, 1990; Battjes et al., 1994; Lambert et al., 1995; Needle et al., 1995).

Studies arising from concern about AIDS

By the mid-1980s, there was sufficient concern about AIDS among drug users, particularly those who were not in treatment, to prompt the spending of tens of millions of dollars to study both the epidemiology of this new disease and interventions for prevention of the spread of the virus. Prior research provided the means to recruit drug users into educational and counselling interventions and to describe the types of behaviours that facilitated the transmission of the virus to other drug users — through sharing of needles and other drug paraphernalia — and to sexual partners. Research aimed at developing effective interventions targeting injecting drug users both in and out of treatment and included both epidemiology and prevention intervention components.

There were two research programmes directed at out-of-treatment drug users. The first, initiated in 1987 and lasting five years, was the National AIDS Demonstration Research programme (NADR). Composed of 41 projects within 61 sites and reaching over 150 000 people, NADR had as its primary objective the evaluation of the efficacy of research-based interventions (Wechsberg et al., 1998). The first published analysis of the findings of this project (Stephens et al., 1993) indicated that, although the programme of interventions was effective in reducing risk associated with drug use, it did not show any impact on sexual risk behaviours. On the basis of this first programme of research, a standard intervention model was developed to be tested against intervention enhancements in the second research programme, Cooperative Agreement for AIDS (CA), implemented in 1990 in 23 sites. In addition to the standard intervention, this second group of projects used targeted sampling strategies, improved instrumentation, standardised research design, improved follow-up strategies and standardised data analysis (Wechsberg et al., 1998).

Observation studies on drug use practices

A tremendous expansion of our knowledge about drug use practices and patterns came about as a result of these two community-based research programmes. Qualitative methods used by NADR proved to be extremely important in documenting that, rather than one transmission vector related to sharing injecting equipment, there were several. Observational studies that took place within the various settings in which drug users shared their needles and drugs led to better descriptions of the many steps involved in the preparation of both drugs and injecting equipment, each creating its own opportunity for transmission: 'indirect sharing' is a term that evolved out of this research (Jose et al., 1993; Koester and Hoffer, 1994). Indirect sharing, in contrast to direct sharing, includes a number of behaviours related to the preparation and use of drugs:

- common use of water, cookers and cottons;
- frontloading (the transfer of drugs from one syringe to another after removing the needle from one syringe and squirting the drug solution from the other into the hub);
- backloading (the transfer of drugs by removing the plunger from the receiving syringe and squirting the drug solution from the other syringe into it); and
- transferring the drug solution from one syringe into a cooker or drug-mixing container and then redrawing it into other syringes.

These observations were explored in a focused initiative supported by the National Institute on Drug Abuse (NIDA), called the Needle Hygiene Study, that covered several geographic sites. Modelled on a PCP study carried out by NIDA in 1979 (Feldman et al., 1979), ethnographic studies were coordinated across the sites using a common protocol developed by a subgroup of the participating ethnographers. The consistency of the findings in a variety of settings provided support for initial observations on what were thought to be unique groups. This new data about other ways of sharing — not only the drug but also the virus — were used to inform existing interventions.

Spread of crack cocaine

In addition, the NADR project found that injecting drugs was not the only drug-related risk for the transmission of HIV. The threat of HIV and AIDS arose head to head with another serious problem that was spreading across the United States: crack cocaine. The HIV prevention studies found that drug users were mixing cocaine with heroin and injecting this drug combination as 'speedball', and that the inclusion of cocaine in the mixture increased the frequency of injection. Furthermore, the use of crack cocaine itself was associated with infection. Exploration of this observation was pursued by another multi-site ethnographic study. The results of this showed consistently that the use of crack cocaine, particularly for women, was associated with increased risky sexual behaviours, including increased number of partners and unprotected sex, as well as with other sexually transmitted diseases (Ratner, 1993).

Another valuable contribution of these projects has been the introduction of social network analysis. The very nature of the transmission of infection from one person to another suggests that studies of dyads and groups focused on risk behaviours were essential to understanding transmission processes. The social-cultural-cognitive contexts of these behaviours needed to be specified, understood and addressed within the prevention intervention, to assure stability of behaviour change (Koester, 1994).

Conclusions

It is clear, then, that qualitative research methods are well-established among United States drug abuse researchers. A combination of qualitative and quantitative approaches enriches the research findings not only from epidemiological studies, but also from intervention studies. This has been exemplified in the discussion of the NADR and CA projects, but also can be seen in other studies conducted by researchers such as Biernacki (1986), Rosenbaum and Murphy (1981; 1990) and Rotheram-Borus et al. (1994).

Although great strides have been made in the area of qualitative research, there is an important continuing debate as to what constitutes 'ethnography' and 'qualitative methods'. There has been a struggle between those forces who wish to make qualitative approaches more 'scientific' and those who want to preserve the 'purity' of the ethnographic approach. Like all other fields that examine human behaviours, ethnographic and other qualitative approaches will, and should, evolve over time, reflecting the experience and knowledge that accumulates over time and embracing new observational and reporting techniques and technologies. An understanding of human behaviour in ever-changing contexts will only be achieved when those who observe it continue to debate the issues and to develop and explore new hypotheses and theories. The debate, however, should not paralyse the field, nor should it create an impression of dissension. Clearly, the field needs to monitor itself, as there is a range of research that is categorised as qualitative that does not comply with existing definitions. This balancing act of debate within the field and the creation of a united force for improved methods is becoming an international effort.

Drug abuse can become the focus for a number of activities in this area that could include annual meetings and cross-national studies. The EMCDDA has taken the lead with its two projects on qualitative research (Fountain and Griffiths, 1997; 1998; see also Chapter 37 in this monograph), two seminars held in July 1997 and October 1998, and the publication of this monograph. It is important that the momentum be maintained.

The author is Adjunct Professor, Department of Sociology, and Senior Research Associate, Center for Health and Social Policy, University of Akron, and former Director, Division of Epidemiology and Prevention Research, National Institute on Drug Abuse (NIDA), USA.

References

Agar, M. H. (1973) *Ripping and Running: a Formal Ethnography of Heroin Addicts,* New York: Seminar Press.

Battjes, R. J. and Pickens, R. W. (Eds.) (1988) *Needle Sharing Among Intravenous Drug Abusers: National and International Perspectives,* Monograph 80, Rockville, MD: NIDA.

Battjes, R. J., Sloboda, Z. and Grace, W. C. (Eds.) (1994) *The Context of HIV Risk Among Drug Users and their Sexual Partners,* Monograph 143, Rockville, MD: NIDA.

Becker, H. S. (1963) *Outsiders: Studies in the Sociology of Deviance,* Glencoe, IL: Free Press.

Biernacki, P. (1986) *Pathways from Heroin Addiction,* Philadelphia, PA: Temple University.

Biernacki, P. and Waldorf, D. (1981) 'Snowball sampling: problems and techniques of chain referral sampling', *Social Methods Research,* 2, 141–163.

Bourgois, P. (1995) 'The political economy of resistance and self-destruction in the crack economy: an ethnographic perspective', *Annals of the NY Academy of Science,* 749, 97–118.

Cary, J. T. and Mandel, J. (1968) 'A San Francisco area speed scene', *Journal of Health and Social Behavior,* 9, 164–174.

Cavan, S. (1972) *Hippies of the Haight,* St. Louis, MO: New Critics Press.

Cleckner, P. J. (1977) 'Cognitive and ritual aspects of drug use among young black urban males', in B. M. DuToit (Ed.) *Drugs, Rituals, and Altered States of Consciousness,* Rotterdam: AA Balkema, pp. 149–168.

Dai, B. (1937) *Opium Addiction in Chicago,* Shanghai: Commercial Press (reprinted, 1970, Montclair, NJ: Patterson Smith).

Feldman, H. W. and Aldrich, M. R. (1990) 'The role of ethnography in substance abuse research and public policy: historical precedent and future prospects', in E. Y. Lambert (Ed.) *The Collection and Interpretation of Data from Hidden Populations,* Monograph 98, Rockville, MD: NIDA.

Feldman, H. W., Agar, M. and Beschner, G. (1979) *Angel Dust: an Ethnographic Study of PCP Users,* Lexington, MA: Lexington Press.

Fields, A. B. (1984) '"Singing weed": the social organization of street-corner marijuana sales', *Urban Life,* 13(2–3), 274–280.

Finestone, H. (1957) 'Cats, kicks, and color', *Social Problems,* 5(1), 39–45.

Fountain, J. and Griffiths, P. (Eds.) (1997) *Inventory, Bibliography, and Synthesis of Qualitative Research in the European Union,* Lisbon/London: EMCDDA/NAC (updated version available on http://www.qed.org.uk).

Fountain, J. and Griffiths, P. (Eds.) (1998) *Coordination of Working Groups of Qualitative Researchers to Analyse Different Drug Use Patterns and the Implication for Public Health Strategies and Prevention,* project report, Lisbon/London: EMCDDA/NAC.

Goldstein, P. J. (1985) 'The drugs–violence nexus: a tri-partite conceptual framework', *Journal of Drug Issues,* 15, 493–506.

Greenwood, J. A. (1971) *Estimating the Number of Narcotic Addicts,* Document SCID-TR-3, Washington DC: Department of Justice.

Hanson, B., Beschner, G., Walters, J. M. and Bovelle, E. (1985) *Life with Heroin: Voices from the Inner City,* Lexington, MA: Lexington Books.

Hughes, P. H., Crawford, G. A., Barker, N. W., Schumann, S. and Jaffe, J. H. (1971) 'The social structure of a heroin copping community', *American Journal of Psychiatry,* 125(5), 551–558.

James, J. (1976) 'Prostitution and addiction: an interdisciplinary approach', *Addictive Diseases,* 2, 601–618.

Johnson, B. D., Goldstein, P. J., Preble, E., Schmeidler, J., Lipton, D. S., Spunt, B. and Miller, T. (1985) *Taking Care of Business: the Economics of Crime by Heroin Abusers,* Lexington, MA: Lexington Books.

Jose, B., Friedman, S. and Neigus, A. (1993) 'Syringe-mediated drug-sharing (backloading): a new risk factor among injecting drug users', *AIDS,* 7, 1653–1660.

Koester, S. K. (1994) 'The context of risk: ethnographic contributions to the study of drug use and HIV', in R. J. Battjes, Z. Sloboda and W. C. Grace (Eds.) *The Context of HIV Risk Among Drug Users and their Sexual Partners,* Monograph 143, Rockville, MD: NIDA.

Koester, S. K. and Hoffer, L. (1994) 'Indirect sharing: additional HIV risks associated with drug injection', *AIDS Public Policy Journal,* 9(2), 100–105.

Lambert, E. Y. (Ed.) (1990) *The Collection and Interpretation of Data from Hidden Populations,* Monograph 98, Rockville, MD: NIDA.

Lambert, E. Y., Ashery, R. S. and Needle, R. H. (Eds.) (1995) *Qualitative Methods in Drug Abuse and HIV Research,* Monograph 157, Rockville, MD: NIDA.

Lindesmith, A. R. (1947) *The Nature of Opiate Addiction,* Evanston, IL: Principia Press.

Lindesmith, A. R. (1980) 'A general theory of addiction to opiate-type drugs', in D. J. Lettieri, M. Sayers and H. W. Pearson (Eds.) *Theories on Drug Abuse: Selected Contemporary Perspectives,* Monograph 30, Rockville, MD: NIDA, pp. 34–37.

National Institute on Drug Abuse (1999) home page (available on http://www.nida.hih.gov).

Needle, R. H., Coyle, S. L., Genser, S. G. and Trotter, R. T. (Eds.) (1995) *Social Networks, Drug Abuse, and HIV Transmission,* Monograph 151, Rockville, MD: NIDA.

Nurco, D. N., Cisin, I. H. and Balter, M. B. (1981) 'Addict careers: 1. A new typology', *International Journal of the Addictions,* 16(8), 1305–1325.

Pearson, P. H., Retka, R. L. and Woodward, J. A. (1976) *Toward a Heroin Problem Index: an Analytical Model for Drug Abuse Indicators,* Department of Health, Education and Welfare (DHEW), pp. 76–367.

Polsky, N. (1967) *Hustler, Beats and Others,* Chicago, IL: Aldine.

Preble, E. and Casey, J. (1969) 'Taking care of business: the heroin user's life on the streets', *International Journal of the Addictions,* 4(1), 1–24.

Ratner, M. (Ed.) (1993) *Crack Pipe as Pimp,* New York: Lexington Press.

Rosenbaum, M. (1981) *Women and Heroin,* New Brunswick, NJ: Rutgers University Press.

Rosenbaum, M. and Murphy, S. (1981) 'Getting the treatment: recycling women addicts', *Journal of Psychoactive Drugs,* 13(1), 1–13.

Rosenbaum, M. and Murphy, S. (1990) 'Women and addiction: process, treatment, and outcome', in E. Y. Lambert (Ed.) *The Collection and Interpretation of Data from Hidden Populations,* Monograph 98, Rockville, MD: NIDA.

Rotheram-Borus, M. J., Luna, G. C., Marotta, T. and Kelly, H. (1994) 'Going nowhere fast: metamphetamine use and HIV infection', in R. J. Battjes, Z. Sloboda and W. C. Grace (Eds.) *The Context of HIV Risk Among Drug Users and their Sexual Partners,* Monograph 143, Rockville, MD: NIDA.

Sloboda, Z. and Kozel, N. J. (1999) 'Frontline surveillance: community epidemiology work group for drug abuse', in M. D. Glantz and C. Hartel (Eds.) *Drug Abuse: Origins and Interventions,* Washington, DC: APA Press.

Soloway, L. H. (1974) 'Methadone and the culture of addiction', *Journal of Psychedelic Drugs,* 6, 1–99.

Stephens, R. C. and McBride, D. C. (1976) 'Becoming a street addict', *Human Organization: Journal for the Society of Applied Anthropology,* 35(1), 85–93.

Stephens, R. C., Simpson, D. D., Coyle, S. L., McCoy, C. B. and the National AIDS Research Consortium (1993) 'Comparative effectiveness of NADR interventions', in B. S. Brown and G. M. Beschner (Eds.) *Handbook on the Risk of AIDS: Injecting Drug Users and Sexual Partners,* Westport, CT: Greenwood Press.

Trotter, R. T., Bowen, A. M. and Potter, J. M. (1995) 'Network models for HIV outreach and prevention programs for drug users', in R. H. Needle, S. L. Coyle, S. G. Genser and R. T. Trotter (Eds.) *Social Networks, Drug Abuse, and HIV Transmission,* Monograph 151, Rockville, MD: NIDA.

Waldorf, D. (1973) *Careers in Dope,* Englewood Cliffs, NJ: Prentice-Hall.

Watters, J. K. and Biernacki, P. (1989) 'Targeted sampling: options for the study of hidden populations', *Social Problems,* 36, 416–430.

Wechsberg, W. M., Desmond, D., Inciardi, J. A., Leukefeld, C. G., Cottler, L. B. and Hoffman, J. (1998) 'HIV prevention protocols: adaptation to evolving trends in drug use', *Journal of Psychoactive Drugs,* 30(3), 291–298.

QUALITATIVE DRUG RESEARCH
IN CENTRAL AND EASTERN EUROPE ([1])

Michael Stauffacher, Dagmar Hedrich, Paul Griffiths and Janusz Sierosławski

Drug use is not a new phenomenon in the central and eastern European countries (CEECs): the intravenous use of home-made opiates and amphetamine-type stimulants, the non-medical use of pharmaceuticals, and solvent use were all found to some extent in most countries in the region during the 1970s and 1980s (EMCDDA, 1998).

However, the scale of the problem was not equivalent to that found in some western countries during this period and, in most CEECs, public health responses remained poorly developed. In public health terms, alcohol abuse has always been perceived as the major substance abuse issue for the region (as well as for the western part of Europe). This remains the case today, but there is now an increasing awareness of the importance of also addressing drug-consumption issues.

Since the collapse of the communist system, both drug problems and responses have changed significantly. Today, drug issues are high on the public agenda in most CEECs. At a policy level, a broad and comprehensive response to drug consumption has been, or is being, formulated. Work is being conducted to reduce both drug trafficking and production, and domestic drug demand. There is a growing awareness that such activity needs to be informed by good epidemiological monitoring. However, given the rapidly changing drug situation and the difficulties in funding the health-care infrastructure (Davis, 1998), it is fair to say that, in general, drug-information systems still require considerable development in the region.

The need for qualitative drug research in the CEECs

The development of national drug demand-reduction strategies — in many cases more or less 'from scratch' — has constituted a major challenge for the CEECs. Investment in demand-reduction activities also has to compete for limited funds with other pressing health-care needs (Davis, 1998). As most countries lack local experience in responding to drug problems, initial activities have largely mirrored responses found elsewhere, notably the experiences of the US and western European countries. With the passing of time, it has become increasingly apparent

---

([1]) The views expressed here are the personal views of the authors, and should in no way be taken to reflect the policies and opinions of the organisations mentioned in this chapter.

that it is important to evaluate the suitability of western models of drug control and treatment to the conditions found in the CEECs. Patterns of drug use are shaped and mediated by the conditions in which they occur. In order to assess the suitability of responses, be they treatment, prevention or harm-reduction responses, it is important to understand the context in which the problems occur.

There has been a tendency to assume that patterns of drug use found in the CEECs are identical to those elsewhere. This ignores the fact that patterns of use are likely to be influenced by the prevailing historical, political, social and economic context in which drug use takes place. It cannot be assumed that models of drug use and responses applicable to western European countries can be applied, without modification, to the CEEC experience. Furthermore, drug problems and their respective responses are different among the countries in the region; each has to find the best strategy on the basis of a local problem assessment reflecting the local context. Whilst epidemiological systems have developed, to date they have largely relied on standard quantitative research techniques (CAN and PG, 1997; Stauffacher, 1999). There is a pressing need to develop a more detailed understanding of patterns of drug use, but this understanding is unlikely to come from quantitative methods alone. What is also required is the development of qualitative studies that can 'fill in the details' of the picture of current drug use.

From a public health perspective, there is a need to react rapidly to emerging trends and recent changes, such as changing patterns of use and the risk of large-scale HIV epidemics (UNAIDS and WHO, 1998). Some work has already been done using rapid assessment and response methodologies. However, assessing the scale of health problems in itself is not enough: capacity has to be built within the different countries to allow for regular follow-up and monitoring of the current situation and tracking of future developments. Again, qualitative methods are likely to play a major role.

Qualitative drug research in the CEECs

In this chapter we will review one attempt to stimulate the development of qualitative research in the region. This programme — conducted under the auspices of the Council of Europe's Pompidou Group and co-funded by the United Nations International Drug Control Programme (UNDCP) — has provided support for training both in qualitative and quantitative research methods and for conducting qualitative studies. It should not be forgotten, however, that much has been done by other organisations, including WHO, UNAIDS, Médecins Sans Frontières, Médecins du Monde and the Soros Foundation, directly or indirectly supporting qualitative inquiry in the CEECs. Most activities have focused on informing responses and assisting in the implementation of rapid interventions, particularly those associated with HIV infection. In the work reported here, the emphasis is more on capacity-building, to enable qualitative research to take place in the coming years. It therefore must be seen as part of a long-term strategy for improving epidemiological capacity. Nevertheless, both approaches are important and should ideally be complementary.

The period before 1996

Until the mid-1990s, qualitative drug research in CEE countries was practically absent. Among the few exceptions are the following (²).

- In Hungary, two research teams (headed by Jozsef Racz and Zsuzsa Elekes) carried out ethnographic research (Racz, 1985; 1992; Elekes, 1991), looking at subcultures of drug users.

- In Poland, Moskalewicz and Sierosławski studied lifestyles of drug users and Sierosławski interviewed drug users in two communities in the framework of a local drug-prevention programme using action-research methodology (Moskalewicz and Sierosławski, 1995; Sierosławski, 1996).

- In Bulgaria, Lazarov and colleagues studied drug use among youth in Sofia (Lazarov and Yanakiev, 1994) and Popov et al. (1994) investigated drug dealers in Varna.

- In Slovenia, Nolimal and colleagues used an ethnographic approach, involving self-help groups, to study temporal and social contexts of heroin use (Nolimal et al., 1993).

- In the Czech Republic, a rapid assessment was conducted (Tyrlik et al., 1996), funded by UNDCP. A fact-finding mission, including ethnographic fieldwork, was conducted in the former Yugoslav Republic of Macedonia (Grund and Nolimal, 1995), financed by the Lindesmith Center.

Projects within the joint Pompidou Group/UNDCP programme

Joint Pompidou Group/UNDCP programme

In the course of the first phase of the programme 'Extension of the multi-city network to central and eastern Europe' (1994–97), selected professionals were trained in drug-use epidemiology. Multidisciplinary groups were also set up to collect and interpret data, and comparable reports based on standard guidelines were produced on drug use in nine cities (Pompidou Group, 1997).

The second phase (1998–99) of this work is designed to consolidate the development of monitoring systems and generate qualitative information on patterns of use and new trends in drug use. It will provide detailed information as a basis for planning and evaluating demand-reduction policies in the CEECs. Consequently, a major part of this phase involves training in qualitative research methods and the actual implementation of qualitative research studies.

Individual qualitative research studies

Research questions and the methods applied are summarised briefly below. All these studies were designed as a response to local needs. Further details can be found in

---

(²) This list only contains studies which served as background to the programme presented in this chapter and is not meant to be exhaustive.

the compilation of the original project protocols (Pompidou Group, 1998). All the projects started in mid-1998 and will end in mid-2000. A compilation of the main research results is expected by the end of 2000. The researchers can be contacted through the Secretariat of the Pompidou Group ([3]).

Figure 1: Studies designed in response to local needs

Researcher	Key research topics				Access		Data collection		
	risk groups	hidden populations	change in use patterns	treatment compliance	snowball	privileged access	in-depth interviews	focus groups	participant observation
Veress (Budapest)	X					X	X		
Varvasovszky (Debrecen)	X					X	X	X	X
Sêkiewicz (Gdansk)	X	X	X		X		X		
Nolimal (Ljubljana)	X	X		X	X		X	X	X
Zuda (Prague)			X	X	X	X	X		
Nesheva (Sofia)	X	X				X	X		
Popov (Varna)	X	X		X	X		X		X
Sierosławski (Warsaw)	X	X	X		X		X		

- Katalin Veress (Budapest, Hungary): 'Drug use among juvenile offenders in Hungary'

This project aims to describe patterns of drug use among the population of juvenile homes; to explore and compare specific risk behaviour as well as preventive possibilities; and to assess their sources of information related to drugs (e.g. the role of the mass media).

- Zsuzsa Varvasovszky (Debrecen, Hungary): 'Qualitative survey of drug problems in Debrecen'

In Debrecen, drugs are most commonly available in the public setting of discos. The study aims to examine the nature and extent of the drug problem among young people; their attitudes towards drugs; and the organisations and institutions dealing with drug problems.

([3]) Pompidou Group, Council of Europe, F-67075 Strasbourg Cedex. Tel. (33) 388 41 20 00, fax (33) 388 41 27 85. E-mail: pompidou.group@coe.int.

• Jacek Sêkiewicz (Gdansk, Poland): 'New patterns of drug use — especially am-phetamines — among the population of drug users in Gdansk'

Since 1990, most drug users in treatment in Poland have had problems with opiates. In recent years, the number of persons using cannabis, amphetamines, LSD and MDMA has grown: a new pattern of drug use has emerged. On the basis of this observation, the project aims to answer the following questions: Are there two distinct subcultures of drug users in Gdansk? If so, what is the relationship between them and what characteristics are associated with the change of the drug of choice?

• Dusan Nolimal (Ljubljana, Slovenia): 'Qualitative study of heroin injectors in Ljubljana'

Although the sharing of needles and syringes seems to have decreased in Ljubljana, more than half of the clients in treatment were never tested for HIV infection. The primary objectives of the study are to assess risk behaviours associated with heroin injection (individually and in relation to social contextual factors) and to identify and initiate effective harm-reduction intervention.

• Tomas Zuda (Prague, Czech Republic): 'Drug careers of long-term drug users in Prague: turning points and readiness to receive help' [4]

In the Czech Republic, there is a lack of information on drug-using careers. The major objective is to describe the most important phases of an individual's drug use history and their context and consequences. This knowledge will be the basis for the preparation of a set of guidelines for local drug policy and low-threshold treatment facilities.

• Eleonora Nesheva (Sofia, Bulgaria): 'Qualitative study amongst users in prisons'

The number of drug users in Bulgarian prisons has increased considerably during recent years. The core questions of the study concern a description of drug use behaviour in prisons; relationships between users, users and other prisoners, and users and prison staff; methods of obtaining drugs; and patterns of use. This knowledge should assist in the establishment and development of programmes for drug-related problems in prisons.

• Gueorgui Popov (Varna, Bulgaria): 'Ethnographies of heroin addiction in a Roma community: the Roma in Varna'

This study attempts to research a relatively recent form of drug-using behaviour among minority communities in Bulgaria which began to increase in the spring of 1995. One aspect of heroin addiction in the Varna Roma community is its culture-specific use-pattern: smoking, rather than injecting, heroin. The field-study will address three primary issues: the identities and personal histories of addicts; culture-specific traits of Roma heroin addiction; and background information about the structure, dynamics and the actors in dealing/trafficking.

---

[4] An identical study will be implemented in Bratislava (Slovak Republic) by Monica Ciutti, allowing for comparative analyses.

• Janusz Sierosławski (Warsaw, Poland): 'Dynamic of drug use patterns in Warsaw'

As the treatment demand-reporting system indicates, home-made opiates hold a dominant position in Warsaw, but more and more addicts are using drugs such as amphetamines, cannabis or hallucinogens. It is possible that this has led to two separate networks of drug users, with different languages, values, symbols and lifestyles. Hence, the study will try to answer the following questions: Are there two separate subcultures of drug users in Warsaw? If so, what relation exists between them and what determines the change in the drug of choice?

Conclusions

The studies listed above illustrate the varied range of topics suitable for qualitative inquiry in the region and also demonstrate the interest of local experts in becoming involved in this kind of research. These studies will form part of the growing, increasingly sophisticated, research base that can now be found in the CEECs. The development of this research base has been accompanied by an increasing level of confidence among local research scientists, who are now prepared to question some of the assumptions made by western European and American commentators on their region. Qualitative research is likely to represent an increasingly important resource for allowing a better understanding of the nature of drug use in the CEECs, thereby informing the development of culturally sensitive interventions. The results of these studies will allow for evidence-based strategies in the field of prevention, treatment and social (re-)integration.

There are certainly many further topics where qualitative methods play a major role. From a demand reduction perspective, the following can be identified:

• detailed assessment of socio-cultural aspects that are relevant in primary prevention (involvement of family, peers, community) to allow the planning of new primary prevention programmes and a further refinement of existing ones;
• evaluation of the functioning of recently established services and treatment methods (e.g. out-patient centres, long-term residential services, methadone maintenance programmes, outreach work); and
• evaluation of the effects of drug policy at local and national level (e.g. studying the balance between drug control and demand reduction).

There are still some problems remaining for qualitative research in the CEECs (some of them similar to those in western countries). In order to sustain the process once initiated, at least the following points need to be addressed.

• The focus of many countries in central and eastern Europe is on national scale prevalence data and other quantitative information. It seems that small-scale and local qualitative drug research does not yet have a high priority. The presentation of research results to local and national policy-makers should (hopefully) contribute to a future priority shift.

- The credibility of qualitative research is as important an issue in central and eastern Europe as it is in the west, where it has been successfully advocated by the EMCDDA for the last few years (Fountain and Griffiths, 1999). If the image of these methods can be improved in the west, better arguments will be provided for promoting them in the CEECs.

- The possibilities both for qualitative research methods in general, and for qualitative research on drug issues within the existing structures of research and education in the CEECs, need to be investigated and further improved. In this respect, international networking between researchers in the field is vital.

- Research in general, and qualitative methods in particular, are having major funding problems in the CEECs (Balàzs et al., 1995; Schimank, 1995). Due to the still critical economic situation in most of these countries and a lack of priority in this area, there is an urgent need for continued external funding.

To conclude, it is evident that further encouragement and development of competence in qualitative research in central and eastern Europe is likely to pay dividends. A comprehensive approach should include the training of individual experts and research teams, and exchanges of experience between researchers across and beyond Europe. It is also important to provide research funding and to support and strengthen qualitative methods within research policies in general. The complementary use of quantitative and qualitative methods will be crucial for the development of effective responses to drug use in a region where the potential for severe drug-related health and social problems remains high.

Michael Stauffacher (freelance researcher/consultant, Zurich) is project coordinator for the Pompidou Group. Dagmar Hedrich (consultant, Lisbon) has developed and implemented the joint PG/UNDCP programme working at the Secretariat of the Pompidou Group. Paul Griffiths (formerly senior research officer at the NAC, London) is project consultant for qualitative research to the Pompidou Group. Janusz Sierosławski (senior researcher at the Institute of Psychiatry and Neurology, Warsaw) is local coordinator in Poland for the Pompidou Group.

References

Balàzs, K., Faulkner, W. and Schimank, U. (1995) 'Transformation of the research system of post-communist central and eastern Europe: an introduction', *Social Studies of Science,* 25, 613–632.

CAN and PG (The Swedish Council for Information on Alcohol and other Drugs and the Council of Europe's Pompidou Group) (1997) *The 1995 ESPAD Report: Alcohol and Other Drug Use Among Students in 26 European Countries,* Stockholm.

Davis, C. (1998) 'Morbidité, mortalité et réformes du système de santé dans les états en transition de l'ex-U.R.S.S. et de l'Europe de l'est', *Revue d'études comparatives Est-Ouest,* 29, 133–185.

Elekes, Z. (1991) 'A survey of drug consumers in Hungary', *Alcohol*, 1–2, 1–55.

EMCDDA (1998) *Annual Report on the State of the Drugs Problem in the European Union 1998*, Luxembourg: Office for Official Publications of the European Communities.

Fountain, J. and Griffiths, P. (1999) 'Synthesis of qualitative research on drug use in the European Union: report on an EMCDDA project', *European Addiction Research*, 5, 4–20 (updated version available on http://www.qed.org.uk).

Grund, J.-P. G. and Nolimal, D. (1995) *A Heroin Epidemic in Macedonia: a report to the Open Society Institute New York and the Open Society Institute Macedonia*, Macedonia and New York: Open Society Institute.

Lazarov, P. and Yanakiev, Y. (1994) *Drug Addiction among Young People as a Risk Factor: Sociology in a Society in Transition*, Sofia.

Moskalewicz, J. and Sierosławski, J. (1995) *Lifestyles of Drug Dependent Persons Living in Poland*, Strasbourg: Pompidou Group, Council of Europe.

Nolimal, D., Globocnik, M., Rebec, A., Krek, M. and Flaker, V. (1993) 'Descriptive epidemiology of the group of street injection drug users in the regions of Koper and Ljubljana in the year 1991', *Zdrav Var*, 32, 161–164.

Pompidou Group (1997) *Extension of the Multi-City Network to Central and Eastern Europe: Qualitative Research among Drug Users*, Strasbourg: Council of Europe.

Pompidou Group (1998) *Extension of the Multi-City Network to Central and Eastern Europe, Phase II: Compilation Qualitative Research Proposals*, Strasbourg: Council of Europe.

Popov, G., Veltcheva, D., Vassilev, G. and Stanchev, B. (1997) 'Socio-cultural characteristics and interrelations of men dealing with illicit drug-traffic in Varna', Medical University of Varna (unpublished; for summary see Pompidou Group, 1997, pp. 5–6).

Racz, J. (1985) 'An example of drug use patterns of a particular subcultural milieu: in an underground group', *Alcohol*, 2, 8–20.

Racz, J. (1992) 'Drug use by the members of youth subcultures in Hungary', *International Journal of Addictions*, 27(3), 289–300.

Schimank, U. (1995) 'Transformation of research systems in central and eastern Europe: a coincidence of opportunities and trouble', *Social Studies of Science*, 25, 633–653.

Sierosławski, J. (1996) 'Badania Narkomanów (Studies on drug users)', in J. Moskalewicz (Ed.) *Badania i ewaluacja 2: Pakiet Prewencyjny — Program Zapobiegania Nrkomanii (Research and Evaluation 2: Prevention Packet — Drug Prevention Programme)*, Warsaw: Institute of Psychiatry and Neurology.

Stauffacher, M. (1999) *Treated Drug Users in 23 European Cities: Trends 1992–1997*, Strasbourg: Pompidou Group, Council of Europe.

Tyrlik, M., Zuda, T., Bem, P. and Power, R. (1996) *Rapid Assessment of the Drug Use Situation in the Czech Republic*, Vienna: United Nations Drug Control Programme.

UNAIDS and WHO (1998) *Report on the Global HIV/AIDS Epidemic*, Geneva: UNAIDS/WHO.

GENERAL CONCLUSIONS

GENERAL CONCLUSIONS

Richard Hartnoll

Qualitative research, pursued under various labels such as anthropology, ethnography or sociology, played an important and distinguished role within the social sciences throughout the 20th century. In the drugs field, however, only in a very few countries, in Europe or elsewhere, is there anything resembling a significant tradition of qualitative research or a body of published studies. In many countries, little or almost no research has been carried out from a primarily qualitative perspective, and even where it has — for example, in the United States and the United Kingdom — this takes second place behind statistical, clinical or biomedical research (Fountain and Griffiths, 1999).

Although there have been some modest attempts in Europe — and also in the United States and Australia — to bring together qualitative researchers in the drugs field into more organised groups or networks, a critical mass has yet to be attained that allows this type of approach to achieve an adequate profile and recognition, either amongst the research community as a whole or amongst the users (and funders) of research. This is regrettable since — as I hope the contributions to this monograph attest and as I mentioned in my introduction — qualitative research and analysis can offer rich insights into the meanings, perceptions, processes and contexts of the 'world of drugs' as well as ways of understanding drug use and responses to it that not only complement quantitative and statistical analyses but make a valuable contribution to them in its own right.

However, much remains to be done if this critical mass is to be achieved and if the full potential and value of qualitative approaches for knowledge and understanding of the drug phenomenon and of societies' responses to it are to be realised. It is therefore essential that the achievements to date are consolidated and used as a foundation for further work.

Directions for the future

The directions which the EMCDDA hopes to pursue in the future fall under three broad headings:

- consolidating and strengthening the European infrastructure for the research community (information exchange, networking and development of resources for qualitative researchers);
- developing collaborative, comparative research on key themes (including the aim of linking research to interested practitioners and other key actors in the specific areas concerned); and

- developing the interface between research and policy (strengthening the profile of qualitative research within policy and research agendas).

Consolidating and strengthening the European infrastructure for the research community

Work in this area includes maintaining and updating the EMCDDA's specialised qualitative research website http://www.qed.org.uk and disseminating reports on studies and conferences. It also involves regularly updating databases on current research projects and researchers, an annotated bibliography of publications and reports, and reviews of the state of the art in qualitative research in the different Member States.

The EMCDDA also intends to develop a more interactive dimension here — for example, by creating discussion groups on innovative methods or specific topics — and to launch a website journal. The overall aim is that this area of activity will serve primarily as a resource to qualitative researchers and strengthen the concept of a European network. Periodic scientific seminars, following those held in Bologna (1996) and Lisbon (1998 and 1999), could help to reinforce this dimension.

Developing collaborative, comparative research on key themes

The EMCDDA foresees developing five specific themes, selected largely on the basis of its early work on qualitative research. These themes are reflected in the main sections of this monograph and are:

- changing patterns and emerging trends in drug use;
- drug markets and drug-related crime;
- risk behaviours and health;
- social exclusion; and
- qualitative research on demand-reduction services and activities.

In the first area, the EMCDDA's review of qualitative research on new drug trends (drawn up by its working group on the topic) is being incorporated into a workplan for the Centre to develop a more coherent structure for monitoring, interpreting and even anticipating changing patterns of drug use and emerging problems. A report from a separate EMCDDA project on identifying, tracking and understanding emerging trends in drug use is also being taken into account. The plan includes a practical dimension, in which qualitative and quantitative information on new trends will be collected, analysed and disseminated in a 'new trends' bulletin. It also includes a more theoretical dimension in which models and theories of the diffusion of innovation will be examined and, if possible, tested.

In the second area, the review of qualitative research on drugs and crime (drawn up by the EMCDDA working group on the topic) is being updated and will be published by the Max-Planck Institute for Foreign and International Criminal Law (Department of Criminology) as a monograph, in cooperation with the EMCDDA. The ideas for research aired by the working group have been adapted and, in 1999, the EMCDDA funded a pilot project on local drug markets and responses to them.

In the third area, the review on risk behaviours and health (drawn up by the EMCDDA working group on the topic) will be published in the EMCDDA's 'Insights' series. The development of work on this theme is still being explored but will probably involve linking it to ongoing EMCDDA projects on drug-related infectious diseases and harm-reduction activities.

The fourth theme, social exclusion, is a more recent addition to the EMCDDA's work. Following the second scientific seminar on qualitative research in Lisbon in 1998 and a small expert meeting in November 1998, the EMCDDA launched a project focusing on minorities, migration, social exclusion and drugs. This aims to 'map' the current situation across the EU, as far as existing information on the topic is available. The follow-up will depend on the results of this mapping exercise, but, as the section on social exclusion in this monograph indicates, this is a broad and challenging issue, and one that is by no means restricted to issues of minorities or migration.

The fifth theme, centring on qualitative research on drug demand-reduction services and activities, is also a recent development at the EMCDDA. This too is a broad and open field where the precise lines of work in the future have yet to be defined. An important dimension, however, will include improved understanding of drug users' perspectives on services, which is especially relevant for planning services and outcome evaluations. It is clear that qualitative research is necessary to achieve an understanding of the apparently contradictory needs of many problem drug users.

Developing the interface between research and policy

It is more difficult to translate the goal of developing the interface between research and policy into concrete activities, but nonetheless it is important to try. As the contribution to this monograph by Virginia Berridge (Chapter 2) indicates, the relationship between research and policy is complex. She suggests that the policy-making process itself should be the subject of research, an idea that may well be worth following up.

There is also a clear need to develop ways in which research can be used to construct qualitative models, not only of the policy-making process itself, but also of the way in which developments in drug use are perceived by different actors and sectors within the process, and of how these developments, mediated by perceptions, influence, and are in turn affected by, changes in policy. The interactive dynamic process between drug use, consequences, perceptions, responses and the various impacts of responses at different levels of the system may be too complex to model adequately using quantitative modelling methods. Complexity theory, discussed by Mike Agar (Chapter 5), offers one possible starting point for exploring this issue. There may well be other approaches in which different policy scenarios can be examined using qualitative methods that offer the sort of flexibility needed to analyse complex and often poorly defined processes.

Finally, there is the need to raise the profile of qualitative research, not only in the policy domain but also in the research, and especially the research-funding, domain. The first prerequisite for this is to have a product that is worth selling.

We trust that publications such as this monograph, and other publications from researchers across Europe, will contribute to this goal. However, this in itself appears insufficient. Finding ways to achieve a critical mass of researchers and research, as well as to cross the often invisible threshold of recognition so that qualitative research is included in research and policy agendas, is a major challenge for the future.

References

Fountain, J. and Griffiths, P. (1999) 'Synthesis of qualitative research on drug use in the European Union: report on an EMCDDA project', *European Addiction Research,* 5, 4–20.

CONTRIBUTORS

CONTRIBUTORS

Michael Agar
University of Maryland
Ethknoworks, Inc.
PO Box 5804
Takoma Park
Maryland 20913
USA
Tel./Fax (1-301) 270 14 38
E-mail: magar@anth.umd.edu

Cas Barendregt
Addiction Research Institute Rotterdam
Heemraadssingel 194
3021 DEM Rotterdam
Netherlands
Tel. (31-10) 425 33 66
Fax (31-10) 276 39 88
E-mail: Barendregt@mgz.fgg.eur.nl

Marina Barnard
Centre for Drugs Misuse Research
University of Glasgow
11 The Square
Glasgow G12 8QG
UK
Tel. (44-141) 339 88 55
Fax (44-141) 339 58 81
E-mail: gkua26@udcf.gla.ac.u

Virginia Berridge
London School of Hygiene and Tropical Medicine
Keppel Street
London WC1E 7HT
UK
Tel. (44-20) 79 27 22 69
Fax (44-20) 76 37 32 38
E-mail: v.berridge@lshtm.ac.uk

Peter Blanken
Central Committee Treatment Heroin Addicts
Stratenum 5th floor
Universiteitsweg 100
3584 CG Utrecht
Netherlands
Tel. (31-30) 253 88 02
Fax (31-30) 253 90 20
E-mail: p.blanken@med.uu.nl

Julian Buchanan
Department of Social Work
University of Central Lancashire
Preston PR1 2HE
UK
Tel. (44-1772) 89 34 69
Fax (44-1772) 89 29 74
E-mail: julianbu@globalnet.ac.uk or J.Buchanan@uclan.ac.uk

Amador Calafat
Irefrea
Rambla, 15, 2°, 3a,
E-07003 Palma de Mallorca
Tel. (34) 971 72 74 34
Fax (34) 971 21 33 06
E-mail: irefrea@correo.cop.es or irefrea@flashnet.it or adicciones@mail.eurociber.es

Anne Coppel
Emergence Espace Tolbiac
60, rue de Tolbiac
F-75013 Paris
Tel. (33) 153 82 81 70
Fax (33) 153 82 81 79
E-mail: coppel@club-Internet.fr

Ton Cramer
Ministry of Public Health, Welfare and Sport
Addiction Policy Division
PO Box 20350
2500 EJ Den Haag
Netherlands
Tel. (31-70) 340 69 38
Fax (31-70) 340 52 33
E-mail: a.cramer@minvws.nl

Tom Decorte
Department of Criminology
University of Ghent
Universiteitstraat 4
B-9000 Ghent
Tel. (32-9) 264 68 37
Fax (32-9) 264 69 88
E-mail: tom.decorte@rug.ac.be

Reiner Domes
Dunckerstr. 22
D-10437 Berlin
Tel./Fax (49-30) 444 10 41
Mobile (49-173) 952 81 31
E-mail: domesr@aol.com

Luís Fernandes
Centro de Ciências do Comportamento Desviante
Universidade do Porto
R. do Campo Alegre, 1055
P-4150 Porto
Tel. (351) 226 07 97 00
Fax (351) 226 07 97 25
E-mail: jllf@psi.up.pt

John Fitzgerald
Department of Criminology
University of Melbourne
Australia
Tel. (61-9344) 94 65
Fax (61-9349) 42 59
Mobile (61-417) 39 19 82
E-mail: johnfitz@ariel.ucs.unimelb.edu.au

Jane Fountain
National Addiction Centre
4 Windsor Walk
London SE5 8AF
UK
Tel. (44-20) 78 48 06 56
Fax (44-20) 77 01 84 54
E-mail: spjejaf@iop.kcl.ac.uk

Mark Gilman
Drugs Prevention Advisory Service (DPAS)
Room 2105
Sunley Tower
Piccadilly Plaza
Manchester M1 4BE
UK
Tel. (44-161) 237 96 34
Fax (44-161) 237 96 57
E-mail: mark.gilman@homeoffice.gsi.gov.uk

Paul Griffiths
UNDCP
Vienna International Centre
PO Box 500
A-1400 Vienna
Tel. (43-1) 260 60 44 34
Fax (43-1) 260 60 58 66
E-mail: paul.griffiths@undcp.org

Fabienne Hariga
Modus Vivendi, asbl
Rue de Haerne 51
B-1040 Brussels
Tel./Fax (32-2) 647 22 12
E-mail: fabienne.hariga@ping.be or modus.vivendi@skynet.be

Richard Hartnoll
EMCDDA
Rua da Cruz de Santa Apolónia, 23/25
P-1149-045 Lisbon
Tel. (351) 218 11 30 00
Fax (351) 218 13 79 43
E-mail: richard.hartnoll@emcdda.org

Dagmar Hedrich
Rua dos Ferreiros à Estrela, 73, 3E
P-1200 Lisbon
Tel. (351) 213 97 04 89
Fax (351) 213 97 04 92
E-mail: dagmar.hedrich@mail.telepac.pt

Mats Hilte
Department of Sociology
University of Lund
Box 23
S-221 00 Lund
Tel. (46-46) 222 94 24
Fax (46-46) 222 94 12
E-mail: mats.hilte@soch.lu.se

Michael Hough
South Bank University
103 Borough Road
London SE1 0AA
UK
Tel. (44-20) 78 15 58 18
Fax (44-20) 78 15 58 22
E-mail: houghjm@unix.sbu.ac.uk

Rhidian Hughes
Department of Social Policy and Social Work
University of York
Heslington
York YO1 5DD
UK
E-mail: rhidian.hughes@ukonline.co.uk

Neil Hunt
Kent Institute of Medicine and Health Sciences
Research and Development Centre
University of Kent at Canterbury
Canterbury
Kent CT2 7PD
UK
Tel. (44-1227) 82 40 90
Fax (44-1227) 82 40 57
E-mail: N.Hunt@ukc.ac.uk

Uwe Kemmesies
Institut für Sozialpaedagogik und Erwachsenenbildung
Universität Frankfurt
Robert Mayer Str. 1
D-60325 Frankfurt am Main
and Adolfsallee 28
D-65185 Wiesbaden
Tel. (49-69) 79 82 28 37
Fax (49-69) 79 82 34 12
E-mail: EwU3Kem@aol.com

Justin Kenrick
Department of Social Anthropology
University of Edinburgh
Adam Ferguson Building
George Square
Edinburgh EH8 9LL
UK
Tel. (44-131) 651 15 30
E-mail: jkenrick@ed.ac.uk

Hilary Klee
Social Research Centre on Health
Manchester Metropolitan University
Elizabeth Gaskell Campus
Hathersage Road
Manchester M13 OJA
UK
Tel. (44-161) 247 25 85
Fax (44-161) 247 68 84
E-mail: h.klee@mmu.ac.uk

Dirk J. Korf
Faculty of Law
University of Amsterdam
'Bonger' Institute of Criminology
PO Box 1030
1000 BA Amsterdam
Netherlands
Tel. (31-20) 525 39 30
Fax (31-20) 525 34 95
E-mail: korf@jur.uva.nl

Ludwig Kraus
IFT Institut für Therapieforschung
Parzivalstr. 25
D-80804 München
Tel. (49-89) 36 08 04 33
Fax (49-89) 36 08 04 69
E-mail: kraus@IFT.Isar.de

Odd Lindberg
Department of Social Science/Social Work
University of Orebro
S-701 92 Orebro
Tel. (46-19) 30 30 94
Fax (46-19) 30 34 84
E-mail: odd.lindberg@hoe.se

Susanne McGregor
Social Policy Research Centre
School of Social Science
University of Middlesex
Queensway
Enfield EN3 4SF
UK
Tel. (44-20) 83 62 61 73
Fax (44-20) 83 62 54 40
E-mail: smacg1@mdx.ac.uk or s.macgregor@mdx.ac.uk

Paula Mayock
The Children's Centre
Áras an Phiarsaigh
Trinity College
Dublin 2
Ireland
Tel. (353-1) 608 26 23
Fax (353-1) 608 23 47
E-mail: pmayock@tcd.ie

Ton Nabben
University of Amsterdam
Faculty of Law
'Bouger' Institute of Criminology
PO Box 1030
1000 Amsterdam
Netherlands
Tel. (31-20) 525 39 46
Fax (31-20) 525 34 95
E-mail: nabben@jur.uva.nl

Aileen O'Gorman
Social Research Consultant
57 Strand Road
Sandymount
Dublin 4,
Ireland
Tel./Fax (353-1) 269 59 40
E-mail: aogorman@connect.ie

Letizia Paoli
Max-Planck-Institut für Auslaendisches und Internationales Strafrecht
Günterstalstr. 73
D-79100 Freiburg im Breisgau
Tel. (49-761) 708 13 11
Fax (49-761) 708 12 94
E-mail: l.paoli@iuscrim.mpg.de

Howard Parker
SPARC
Social Policy and Social Work
Williamson Building
Manchester University
Manchester M13 9PL
UK
Tel. (44-161) 275 47 83
Fax (44-161) 275 49 22
E-mail: howard.parker@man.ac.uk or e-sparc@man.ac.uk

Kamlesh Patel
Faculty of Health
University of Central Lancashire
Preston PR1 2HE
UK
Tel. (44-1274) 72 82 41 or (44-1274) 73 91 81
Fax (44-1274) 72 82 41
Mobile (44-802) 56 31 36
E-mail: zr83@dial.pipex.com

Catherine Pérez
Centre for Epidemiological Studies on AIDS of Catalonia (Ceescat)
Hospital Universitari Germans Trias i Pujol
Ctra. de Canyet sn
E-08916 Badalona
Tel. (34) 934 97 88 91, ext. 3481, or (34) 934 97 89 48
Fax (34) 934 97 88 89
E-mail: kperez@ceescat.hugtip.scs.es

Robert Power
Department of STDs
University College London
Mortimer Market Centre
Mortimer Market
London WC1E 6AU
UK
Tel. (44-20) 73 80 99 49
Fax (44-20) 73 88 41 79
E-mail: rpower@gum.ucl.ac.uk

Tim Rhodes
Centre for Research on Drugs and Health Behaviour
Imperial College School of Medicine
200 Seagrave Road
London SW6 1RQ
UK
Tel. (44-20) 88 46 65 03
Fax (day) (44-20) 88 46 65 05, (evening) (44-20) 84 42 42 81
E-mail: t.rhodes@ic.ac.uk

Anna Rodés
Centre for Epidemiological Studies on AIDS of Catalonia (Ceescat)
Hospital Universitari Germans Trias i Pujol
Ctra. de Canyet sn
E-08916 Badalona
Tel. (34) 934 97 88 91, ext. 3481, or (34) 934 97 89 48
Fax (34) 934 97 88 89
E-mail: arodes@ceescat.hugtip.scs.es

Nuria Romo Aviles
Escuela Andaluza de Salud Publica
Campus Universitario de Cartuja
Ap. Correos 2070
E-18080 Granada
Tel. (34) 58 16 10 44
Fax (34) 58 16 11 30 or (34) 58 16 11 42
E-mail: nromo@easp.es

Michel Schiray
CIRED MSH
54, Boulevard Raspail
F-75006 Paris
Tel. (33) 149 54 21 85
Fax (33) 145 48 83 53
E-mail: schiray@msh-paris.fr

Janusz Sierosławski
Institute of Psychiatry and Neurology
Sobieskiego 1/9
Poland
Tel. (48-22) 42 27 00
Fax (48-22) 642 75 01 or (48-22) 642 53 75
E-mail: sierosla@ipin.edu.pl

Zili Sloboda
255 Sloboda Avenue
Mansfield
OH 44906
USA
Tel. (1-419) 529 83 74
Fax (1-419) 529 83 24
E-mail: Zsloboda@aol.com

Karen Ellen Spannow
Centre for Alcohol and Drug Research
Aarhus University
Jens Baggesensvej 43–45
DK-Århus 8200 N
Tel. (45) 86 10 85 55
Fax (45) 86 10 85 58
E-mail: canfkesp@aau.dk

Michael Stauffacher
Riedmattstr. 4
CH-8055 Zurich
Tel. (41-1) 461 38 90
E-mail: michael.stauffacher@active.ch

Paolo Stocco
Irefrea Italia
Via Orsera, 4
I-30126 Lido of Venice
Tel. (39) 04 15 26 88 22
Fax (39) 04 15 26 78 74
E-mail: p.stocco@doge.it

Bengt Svensson
Department of Sociology
Malmö hogskola
Halsa och samhalle
Avdelningen for Socialt arbete
S-205 06 Malmö
Tel. (46-40) 665 74 63
Mobile (46-70) 513 72 79
E-mail: bengt.svensson@soch.lu.se

Louisa Vingoe
National Addiction Centre
4 Windsor Walk
London SE5 8AF
UK
Tel. (44-20) 77 40 52 31
Fax (44-20) 79 19 27 51
E-mail: l.vingoe@iop.kcl.ac.uk

Urban Weber
Integrative Drogenhilfe e. V.
Dept IDH International
Niddastr. 49
D-60329 Frankfurt
Tel. (49-69) 24 00 24 48
Fax (49-69) 24 00 24 33
Mobile (49-171) 525 58 61
E-mail: u.weber@idh-frankfurt.de

Sam Wright
Social Research Centre on Health
Manchester Metropolitan University
Elizabeth Gaskell Campus
Hathersage Road
Manchester M13 OJA
UK
Tel. (44-161) 247 25 91
Fax (44-161) 247 63 94
E-mail: s.j.wright@mmu.ac.uk

Lee Young
Department of Sociology
University of Liverpool
Liverpool L69 3BX
UK
Tel. (44-151) 794 20 00
Fax (44-151) 794 29 97
E-mail: young@liverpool.ac.uk or younglk@globalnet.co.uk

Linda Zuidmulder
Addiction Research Institute Rotterdam
Heemraadssingel 194
3021 DEM Rotterdam
Netherlands
Tel. (31-10) 425 33 66
Fax (31-10) 276 39 88

PRACTICAL INFORMATION

Address
European Monitoring Centre for Drugs and Drug Addiction (EMCDDA)
Rua da Cruz de Santa Apolónia 23–25
P-1149-045 Lisbon

Telephone
(351) 218 11 30 00

Fax
(351) 218 13 17 11

E-mail
info@emcdda.org

Website
http://www.emcdda.org

EMCDDA, July 2000

European Monitoring Centre for Drugs and Drug Addiction

EMCDDA Scientific Monograph Series No 4
Understanding and responding to drug use: the role of qualitative research

Luxembourg: Office for Official Publications of the European Communities

2000 — 350 pp. — 16 x 24 cm

ISBN 92-9168-088-5

Price (excluding VAT) in Luxembourg: EUR 18